Learning Analytics

This book explores how data science, which involves preparing, analyzing, visualizing, and interpreting data, can revolutionize the field of education. The authors delve into how schools and universities can analyze data to improve teaching methods, enhance student learning, and design effective evaluations.

Learning Analytics: Shaping the Future of Education with Data Science examines how machine learning algorithms can analyze individual student performance data to tailor personalized adaptive learning paths, ensuring the best educational experience. Through real-world examples, this book discusses how valuable insights and opportunities can be gained through the application of data science in educational environments. The authors discuss the application of natural language processing (NLP) to analyze educational content, providing insights into language usage, comprehension levels, and improving the effectiveness of instructional materials and examines computer vision in classroom dynamics to measure student engagement. The book also exposes the reader to the crucial role of cybersecurity in safeguarding sensitive student and institutional information, ensuring a secure learning environment, and protecting against cyber threats. It also addresses the ethical considerations and privacy concerns associated with collecting, analyzing, and making decisions from educational data. Finally, it emphasizes the importance of responsible practices to protect the rights and well-being of students and educators.

The book is intended for engineers from computer science, government policymakers, institutions, and educational stakeholders. It shows how computer science, statistics, and data can personalize learning, improve educational tools, enhance classroom dynamics, secure academic records with blockchain, and ensure online safety.

Future Generation Information Systems

Series editor- Bharat Bhushan

With the evolution of future generation computing systems, it becomes necessary to occasionally take stock, analyze the development of its core theoretical ideas, and adapt to radical innovations. This series will provide a platform to reflect the theoretical progress, and forge emerging theoretical avenues for the future generation information systems. The theoretical progress in the Information Systems field (IS) and the development of associated next generation theories is the need of the hour. This is because Information Technology (IT) has become increasingly infused, interconnected and intelligent in almost all context.

Industry 6.0: Technology, Practices, Challenges, and Applications
Kishor Kumar Reddy C, Srinath Doss, Lavanya Pamulaparty, Kari J Lippert and Ruchi Doshi

Convergence of Deep Learning and Artificial Intelligence in Internet of Things
Ajay Rana, Arun Rana, Sachin Dhawan, Sharad Sharma and Ahmed A. Elngar

Next Generation Communication Networks for Industrial Internet of Things Systems
Sundresan Perumal, Mujahid Tabassum, Moolchand Sharma and Saju Mohanan

Artificial Intelligence and Optimizing Techniques for Smart Information System Generations
Edited by: Aleem Ali, Rajdeep Chakraborty and Nawaf R. Alharbe

Artificial Intelligence for Healthcare Applications
Edited by: Anoop V.S, Suhasini Verma and Usharani Hareesh Govindarajan

Next Generation Data Driven Business 4.0 using the Internet of Things Blockchain and Interconnected Devices
Edited by: Hemant Kumar Saini, Rupali A Mahajan and Dac-Nhuong Le

Industry 5.0: Emerging Paradigms for Business, Technology, and Society
Edited by: Deergha Sharma, Manisha Gupta, Raj K Kovid, Thipendra P Singh, Pradeep Kumar and Ahatsham Hayat

Learning Analytics: Shaping the Future of Education with Data Science
Edited by: Mohd Anas Wajid and Claudia Camacho-Zuñiga

Learning Analytics

Shaping the Future of Education with Data Science

Edited by
Mohd Anas Wajid and
Claudia Camacho-Zuñiga

CRC Press
Taylor & Francis Group
Boca Raton London New York

CRC Press is an imprint of the
Taylor & Francis Group, an **informa** business

Designed cover image: Mohd Anas Wajid

First edition published 2026
by CRC Press
2385 NW Executive Center Drive, Suite 320, Boca Raton FL 33431

and by CRC Press
4 Park Square, Milton Park, Abingdon, Oxon, OX14 4RN

CRC Press is an imprint of Taylor & Francis Group, LLC

ISBN: 978-1-041-15193-7 (hbk)
ISBN: 978-1-041-15194-4 (pbk)
ISBN: 978-1-003-67825-0 (ebk)

DOI: 10.1201/9781003678250

Typeset in Times
by Apex CoVantage, LLC

Contents

About the Editors

Dr. Mohd Anas Wajid is a postdoctoral research associate in Data Science at TEC de Monterrey, Mexico. He received his PhD degree in computer science from Aligarh Muslim University, India. He was awarded with the MITACS-SICI Globalink Research Award by Mitacs in collaboration with HRD ministry, Government of India, to do a project at the University of Athabasca, Edmonton, Alberta, Canada. The ACM India Council named him an ACM India Anveshan Setu Fellow, and he received a fellowship to conduct a part of his research at IIIT-Delhi. His contribution to neutrosophic research earned him a diploma from the Neutrosophic Science International Association (NSIA), University of New Mexico, United States (USA). He has keen interest in soft computing, machine learning, data science, information retrieval, and neutrosophy. He has academic as well as industrial experience.

Prof. Claudia Camacho-Zuñiga is a researcher at the Institute for the Future of Education and a professor at the School of Engineering at Tecnologico de Monterrey, Mexico. She is a leader in research, innovation, and transformation in higher education with over 29 years of experience in the field. Since 2014, Professor Camacho-Zuñiga has been a driving force in educational innovation and research in Mexico and Latin America; she has leveraged her expertise in teaching and data science tools to foster a passion for science, ethical and civic engagement, and appreciation for diversity of knowledge and people among undergraduate students and academia.

Contributors

Alario-Hoyos, Carlos
Universidad Carlos III de Madrid
Department of Telematics Engineering
Madrid, Spain

Álvarez-Pérez, Hugo Alberto
School of Business
Tecnológico de Monterrey, Mexico

Atique, Saim
Jamia Urdu College of Education
Aligarh, Uttar Pradesh, India

Ayón-Muñoz, Luisa Reyna Beatriz
Universidad Autónoma del Estado de México (UAEM)
Centro Universitario UAEM Valle de Chalco

Calderon, Andres A.
Fellow and Adjunct Faculty
Tulane University, USA

Camacho-Zuñiga, Claudia
Tecnologico de Monterrey
Institute for the Future of Education
Monterrey, Mexico

Cardona-Reyes, Hector
Center for Research in Mathematics
Zacatecas, México

Coronado, Yaxk'in U Kan
Centro Transdisciplinario de Investigación
Desarrollo e innovación, Universidad La Salle México

Cortes, Aldo A.
School of Engineering and Sciences
Instituto Tecnologico y de Estudios Superiores de Monterrey
Chihuahua, México

Dadoriya, Nisha
Department of Computer Science
O P Jindal University, India

Delgado-Kloos, Carlos
Universidad Carlos III de Madrid
Department of Telematics Engineering
Madrid, Spain

Espinoza Salinas, Ariana
Department of Computer Science
CICESE, Ensenada, Mexico

Faiz, Mohd.
JIIU's Jamia College of Education
Akkalkuwa, Nandurbar
Maharashtra, India

Favela, Jesus
Department of Computer Science
CICESE, Ensenada, Mexico

Ferrari-Díaz, Martina
Facultad de Humanidades y Ciencias Sociales
Universidad La Salle México

García-Castelán, Rosa María Guadalupe
School of Engineering and Science
Tecnologico de Monterrey, Cd. de México, Mexico

García-López, Iván Miguel
Escuela de Ingeniería y Ciencias
Tecnológico de Monterrey, Mexico

García-Peñalvo, Francisco J.
Computer Science Department
GRIAL Research Group
Universidad de Salamanca, Spain

Gonzalez-Nucamendi, Andres
School of Engineering and Science
Tecnologico de Monterrey
Cd. de México, Mexico
Universidad Nacional Autónoma de México (UNAM)
Mexico City, Mexico

Imran
JIIU's Jamia College of Education
Akkalkuwa, Nandurbar
Maharashtra, India

Jerez-Yañez, Oscar
Universidad de Chile
Department of Health Sciences Education, Santiago, Chile

Jiménez-Botello, Luis Clemente
Facultad Mexicana de Medicina, Universidad La Salle México
CDMX, México
and
Universidad de Salamanca
Salamanca, Spain

Kamal, Amjad
JIIU's Jamia College of Education
Akkalkuwa, Nandurbar
Maharashtra, India

Lara-Álvarez, Carlos Alberto
Center for Research in Mathematics
Zacatecas, México

Levchuk, Oleksiy
Department of Computer Science
CICESE, Ensenada, Mexico

López-Botello, Cynthia Karyna
Tecnologico de Monterrey
Institute for the Future of Education

Lopez Hurtado, Isabel
Department of Computer Science
CICESE, Ensenada, Mexico

Lozoya, Camilo
School of Engineering and Sciences.
Instituto Tecnologico y de Estudios Superiores de Monterrey
Chihuahua, México

Martínez-Reyes, Magally
Universidad Autónoma del Estado de México (UAEM)
Centro Universitario UAEM Valle de Chalco

Melendez-Anzures, Frank E.
Tecnologico de Monterrey
Institute for the Future of Education
Monterrey, Mexico

Morales-Chan, Miguel A.
Universidad Galileo
GES Department, Guatemala

Morán-Mirabal, Luis Fernando
Tecnologico de Monterrey
Institute for the Future of Education

Neri, Luis
School of Engineering and Science
Tecnologico de Monterrey
Cd. de México, Mexico

Nieto Jalil, José Manuel
Tecnológico de Monterrey
School of Engineering and Sciences
Mexico

Noguez, Julieta
School of Engineering and Science, Tecnologico de Monterrey
Cd. de México, Mexico
and
Universidad Nacional Autónoma de México (UNAM)
Mexico City, Mexico

Nosedal-Sanchez, Jenaro
School of Engineering and Sciences
Instituto Tecnologico y de Estudios Superiores de Monterrey
Chihuahua, México

Olmos-Peña, Samuel
Universidad Autónoma del Estado de México (UAEM)
Centro Universitario UAEM Valle de Chalco

Pandey, Swapnil
Department of Computer Science and Information Systems
Birla Institute of Technology and Science, India

Parra-González, Ezra Federico
Center for Research in Mathematics
Zacatecas, México

Pineda, Oscar Alfredo
FUSADES
Departamento de Estudios Legales
El Salvador

Ramírez-Montoya, María Soledad
Benemérita Escuela Normal de Coahuila, Saltillo, México

Robledo-Rella, Víctor
School of Engineering and Science
Tecnologico de Monterrey
Cd. de México, Mexico

Rodríguez Molina, Joaquín Ernesto
FUSADES
Departamento de Estudios Legales, El Salvador

Ruiz-Ramírez, Jessica Alejandra
Tecnologico de Monterrey
Institute for the Future of Education

Serrano, Julio
University of Vaasa, Finland

Solano-Romo, Lizeth
Autonomous University of Aguascalientes, Mexico

Tamayo-Preval, Dayannis
Tecnologico de Monterrey
Institute for the Future of Education

Vaish, Arti
Department of Computer Science
O P Jindal University, India

Valverde-Rebaza, Jorge
School of Engineering and Science
Tecnologico de Monterrey
Cd. de México, Mexico

Vazquez, Roberto A.
Centro Transdisciplinario de Investigación
Desarrollo e innovación
Universidad La Salle México

Wajid, Mohd Anas
Institute for the Future of Education
Tecnologico de Monterrey
Monterrey, Mexico

Zavala, Genaro
Tecnologico de Monterrey
Institute for the Future of Education
Monterrey, Mexico
Universidad Andres Bello, School of Engineering, Santiago, Chile

Preface

In the book *Learning Analytics: Shaping the Future of Education with Data Science*, the authors explore how data science, which involves preparing, analyzing, visualizing, and interpreting data, can revolutionize the field of education. They delve into how schools and universities can analyze data to improve teaching methods, enhance student learning, and design effective evaluations.

If educational institutions could use data to understand which teaching techniques work best, identify areas where students may need extra support, and even predict academic performance trends, they would take better and informed decisions. Through real-world examples, this book discusses how valuable insights and opportunities can be gained through the application of data science in educational environments. In simpler terms, the purpose of the book is to equip educational institutions with the power of information, programming, and statistics to make our education system smarter, more effective, and better tailored to the needs of administrative personnel, learners, and faculty.

In this proposed book each chapter offers a unique perspective on how different areas of data science contribute to the evolving landscape of education. Following this is a brief overview of some chapters to exemplify how data science could be employed in the field of education. The proposed book emphasizes on machine learning for personalized learning paths. It will evidence how machine learning algorithms can analyze individual student performance data to tailor personalized adaptive learning paths, ensuring the best educational experience.

It also sheds light on natural language processing in educational content. It explores the application of natural language processing (NLP) to analyze educational content, providing insights into language usage, comprehension levels, and improving the effectiveness of instructional materials.

The book focuses on computer vision in classroom dynamics. It delves into the use of computer vision technology to analyze classroom dynamics, track student engagement, and optimize physical and virtual learning environments for better educational outcomes. Whereas Chapter 4 focusses on blockchain for academic credentialing. It mainly deals with the integration of blockchain technology in securely managing academic credentials, ensuring the integrity of educational records, and streamlining the verification process for employers and institutions.

It deals with cybersecurity for educational platforms. It exposes the reader to the crucial role of cybersecurity in safeguarding sensitive student and institutional information, ensuring a secure learning environment, and protecting against cyber threats in the digital realm of education. It also focusses on human-computer interaction in educational tools. It explores how advances in human-computer interaction influence the design and usability of educational tools, making them more intuitive and engaging for both students and educators.

The proposed book highlights data ethics and privacy in education. It addresses the ethical considerations and privacy concerns associated with collecting, analyzing, and making decisions from educational data. It emphasizes the importance of responsible practices to protect the rights and well-being of students and educators, that is, adhesion to IDEA guidelines (inclusion, diversity, equity, and accessibility).

By weaving insights from these various data science domains into the discussion, the proposed book provides a comprehensive overview of how interdisciplinary approaches contribute to shaping the future of education. It offers a holistic perspective on the synergies between data-driven methodologies and computer science, fostering a deeper comprehension of the defiant educational landscape in the digital era.

AI USAGE DECLARATION

The authors used AI-assisted tools for limited editorial support, including language refinement and structural feedback. Grammarly Pro Version 1.2.201 was used to support grammar correction and stylistic editing. All arguments, interpretations, and final text remain the sole responsibility of the authors.

1 Use of Virtual Reality in Learning Environments and Its Impact on Mental Health

Yaxk'in U Kan Coronado, Martina Ferrari-Díaz, and Roberto A. Vazquez

1.1 INTRODUCTION

The COVID 19 pandemic represented a set of challenges internationally in different dimensions. In the educational sector, the transition from in-person to virtual classes was necessary, which posed a challenge for various educational stakeholders. It is reported that in Mexico, during the 2020–2021 school year, 1.8 million people did not enroll due to COVID-19 (National Institute of Statistics and Geography [INEGI], 2020). Many of the causes of school dropouts are related to economic issues; however, a decrease in the quality of learning compared to in-person classes, a lack of follow-up by teachers, and a decrease in peer interaction are also reported as disadvantages of virtual lessons (INEGI, 2020). In many cases, confinement meant forgoing the possibility of conducting practical sessions, which could have undermined a range of learning experiences for professionals in training.

Therefore, virtual reality (VR) is proposed as a potential alternative to ensure educational quality in this context of social changes related to virtual education. The use of VR addresses the possibility of more active participation of educational stakeholders through its three pillars: realism, engagement, and interactivity, which allow immersion (Sousa-Ferreira et al., 2021).

VR is an emerging technology that provides computer-generated simulations of real-life environments and enables interactions in apparent real time (Marougkas et al., 2023). In education, VR can promote collaborative distance learning through an immersive experience, which can enhance creativity and engagement in classrooms (Marougkas et al., 2023).

Currently, the educational system seeks to reach more people, regardless of their geographic location. However, online experience may lack certain advantages that in-person learning offers. VR has been proposed as a potential alternative to promote the immersive experience and motivation that in-person learning offers, despite the spatial distance (Portuguez-Castro & Santos Garduño, 2024). Its incorporation into educational spaces is becoming increasingly relevant in vocational training environments.

DOI: 10.1201/9781003678250-1

Any new educational proposal requires addressing the advantages and disadvantages of its implementation. A recent literature review by Lin et al. (2024), which analyzed the impact of VR use on student engagement (cognitive, behavioral, and affective) and academic performance, found that VR promoted the understanding of abstract concepts that require a higher level of complexity. The authors also found that VR is related to increased affective interaction. Furthermore, these positive effects were more evident in students with learning difficulties (Lin et al., 2024).

Papanastasiou et al. (2018) reported that VR promotes independent learning, enables multisensory learning, improves spatial skills, confidence, satisfaction with the learning process, and can help reduce the cognitive load of certain content. These improvements are believed to be potentially applicable to real-world problem-solving (Papanastasiou et al., 2018).

However, despite the reported benefits of VR applied to education, several limitations and disadvantages are also recognized. One challenge for implementing VR in the educational sector is the high cost of the equipment, which limits its possible incorporation at different levels (Javaid et al., 2024). Likewise, constant monitoring of technological advances is required, and there is a need for instruction and training for its proper use by the various educational stakeholders (Javaid et al., 2024; Lin et al., 2024). On the other hand, it has been considered that the purposes of learning can be distorted. For example, the excessive use of "gamification" can disconnect classes from educational content (Marougkas et al., 2023). Furthermore, VR may not fully capture the face-to-face experiences that occur in everyday interactions (Marougkas et al., 2023), which may limit the generalization of learning.

Most studies describing the limitations of VR use in education focus on technical and pedagogical difficulties. However, if VR will be implemented on a daily and frequent basis, it is necessary to consider the effects on users' health, which has been underreported. Some potential health effects have been reported after prolonged exposure (more than one hour) to these technologies, such as eye pain, nausea, and vestibular problems (Marougkas et al., 2023). Some discomfort due to the weight of the equipment has also been reported during prolonged sessions (Javaid et al., 2024). These effects could be mitigated by implementing breaks and guidelines for responsible VR use (Marougkas et al., 2023). Recent studies suggest that the average time use of devices should be between 20 and 40 minutes (Meta Horizon, 2025).

Although the effects on mental health are less described than those on physical health, potential effects have been found (Javaid et al., 2024). For example, symptoms of alienation have been reported in samples of 80 individuals, where a feeling of unrealization or detachment from reality is associated with VR use for up to three hours, even after a single session (Peckmann et al., 2022). These symptoms, rather than a disorder, are considered experiences of depersonalization/derealization in healthy people as a transient stress response. Peckmann et al. (2022) found a greater experience of depersonalization/derealization in groups that played with VR than those that played with a computer, although this was not statistically significant, nor were any long-term symptoms observed.

Given the findings of these potential effects on mental health, even if the symptoms were mild and transient, it is recommended to include a brief assessment in studies where VR is implemented in the educational setting.

The aim of this research is to evaluate the levels of engagement and mental health impacts in college students after using VR for learning purposes. To gain greater clarity regarding the influence of VR on these variables, we propose establishing groups with two different educational modalities, considering a population divided into three groups: two groups will participate in a class using VR equipment, and one group will participate in a regular in-person class. Furthermore, a series of instruments will be applied previous and after the class to evaluate the affective state (positive and negative affect scale [PANAS]), possible symptoms of depersonalization associated with the use of VR (scale of Cambridge depersonalization), and an adaptation of the student engagement scale to assess the levels of motivation in the various learning modalities.

1.2 METHODS

This research is focused on evaluating the engagement and depersonalization-derealization symptoms in college students using virtual reality for educational purposes. Through this research we expect to give an answer to the question: How does the use of VR influence learning, engagement, and the presence of depersonalization-derealization symptoms in university students in the educational setting? To achieve this, a quasi-experimental design with an exploratory scope was proposed.

1.2.1 Subjects of Study

The sample selection was non-probabilistic and based on convenience. Volunteer students from various undergraduates from La Salle University were invited to participate. Those interested in participating and met inclusion criteria were selected for the study after they had signed the corresponding informed consent form.

In this preliminary experimental setup, a sample size composed of four participants per experimental group was proposed according to the next inclusion and exclusion criteria described in Table 1.1.

We also considered elimination criteria when a participant reported discomfort at any point during the experimental procedure.

TABLE 1.1
Inclusion and Exclusion Criteria

Exclusion Criteria	Inclusion Criteria
1. History of motion sickness and/or vestibular problems.	1. Undergraduate students at La Salle University.
2. History of epilepsy or seizures triggered by visual stimuli.	2. 18 years or more.
3. History of visual problems (double vision).	3. Agree to participate in the study.
4. History of claustrophobia or anxiety triggered by enclosed spaces.	4. Sign informed consent.

1.2.2 Variables of Study

Several variables were defined to evaluate the engagement and depersonalization-derealization symptoms in college students using virtual reality for educational purposes.

1. Independent variable: learning modality (VR or in-person lessons)
2. Dependent variable: affective state, depersonalization-derealization symptoms, and engagement
3. Control variables: cybersickness or physical discomfort, immersive experience

Table 1.2 and 1.3 describe the conceptual definition and operational definition of the independent and dependent variables.

TABLE 1.2
Independent Variables

Variable	Conceptual Definition	Operational Definition
Learning environment	Teaching and learning modalities (virtual reality and in-person classes) represent alternative educational environments. Comparing them allows for an analysis of how technology and prior experience influence students' learning, participation, and subjective experience.	Three groups will be formed with different educational modalities. Two will be part of the experimental group using VR equipment. There will be two subgroups: (a) Students with prior experience using VR, (b) Students without prior experience using VR. The third group will participate in a regular in-person class.

TABLE 1.3
Dependent Variables

Variable	Conceptual Definition	Operational Definition
Affective state	A person's momentary emotional experience, which can manifest itself in the form of positive emotions (enthusiasm, energy, satisfaction) or negative emotions (stress, sadness, discomfort).	Positive and Negative Affect Scale (PANAS)
Depersonalization-derealization symptoms	A series of alterations in the perception of the self, in which the person experiences sensations of unreality, disconnection, or strangeness regarding themselves or their immediate surroundings.	Cambridge Depersonalization Scale (selected items)
Engagement	Level of cognitive, emotional, and behavioral involvement that the student demonstrates in academic activities, reflecting their interest, motivation, and effort toward learning.	Student Engagement Scale

1.2.3 Data Collection Techniques

Data will be collected using the Kobotoolbox platform (Kobotoolbox, 2025), which allows for secure and organized online data collection, free of charge, and with the guarantee that the data can be deleted from the server if required. It also allows for real-time visualization of data as it is collected and its automatic analysis using some statistical functions. It also allows for digital control of the digital capture of informed consent forms and controls that would anonymize the information if required, given automatic data preprocessing. Questionnaires will be administered to the three groups (VR without prior experience, VR with prior experience, and in-person lessons).

1.2.4 Procedure

First, an open invitation was extended to students interested in participating in the research project. Those who met the inclusion criteria and signed the informed consent form were selected. Participants in the experimental groups were later divided into groups who never had contact with VR equipment and those with more experience with this technology. The remaining group participants were assigned to the in-person lesson. They first completed an online form requesting sociodemographic information and assessing the different variables of interest. Then, they attended the lesson in the learning environment of the correspondent group and then completed another online form posterior to the lesson.

The class consisted of reviewing strategies to improve attention processes: from a theoretical perspective on what attention is and how to improve it using a PowerPoint presentation. Later, a short video about the state of "Flow" related to attention was presented. Finally, they completed an object-finding task through a screen for the in-person modality, and through VR headsets for the VR environment.

The same class was carried out across the different educational modalities and lasted around 20 minutes.

1.2.5 Data Analysis

The initial data analysis was performed with statistical frameworks using the statistical package available in R to test the relevance of the data according to the scales of PANAS and depersonalized test of Cambridge. Additionally, the cybersickness and flow state instruments were only applied to the virtual classroom.

As a preliminary experimental setup, the means of the results from the different variables of interest between pre-class and post-class across the learning modalities were compared: positive and negative affective states scores of the PANAS, the Cambridge depersonalization scale, and the study engagement scale.

1.3 RESULTS

As a preliminary experimental setup, the sample consisted of a total of 11 students: four for the VR-prior experience modality group, four for the VR-less prior experience, and three for the in-person modality.

The in-person group (Figure 1.1) and the VR with less prior experienced group (Figure 1.2) presented a decrease in both positive and negative affective states after the lesson, which contrasts with the VR with prior experience group (Figure 1.3) that showed a trend of more positive affective states and a decrease in negative ones.

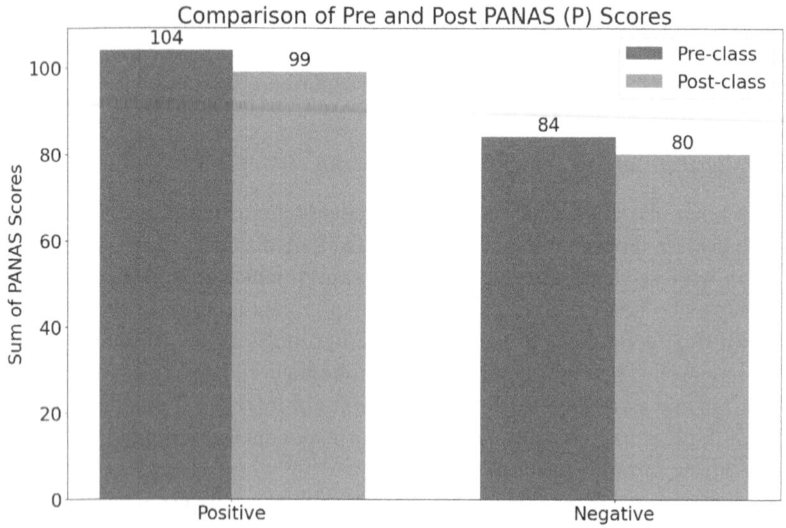

FIGURE 1.1 Comparative between negative and positive scores previous and after class presential modality.

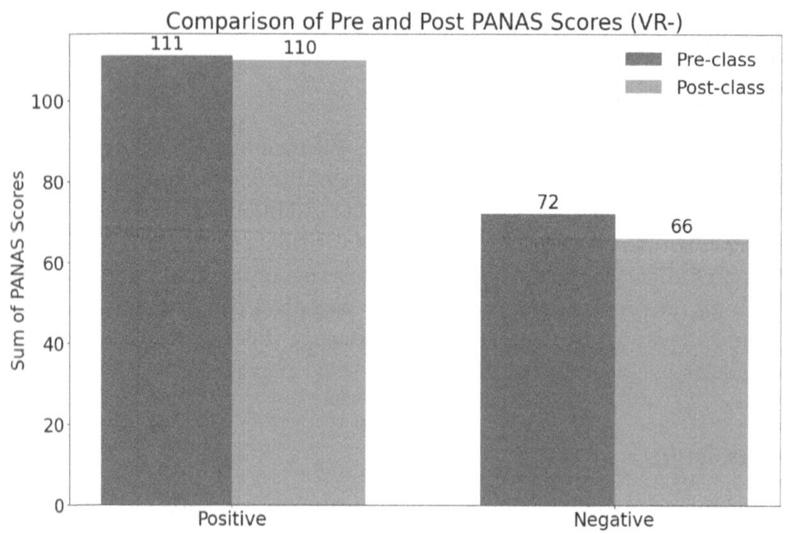

FIGURE 1.2 Comparative between negative and positive scores previous and after class VR less experienced modality.

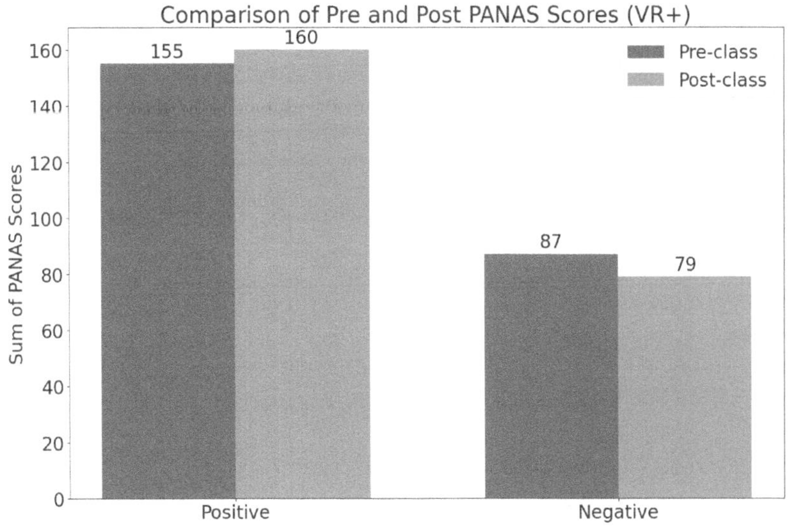

FIGURE 1.3 Comparative between negative and positive scores previous and after class VR more experienced modality.

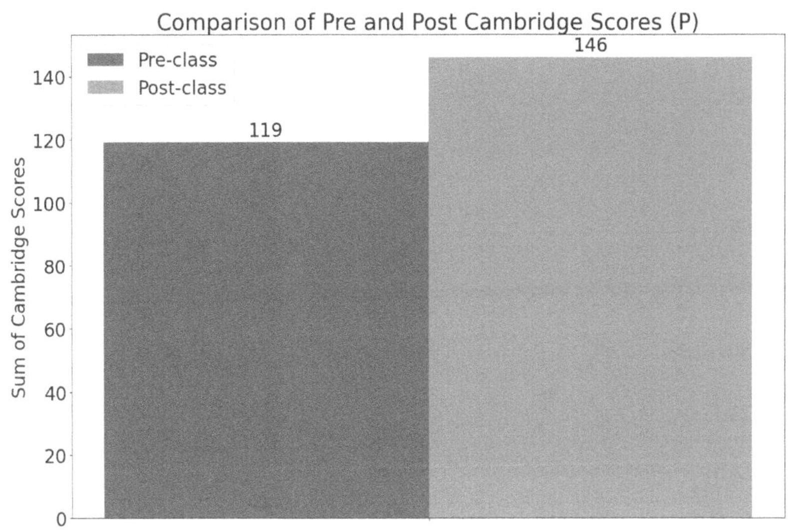

FIGURE 1.4 Comparative between Cambridge depersonalization scores in presential modality, previous and after class VR modality.

The in-person group showed an increase of depersonalization symptoms after the lesson (Figure 1.4), while both the VR less experienced group (Figure 1.5) and the more experienced group presented a decrease in these symptoms (Figure 1.6).

Regarding the academic engagement, the group with more experience with VR showed less academic engagement than the group with less experience with VR (Figure 1.7)

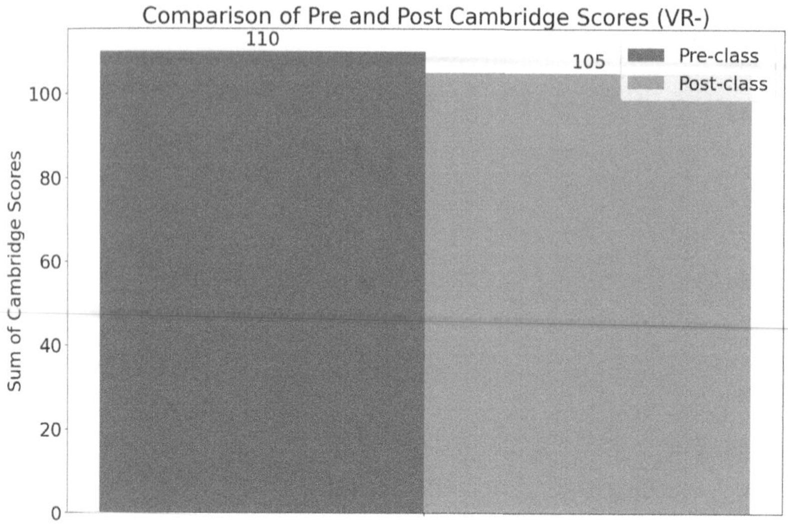

FIGURE 1.5 Comparative between Cambridge depersonalization scores in VR less experienced, previous and after class VR modality.

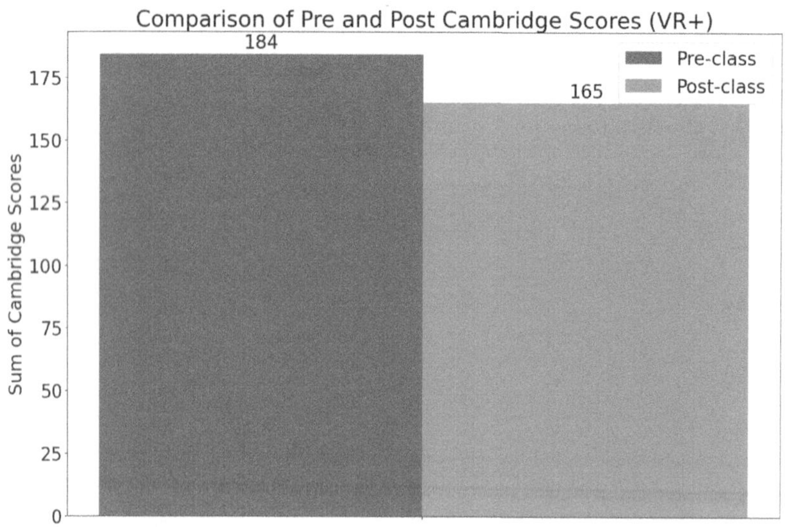

FIGURE 1.6 Comparative between Cambridge depersonalization scores in VR more experienced, previous and after class VR modality.

and the in-person modality group, which had a greater academic engagement compared to the less experienced group (Figure 1.8).

1.4 DISCUSSION

This preliminary experimental setup study is the first effort to show the comparison between two learning modalities, between the in-person lessons and the use of VR

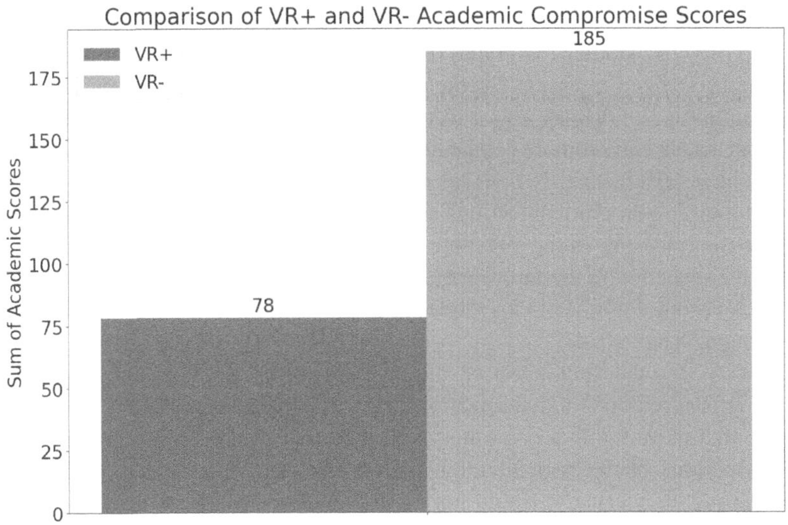

FIGURE 1.7 Comparative between academic engagement scores in VR more and less experienced, after class VR modality.

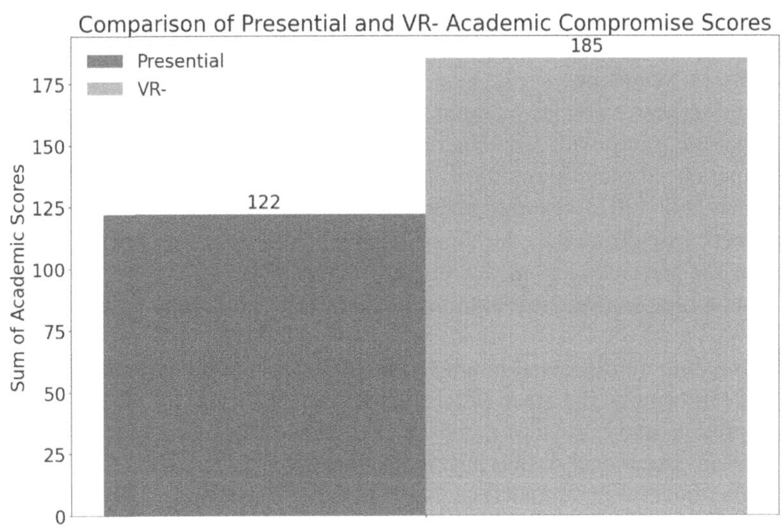

FIGURE 1.8 Comparative between academic engagement scores in VR less experienced and presential modality, after class.

headsets, trying to emulate the same situation in equivalence of conditions in the mental health of students.

The results of the PANAS, allowed comparison between the different modalities, before and after the lesson: the in-person group and the VR less experienced group showed more positive emotions before the lesson, and a decrease after it. However, the more experienced group with the use of VR presented a positive increment in the experience and a decrease in negative emotions after the class. This result is consistent with previous studies that found that the use of VR was related to more positive affect and focalized attention (Neumann & Moffitt, 2018). Other studies reported the potential use of VR as a tool to enhance mental health (Maples-Keller et al., 2017), because it can promote engagement, and the interaction on personalized, real-world contexts (Bell et al., 2020). Our study found a subtle trend of positive affective changes even in non-clinical settings as learning environments.

The better outcome in the VR more experienced group in positive affective states may be associated with the familiarity with this technology, which has been demonstrated can promote the flow experience and the intention to continue to play and use VR (Yang & Xiao, 2024).

Contrary to what Peckmann et al. (2022) reported about an increased experience of depersonalization/derealization in groups that played with VR as opposed to those that played with a computer, we found that the in-person group presented more symptoms of depersonalization than both VR groups. These findings seem counterintuitive, because it would not be expected to observe a higher sensation of unreality or disconnection in a presential setting rather than a VR setting. However, it is important to note that it was the first time the students who participated in the experiment were in the place where the lesson was given. This condition may explain the feelings of strangeness regarding themselves, or their immediate surroundings reported by the in-person group. Additionally, the results of Peckmann et al. (2022) about the depersonalization symptoms were not statistically significant, nor reported any long-term symptoms.

Another crucial variable we wanted to address was academic engagement; we found that the group with less experience in VR exhibited higher scores, and the more experienced group showed the lowest scores. These results may support what Marougkas et al. (2023) reported about how the excessive use of "gamification" can disconnect classes from the educational content. Even if the group with more experience in VR presented less symptoms of depersonalization, less negative affective states and more positive ones, in terms of motivation, satisfaction, and approach to the knowledge of the lesson. For instance, the group with more experience in VR tended to get more distracted by all the possibilities that the platform provided to them, like drawing in the space and using the laser pointer.

The present study provides a general overview of the relationship between the use of VR in educational settings and mental health variables. The selection of three groups that underwent similar lessons differing only in the modality of the lesson allows us to compare their results. However, this study has some limitations that must be considered, like the sample size and the scope of the study is exploratory.

Future studies must enlarge the sample to perform some statistical analysis and to better understand the possible relationships between the variables. Another relevant variable not included in the present study was an assessment of the teacher performance, which could provide data to help include all educational stakeholders in these new approaches.

Exploring the advantages and disadvantages of VR can help to promote the incorporation of new devices in education, which could enhance teaching and learning processes, understanding the limitations and possibilities of these innovative technologies.

1.5 CONCLUSIONS

This preliminary research reveals some interesting contrasts between the different learning modalities and their impact on student affective states and academic engagement.

While the VR-prior experience group showed increased positive affective states and decreased negative affective states, the in-person group exhibited an increase in depersonalization symptoms after the lesson. In contrast, both the VR-less experienced and VR-more experienced groups presented a decrease in depersonalization symptoms.

Regarding academic engagement, the surprising finding is that the group with more VR experience actually showed less academic engagement compared to the group with less VR experience, as well as the in-person modality group, which had the greatest academic engagement.

These results suggest that prior experience with VR technology may not automatically translate to higher academic engagement in VR-based learning environments. The decreased depersonalization symptoms in the VR-experienced groups indicate that familiarity with the technology can mitigate negative affective states but does not necessarily lead to higher academic engagement compared to traditional in-person learning or VR-less experienced groups.

Overall, the findings highlight the complex interplay between prior VR experience, affective states, and academic engagement in educational settings. Further research is needed to better understand how VR-based learning impacts students with varying levels of familiarity with this technology.

Future research in this area should aim to increase the sample size of the experimental groups to provide more robust and generalizable results. The current preliminary study had a relatively small number of participants, with only 4 in the VR-prior experience group, 4 in the VR-less prior experience group, and 3 in the in-person group. Expanding the sample size would help to validate the trends observed and allow for more reliable statistical analysis.

Additionally, it would be valuable to consider the role of teacher experience with VR technology as another factor in academic engagement and affective outcomes. The current study focused only on student-level variables, but the level of comfort and expertise that instructors have in designing and delivering VR-based lessons may also play a significant role in influencing student engagement and experiences.

Expanding the research in these directions—larger sample sizes and the inclusion of teacher VR experience as a variable—would help build a more comprehensive understanding of the complex relationship between prior VR experience, affective states, and academic engagement in technology-enhanced learning environments.

ACKNOWLEDGMENTS

The authors thank Universidad La Salle México for the economic support for the correct development of this research.

REFERENCES

Bell, I. H., Nicholas, J., Alvarez-Jimenez, M., Thompson, A., & Valmaggia, L. (2020). Virtual reality as a clinical tool in mental health research and practice. *Dialogues in Clinical Neuroscience*, 22(2), 169–177. https://doi.org/10.31887/DCNS.2020.22.2/lvalmaggia

Instituto Nacional de Estadística y Geografía, INEGI. (2020). Encuesta para la Medición del Impacto COVID-19 en la Educación (ECOVID-ED) 2020. *Recuperado el 20 de junio de 2025 de.* https://www.inegi.org.mx/contenidos/investigacion/ecovided/2020/doc/ecovid_ed_2020_nota_tecnica.pdf

Javaid, M., Haleem, A., Singh, R. P., & Dhall, S. (2024). Role of Virtual Reality in advancing education with sustainability and identification of Additive Manufacturing as its cost-effective enabler. *Sustainable Futures.* https://doi.org/10.1016/j.sftr.2024.100324

Kobo Toolbox. (2025, Julio 29). *Kobotoolbox.* https://www.kobotoolbox.org

Lin, X. P., Li, B. B., Yao, Z. N., Yang, Z., & Zhang, M. (2024). The impact of virtual reality on student engagement in the classroom-a critical review of the literature. *Frontiers in Psychology.* https://doi.org/10.3389/fpsyg.2024.1360574

Maples-Keller, J. L., Bunnell, B. E., Kim, S. J., & Rothbaum, B. O. (2017). The use of virtual reality technology in the treatment of anxiety and other psychiatric disorders. *Harvard Review of Psychiatry*, 25(3), 103–113. https://doi.org/10.1097/HRP.0000000000000138

Marougkas, A., Troussas, C., Krouska, A., & Sgouropoulou, C. (2023). Virtual reality in education: A review of learning theories, approaches and methodologies for the last decade. *Electronics*, 12(13), 2832. https://doi.org/10.3390/electronics12132832

Meta Horizon. (2025, julio 24). *Building Content to Optimize User Time: 20–40 Minute "Goldilocks" Session Length on Meta Quest.* https://developers.meta.com/horizon/blog/optimize-user-time-goldilocks-session-length-meta-quest/

Neumann, D. L., & Moffitt, R. L. (2018). Affective and attentional states when running in a virtual reality environment. *Sports (Basel, Switzerland)*, 6(3), 71. https://doi.org/10.3390/sports6030071

Papanastasiou, G. P., Drigas, A., Skianis, C., Lytras, M. D., & Papanastasiou, E. (2018). Virtual and augmented reality effects on K-12, higher and tertiary education students' twenty-first century skills. *Virtual Reality*, 23, 425–436. https://doi.org/10.1007/s10055-018-0363-2

Peckmann, C., Kannen, K., Pensel, M. C., Lux, S., Philipsen, A., & Braun, N. (2022). Virtual reality induces symptoms of depersonalization and derealization: A longitudinal randomised control trial. *Computers in Human Behavior*, 131, C. https://doi.org/10.1016/j.chb.2022.107233

Portuguez-Castro, M., & Santos Garduño, H. (2024). Beyond traditional classrooms: Comparing virtual reality applications and their influence on students' motivation. *Education Sciences*, 14(9), 963. https://doi.org/10.3390/educsci14090963

Sousa-Ferreira, R., Campanari-Xavier, R. A., & Rodrigues-Ancioto, A. S. (2021). La realidad virtual como herramienta para la educación básica y profesional. *Revista Científica General José María Córdova*, 19(33), 223–241. https://doi.org/10.21830/19006586.728

Yang, L., & Xiao, D. (2024). Embodied echoes: Navigating the familiarity in continued intention to play VR game. *Frontiers in Human Neuroscience*, 18, 1495845. https://doi.org/10.3389/fnhum.2024.1495845

2 AI-Driven Adaptive Learning

Architecture, Governance, and a Road Map for Scalable Personalization

Andres A. Calderon, Julio Serrano, Joaquín Ernesto Rodríguez Molina, and Oscar Alfredo Pineda

2.1 INTRODUCTION

AI refers to computational systems that display intelligent behavior by analyzing their environment and taking actions, with some degree of autonomy, to achieve specific goals (Serrano et al., 2024). In education, this capability transcends simple automation and needs a more operational definition which frames AI as *automation based on associations* (Cardona et al., 2023). The shift is twofold: first, from merely *capturing* data (e.g., storing grades in a spreadsheet) to actively *detecting patterns* within that data (e.g., identifying behaviors that correlate with student success); and second, from providing passive *access* to instructional resources (e.g., a folder of PDFs in a Learning Management System) to *automating decisions* about the instructional process itself (Cardona et al., 2023). This delegation of decision-making responsibility to a machine marks a turning point from a passive tool into an active and engaged player in education.

The field of AIEd has two primary missions: *education for understanding AI,* which focuses on developing AI literacy among students and educators, and *education using AI,* which involves the application of AI technologies to enhance teaching and learning (Paek & Kim, 2021). This chapter focuses on exploring how AI serves as an engine for pedagogical innovation.

The growing importance of this field is underscored by significant economic investment and projected growth, with the global market for AIEd in education estimated to reach $12.6 billion by 2027 (Krstić et al., 2022). This and other investment commitments toward AI in general demonstrate that AI is not a passing fad, but a foundational element of the future of educational landscape and our lives.

Adaptive learning is a data-driven pedagogical methodology that utilizes technology, particularly AI and machine learning algorithms, to orchestrate interaction with the learner and deliver customized resources and learning activities in real-time

DOI: 10.1201/9781003678250-2

(Gligorea et al., 2023). The main principle of an adaptive learning system is its capacity to *dynamically adjust to the level or type of course content based on an individual's abilities or skill attainment* (Capuano & Caballé, 2020). AIEd is designed to address the individual needs of each learner by tailoring educational content, instructional strategies, and assessment methods (Gligorea et al., 2023). The ultimate goal of AIEd is to transform the student from a *passive receptor of information to collaborator in the educational process* (Spector, 2014). This approach is fundamentally an attempt to solve the long-standing challenge of providing personalized, one-on-one tutoring at scale, using technology to emulate the way a human tutor diagnoses a student's understanding and adjusts instruction accordingly (Hakkal & Ait Lahcen, 2021).

AIEd has evolved from simple digital tools into increasingly sophisticated systems that analyze, predict, and create to personalize learning. The first wave primarily driven by machine learning (ML) algorithms enabled predictive analytics and automated assessment by uncovering patterns in student data. ML uses algorithms trained on large datasets to identify complex patterns and make predictions or decisions without being explicitly programmed for every contingency (Majumder, 2025). In education, ML analyzes student data to forecast future trends and outcomes, thereby enabling proactive and data-informed interventions (Gašević et al., 2015).

The next evolutionary stage was powered by natural language processing (NLP), and it introduced more natural communication through essay scoring, chatbots, and conversational support. NLP gave computers the ability to understand, interpret, and generate human language in both text and speech (J. Sun et al., 2022). In education, NLP served as the critical bridge enabling more natural and sophisticated interactions between humans and machines. The most recent shift toward Generative AI (GenAI) moved AI capabilities beyond prediction and interaction to creation, producing new, tailored content and GenAI started to become our learning and knowledge companions. GenAI is built on large language models (LLMs) like GPT-5, making a shift from simply predicting outcomes to creating new ideas. Instead of merely analyzing existing data to make a prediction, the new GenAI models learns patterns from vast datasets to generate entirely new and original content, including text, images, audio, and code (Mittal et al., 2024).

Together, these stages illustrate the progression of AI from analysis to communication to creativity, each deepening the potential for truly personalized education. The emergence of GenAI, however, represents a qualitative leap with multiple reviews demonstrating identify automated content generation as a clear capability of GenAI, while simultaneously warning that pedagogical soundness, assessment validity, bias, and governance are the emergent limitations to meaningful personalization. GenAI systems are no longer limited to just selecting from a predefined set of resources, but systems can create novel educational content in real-time. This suggests that the very definition of "personalized content" is expanding. The primary bottleneck for personalization is thus shifting away from the time and cost of creating a diverse content library, which can now be generated algorithmically and quickly evolving toward the pedagogical expertise required to design effective prompts and the ethical frameworks needed to govern AI's creative autonomy.

Traditional e-learning and adaptive learning diverge sharply in how the two approaches embody different pedagogical philosophies. Traditional e-learning typically offers a linear and predetermined learning path, where all students progress through the same sequence of modules in a fixed order (Serrano et al., 2024). By contrast, adaptive learning provides dynamic, personalized pathways that adjust in real time to each learner's needs based on their performance and interactions (Gligorea et al., 2023). Content delivery in adaptive systems is individualized, aligning materials with a learner's specific gaps, preferences, and styles (Parveen et al., 2025), while traditional systems provide uniform, static resources that remain the same for all students (Gligorea et al., 2023). Pacing is another point of distinction: adaptive platforms allow learners to move at their own pace, accelerating or remediating based on mastery (Sadaf Saleem et al., 2025), but traditional models either follow rigid schedules or leave pacing unguided by the system (Gligorea et al., 2023). Feedback in adaptive learning is immediate and instructional, often with scaffolding to explain why an answer is right or wrong (Laak & Aru, 2025), while traditional systems usually provide delayed, generic feedback after assessments (Sridharan et al., 2021). Data usage also reflects this contrast where adaptive systems continuously analyze interaction data to update learner models and tailor instruction (Gligorea et al., 2023), while traditional platforms rely on post-hoc data analysis mainly for grading (Huang et al., 2025). Finally, the underlying technology differs fundamentally since adaptive learning depends on AI/ML algorithms and dynamic learner models (Romero & Ventura, 2020), while traditional e-learning relies on static content repositories within learning management systems (LMS), functioning as containers rather than adaptive engines (Romero & Ventura, 2020).

The current trajectory of AIEd capabilities suggests curriculum shifts from a fixed, static framework to a dynamic, co-created artifact shaped by the continuous interaction of learners, educators, and generative AI partners. In such an environment, learning materials and pathways evolve in real time, reflecting both individual learner needs and broader instructional goals. However, realizing this vision requires more than technical sophistication; it demands deep pedagogical insight to design the rules, models, and frameworks that underpin the AI's "tutoring" decisions, ensuring that automation remains aligned with sound educational practice (Bayly-Castaneda et al., 2024).

Ultimately, the importance of AIEd lies in their ability to transform instruction from static sequences into dynamic, personalized, and optimized learning experiences. By continuously collecting data, analyzing it through sophisticated models, and adjusting in real time, AI personalizes pacing, content, and feedback in ways that were once unimaginable in traditional classrooms (Vorobyeva et al., 2025; Huang et al., 2025). This continuous data-analysis-adaptation cycle not only enables mastery-based progression but also turns every learner interaction into a formative assessment, dissolving the boundaries between teaching and testing (Sangrà et al., 2012; Raza, 2023). Such advances underscore that personalization in education is no longer a theoretical aspiration but a scalable reality (Guskey, 2007; Laak & Aru, 2025).

The next section examines the system architecture of AI-driven adaptive learning, focusing on its three foundational components: the learner model, the domain model, and the adaptation engine (Imhof et al., 2020).

2.2 SYSTEM ARCHITECTURE OF AI-DRIVEN ADAPTIVE LEARNING SYSTEMS

The system architecture of AIEd is represented by the convergence of educational theory, artificial intelligence, data science, and system engineering, creating personalized educational experiences through sophisticated technical architectures. These systems fundamentally rely on four interconnected core components:

1. Learner model that tracks the learner's progress and characteristics;
2. Domain models that structure educational content and knowledge ontological relationships;
3. Adaptation engine that makes real-time decisions about content presentation based on objectives;
4. Control mechanism through a "Human-in-the-loop" (HITL) framework that ensures educators and, to some extent learners, retain ultimate authority and informational oversight within adaptive learning systems.

The learner model tracks data associated with learning styles, cognitive levels, and behavioral attributes, which are dynamically updated as learners progress through their content and objectives. This model is essential for predicting future performance and making pedagogical decisions, often using machine learning algorithms to adapt to individual learning styles and preferences (Villegas-Ch et al., 2024; Eglington & Pavlik, 2023; Essa et al., 2023). The domain model represents the knowledge structure, including the ontology and prerequisite relations among learning items. This framework is essential for the effective design and development of logical learning paths that guide learners through their educational journey (Liu et al., 2019). This domain model opens the door for sophisticated reasoning that can maintain a knowledge graph of the curriculum and the learner's mastery of each concept, powering an adaptation engine that is more pedagogically informed and allowing for better adaptation. This brings us to the Adaptation Engine, which uses decision logic that can span from deterministic expert system; rule-based systems; to dynamic, adaptive, and intelligent techniques that provide a deeper level of adjustment to the particular needs of the learner. This adaptation is accomplished by tailoring and personalizing learning paths for each individual user through the analysis of learner's unique preferences, strengths, and weaknesses and, with the logical learning paths presented by the ontologies of the domain model, create customized educational experiences that optimize engagement and effectiveness. Lastly, the control mechanism which ensures that human expertise remains at the center of the learning process. This framework is called the human-in-the-loop (HITL) and positions AIEd as an assistant to human educators and learners, rather than a replacement. It provides educators with decision support tools for monitoring progress and intervening when needed, while giving learners guided autonomy over their educational journey. This machine-human partnership ensures alignment with pedagogical goals and that the AIEd learning experience remains grounded in human guidance and oversight.

The integration with learning management systems (LMS) embeds the AI functionality directly into the LMS environment, leveraging the LMS's existing data structures, learning elements, APIs, and integration points. The AI effectively adapts to the LMS constraints, using the platform's own constructs of courses, modules, users, gradebook, and student information to perform its tasks.

Ideally the adaptive learning AI layer is designed to seamlessly incorporate personalized study paths into existing LMS infrastructures. This involves creating cohesive content that adapts to individual implementation standards, that allow for the definition of learner capabilities, preferences, and learning speeds, often using near real-time data and feedback mechanisms to rank and select appropriate learning materials within the LMS (Sridharan et al., 2021; Conlan, 2000; Sayed et al., 2023). The learner model is continuously updated allowing for the adjustment of learning paths based on ongoing assessments and feedback, ensuring that the system remains responsive and focused on the evolving needs of the learners by enhancing engagement and academic performance.

The integration of adaptive learning technologies into LMS platforms is facilitated by model-based approaches that ensure the adaptability and scalability of the system, allowing for a personalized and effective learning experience across diverse educational contexts (Conlan, 2000). The complexity of adaptive learning systems comes from their need to process multiple domain data streams, maintain complex state information, and make real-time decisions while ensuring transparency and user control (Vagale et al., 2020); therefore, current implementations emphasize human-in-the-loop (HITL) approaches until standards and controls can replace human judgment. Another set of complexities comes from having to build adaptive learning systems around LMS constraints, with limited portability, narrow data scope unaware of learner's interactions with external systems outside the LMS, and with the learner's model and data largely residing inside the LMS with no portability.

2.3 LEARNER MODELS

Learner models in adaptive systems capture student characteristics through structured data representations. The IEEE's Public and Private Information for Learners (PAPI) standard (Zine et al., 2019) advocates for attributes including personal information, relationships with others that are relevant to the learning context, security preferences, performance metrics, and portfolio data. Modern implementations extend these basic structures to include learning style preferences, cognitive load indicators, and temporal learning patterns (Pan et al., 2021).

Contemporary learner models employ overlay architectures where students' knowledge is represented as a subset of the domain knowledge space. These models use algebraic lattice structures to represent task complexity and competency relationships, enabling fine-grained tracking of learning progress across interconnected concepts. The data structures usually encompass performance vectors which are time-series data that captures assessment scores, completion times, error patterns, and learning style profile that are multi-dimensional representations of cognitive preferences using frameworks like the Felder and Silverman Learning Style (Pan et al., 2021), knowledge state matrices which are probabilistic representations of concept mastery levels, and behavioral indicators such as patterns of interaction, navigation sequences, and temporal engagement metrics.

Learner model updates occur through multiple mechanisms operating at different temporal scales. Real-time updates capture immediate interactions and performance indicators, while scheduled processing mechanisms handle more complex analytical computations (H. Sun et al., 2022). The update algorithms typically employ Bayesian inference to maintain probabilistic knowledge states, with some systems implementing knowledge tracing algorithms like attentive knowledge tracing (AKT) (Gudoniene et al., 2022) for more sophisticated state estimation.

This dynamic adaptation requires continuous model refinement based on new evidence. Systems implement forgetting curves to account for knowledge decay over time and the use of reinforcement learning approaches to optimize the balance between exploration of new content and exploitation of known effective strategies. Clearly the challenge lies in maintaining temporal and contextual model accuracy and balance while avoiding overfitting to recent interactions.

2.4 DOMAIN MODELS

Domain models in adaptive learning systems increasingly rely on ontological representations for their data structure to capture both explicit knowledge relationships and implicit pedagogical dependencies (Popescu et al., 2008). These ontologies typically employ hierarchical structures with multiple relationship types including prerequisite dependencies, conceptual similarities, and difficulty progressions (Zang & Ma, 2022). The representation of knowledge within domain models is crucial for facilitating effective learning experiences, as it allows for the identification of complex interdependencies among educational content.

Modern domain models implement sophisticated mapping mechanisms to align content with curriculum standards and learning objectives. These systems use semantic annotation approaches that tag learning objects with relevant metadata, enabling dynamic content discovery and sequencing (Gudoniene et al., 2022).

The mapping process typically involves multilayered ontologies where domain specific knowledge connects to broader educational frameworks through standardized vocabularies. This approach enables interoperability across different educational systems while maintaining domain-specific granularity. By evaluating factors like scalability, vendor dependence, desired AI sophistication of ontologies, and the diversity of learning tools, decision-makers can determine which approach best fits their need, but the sunken cost and investments in their current LMS will be a significant determining factor for the implementation of the domain layer.

2.5 ADAPTATION ENGINES

Adaptation engines generally rely on expert-defined rule systems, also known as expert systems, that encode pedagogical knowledge as conditional logic (Shabalin & Nikolaychuk, 2022). These expert systems implement decision trees, or production rule systems, that map learner characteristics and performance indicators to specific instructional strategies. While interpretable and controllable, rules-based systems struggle with adaptability demands and the complexity of real-world learning scenarios, making these systems brittle and with a high maintenance cost.

To address these challenges, recent advancements in adaptive learning systems have introduced machine learning techniques that enhance the adaptability and efficiency of adaptation engines, promoting more effective educational interventions. These systems have used collaborative filtering approaches to identify similar learners to recommend content based on peer success patterns, while other content-based filtering analyzes learning object characteristics to match student preferences.

Reinforcement learning has shown promising results, with systems like the adaptive learning path navigation (ALPN) system using entropy-enhanced proximal policy optimization (EPPO) algorithms to optimize content recommendations (Chen et al., 2023). This type of system models the learning process as a Markov decision process, where the adaptation engine learns and develops optimal policies through close interaction with learners.

Designing adaptation engines requires striking the right balance between responsiveness, scalability, and long-term maintainability. Modern implementations often employ microservices architectures that separate different adaptation concerns into independent levels of abstraction within scalable components. Architectural patterns can be classified as: event-driven architectures for quick responses to learner actions, plugin-based systems that support flexible and expandable approaches, and distributed processing models that handle complex computations across various services.

2.5.1 Control Mechanisms

Modern adaptive learning systems increasingly emphasize transparency in their decision-making processes which includes providing learners and instructors with explanations for content recommendations, visualizations of learning progress, and mechanisms for understanding system behavior. The main challenge lies in making complex algorithmic decisions understandable to non-technical users without compromising the system's effectiveness.

To be effective, these adaptive systems require a balance that provide multiple levels of user control, from high-level preference settings to fine-grained content selection. Additionally adaptive systems must provide learner controls to override system recommendations, adjust adaptation parameters, and maintain control over their learning paths, while providing instructors the ability to monitor system behavior, adjust adaptation rules, and intervene when necessary (Schoenherr, 2021).

The idea of a "human-in-the-loop" (HITL) means that AI ought to function as an aid to enhance human decision-making instead of replacing it. This method requires thoughtful interface design that delivers relevant information with clear methods for human supervision and involvement. These control mechanisms highlight the central principle that adaptive learning must remain a partnership between human judgment and algorithmic intelligence. Transparency, multi-level user controls, and HITL design ensure that learners retain their agency, instructors maintain knowledge relevance and provide human depth to the learning experience, and AI functions as a collaborator rather than a replacement. With this foundation in place, the discussion can now turn to how these mechanisms are embedded within broader learning infrastructures, pedagogical frameworks, and institutional strategies.

Explainability and feedback loops are central to responsible adaptive learning design, with human-centric explainable AI providing interpretable outputs and feedback channels that allow educators to see why the system adapted content or recommended a particular intervention. To make this actionable, instructor tooling should include real-time dashboards that visualize performance trends and detect model drift, configurable alerts for at-risk learners or anomalous outputs, and rule editors that enable instructors to adjust adaptation parameters or override automated choices. Ultimately, the role of educator expertise remains paramount: educators should help define learning objectives, validate system recommendations, and tune adaptation policies of systems.

2.6 INTEGRATION PROTOCOLS AND SYSTEM ARCHITECTURE

Learning management systems (LMS) rely on a variety of interoperability standards and application programming interfaces (API) protocols to exchange data with other systems in real or near real time. These standards ensure that data associated with courses, user information, grades, and learning activities can be shared across platforms. Service-oriented architecture (SOA) and RESTful APIs provide the technical foundation for these integrations, while specifications such as QTI (Question and Test Interoperability) and SCORM (Sharable Content Object Reference Model) enable content portability. Additional standards, including xAPI (Experience API, also known as Tin Can API), LTI (Learning Tools Interoperability), OneRoster, and OpenAPI-based LMS web services, support real-time data exchange across diverse educational technologies.

Building on this foundation, widely adopted e-learning standards each address specific aspects of interoperability. The QTI (Question and Test Interoperability) and SCORM (Sharable Content Object Reference Model) focus on packaging course content and assessments into a portable format that any compliant LMS can import and track. The xAPI enables the collection of detailed learning experience records from multiple sources in a unified format, often storing them in a learning record store for analysis beyond the LMS. LTI provides a standard method for integrating third-party learning tools into an LMS, enabling features like single sign-on and grade pass-back between the external tool and the LMS. The OneRoster specification standardizes the exchange of roster and gradebook data, such as student enrollments and scores, between systems like student information systems and LMS. Together, these standards and protocols enable real-time interoperability, allowing an LMS to function as part of a broader adaptive learning technology ecosystem.

Modern educational technology ecosystems require AIEd systems to integrate with existing learning management systems, content repositories, and assessment platforms (Anido et al., 2003). This necessitates distributed architectures that can operate across organizational boundaries while maintaining data privacy and security by leveraging these complementary standards. This integrated approach transforms the LMS from a standalone course delivery tool into a central hub of a connected, data-driven educational ecosystem that can evolve alongside pedagogical innovations while safeguarding privacy and maintaining trust across organizational boundaries. Any next-generation AI adaptive learning platform that is to be integrated into existing LMS must ensure that the three pillars of learner, content, path remain aligned yet decoupled, allowing for intelligent agents mediating their interaction and continuous feedback loops driving improvement.

2.7 PEDAGOGICAL AND TECHNICAL CORE

This section serves as a foundational core of the educational views on AI adaptive learning, by merging the pedagogical principles that motivate adaptive learning with the technical and algorithmic machinery that brings it to life. The architecture of modern adaptive systems is deconstructed into four interconnected pillars: the learner model with the application of mastery learning principles, the construction of dynamic learner and domain models, the implementation of adaptive sequencing and feedback, and the critical control role of the HITL. By examining each pillar, this analysis will illustrate how data science and AI are not merely tools but are integral to realizing the long-held educational ideal of personalized instruction at scale, a vision famously articulated by Benjamin Bloom (B. S. Bloom, 1984).

By shifting the focus from a fixed-time, cohort-based model of progression to an individualized, competency-based one, mastery learning creates a framework where technology can be leveraged to provide tailored support at scale.

2.8 MASTERY LEARNING: ENSURING PROFICIENCY FOR ALL

Mastery learning is an instructional approach that assumes nearly all students can learn a subject given sufficient time and appropriate teaching strategies (Guskey, 2007).

Pioneered by Benjamin Bloom in the 1960s, mastery learning was Bloom's attempt to adapt the most powerful aspects of one-to-one tutoring and individualized instruction for standard classrooms (B. Bloom, 1968). Instead of the traditional model where teachers move on after a unit regardless of who has or hasn't mastered the material, mastery learning proposes that students should progress at their own pace, receiving additional support until they reach a pre-defined mastery level on each unit or skill before advancing. Bloom observed that while students vary in learning speed and style, if educators provide the necessary time and appropriate learning conditions, nearly all students can achieve a high level of understanding. This was dramatically illustrated by Bloom's famous finding that students who received one-to-one mastery-oriented tutoring performed two standard deviations better than those in conventional classes (the *2 sigma problem*), essentially moving the average tutored student to the 98th percentile of the control group (B. S. Bloom, 1984). Such results show the potential of mastery learning to close achievement gaps. The "problem" was not a pedagogical one but a logistical one: replicating this level of individualized tutoring on a large scale was deemed "too costly for most societies to bear" (B. S. Bloom, 1984). With AIEd adaptive learning systems represent the most sophisticated technological attempt to solve this logistical challenge.

The mastery learning pedagogy is implemented through a cyclical process involving three core components as follows. First, a diagnostic pre-assessment establishes a baseline for a student's set knowledge and identifies their appropriate starting point in the learner's journey. Second, frequent and low-stakes formative assessments are used to measure progress and provide immediate feedback as part of the learning experience. Third, based on the outcomes of these assessments, the system provides high-quality corrective instructions (or enrichment activities) to address specific learning gaps or deepen understanding on more complex topics (Guskey, 2007). This direct mapping of the pedagogical cycle onto the functional architecture of adaptive systems reveals a crucial point: adaptive learning technology is not a new pedagogy. Rather, it is the first truly scalable mechanism for implementing a proven teaching philosophy, repositioning AI not as a replacement for educational principles but as a powerful executor of them.

2.9 ALGORITHMIC IMPLEMENTATION OF "MASTERY LEARNING"

A central technical challenge in operationalizing mastery learning is moving beyond the simple rule base of "test scores" to precisely and dynamically define when "mastery" has been achieved (Rusman et al., 2023). Adaptive systems address this by defining mastery not as a single score, but as a "continuously updated probability" that a student has acquired a skill (Corbett & Anderson, 1995).

When the probability of mastery surpasses a threshold, the system progresses the student to the next concept (Corbett & Anderson, 1995). This technical definition and its alignment with the pedagogical goal and learner objectives are critical, as a poorly defined threshold can result in "pseudo-mastery," where students are advanced without a solid foundation (Pearson & Flory, 2014).

To make these mastery probability estimations, systems primarily employ two statistical frameworks. Item response theory (IRT) is a powerful psychometric framework used to model the relationship between a learner's proficiency in a specific skill and their responses to individualized assessment items (Reid et al., 2007). Unlike traditional testing, IRT analyzes performance at the item level and uses a mathematical function known as the item characteristic curve to describe the probability of a student answering an item correctly based on their ability (Reid et al., 2007). Different IRT models, such as the One-Parameter Logistic Model (1PL), Two-Parameter Logistic Model (2PL), and Three-Parameter Logistic Model (3PL), add parameters to account for item difficulty, discrimination, and the probability of guessing, respectively (Reid et al., 2007). IRT is the core engine behind Computerized Adaptive Tests (CAT), which efficiently measures ability by selecting items whose difficulty is closely matched to the student's current estimated ability, thereby requiring fewer items to achieve a precise measurement (Ihichr et al., 2024; Reid et al., 2007).

Alternatively, learning curves provide a complementary method for modeling and predicting mastery. A learning curve graphically represents the relationship between practice opportunities and a performance metric, such as error rate. In the field of educational data mining, raw empirical learning curves can be noisy, so models such as the Additive Factor Model (AFM) are used to filter out noise and generate a smooth, predicted learning curve (Anderson et al., 1997; Ikeda et al., 2006). By analyzing the parameters of this predicted curve—including its initial difficulty (height) and rate of learning (slope)—the system can estimate how many practice opportunities are needed for mastery and identify when a student is deviating from their expected learning trajectory (Anderson et al., 1997). This provides the system with a robust predictive capability.

The success of adaptive systems hinges on this duality: the pedagogical ideal of mastery is made tangible and actionable through a technical, probabilistic definition. The degree to which these two meanings of mastery align is a primary determinant of the system's effectiveness.

2.9.1 Learner Model: Dynamic Learner Portrait

The learner model is a central component for individualization in an adaptive system, functioning as a "dynamic repository of information" about the learner provided (Padayachee, 2002). This model is constructed from a continuous streams of data, which includes explicit performance data, implicit behavioral data, and demographic or static data (Aammou et al., 2016). To transform this data into a meaningful representation of student knowledge, adaptive systems use various "knowledge tracing" models. The Bayesian Knowledge Tracing (BKT) is a probabilistic model that conceptualizes a learner's knowledge of a skill as a binary latent variable ("mastered" or "not mastered") (Corbett & Anderson, 1995). This model uses Bayesian inference to update the probability that a student is in the mastered state, and its parameters have clear pedagogical interpretability (Corbett & Anderson, 1995). The Performance Factor Analysis (PFA) is a statistical alternative to BKT that uses logistic regression to model a learner's performance with a continuous logit value representing the strength for a given knowledge component, making it suitable for problems with multiple knowledge components used for performance prediction for the next attempt (Eglington & Pavlik, 2023; Pavlik et al., 2009). The Deep Knowledge Tracing (DKT) is a more recent and powerful approach which utilizes recurrent neural networks (RNNs) to create a high-dimensional vector representation of the learner's knowledge state across all skills (Piech et al., 2015). DKT can achieve superior accuracy on large datasets but is a "black box" model that lacks the interpretability of BKT or (Piech et al., 2015).

2.9.2 Domain Model: The Subject Matter

The domain model is the system's expert knowledge base, containing the concepts, skills, and relationships of the subject matter (Padayachee, 2002). This model serves as the canonical and ontological map of the curriculum, providing the structure against which student knowledge is measured (Padayachee, 2002; Piech et al., 2015). The effectiveness of an adaptive system is dependent on the domain knowledge representation. Common methods for representing domain knowledge include knowledge graphs (KGs) and prerequisite maps. A knowledge graph represents a domain as a network of nodes with concepts and skills where and edges represent the relationships. The most critical relationship in an educational context is "is prerequisite of," which defines the dependency structure of the curriculum (Zhou et al., 2023). This structure guides the system in determining which topics are pedagogically available for a student to learn next. A more formal and semantically rich structure is provided by Ontologies, which are explicit specifications of the terms and relationships within a domain, enabling more intelligent reasoning about the content (Cheung et al., 2010).

The personalization stems from the continuous back and forth interaction between the learner model and the domain model. A student's interaction is mapped to specific knowledge components (KCs) in the domain model, and their performance is used to update the mastery estimates for those KCs in the learner model (Guerra et al., 2016; Pavlik et al., 2009). The system then consults the domain model's prerequisite map to identify the set of KCs that are now available to the student, and its adaptation engine selects the next optimal learning activity. This fundamental co-dependency between learner and domain models highlights a critical design consideration: the quality and granularity of one model directly constrain the effectiveness of the other.

The use of semantic web technologies can enhance the interoperability of domain models, allowing for more effective alignment with curriculum standards and facilitating the dynamic discovery of learning content (Bittencourt et al., 2009). Domain models based on ontologies offer rigorous semantic definition that enable precise algorithmic reasoning but are notoriously time-consuming and complex to develop and maintain, so they have been rarely used in practical e-learning systems due to these challenges. On the other hand, semantic or concept maps are intuitive and simpler to create and widely used by educators to visualize and organize course knowledge. Semantic maps have lower barriers to adopting adaptive learning, since educators can contribute directly to the domain model without needing a semantic technologist.

2.9.3 Adaptation Engine: Sequencing and Feedback

With a representation of the student and the subject matter, the system can guide the learning process. This is done through adaptive sequencing, which determines the optimal path through the curriculum, and adaptive feedback, which provides immediate, tailored support at each step. These two functions work in tandem to deliver "just-in-time" instruction, ensuring the learner receives the right content and guidance at the precise moment of need (Nahum-Shani et al., 2018).

2.9.3.1 Sequencing

The adaptation engine is the algorithmic component that synthesizes information from the learner and domain models to decide which piece of content element or activity to present next (Padayachee, 2002; Ullah et al., 2025). The strategies for sequencing vary significantly in their complexity and underlying logic.

Rule-Based Expert Systems represent the most straightforward approach where the learning path is determined by a set of explicit, predefined "if-then" rules authored by domain experts (Shute & Zapata-Rivera, 2012). While this approach is transparent and predictable, it is often brittle and difficult to scale, as it can only account for scenarios anticipated by the author (Shute & Zapata-Rivera, 2012) and is domain specific. A data-driven approach establishes the sequencing task as forecasting (a prediction problem) and uses machine learning (ML) classifiers to accomplish this. These ML models are trained on historical data to predict the optimal next item for a learner with a given knowledge state (Yu et al., 2020). This ML method is more flexible than the rule-based system, but it often optimizes for a local, short-term outcome (e.g., success on the very next problem) and functions as a "black box" (Yu et al., 2020). Reinforcement learning (RL) models represent the most sophisticated approach, aiming to optimize long-term learning outcomes rather than local short-term success. The system acts as an "agent" that learns an optimal "policy" for selecting activities based on the student's current knowledge (Reddy et al., 2023; Shawky & Badawi, 2019). The RL's objective is to maximize a cumulative "reward" over entire learning sessions that are marked by a final mastery or sustained engagement. While RL is theoretically powerful, it is also the most complex and data-hungry approach, requiring massive datasets and sophisticated simulations for effective training.

2.9.3.2 Feedback

Effective learning occurs through immediate and targeted feedback; this is a key feature of adaptive AIEd systems. These systems move beyond simple feedback to provide more nuanced and useful guidance to the learner and instructor. While basic feedback types include knowledge of result (KR) (correct/incorrect) and knowledge of correct response (KCR) (providing the right answer), the most pedagogically valuable form is elaborated feedback, which explains *why* a response was correct or incorrect.

With the advent of large language models (LLMs) a paradigm shift in the potential for automated feedback has emerged. LLMs can generate dynamic, personalized, and conversational guidance in real-time, moving beyond pre-scripted, template-based responses (Chaszczewicz et al., 2024). Research has shown that LLM-generated feedback can be nearly as accurate as human feedback while drastically reducing cost and response time, which allows for instant, high-quality feedback at a scale impossible for a single human teacher (Bewersdorff et al., 2023).

However, LLMs also introduce significant risks. As probabilistic models, they can "hallucinate," confidently generating feedback that is factually incorrect or pedagogically unsound (Baidoo-Anu & Owusu Ansah, 2023; Kasneci et al., 2023). LLMs can also lack the deep contextual awareness of a human teacher and struggle with complex, multi-step reasoning. These and other limitations highlight the critical need for a human in the loop for validation and oversight (Kasneci et al., 2023).

The shift from template-based to generative feedback, while promising, underscores the new responsibilities and quality control measures required in system design.

2.9.4 Human Control Mechanism: Closing the Loop

The most effective adaptive systems are not fully autonomous; they are designed as human in the loop (HITL) systems, where the expertise and judgment of human educators and the agency of learners are integral to managing and controlling learning outcomes. The HITL creates a partnership between AI-driven automation and human intelligence (Sottilare et al., 2018).

2.9.4.1 The Role and Agency of the Human

HITL architectures can also give learners structured agency with choices and configurable support, while preserving curricular relevance and ethical alignment.

Adaptive platforms are designed as "co-bots," which are collaborative partners that augment, rather than replace, the teachers. The primary user interface is the teacher dashboard, a learning analytics tool that provides educators with real-time, actionable insights. These dashboards offer metrics for a high-level of awareness and provide visual indicators of student progress and status (Van Der Scheer & Visscher, 2018). Automated alerts serve as early warning system, flagging students who show patterns of struggle or off-task behavior (Arnold & Pistilli, 2012). For diagnosis, teachers can "drill down" into a deep dive view of an individual student's performance history and error patterns to understand the "why" behind learner struggles. The dashboard also facilitates data-driven interventions by aggregating class-wide trends, diagnosis with deeper views into patterns with reports on common misconceptions, enabling teachers to make informed decisions about targeted mini-lessons or small-group instruction (Van Der Scheer & Visscher, 2018).

The level of control afforded to the learner is a critical aspect of system design. Providing learners with a sense of agency has shown increased motivation and engagement (Bray & McClaskey, 2016). However, unconstrained choice can be counterproductive for novice learners who may lack the skills to make effective learning decisions, a problem known as the "expert-novice problem" (Prusak & Shriki, 2023). To mitigate this, effective systems employ a model of "constrained choice" or "guided autonomy." The AIEd curates a small, pedagogically appropriate list of recommended next steps that act as "guardrails" which the learner can use to make their final selection (Hooshyar et al., 2020; Rivero et al., 2013). This approach balances the motivational benefits of learner choice with the pedagogical necessity of a structured learning path.

2.9.4.2 Designing Effective HITL Systems

The design of successful HITL educational system is guided by several key principles. The fundamental principle is Synergy, not Replacement, where the AIEd should complement the human's strengths. While the AIEd excels at rapid data processing and executing sequencing algorithms at scale, it is the human teacher who can build relationships, provide necessary emotional support, and address complex, nuanced misunderstandings that data assisted AIEd alone cannot reveal (Sottilare et al., 2018).

Data transparency and interpretability are important since both teachers and learners must be able to trust and effectively use the system's outputs. This is a significant challenge for "black box" models, where the reasoning behind a recommendation can be opaque or invisible (Piech et al., 2015). Effective dashboards must translate complex analytics into clear, actionable visualizations to support transparency.

The principle of gradual release of responsibility is important learner agency, so that progressive autonomy and control is provided as students develop the maturity and "self-regulation" to manage their own learning effectively. This approach moves from a highly structured, system-driven path toward a more autonomous one, where the teacher performs the role of a facilitator or coach that supports the learners' journey.

Lastly, the design must always maintain the centrality of the teacher as the ultimate authority in the classroom (Sottilare et al., 2018). The AI provides recommendations and alerts, but the teacher must retain the control to override, customize, and adapt the system's behavior to fit their pedagogical philosophy and the unique context of their classroom (Sottilare et al., 2018).

The successful implementation of adaptive learning technology reveals a paradox concerning the teacher's role (Peters & Buckmiller, 2014). While the system automates rote tasks such as content delivery and assessment, it simultaneously increases the cognitive and managerial complexity of the teacher's responsibilities. Alison King introduced the distinction between the "sage on the stage" and the "guide on the side," recognizing the need to evolve the teacher's role back in 1993 (King, 1993). This evolution toward AIEd requires the teacher to constantly monitor data from dashboards, diagnose individual student needs, provide targeted interventions, and address the motivational and metacognitive needs of each learner (Bai et al., 2021; Gašević et al., 2015). This requires professional development that extends beyond software training to encompass the deep pedagogical and classroom management strategies required to run a differentiated, mastery-based classroom effectively to transform education from a static, one-size-fits-all model into a dynamic, personalized ecosystem as articulated by Benjamin Bloom (B. S. Bloom, 1984).

2.10 REFRAMING THE TRADITIONAL EDUCATION PROBLEM

The convergence of data science and learning are catalyzing a profound, abrupt, and disruptive paradigm shift for our education institutions, forcing established structures to reconsider their pedagogical practices from current standardized delivery and regulated practices to a dynamic, responsive, and deeply personalized experiences. For decades, the promise of individualized instruction, long considered the gold standard for mastery, was constrained by the irrefutable limitations of the traditional classroom. AIEd and the rich data streams from modern learning environments are disrupting this "one size fits all" educational traditional model, making this vision of individualized learning attainable at scale, therefore solving the "2 Sigma Problem" (B. S. Bloom, 1984).

2.10.1 Current Educational System

A critical analysis of the current educational landscape reveals that many efforts go toward adopting technology to modernize rather than undertaking a necessary systemic transformation. The traditional educational model is fundamentally misaligned with the dynamic, learner-centric needs of the modern era, as its core structure is a legacy of the one-to-many instructional model. That all students must follow regardless of their individual needs results in an educational system where students who grasp concepts quickly become disengaged, and those who struggle are often forced to move on with their cohort, leading to the accumulation of critical knowledge gaps that hinder future learning.

Traditional LMS e-learning systems and their technology designs largely digitize this conventional model, functioning as a passive content delivery channel, like a "digital filing cabinet" for course materials rather than an active, intelligent agent to support the individual needs of the learner. These systems have continued to evolve to integrate with other systems to provide further support for existing educational needs like calculating final grades, maintaining attendance records, identifying plagiarism in assignments, but inform real-time instructional adjustments for both learners and educators.

The failure to transform the underlying pedagogical model means that technology is often bolted onto the existing structure, limiting its potential to solve problems at a fundamental level. A true transformation, in contrast, requires redefining the very concepts of a teacher, a student, the learning path, a grade, and a classroom. The traditional model is not merely inefficient; it is philosophically and structurally incompatible with the goal of achieving universal mastery.

2.10.2 Scalable Personalized Education

This cycle begins with the collection of a vast and granular stream of data from every student interaction, from quiz answers to clickstream patterns and time spent on tasks (Huang et al., 2025). These data are fed into the AIEd engine, which continuously updates a learner model that contains inferences about their knowledge state, misconceptions, and learning preferences (Vorobyeva et al., 2025).

This cyclical process fundamentally redefines the concept of assessment. In traditional education, assessment is typically a discrete, summative event that occurs *after* instruction is complete (Gligorea et al., 2023), but AIEd collapses this structure, as every interaction becomes a micro-assessment that immediately informs the next instructional move. This collapses the traditional "teach-then-test" cycle into a single, continuous, and integrated dialogue focused on formative development rather than summative judgment (Sangrà et al., 2012).

The road map for the evolution of AIEd must start with the definition of an extensible common AIEd data model which abstracts out the current regulated structure of institutions and the current LMS implementations, from the evolutionary nature of AIEd centered around the core learner data model, domain data models, adaptation engine data model, and the data model for control mechanism and governance.

2.10.3 The Common AIEd Data Model

The road map for adoption of AIEd must move beyond a fragmented landscape of proprietary, "bolted-on" standards and solutions that continue to perpetuate the structures of the past through integrations. The current ecosystem of technologies is fragmented and involves proprietary solutions that are embedded within existing learning management systems (LMSs), with limited portability and narrow data scope to realize the potential of AIEd. For example, this "bolt on" approach creates data silos that prevent the creation of a modern learner centered "digital twin," a dynamic, context aware, portable, and ever evolving profile of a learner that can be seamlessly transferred between different educational systems (Anido et al., 2003).

The foundation for this Common AIEd Data Model (CAIDM) data model already exists within a suite of interoperability standards and application programming interfaces (APIs). Protocols like xAPI (Experience API), LTI (Learning Tools Interoperability), and OneRoster provide the technical means for real-time data exchange across diverse educational technologies, but these data models are not extensible; therefore, alignment of data requirements of new AIEd emerging capabilities cannot be easily collected and integrated into an ecosystem of technologies to support the learning experience. Existing standards excel at interoperability for today's typical educational records and supporting "plug-in" based integrations, but they fall short of enabling a new learning paradigm that is prudent, adaptive, personalized, and open.

An extensible common data model would serve as the central way to identify the data needs for interoperability across multiple systems, allowing for the creation of a unified data layer that captures the learner's evolving journey and skill acquisition across various educational contexts, and satisfy the needs of the four interconnected core components of AIEd.

This is not a technical convenience; it is the enabler of true lifelong learning. A fragmented, proprietary or industry fitting data landscape is a systemic barrier to the vision of a learner whose digital profile evolves alongside their knowledge and skills, a profile that can be ported from system to system to support a continuous, lifelong learning journey that is facilitated by experts in human learning and has the controls to validate the skill and capabilities for the mastery of knowledge. Designing a system that from the outset utilizes this extensible data model ensures that the entire learning ecosystem is built to support the evolutionary needs of learners, rather than serving the constraints of proprietary solutions or institutions.

Furthermore, this is not a replacement but would complement and extend existing work by harnessing the best emerging AIEd concepts around ontologies, ownership of learner data and outcomes, and would facilitate the adoption or transformation by institutions at different levels of maturity.

This is not a trivial undertaking, success will require collaboration, iterative refinement, and demonstrable value, but the potential benefits for democratizing knowledge and improving learning outcomes are immense. In short, the vision of a CAIDM is *essential* to shaping the "to-be" of education.

2.11 AIED ADOPTION ROAD MAP

The successful institutional adoption of AIEd is not merely another "technical project" but a deliberate, phased process of socio-technical and cultural transformation. A phased road map is, by design, a risk mitigation strategy that navigates the complexity of implementing a new pedagogy (Ferguson et al., 2014). This sequential approach is based on a logical progression that prioritizes the development of human capacity and trust before the full implementation of technological platforms which adheres to the ITIL people, process, technology.

2.11.1 Phase 0—Strategic Foundations for Ethical and Sustainable Adoption

The most critical work occurs before the first step of implementation. This phase focuses on the strategic, human, and ethical structures necessary for responsible and long-term sustainability. This requires commitment from senior leadership at all levels of the industry, to establish global, country, regional, local, and institutional priorities. It also requires stakeholder engagement from the outset and an honest assessment of institutional readiness across the cultural, human resources, infrastructure, and governance (Lang et al., 2017). The establishment of a foundational governance and ethical framework for data privacy and use is indispensable (Soffer & Cohen, 2024). Without this pre-work, the initiative is likely to generate distrust among participants, leading to resistance and most likely failure (Soffer & Cohen, 2024).

2.11.2 Phase I—Building Data Literacy and a Culture of Evidence

The first operational phase is designed to be a non-invasive introduction to learning analytics. The main objective is to cultivate a data-informed culture and build data literacy without demanding immediate changes in teaching practice (Dixon et al., 2025). The focus is on descriptive analytics that leverage all existing data from gradebooks and LMS to generate new perspectives for educators (Dourado et al., 2021). The primary tool for this phase is a faculty-facing learning analytics dashboard (LAD), which must be designed to support pedagogical inquiry rather than simply present data in a vacuum (Dourado et al., 2021).

Integrating CAIDM into the initial phase of AIEd adoption emerges as a critical enabler for the maximizing of initiative's intended values. By establishing an extensible, unified data foundation, CAIDM ensures that the learning analytics dashboard (LAD) can draw on a comprehensive learner profile, yielding immediate pedagogical insights and interventional value. This unified approach allows educators to begin practicing emerging AIEd concepts in a low-stakes, conceptual environment, akin to rehearsing with a Monopoly" game simulation before entering the real world of AIEd thereby building data literacy, trust, and human capacity from the outset. Furthermore, designing the system around a CAIDM from the start mitigates the fragmentation of proprietary data silos, enabling the creation of a portable, evolving digital learner profile that supports truly lifelong and personalized learning journeys. In effect, the deliberate use of CAIDM in this introductory phase not only reinforces the ethical, human-centered principles underlying the AIEd road map but also lays a durable socio-technical foundation for the sustainable and transformative future of education.

2.11.3 Phase II—Experimentation Through Low-Stakes Adaptive Practice

The following phase focuses on developing competence and confidence through the low-stakes adaptive experiences. This phase represents a crucial transition from passive observation to active experimentation (Beverson, 2023). The guiding principle is to introduce adaptive functionalities in "low-stakes" scenarios, where the impact of potential failures is minimal and the focus is on learning and exploration (Beverson, 2023). The literature offers a typology of such interventions, including personalized resource recommendations and gamified adaptive practice activities that are decoupled from high-stakes summative assessments (Wei et al., 2021). This phase functions as a crucial "sandbox" for the participants to identify and resolution of technical and pedagogical problems, including algorithmic bias if AI is being used, before a large-scale deployment (Beverson, 2023). The success of this phase is critical, as positive experiences will provide the motivation and confidence needed to embrace the complexity of full implementation (Beverson, 2023).

By embedding the CAIDM from the outset, institutions can systematically track the completeness, consistency, and accuracy of data streams feeding into the LAD. This not only ensures that early descriptive analytics are meaningful but also allows the CAIDM itself to function as a maturity model, offering benchmarks of institutional readiness and data quality prior to full implementation. In doing so, early adoption phases become diagnostic as well as developmental, creating a feedback loop where deficiencies are identified and remediated before advancing to more complex adaptive and AI-driven pedagogical interventions.

2.11.4 Phase III—Institutionalization of Adaptive Learning at Scale

This final phase represents the culmination of the road map, where a fully adaptive learning environment is implemented at scale. This goes beyond isolated interventions to encompass the dynamic and continuous sequencing of the entire learning experience ("Adaptive Learning," 2021). From a human perspective, this phase demands a profound transformation of the participant roles. Teachers from "sage on the stage" to "expert guide" or "learning orchestrator," requiring advanced professional development focused on data interpretation, ethical supervision, learning governance and supervision, and strategic intervention (Simon & Zeng, 2024).

The CAIDM serves as a critical enabler by providing a robust technical backbone for adaptive learning at scale. It ensures interoperability and real-time data exchange across the institution's diverse educational technologies, effectively allowing all systems to "speak" a common language. This unified data model can function like a dynamic digital twin of each learner's journey, continuously updating a comprehensive learner profile for the different domains that fuel predictive analytics for personalized interventions. Technically, CAIDM's standardized schema makes integration and data flow frictionless: data can be extracted and transferred via APIs without loss of fidelity or control, freeing the institution from vendor lock-in. New tools and AI-driven platforms can be easily "plugged into" the extensible ecosystem, thereby future-proofing the learning environment. On the human side, CAIDM empowers transformative pedagogy by supporting adaptive pathways and informed decision-making by all roles. Educators gain a holistic, real-time view of student progress and competencies across systems, enabling timely, data-driven interventions that improve learner success. Learners, in turn, become key actors in this ecosystem: with a portable digital learner record underpinned by CAIDM, they can carry their achievements and personalized data across platforms and even institutions, fostering continuity and ownership of learning. At an institutional level, a common data model streamlines coordination and governance, unified standards make it easier to enforce data privacy, ethics, and accountability at scale. Additionally, any analytics tools or dashboards developed around the CAIDM are inherently shareable and interoperable; innovations can propagate across departments, institutions, and communities as everything adheres to the same blueprint. In sum, by Phase III the CAIDM not only supports the technical interoperability required for a fully adaptive learning environment but also catalyzes the human and organizational transformations needed to ensure responsible sustainment.

2.12 GOVERNANCE

The implementation of AI in education, while offering immense potential, is not merely a technical challenge but a profound ethical and governance one. A robust governance framework is not a barrier to innovation, but a prerequisite for it, building the necessary trust and accountability among all stakeholders (Soffer & Cohen, 2024). Static governance models are inadequate for the dynamic environment of AIEd. An effective governance framework must be adaptive, based on principles of flexibility, continuous learning, and broad stakeholder participation in policy creation and review (Martikalini, 2024). The most effective adaptive systems are not fully autonomous; they are designed as human in the loop (HITL) systems, where the expertise and judgment of educators and the agency of learners are integral to managing and controlling learning outcomes (Sottilare et al., 2018). This paradigm creates a synergistic partnership that ensures technology serves to augment human expertise rather than replace it (Sottilare et al., 2018).

Through sophisticated LAD dashboards, educators are empowered to monitor progress, diagnose misconceptions, and deliver targeted, data-informed interventions (Van Der Scheer & Visscher, 2018). The AIEd acts as a "co-bot," a collaborative partner that excels at rapid data processing and executing sequencing algorithms at scale, freeing the human educator to focus on tasks that require uniquely human skills, such as building relationships, providing emotional support, and addressing complex, nuanced misunderstandings (Sottilare et al., 2018). The educator maintains the ultimate authority to override, customize, and adapt the system's behavior to fit the pedagogical philosophy and the unique context of the learner needs (Sottilare et al., 2018).

As mentioned before, giving learners a sense of agency is strongly correlated with their motivation and engagement (Bray & McClaskey, 2016). To mitigate the risk of unfettered choice being counterproductive for novice learners, effective systems use a model of "constrained choice," that needs to be governed and configured. Helping learners engage in their role as part of AIEd balances the motivational benefits of learner choice with the pedagogical necessity of a structured learning path, an educational experience that supports learners in their lifelong learning journey.

The successful implementation of AIEd requires a holistic, continuous evaluation strategy that moves beyond a narrow focus on learning outcomes (Naseer et al., 2025). A comprehensive evaluation must treat compliance with regulations, effectiveness, equity, and trust as interdependent dimensions. A critical challenge is the detection and mitigation of algorithmic bias, which occurs when a model makes inequitable predictions across different identity groups (Zambrano et al., 2024). An algorithm optimized solely for predictive accuracy can learn biased patterns from historical data and interactions, potentially reinforcing the very achievement gaps the system was intended to close (Obed Boateng & Bright Boateng, 2025). A robust evaluation strategy must not only check for bias post-development but also ensure that governance for fairness is built into the entire life cycle surrounding the use of adaptive technologies.

FUSADE, in its "Path to Inclusive Digital Transformation in El Salvador" (2023), argues that AIEd governance catalyzes innovation when it uses privacy-by-design principles to build trust over mere compliance and presents a balanced governance approach to the massive collection of sensitive student data (Path to Inclusive Digital Transformation in El Salvador, 2023). Such a model must coherently integrate the legal precision of the EU's General Data Protection Regulation (GDPR), the policy guidance of the Organization for Economic Co-operation and Development (OECD) Principles on AI, and the ethical imperatives of the United Nations Educational, Scientific and Cultural Organization (UNESCO) Recommendation on the Ethics of AI (Regulation (EU) 2016/679 of the European Parliament and of the Council of 27 April 2016 on the Protection of Natural Persons with Regard to the Processing of Personal Data and on the Free Movement of Such Data, and Repealing Directive 95/46/EC (General Data Protection Regulation), 2016). Together, these frameworks provide a road map for developing systems that are not only pedagogically effective but also legally sound, ethically responsible, and socially accepted.

The principles of the GDPR must directly inform the architecture of the AIEd system. The principle of "Data Protection by Design and by Default" (Regulation (EU) 2016/679 of the European Parliament and of the Council of 27 April 2016 on the Protection of Natural Persons with Regard to the Processing of Personal Data and on the Free Movement of Such Data, and Repealing Directive 95/46/EC (General Data Protection Regulation), 2016) mandates that the learner model adhere to minimal use, collecting only information strictly necessary for defined and legitimate pedagogical purposes (purpose limitation principle, Art. 5). Special attention must be paid to the processing of data from minors; under Article 8 of the GDPR, offering these services directly to children below a certain age requires technical and procedural mechanisms to obtain and verify consent from a parent or guardian. Furthermore, the system must be engineered to facilitate the exercise of student rights, including the right of access to their complete profile, the right to erasure, and the right to data portability (Art. 20), which allows students to carry their learning history with them as proposed by CAIDM.

The "Adaptation Engine" functions as an automated decision-making system, which activates specific protections under Article 22 of the GDPR and aligns with the OECD's principles of "Transparency and Explainability" (Regulation (EU) 2016/679 of the European Parliament and of the Council of 27 April 2016 on the Protection of Natural Persons with Regard to the Processing of Personal Data and on the Free Movement of Such Data, and Repealing Directive 95/46/EC (General Data Protection Regulation), 2016). This means the engine cannot be an inscrutable "black box." The HITL framework and educator dashboards are not just pedagogical best practices; they are essential mechanisms for guaranteeing a student's right to receive a meaningful explanation of algorithmic recommendations and the ability to challenge them. This materializes UNESCO's principle of "Human Oversight and Determination," ensuring that technology augments the educator's capacity rather than supplanting their judgment and ultimate responsibility (Recommendation on the Ethics of Artificial Intelligence, 2021).

Finally, the governance framework must proactively address the risk of algorithmic bias, a central concern for both the OECD and UNESCO (Recommendation on the Ethics of Artificial Intelligence, 2021; OECD Council Recommendation on Artificial Intelligence, 2024). An algorithm optimized solely for predictive accuracy can learn and amplify historical biases present in training data, reinforcing the very performance gaps the system was intended to close. Therefore, governance must include procedures for regular fairness audits and algorithmic impact assessments. As clearly articulated by the UNESCO, these protective measures are not merely technical; they are intrinsically linked to the goal of education: to foster human potential in a just and equitable manner, respecting the dignity and autonomy of every student (Recommendation on the Ethics of Artificial Intelligence, 2021).

The use of CAIDM can strengthen governance by centralizing identity and access management (IAM) within the data exchange framework, ensuring that all exchanges of AIEd data are mediated under consistent rules of control. By adopting "minimal use" principles, the CAIDM configuration enforces that only the data required for a given transaction is shared, reducing exposure and risk of having to share all data elements with LMSs. Built-in best practices such as role-based access control (RBAC) allow organizations to further define and enforce fine-grained permissions, aligning data access with institutional responsibilities and ethical priorities. In this way, CAIDM not only standardizes technical interoperability but also embeds IAM and data governance mechanism that maintains institutional oversight, preserves learner trust, and ensures that AIEd innovation operates within a security, transparency, privacy, and accountability first data environment.

Having a CAIDM enables communities of practice to share and reuse role-based access control (RBAC) definitions across institutions. These shared definitions act as governance templates that can be tailored to local needs, while ensuring consistent rules for who can access what data at every level of the organization. In effect, governance is strengthened not only through centralized IAM and RBAC over CAIDM data, but also through a collaborative ecosystem where identity and access practices evolve collectively and remain portable across contexts and jurisdictions.

2.13 CONCLUSION AND FUTURE DIRECTIONS

The convergence of data science and AIEd has presented a revolutionary model for education, offering a path to solve the long-standing "2 sigma problem" and democratize the benefits of personalized, mastery-based instruction. This new educational change is not merely a technological upgrade but a fundamental paradigm shift that redefines the roles of students, teachers, and the very structure of the curriculum. The AIEd engine, with its four interconnected pillars, creates a continuous cycle of data-analysis-adaptation that collapses the traditional "teach-then-test" model into a single, integrated dialogue focused on formative development rather than summative judgment of adherence to academic compliance. This groundbreaking change affords us the long-sought solution to provide individualized learning at-scale, making a vision once deemed too costly for most societies to bear a viable reality.

This seismic transformation presents educators with a new set of opportunities and responsibilities that they must actively own. The role of the educator is evolving from a "sage on the stage" to a "guide on the side." AIEd automates repetitive tasks like content delivery and sequencing, which frees the educator to focus on higher-order responsibilities such as providing targeted interventions, building relationships that support learners, and addressing the motivational and emotional needs of each learner. This is not a passive role; it requires educators to become "pedagogical architects" for AIEd, actively designing effective configurations and ethical frameworks to govern the system's creative autonomy.

The curriculum shifts from a static framework to a dynamic, co-created artifact, with the educator and their objectives at the center, ensuring that the technology is a faithful and ethical executor of sound instructional design. This is the ultimate form of "owning" the new educator role, and this journey of ownership with AIEd as a co-pilot is a critical component of professional development and growth.

The vision for the future of education is a powerful one: an ecosystem where every learner's journey is unique and optimized for their individual needs. This future is contingent upon a bold, strategic act of transformation by existing organizations. A truly transformative AIEd ecosystem cannot be realized within a fragmented landscape of proprietary and "bolted-on" solutions. The current ecosystem creates data silos that prevent the creation of a portable, complete learner profile (a "digital twin") that can follow a student throughout their lifelong learning journey. Existing interoperability standards are limited, and the inertia of past investments, or "institutional sunken cost," is a systemic barrier to progress that perpetuates an outdated, inefficient, and legacy model of education.

The Common AIEd Data Model (CAIDM) and a collaborative environment are the strategic linchpins of this transformation, providing the unified data layer necessary to break the siloed and proprietary mold. CAIDM is not a simple technical fix, but the enabler of a portable learner centered profile and a community-driven approach of educators that promote a healthy balance of educational progress through governance and adoption. The CADIM model can further increase the ability to benchmark performance and effectiveness against others, fostering a collaborative and competitive environment that drives innovation. The CADIM can also serve as a testbed to build new capabilities and a marketplace for AIEd services, acting as a portal for learning content that is suitable for the next best fit for the learner and the consumer (beneficiary of skills, generally an employer). The CADIM frees institutions from vendor lock-in and future-proofs their learning environment.

The building blocks for transformation are already in place. The challenge before us is to redirect energy from preserving institutions and proprietary technologies toward advancing true mastery of learning and supporting individual learning paths. Choosing to act is not about loss, but about unlocking the system's full potential. The risks of inaction, allowing the system to continue falling short of its potential, are far greater than the discomfort of risk and change. By contrast, the rewards of a responsible, thoughtful, and necessary institutional and cultural transformation are immense. The time to embrace that transformation is now.

REFERENCES

Aammou, S., Khaldi, M., & Novaes Carvalho, R. (2016). Learner modeling in adaptive educational systems: A comparative study. *International Journal of Modern Education and Computer Science*, *8*(3), 1–10. https://doi.org/10.5815/ijmecs.2016.03.01

Adaptive Learning. (2021). [Instructional Technology and Design Services Website]. *Adaptive Learning*. https://www.montclair.edu/itds/digital-pedagogy/pedagogical-strategies-and-practices/adaptive-learning/

Anderson, J. R., Matessa, M., & Lebiere, C. (1997). ACT-R: A theory of higher level cognition and its relation to visual attention. *Human–Computer Interaction*, *12*(4), 439–462. https://doi.org/10.1207/s15327051hci1204_5

Anido, L., Caeiro, M., Rodriguez, J. S., & Santos, J. M. (2003). Modelling and specification of interfaces for standard-driven distributed software architectures in the e-learning domain. In A. Coen-Porisini & A. Van Der Hoek (Eds.), *Software Engineering and Middleware* (Vol. 2596, pp. 68–89). Springer. https://doi.org/10.1007/3-540-38093-0_5

Arnold, K. E., & Pistilli, M. D. (2012). Course signals at Purdue. In *Proceedings of the 2nd International Conference on Learning Analytics and Knowledge* (p. 267). https://doi.org/10.1145/2330601.2330666

Bai, S., Hew, K. F., Sailer, M., & Jia, C. (2021). From top to bottom: How positions on different types of leaderboard may affect fully online student learning performance, intrinsic motivation, and course engagement. *Computers & Education*, *173*, 104297. https://doi.org/10.1016/j.compedu.2021.104297

Baidoo-Anu, D., & Owusu Ansah, L. (2023). Education in the era of generative artificial intelligence (AI): Understanding the potential benefits of ChatGPT in promoting teaching and learning. *SSRN Electronic Journal*. https://doi.org/10.2139/ssrn.4337484

Bayly-Castaneda, K., Ramirez-Montoya, M.-S., & Morita-Alexander, A. (2024). Crafting personalized learning paths with AI for lifelong learning: A systematic literature review. *Frontiers in Education*, *9*, 1424386. https://doi.org/10.3389/feduc.2024.1424386

Beverson, J. (2023). *Literature Review on Low Stakes Testing and Course Performance* (Literature Review No. RRN 2621). Crafton Hills College, Office of Institutional Effectiveness, Research, and Planning. https://www.craftonhills.edu/about-chc/research-and-planning/documents/rrn2621_literature_review_low_stakes_testing.pdf

Bewersdorff, A., Seßler, K., Baur, A., Kasneci, E., & Nerdel, C. (2023). Assessing student errors in experimentation using artificial intelligence and large language models: A comparative study with human raters. *Computers and Education: Artificial Intelligence*, *5*, 100177. https://doi.org/10.1016/j.caeai.2023.100177

Bittencourt, I. I., Costa, E., Braz, L., Pacheco, H., & Dicheva, D. (2009). Supporting interoperability between web-based educational systems. In *2009 39th IEEE Frontiers in Education Conference* (pp. 1–6). https://doi.org/10.1109/FIE.2009.5350551

Bloom, B. (1968). Learning for mastery. Instruction and curriculum. *Regional Education Laboratory for the Carolinas and Virginia*. https://eric.ed.gov/?id=ED053419

Bloom, B. S. (1984). The 2 sigma problem: The search for methods of group instruction as effective as one-to-one tutoring. *Educational Researcher, 13*(6), 4. https://doi.org/10.2307/1175554

Boateng, O., & Boateng, B. (2025). Algorithmic bias in educational systems: Examining the impact of AI-driven decision making in modern education. *World Journal of Advanced Research and Reviews*, *25*(1), 2012–2017. https://doi.org/10.30574/wjarr.2025.25.1.0253

Bray, B., & McClaskey, K. (2016). *How to Personalize Learning*. Corwin. https://www.corwin.com/books/how-to-personalize-learning-250714

Capuano, N., & Caballé, S. (2020). Adaptive learning technologies. *AI Magazine*, *41*(2), 96 98. https://doi.org/10.1609/aimag.v41i2.5317

Cardona, M., Rodriguez, R., & Ishmael, K. (2023). *Artificial Intelligence and Future of Teaching and Learning: Insights and Recommendations*. U.S. Department of Education, Office of Educational Technology.

Chaszczewicz, A., Shah, R. S., Louie, R., Arnow, B. A., Kraut, R., & Yang, D. (2024). Multi-level feedback generation with large language models for empowering novice peer counselors (No. arXiv:2403.15482). *arXiv*. https://doi.org/10.48550/arXiv.2403.15482

Chen, J.-Y., Saeedvand, S., & Lai, I.-W. (2023). Adaptive learning path navigation based on knowledge tracing and reinforcement learning (version 2). *arXiv*. https://doi.org/10.48550/ARXIV.2305.04475

Cheung, R., Wan, C., & Cheng, C. (2010). An ontology-based framework for personalized adaptive learning. In X. Luo, M. Spaniol, L. Wang, Q. Li, W. Nejdl, & W. Zhang (Eds.), *Advances in Web-Based Learning—ICWL 2010* (Vol. 6483, pp. 52–61). Springer. https://doi.org/10.1007/978-3-642-17407-0_6

Conlan, O. (2000). Novel components for supporting adaptivity in education systems—Model-based integration approach. In *Proceedings of the Eighth ACM International Conference on Multimedia* (pp. 519–520). https://doi.org/10.1145/354384.376509

Corbett, A. T., & Anderson, J. R. (1995). Knowledge tracing: Modeling the acquisition of procedural knowledge. *User Modelling and User-Adapted Interaction*, *4*(4), 253–278. https://doi.org/10.1007/BF01099821

Dixon, N., Howe, R., & Richter, U. M. (2025). Exploring learning analytics practices and their benefits through the lens of three case studies in UK higher education. *Research in Learning Technology*, *33*. https://doi.org/10.25304/rlt.v33.3127

Dourado, R. A., Rodrigues, R. L., Ferreira, N., Mello, R. F., Gomes, A. S., & Verbert, K. (2021). A teacher-facing learning analytics dashboard for process-oriented feedback in online learning. In *LAK21: 11th International Learning Analytics and Knowledge Conference* (pp. 482–489). https://doi.org/10.1145/3448139.3448187

Eglington, L. G., & Pavlik, P. I. (2023). How to optimize student learning using student models that adapt rapidly to individual differences. *International Journal of Artificial Intelligence in Education*, *33*(3), 497–518. https://doi.org/10.1007/s40593-022-00296-0

Essa, S. G., Celik, T., & Human-Hendricks, N. E. (2023). Personalized adaptive learning technologies based on machine learning techniques to identify learning styles: A systematic literature review. *IEEE Access*, *11*, 48392–48409. https://doi.org/10.1109/ACCESS.2023.3276439

Ferguson, R., Clow, D., Macfadyen, L., Essa, A., Dawson, S., & Alexander, S. (2014). Setting learning analytics in context: Overcoming the barriers to large-scale adoption. In *Proceedings of the Fourth International Conference on Learning Analytics and Knowledge* (pp. 251–253). https://doi.org/10.1145/2567574.2567592

Gašević, D., Dawson, S., & Siemens, G. (2015). Let's not forget: Learning analytics are about learning. *TechTrends*, *59*(1), 64–71. https://doi.org/10.1007/s11528-014-0822-x

Gligorea, I., Cioca, M., Oancea, R., Gorski, A.-T., Gorski, H., & Tudorache, P. (2023). Adaptive learning using artificial intelligence in e-learning: A literature review. *Education Sciences*, *13*(12), 1216. https://doi.org/10.3390/educsci13121216

Gudoniene, D., Staneviciene, E., & Motiejunas, L. (2022). The interoperability of learning object design, search and adaptation processes in the repositories. *Applied Sciences*, *12*(7), 3628. https://doi.org/10.3390/app12073628

Guerra, J., Hosseini, R., Somyurek, S., & Brusilovsky, P. (2016). An intelligent interface for learning content: Combining an open learner model and social comparison to support self-regulated learning and engagement. In *Proceedings of the 21st International Conference on Intelligent User Interfaces* (pp. 152–163). https://doi.org/10.1145/2856767.2856784

Guskey, T. R. (2007). Closing achievement gaps: Revisiting Benjamin S. Bloom's "Learning for Mastery". *Journal of Advanced Academics, 19*(1), 8–31. https://doi.org/10.4219/jaa-2007-704

Hakkal, S., & Ait Lahcen, A. (2021). An overview of adaptive learning fee-based platforms. In *Proceedings of the 2nd International Conference on Big Data, Modelling and Machine Learning* (pp. 222–226). https://doi.org/10.5220/0010731400003101

Hooshyar, D., Pedaste, M., Saks, K., Leijen, Ä., Bardone, E., & Wang, M. (2020). Open learner models in supporting self-regulated learning in higher education: A systematic literature review. *Computers & Education, 154*, 103878. https://doi.org/10.1016/j.compedu.2020.103878

Huang, J., Xin, Y. P., & Chang, H. H. (2025). The application of machine learning to educational process data analysis: A systematic review. *Education Sciences, 15*(7), 888. https://doi.org/10.3390/educsci15070888

Ihichr, A., Oustous, O., Idrissi, Y. E. B. E., & Lahcen, A. A. (2024). A systematic review on assessment in adaptive learning: Theories, algorithms and techniques. *International Journal of Advanced Computer Science and Applications, 15*(7). https://doi.org/10.14569/IJACSA.2024.0150785

Ikeda, M., Ashley, K. D., & Chan, T.-W. (2006). *Intelligent Tutoring Systems: 8th International Conference, ITS 2006, Jhongli, Taiwan, June 26–30, 2006. Proceedings.* Springer-Verlag Berlin Heidelberg.

Imhof, C., Bergamin, P., & McGarrity, S. (2020). Implementation of adaptive learning systems: Current state and potential. In P. Isaias, D. G. Sampson, & D. Ifenthaler (Eds.), *Online Teaching and Learning in Higher Education* (pp. 93–115). Springer International Publishing. https://doi.org/10.1007/978-3-030-48190-2_6

Kasneci, E., Sessler, K., Küchemann, S., Bannert, M., Dementieva, D., Fischer, F., Gasser, U., Groh, G., Günnemann, S., Hüllermeier, E., Krusche, S., Kutyniok, G., Michaeli, T., Nerdel, C., Pfeffer, J., Poquet, O., Sailer, M., Schmidt, A., Seidel, T., . . . & Kasneci, G. (2023). ChatGPT for good? On opportunities and challenges of large language models for education. *Learning and Individual Differences, 103*, 102274. https://doi.org/10.1016/j.lindif.2023.102274

King, A. (1993). From sage on the stage to guide on the side. *College Teaching, 41*(1), 30–35. https://doi.org/10.1080/87567555.1993.9926781

Krstić, L., Aleksić, V., Krstić, M., & Academy of Vocational Studies Southern Serbia, Department of Higher Business School. (2022). Artificial intelligence in education: A review. In *Proceedings TIE 2022* (pp. 223–228). https://doi.org/10.46793/TIE22.223K

Laak, K.-J., & Aru, J. (2025). AI and personalized learning: Bridging the gap with modern educational goals (No. arXiv:2404.02798). *arXiv*. https://doi.org/10.48550/arXiv.2404.02798

Lang, C., Siemens, G., Wise, A., & Gašević, D. (Eds.). (2017). *Handbook of Learning Analytics* (1st ed.). Solar Society for Learning Analytics Research. https://doi.org/10.18608/hla17

Liu, Q., Tong, S., Liu, C., Zhao, H., Chen, E., Ma, H., & Wang, S. (2019). Exploiting cognitive structure for adaptive learning. In *Proceedings of the 25th ACM SIGKDD International Conference on Knowledge Discovery & Data Mining* (pp. 627–635). https://doi.org/10.1145/3292500.3330922

Majumder, R. Q. (2025). Machine learning for predictive analytics: Trends and future directions. *International Journal of Innovative Science and Research Technology*, 3557–3564. https://doi.org/10.38124/ijisrt/25apr1899

Martikalini, C. (2024). Policy learning in collaborative government: A framework for adaptive and resilient public policy. *Edelweiss Applied Science and Technology*, *8*(6), 9142–9157. https://doi.org/10.55214/25768484.v8i6.3954

Mittal, U., Sai, S., Chamola, V., & Sangwan, D. (2024). A comprehensive review on generative AI for education. *IEEE Access*, *12*, 142733–142759. https://doi.org/10.1109/ACCESS.2024.3468368

Nahum-Shani, I., Smith, S. N., Spring, B. J., Collins, L. M., Witkiewitz, K., Tewari, A., & Murphy, S. A. (2018). Just-in-time adaptive interventions (JITAIs) in mobile health: Key components and design principles for ongoing health behavior support. *Annals of Behavioral Medicine*, *52*(6), 446–462. https://doi.org/10.1007/s12160-016-9830-8

Naseer, F., Khan, M. N., Addas, A., Awais, Q., & Ayub, N. (2025). Game mechanics and artificial intelligence personalization: A framework for adaptive learning systems. *Education Sciences*, *15*(3), 301. https://doi.org/10.3390/educsci15030301

OECD Council Recommendation on Artificial Intelligence. (2024). *Organisation for Economic Co-operation and Development*. https://legalinstruments.oecd.org/en/instruments/OECD-LEGAL-0449

Padayachee, I. (2002). Intelligent tutoring systems: Architecture and characteristics. *South African Journal of Education*.

Paek, S., & Kim, N. (2021). Analysis of worldwide research trends on the impact of artificial intelligence in education. *Sustainability*, *13*(14), 7941. https://doi.org/10.3390/su13147941

Pan, D., Hussain, A., Nazir, S., & Khan, S. (2021). A computationally efficient user model for effective content adaptation based on domain-wise learning style preferences: A web-based approach. *Complexity*, *2021*(1), 6634328. https://doi.org/10.1155/2021/6634328

Parveen, K., Obidallah, W., Alghamdi, A., Alduraywish, Y., & Shafiq, M. (2025, November 3). Gesture-enhanced adaptive learning platform for personalized AI-driven education. *Interactive Learning Environments*. https://doi.org/10.1080/10494820.2025.2542897

Path to Inclusive Digital Transformation in El Salvador. (2023). *FUSADES*. https://fusades.org/publicaciones/Camino_Transf_Digital_2023.pdf

Pavlik, P. I., Hao, C., & Koedinger, K. R. (2009). Performance factors analysis—a new alternative to knowledge tracing. In *Frontiers in Artificial Intelligence and Applications*. IOS Press. https://doi.org/10.3233/978-1-60750-028-5-531

Pearson, J., & Flory, M. (2014). *Beyond Proficient How Three High Schools in Kentucky Implement Mastery Learning* (No. IRM-2014-U-008147). CNA. https://files.eric.ed.gov/fulltext/ED555565.pdf

Peters, R., & Buckmiller, T. (2014). Our grades were broken: Overcoming barriers and challenges to implementing standards-based grading. *Journal of Educational Leadership in Action*, *2*(2). https://doi.org/10.62608/2164-1102.1070

Piech, C., Spencer, J., Huang, J., Ganguli, S., Sahami, M., Guibas, L., & Sohl-Dickstein, J. (2015). Deep knowledge tracing (No. arXiv:1506.05908). *arXiv*. https://doi.org/10.48550/arXiv.1506.05908

Popescu, E., Badica, C., & Trigano, P. (2008). Learning objects' architecture and indexing in WELSA adaptive educational system. *Scalable Computing: Practice and Experience*, *9*(1), 11–20.

Prusak, A., & Shriki, A. (2023). "Correspondence with the professor": A didactic-pedagogical tool that allows listening to student voice. *Creative Education*, *14*(7), 1379–1410. https://doi.org/10.4236/ce.2023.147088

Raza, F. (2023). *AI in Education: Personalized Learning and Adaptive Assessment*. Unpublished. https://doi.org/10.13140/RG.2.2.24796.77446

Recommendation on the Ethics of Artificial Intelligence. (2021). *United Nations Educational, Scientific and Cultural Organization*. https://unesdoc.unesco.org/ark:/48223/pf0000381137

Reddy, P., Chaudhary, K., & Hussein, S. (2023). A digital literacy model to narrow the digital literacy skills gap. *Heliyon*, *9*(4), e14878. https://doi.org/10.1016/j.heliyon.2023.e14878

Regulation (EU) 2016/679 of the European Parliament and of the Council of 27 April 2016 on the Protection of Natural Persons with Regard to the Processing of Personal Data and on the Free Movement of Such Data, and Repealing Directive 95/46/EC (General Data Protection Regulation). (2016). *European Parliament, & Council of the European Union*. https://eur-lex.europa.eu/legal-content/EN/TXT/?uri=CELEX%3A32016R0679&qid=1756609859134

Reid, C. A., Kolakowsky-Hayner, S. A., Lewis, A. N., & Armstrong, A. J. (2007). Modern psychometric methodology: Applications of item response theory. *Rehabilitation Counseling Bulletin*, *50*(3), 177–188. https://doi.org/10.1177/00343552070500030501

Rivero, M., Rogosin, S. V., Tenreiro Machado, J. A., & Trujillo, J. J. (2013). Stability of fractional order systems. *Mathematical Problems in Engineering*, *2013*, 1–14. https://doi.org/10.1155/2013/356215

Romero, C., & Ventura, S. (2020). Educational data mining and learning analytics: An updated survey. *WIREs Data Mining and Knowledge Discovery*, *10*(3), e1355. https://doi.org/10.1002/widm.1355

Rusman, A., Mas'udi, M. M., Hermoyo, R. P., Yarno, Yunianti, S., & Rafsanjani, H. (2023). Education transformation in 5.0 society development era, 020050. https://doi.org/10.1063/5.0141657

Saleem, S., Aziz, M. U., Iqbal, M. J., & Abbas, S. (2025). AI in education: Personalized learning systems and their impact on student performance and engagement. *The Critical Review of Social Sciences Studies*, *3*(1), 2445–2459. https://doi.org/10.59075/c35qa453

Sangrà, A., Vlachopoulos, D., & Cabrera, N. (2012). Building an inclusive definition of e-learning: An approach to the conceptual framework. *The International Review of Research in Open and Distributed Learning*, *13*(2), 145. https://doi.org/10.19173/irrodl.v13i2.1161

Sayed, W. S., Noeman, A. M., Abdellatif, A., Abdelrazek, M., Badawy, M. G., Hamed, A., & El-Tantawy, S. (2023). AI-based adaptive personalized content presentation and exercises navigation for an effective and engaging e-learning platform. *Multimedia Tools and Applications*, *82*(3), 3303–3333. https://doi.org/10.1007/s11042-022-13076-8

Schoenherr, J. R. (2021). Designing ethical agency for adaptive instructional systems: The FATE of learning and assessment. In R. A. Sottilare & J. Schwarz (Eds.), *Adaptive Instructional Systems. Design and Evaluation* (Vol. 12792, pp. 265–283). Springer International Publishing. https://doi.org/10.1007/978-3-030-77857-6_18

Serrano, J. C., Diduc, S., Šilenskytė, A., Stephens, M., & Nava-Aguirre, K. M. (2024). Fostering awareness of social sustainability in digital business. In A. Šilenskytė, M. Cordova, M. A. Schmitz, & S. M. Toh (Eds.), *The Palgrave Handbook of Social Sustainability in Business Education* (pp. 147–166). Springer Nature Switzerland. https://doi.org/10.1007/978-3-031-50168-5_8

Shabalin, A., & Nikolaychuk, O. (2022). Adaptation of the educational process using a rule-based system. In *2022 VIII International Conference on Information Technology and Nanotechnology (ITNT)* (pp. 1–6). https://doi.org/10.1109/ITNT55410.2022.9848764

Shawky, D., & Badawi, A. (2019). Towards a personalized learning experience using reinforcement learning. In A. E. Hassanien (Ed.), *Machine Learning Paradigms: Theory and Application* (Vol. 801, pp. 169–187). Springer International Publishing. https://doi.org/10.1007/978-3-030-02357-7_8

Shute, V. J., & Zapata-Rivera, D. (2012). Adaptive educational systems. In P. J. Durlach & A. M. Lesgold (Eds.), *Adaptive Technologies for Training and Education* (1st ed., pp. 7–27). Cambridge University Press. https://doi.org/10.1017/CBO9781139049580.004

Simon, P. D., & Zeng, L. M. (2024). Behind the scenes of adaptive learning: A scoping review of teachers' perspectives on the use of adaptive learning technologies. *Education Sciences, 14*(12), 1413. https://doi.org/10.3390/educsci14121413

Soffer, T., & Cohen, A. (2024). Privacy versus pedagogy—students' perceptions of using learning analytics in higher education. *Australasian Journal of Educational Technology*. https://doi.org/10.14742/ajet.9130

Sottilare, R. A., Graesser, A. C., Hu, X., & Sinatra, A. M. (2018). *Design Recommendations for Intelligent Tutoring Systems: Volume 6—Team Tutoring*. US Army Research Laboratory.

Spector, J. M. (2014). Conceptualizing the emerging field of smart learning environments. *Smart Learning Environments, 1*(1), 2. https://doi.org/10.1186/s40561-014-0002-7

Sridharan, S., Saravanan, D., Srinivasan, A. K., & Murugan, B. (2021). Adaptive learning management expert system with evolving knowledge base and enhanced learnability. *Education and Information Technologies, 26*(5), 5895–5916. https://doi.org/10.1007/s10639-021-10560-w

Sun, H., Zheng, Q., Zhang, H., & Pan, H. (2022). Learner modeling framework based on learning analytics. In *2022 IEEE 2nd International Conference on Data Science and Computer Application (ICDSCA)* (pp. 64–68). https://doi.org/10.1109/ICDSCA56264.2022.9988517

Sun, J., Song, T., Song, J., & Peng, W. (2022). Improving automated essay scoring by prompt prediction and matching. *Entropy, 24*(9), 1206. https://doi.org/10.3390/e24091206

Ullah, N., Khan, J. A., De Falco, I., & Sannino, G. (2025). Explainable artificial intelligence: Importance, use domains, stages, output shapes, and challenges. *ACM Computing Surveys, 57*(4), 1–36. https://doi.org/10.1145/3705724

Vagale, V., Niedrite, L., & Ignatjeva, S. (2020). Implementation of personalized adaptive e-learning system. *Baltic Journal of Modern Computing, 8*(2). https://doi.org/10.22364/bjmc.2020.8.2.06

Van Der Scheer, E. A., & Visscher, A. J. (2018). Effects of a data-based decision-making intervention for teachers on students' mathematical achievement. *Journal of Teacher Education, 69*(3), 307–320. https://doi.org/10.1177/0022487117704170

Villegas-Ch, W., García-Ortiz, J., & Sánchez-Viteri, S. (2024). Personalization of learning: Machine learning models for adapting educational content to individual learning styles. *IEEE Access, 12*, 121114–121130. https://doi.org/10.1109/ACCESS.2024.3452592

Vorobyeva, K. I., Belous, S., Savchenko, N. V., Smirnova, L. M., Nikitina, S. A., & Zhdanov, S. P. (2025). Personalized learning through AI: Pedagogical approaches and critical insights. *Contemporary Educational Technology, 17*(2), ep574. https://doi.org/10.30935/cedtech/16108

Wei, X., Sun, S., Wu, D., & Zhou, L. (2021). Personalized online learning resource recommendation based on artificial intelligence and educational psychology. *Frontiers in Psychology, 12*, 767837. https://doi.org/10.3389/fpsyg.2021.767837

Yu, R., Gong, Y., He, X., An, B., Zhu, Y., Liu, Q., & Ou, W. (2020). Personalized adaptive meta learning for cold-start user preference prediction (version 1). *arXiv*. https://doi.org/10.48550/ARXIV.2012.11842

Zambrano, A. F., Zhang, J., & Baker, R. S. (2024). Investigating algorithmic bias on bayesian knowledge tracing and carelessness detectors. In *Proceedings of the 14th Learning Analytics and Knowledge Conference* (pp. 349–359). https://doi.org/10.1145/3636555.3636890

Zang, Z., & Ma, T. (2022). Research and application of mathematical knowledge graph based on ontology learning. In Q. Liu, X. Liu, J. Cheng, T. Shen, & Y. Tian (Eds.), *Proceedings of the 12th International Conference on Computer Engineering and Networks* (Vol. 961, pp. 1387–1394). Springer Nature Singapore. https://doi.org/10.1007/978-981-19-6901-0_147

Zhou, J., Mao, S., Yang, G., Tang, B., Xie, Q., Lin, L., Wang, X., & Wang, D. (2023). RL-MPCA: A reinforcement learning based multi-phase computation allocation approach for recommender systems. In *Proceedings of the ACM Web Conference 2023* (pp. 3214–3224). https://doi.org/10.1145/3543507.3583313

Zine, O., Derouich, A., & Talbi, A. (2019). IMS compliant ontological learner model for adaptive e-learning environments. *International Journal of Emerging Technologies in Learning (iJET)*, *14*(16), 97. https://doi.org/10.3991/ijet.v14i16.10682

3 Enhancing AI Model Reliability

Mitigating Synthetic Data Risks With Hybrid Data and Explainable AI

Nisha Dadoriya, Arti Vaish, and Swapnil Pandey

3.1 INTRODUCTION AND BACKGROUND

The landscape of intelligent systems also grows ever faster, and synthetic data is influential, whether in the installation or the results of various applications. The findings of synthetic data receive considerable attention in the field of ethics and law, as well as the imperative need to implement protective mechanisms to maintain fairness and eliminate biases in the evolution of artificial intelligence systems (Adjei et al., 2024). Although synthetic data has eliminated data availability problems in AI and ML systems, it is not wholly reliable; it does not make any modifications to the original data but replaces the value of all real content (Clark et al., 2025), leading to problems such as misrepresentation of features, bias, etc. Although machine learning models require satisfactory data inputs, many practical applications deal with several data-related issues. It has led to problems of under-fitting, poor quality, and inadequacy, along with restricted data access due to privacy concerns and security. These problems are overcome by synthetic data creation and enabled data sharing (Kanagarla, 2024). Considering all these problems, we have emerged with an approach that can safeguard the advantages of synthetic data while simultaneously reducing its potential hazards.

The problems of unbalanced data can be resolved in three ways: hybrid dataset techniques, data-level, and algorithm-level approaches (Altalhan et al., 2025; Johnson & Khoshgoftaar, 2019; Sagana et al., 2024). In this research, we have primarily focused on the impact of hybrid data, which we created by combining both data, enhancing the stability of AI models or increasing the reliability of the performance level. Hybrid data can also enhance the scalability of synthetic data feature presentation, bias reduction, and model consistency through real-world data, which can be achieved with both datasets. The hybrid data approach is for data augmentation and model accuracy performance by enabling the right combination. XAI techniques such as SHAP (Salih et al., 2025; Thulasiram, 2025) use the impact of synthetic or hybrid data to evaluate the decision-making process in AI model decisions. XAI

DOI: 10.1201/9781003678250-3

studies the insights into the entire process and the increased visibility before and after hybrid implementation. These frameworks improve clarity in decision-making by checking the value of the features (Silva, 2025), making the model understandable and trustworthy to users.

In our chapter, we used accuracy, recall, F1 score, and precision, which are also named evaluation metrics in this chapter. Here, we note recall as the actual positive rate, accuracy is the correctly predicted observations, precision is the total predicted positive, and F1-score, which is the mean of precision and recall. These are the other comprehended names of evaluation metrics. We also documented real data as actual data, authentic data, realistic data, real world data; and so-called synthetic data as generated data, artificial datasets, and simulated data.

This chapter produces an extensive performance evaluation of the study models conducted by calculating their accuracy, recall, precision, and F1-score across all datasets (Naidu et al., 2023). Explainable AI analysis confirms that our study predicts the effect of synthetic or hybrid data by reducing risk through better interpretation. This research leads to the creation of better, more reliable AI models by integrating artificial and real-world data, enhancing performance improvements, and increasing the model's efficiency.

Synthetic data are being used in various fields for application in AI model training. This has almost solved the data availability problem, but it has also brought some difficulties related to inconsistency concerns by reducing the stability of the model (Vatsavayi, 2025).

3.1.1 Generated Data in Model Training

Artificial data can be used instead of authentic data to overcome data availability concerns (Latner et al., 2024; Marwala, 2024). The technologies used to create synthetic data include rule-based generation for GANs (generative adversarial networks) (Bhat and Nanjundegowda, 2025; Emadi et al., 2025; Kiran et al., 2025) and VAEs (variational autoencoders) (Mienye and Swart, 2025; Wang et al., 2025), as well as generative AI and additional datasets from the real world. Image data augmentation has many benefits through GANs (Sapkota et al., 2025), which show great potential in these fields. VAEs work best for probabilistic structure data (Chen, 2025), yet many studies suggest that synthetic data cannot be completely relied upon as a model (Vatsavayi, 2025; Baiardi et al., 2025).

3.1.2 Risks in Synthetic Data

The advantages of artificial data only need to be carefully analyzed so that the uncontrolled excitement caused by it can be prevented. In addition to improving data accessibility while protecting privacy, synthetic data presents positive and negative political and governance challenges (Fitzgerald, 2024). Its use also poses risks as it reduces the robustness of the model while features evolve. Research shows that synthetic data rarely maintains unpredictable elements to create stable models (Gomes et al., 2025; Nikolenko et al., 2021). During synthetic data training sessions, various cybersecurity models struggle to recognize threats, with dissimilarities between the generated and real-world security attacks (Baiardi et al., 2025). Studies using synthetic data have faced growing questions about their prior problems, as the propensity was present in both synthetic and real datasets (Momha, 2025; Steinhoff Hind, 2025).

3.1.3 Hybrid Data Approach

Introduced a hybrid approach by combining natural (real-world) and simulated data that is reliable and improves model quality. According to research, hybrid data performs better in image classification by eliminating the weakness of synthetic data. Several research studies have found that the language of the NLP hybrid method interprets well, so it strengthens the actions of authentic and artificially generated datasets (Ghanadian et al., 2025; Koç et al., 2025). This method brings beneficial findings for fields that often face ethical and regulatory concerns, such as healthcare (Mennella et al., 2024; Suhag, 2024), education (Tkachenko, 2024), cyber security, finance, and autonomous systems (Deng & Deng, 2023). Precise evaluation data is required to achieve the maximum possible benefit of hybrid data. Actions using structured hybrid data achieve high accuracy, reliability and reduce the risks of using only synthetic data.

3.1.4 Explainable AI for Data Analysis and Understanding

Expert systems require interpretability at maximum power levels; using explainability to evaluate AI models is crucial. An understanding of this is to use techniques such as SHAP and LIME to detect anomaly vs consistency in data (Kalusivalingam et al., 2021; Vimbi et al., 2024). According to the research, XAI provides a method to detect manipulation of artificial data by contrasting synthetic and real data (Munteanu et al., 2025; Ramesh et al., 2025). In this work, we evaluate the before and after unification of hybrid data to check the explanation of hybrid data for comparing SHAP values for real and synthetic datasets. This approach helps to find out whether the hybrid data model improves model transparency and whether it gives a misleading explanation.

3.1.5 Our Contributions

Preliminary studies to investigate synthetic data risks exist in the research literature (Altalhan et al., 2025; Johnson and Khoshgoftaar, 2019; Sagana et al., 2024), but investigation using systematic performance metrics and analytical analysis of both real, artificial, and hybrid datasets remains difficult. This research work aims to address the existing gap.

- Comparative performance analysis: Systematically compared real, synthetic, and hybrid datasets by taking datasets from multiple domains and analyzing them by calculating performance metrics.
- Explainability assessment: Using the SHAP XAI techniques, we observe how synthetic or hybrid data affects the explicability of the model.
- Reduce the risk of synthetic data: We present a structured approach that integrates hybrid data through a model that balances synthetic and real data and reduces the risk by increasing the model's reliability.

3.2 METHODOLOGY

This section outlines our systematic research process that evaluates the performance outcome of artificial data in generative models and demonstrates the role of hybrid data and synthetic explanations in managing these impacts. Samples created from synthetic data are effective even when real data lack completeness. However, their effectiveness is not particular when training the model because they contain inconsistent biases (Baiardi et al., 2025; Fitzgerald, 2024; Gomes et al., 2025; Momha, 2025; Nikolenko et al., 2021). To address this challenge, we introduce a hybrid data strategy that blends real world and generated data with the primary objective of improving model efficiency and maintaining the reliability of real data. This research applies a multistep workflow as shown in Figure 3.1.

3.2.1 Dataset Collection

In our research, we relied on the data for in-depth analysis. These datasets were selected because they have mixed feature sets containing numerical as well as categorical variables suitable for classification purposes. Hence, it provides an optimal basis for direct synthetic datasets in the AI model. Each dataset contains various features in addition to target labels that support classification tasks.

3.2.2 Synthetic Dataset Generation

In this analysis, we employed GANs and VAEs to create synthetic data for artificial data generation (Bhat and Nanjundegowda, 2025; Emadi et al., 2025; Kiran et al., 2025; Mienye and Swart, 2025; Wang et al., 2025). VAEs go from learning distributions in probabilistic content to real-world information to perform this process (Chen, 2025), while GANs function uses a two-part generator architecture in which one creates synthetic data and the other differentiates between real or synthetic samples (Vyas and Pandey, 2025). They refine their output and distribute data like the

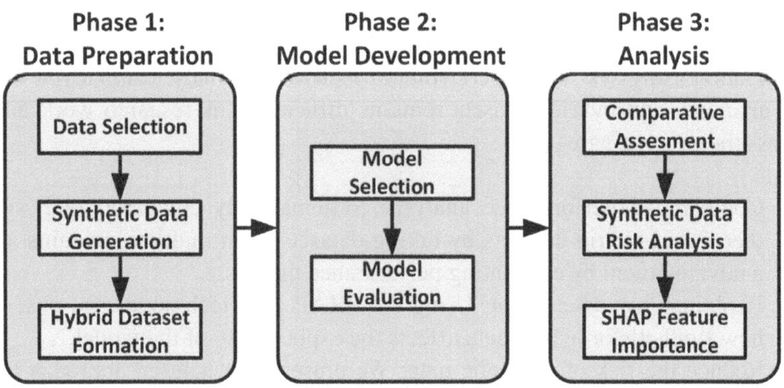

FIGURE 3.1 Multistep framework for synthetic data integration in AI model training with hybrid data and XAI analysis.

real world. The models preserve the quality of the data by achieving distributional understanding, yet they have several risks, like distributional shifts, privacy concerns where synthetic samples are derived from real data patterns but are inconsistent, and biases that affect the robustness of the AI model.

3.2.3 Hybrid Dataset Creation

In this study, we create hybrid datasets that integrate artificial and real instances to reduce the risks of generated datasets. This method integrates synthetic data with real-world info, thereby maintaining the results of data distribution while enhancing the reliability of genuine data and the benefits of artificially created data (Bauer et al., 2024). The main goal of hybrid data creation is to obtain synthetic diversity along with natural patterns from authentic real-world samples (Latner et al., 2024). When synthetic samples are included in the training, AI models achieve better generalization because their portion is also real-world and shares a particular ratio, thus preventing artificial patterns from dominating. The datasets become more operable for classification, which requires more robust performance variability.

3.2.4 Model Training and Performance Calculation

To train our dataset (Pal, 2005), we include synthetic data or a synthesized combination of these along with these three variant real samples. For the evaluation process, the model training data covers about 80% of the whole dataset, whereas the remaining 20% of the data is used for testing. To investigate the implementation of each dataset, we calculated accuracy, precision, and F1-score Naidu et al. (2023). The result of the generated data showed a decrease identical to the realistic data, which signifies a high risk. This research was studied through three datasets in which the risk caused by synthetic data was quantified. Along with this, the benefits of synthetic data were taken positively and combined with real data to use them in training and on that basis.

3.2.5 XAI Analysis and Improvement Evaluation

By analyzing with explainable AI techniques like SHAP (Salih et al., 2025; Thulasiram, 2025), what happened pre- and post-integration of hybrid data formation was found out. SHAP values evaluation was analyzed for model assessment so that decision-making is efficient. Such as analyzing the risks involved in synthetic data and then using the positive response from hybrid data creation and analyzing the overall performance of the model through metrics scores.

3.3 RESULTS AND FINDINGS

3.3.1 Comparative and Comprehensive Implementation Analysis

The evaluation process confirmed that synthetic data contain risk when compared to real data, which can be seen in Table 3.1, that has a negative effect on model performance, and the result of Table 3.2 verified that hybrid datasets perform better than generative dataset because they are integrated with real data.

TABLE 3.1
Synthetic Data Risk over Real Data

Dataset	Accuracy Risk	Precision Risk	Recall Risk	F1 Score Risk
Iris	0.4000	0.4175	0.4000	0.4410
Wine	0.4722	0.4360	0.4722	0.4646
Cancer	0.2105	0.1995	0.2105	0.2170

TABLE 3.2
Performance Improvement of Hybrid Data over Synthetic Data

Dataset	Metric	Absolute Improvement	% Improvement
Iris	Accuracy	0.2444	40.74%
	Precision	0.2714	46.57%
	Recall	0.2444	40.74%
	F1 Score	0.2862	51.23%
Wine	Accuracy	0.3241	61.42%
	Precision	0.2965	52.55%
	Recall	0.3241	61.42%
	F1 Score	0.3112	58.12%
Cancer	Accuracy	0.1579	20.91%
	Precision	0.1466	19.15%
	Recall	0.1579	20.91%
	F1 Score	0.1638	21.89%
Average	Accuracy	**0.2421**	**41.02%**
	Precision	**0.2382**	**39.42%**
	Recall	**0.2421**	**41.02%**
	F1 Score	**0.2537**	**43.74%**

The real dataset shows precision, recall, and f1-score value along with perfect accuracy, whereas synthetic data shows the worst metrics score in comparison. Table 3.1 shows the vulnerabilities of the simulated data as opposed to the realistic data.

It shows that the wine dataset has the highest attrition, indicating that synthetic data gradually degrade the performance of the model.

Table 3.2 shows the performance improvement when using hybrid data instead of purely synthetic data.

The performance of the datasets for iris, wine, and cancer is shown in Table 3.3, which is a complete comparative analysis of the evaluation metrics scores taken in the research study. It showed that the accuracy of real data was 1.00, which was perfect, but the synthetic data had the highest score only up to 0.6. Whereas the accuracy score of the hybrid approach, which was created by merging real and synthetic samples, was raised to 0.844, which is more beneficial for the system.

3.3.2 SHAP-Based Explainability Analysis

After utilizing generated data, we used the SHAP-based explainable AI approach to advance the model's interpretability. SHAP value evaluation shows which model features determine the most important factor in decision-making. SHAP datasets value calculation works on each dataset, including synthetic, real, and hybrid datasets of each domain. An enhancement in SHAP value was observed in the evaluated datasets through hybrid data approach (Chinnaraju, 2025; Oblizanov et al., 2023).

SHAP value improvement was 0.093 in the iris dataset before but increased to 0.109 after hybrid data. Similarly, it increased from 0.030 to 0.036 in wine and from 0.014 to 0.016 in cancer. This proves that hybrid features improve the interpretability of the model as it is more reliable.

3.3.3 Results

Our research confirmed that the hybrid data collection method performs much better than synthetic data collection. Systems with real datasets provide the best outcome, but hybrid datasets are an alternative, which are a combination of actual patterns and large-scale generative data. The results presented in Table 3.3 show that hybrid data deliver approximately 90% accuracy, which is in no way better than synthetic. This adoption eliminates the synthetic limitation by successfully enhancing the hybridization model. On the basis of SHAP explanation, hybrid datasets maintain more important characteristics than individual synthetic data.

TABLE 3.3
Performance Evaluation on Real, Synthetic, and Hybrid Data

		Iris		
Type	**Acc**	**Prec**	**Rec**	**F1**
Real	1.000	1.000	1.000	1.000
Synth	0.600	0.5825	0.600	0.5590
Hybrid	0.8444	0.8539	0.8444	0.8452
		Wine		
Type	**Acc**	**Prec**	**Rec**	**F1**
Real	1.000	1.000	1.000	1.000
Synth	0.5278	0.5640	0.5278	0.5354
Hybrid	0.8519	0.8605	0.8519	0.8466
		Cancer		
Type	**Acc**	**Prec**	**Rec**	**F1**
Real	0.9649	0.9652	0.9649	0.9647
Synth	0.7544	0.7657	0.7544	0.7477
Hybrid	0.9123	0.9123	0.9123	0.9115

Figure 3.1 and Figure 3.2 show the performance comparison assessment and the SHAP value assessment. The assessment validates how the hybrid dataset proved to be an effective methodology and measures significant changes in all metrics in the comparison that enhance the system's decision-making, which makes the model trustworthy and maintains its interpretability.

3.3.4 Key Findings

This research proves that by joining a synthetic sample with a real sample, an optimal method provides for better performance, which reduces the risk caused by synthetic data. The hybrid data model introduces more dependable predictive models, as these eliminate the systematic problems caused by the use of synthetic data, which is independent (Figure 3.2). The evaluation calculation Table 3.1 explains the difference between artificial data and actual data by calculating risk, and Table 3.2 shows the improvement in this through the hybrid approach. The SHAP-based technique gives better feature explanations through the feature value of each dataset. We can see the effects of hybridization through Table 3.4.

This also becomes a useful solution for AI applications, as confirmed in Table 3.2 that each dataset improves the hybrid model. The research findings validate that hybrid data is a better approach than synthetic data as it generates trustworthy feature distribution characteristics as well as optimal model performance. AI models will prove to be even more suitable for the real world when this hybrid data is used instead of synthetic data; along with this, the model risk will start reducing, and interpretability will increase (Figure 3.3).

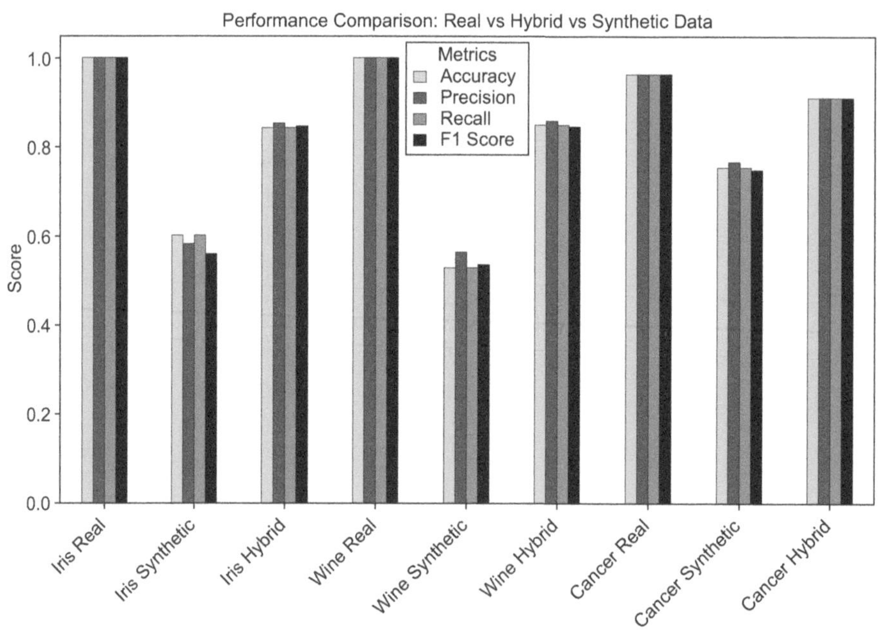

FIGURE 3.2 Comparative analysis of iris, wine, and cancer dataset by performance metrics.

TABLE 3.4
XAI Results—Mean SHAP Values and % Improvement

Dataset	Phase	Mean SHAP Value	% SHAP Improvement
Iris	Synthetic (Before)	0.0934	–
	Hybrid (After)	0.1099	+17.64%
Wine	Synthetic (Before)	0.0303	–
	Hybrid (After)	0.0364	+20.13%
Cancer	Synthetic (Before)	0.0141	–
	Hybrid (After)	0.0164	+16.31%

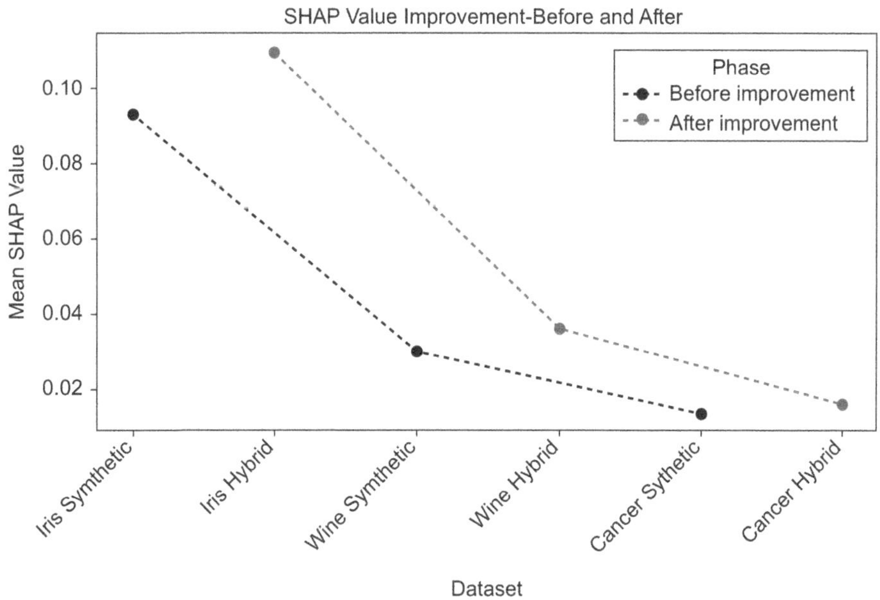

FIGURE 3.3 XAI analysis by SHAP value.

3.4 CONCLUSION

This research confirms synthetic data risks in AI training and presents a hybrid data method that tackles these vulnerabilities. Synthetic data also provides many benefits, the primary advantages of which are improving data accessibility and enhancing the diversity potential. Our study showed that combining synthetic and real data and using a hybrid model implementation enhances model performance, especially accuracy, precision, and F1-score. In the analysis of the SHAP-based XAI technique, both synthetic and hybrid datasets were used in interpretable model training. When only synthetic data was used, it predicted feature values which gave unreliable outcome in decision-making but model training with hybrid data gave more understandable result as it keeps the contribution of crucial elements and also delivers better real-world performance.

This study proves that real-world data must be used in model training so that it can be made reliable and accurate. Although synthetic data helps in creating additional resources, its exclusive use also produces fluctuations. Hybrid dataset implementation shows success in various domains because it takes authentic patterns from actual data, creating AI models with flexible functionality and dependable interpretation.

3.4.1 Future Work

Future research should focus on hybrid data methods by integrating techniques such as adversarial data filtering and dynamic weight calculations to improve the quality of datasets. Synthetic data producing methods must be tested along with hybridization methods for AI applications. These research directions are leading to AI systems that maintain safety and reliability through effective management of synthetic risk benefits.

REFERENCES

Adjei, J. K., Owusu, H., & Yeboah, C. (2024). Generative AI-induced synthetic data: Explicating the ethical implications.

Altalhan, M., Algarni, A., & Turki-Hadj Alouane, M. (2025). Imbalanced data problem in machine learning: A review. *IEEE Access*.

Baiardi, F., Ruggieri, S., & Sammartino, V. (2025). AI-enabled cybersecurity using synthetic data. In *2025 IEEE International Conference on Pervasive Computing and Communications Workshops and Other Affiliated Events (PerCom Workshops)* (pp. 140–145). IEEE Computer Society.

Bauer, A., Trapp, S., Stenger, M., Leppich, R., Kounev, S., Leznik, M., . . . & Foster, I. (2024). Comprehensive exploration of synthetic data generation: A survey. *arXiv preprint arXiv:2401.02524*.

Bhat, R., & Nanjundegowda, R. (2025). A review on comparative analysis of generative adversarial networks' architectures and applications. *Journal of Robotics and Control (JRC)*, *6*(1), 53–64.

Chen, T. (2025). Probabilistic latent variable models: Principles and foundations for modern generative AI. *Available at SSRN 5244929*.

Chinnaraju, A. (2025). Explainable AI (XAI) for trustworthy and transparent decision-making: A theoretical framework for AI interpretability. *World Journal of Advanced Engineering Technology and Sciences*, *14*(3), 170–207.

Clark, J., Barton, B., Albarqouni, L., Byambasuren, O., Jowsey, T., Keogh, J., . . . & Jones, M. (2025). Generative artificial intelligence use in evidence synthesis: A systematic review. *Research Synthesis Methods*, 1–19,

Deng, H, & Deng, H. (2023). *Exploring Synthetic Data for Artificial Intelligence and Autonomous Systems: A Primer.*

Emadi, M., Moghtadaiee, V., & Alishahi, M. (2025). *From Real to Synthetic: GAN and DPGAN for Privacy Preserving.*

Fitzgerald, A. (2024). Why synthetic data can never be ethical: A lesson from media ethics. *Surveillance & Society*, *22*(4), 477–482.

Ghanadian, H., Nejadgholi, I., & Al Osman, H. (2025). Improving suicidal ideation detection in social media posts: Topic modeling and synthetic data augmentation approach. *JMIR Formative Research*, *9*, e63272.

Gomes, A., Islam, N.M., & Karim, M.R. (2025). Data-driven environmental risk management and sustainability analytics. *Journal of Computer Science and Technology Studies*, *7*(3), 812–825.

Johnson, J.M., & Khoshgoftaar, T.M. (2019). Survey on deep learning with class imbalance. *Journal of Big Data*, *6*(1), 1–54.

Kalouli, A.-L., Crouch, R., & De Paiva, V. (2020). Hy-NLI: A hybrid system for natural language inference. In *Proceedings of the 28th international conference on computational linguistics* (pp. 5235–5249).

Kalusivalingam, A.K., Sharma, A., Patel, N., & Singh, V. (2021). Leveraging shap and lime for enhanced explainability in AI-driven diagnostic systems. *International Journal of AI and ML*, *2*(3).

Kanagarla, K. (2024). The role of synthetic data in ensuring data privacy and enabling secure analytics. *Available at SSRN 5012479.*

Kiran, A., Rubini, P., & Kumar, S.S. (2025). Comprehensive review of privacy, utility and fairness offered by synthetic data. *IEEE Access.*

Koç, C., Özyurt, F., & Iantovics, L.B. (2025). Survey on latest advances in natural language processing applications of generative adversarial networks. *Wiley Interdisciplinary Reviews: Data Mining and Knowledge Discovery*, *15*(1), e70004,

Latner, J., Neunhoeffer, M., & Drechsler, J. (2024). Generating synthetic data is complicated: Know your data and know. In *Privacy in statistical databases: International conference, PSD 2024, Antibes Juan-Les-Pins, France, September 25–27, 2024, proceedings* (Vol. 14915, p. 115).

Marwala, T. (2024). Synthetic versus authentic data. In *The balancing problem in the governance of artificial intelligence* (pp. 105–120). Springer.

Mennella, C., Maniscalco, U., De Pietro, G., & Esposito, M. (2024). Ethical and regulatory challenges of AI technologies in healthcare: A narrative review. *Heliyon*, *10*(4).

Mienye, I.D., & Swart, T.G. (2025). Deep autoencoder neural networks: A comprehensive review and new perspectives. *Archives of Computational Methods in Engineering*, 1–20.

Momha, M. (2025). The synthetic mirror–synthetic data at the age of agentic AI. *arXiv preprint arXiv:2506.13818.*

Munteanu, D., Moldovanu, S., & Miron, M. (2025). The explanation and sensitivity of AI algorithms supplied with synthetic medical data. *Electronics*, *14*(7), 1270.

Naidu, G., Zuva, T., & Mmbongeni Sibanda, E. (2023). A review of evaluation metrics in machine learning algorithms. In *Computer Science On-Line Conference* (pp. 15–25). Springer.

Nikolenko, S.I., et al. (2021). *Synthetic data for deep learning* (Vol. 174). Springer.

Oblizanov, A., Shevskaya, N., Kazak, A., Rudenko, M., & Dorofeeva, A. (2023). Evaluation metrics research for explainable artificial intelligence global methods using synthetic data. *Applied System Innovation*, *6*(1), 26.

Pal, M. (2005). Random forest classifier for remote sensing classification. *International Journal of Remote Sensing*, *26*(1), 217–222.

Ramesh, G., et al. (2025). Enhancing water quality monitoring with explainable AI and WGAN-based data augmentation. *Remote Sensing in Earth Systems Sciences*, *8*(2), 423–434.

Sagana, C., Manjula Devi, R., Sangeetha, M., Kiruthick Kumar, K., Lalit, K., & Manyu Sameera, N. (2024). Ensemble model-based crop recommendation system with data generation using GAN. In *International Conference on Artificial Intelligence and Smart Energy* (pp. 310–321). Springer.

Salih, A.M., Raisi-Estabragh, Z., Galazzo, I.B., Radeva, P., Petersen, S.E., Lekadir, K., & Menegaz, G. (2025). A perspective on explainable artificial intelligence methods: Shap and lime. *Advanced Intelligent Systems*, *7*(1), 2400304.

Sapkota, R., Raza, S., Shoman, M., Paudel, A., & Karkee, M. (2025). Image, text, and speech data augmentation using multimodal LLMs for deep learning: A survey. *arXiv e-prints*, arXiv–2501.

Silva, H.O. (2025). Explainability in machine learning models: A shap-driven framework for misclassification analysis and feature selection.

Steinhoff, J., & Hind, S. (2025). Simulation and the reality gap: Moments in a prehistory of synthetic data. *Big Data & Society, 12*(1), 20539517241309884.

Suhag, D. (2024). Regulatory and ethical considerations. In *Handbook of biomaterials for medical applications, volume 2: Applications* (pp. 355–372). Springer.

Thulasiram, P.P. (2025). Explainable artificial intelligence (XAI): Enhancing transparency and trust in machine learning models.

Tkachenko, N. (2024). Opportunities for synthetic data in nature and climate finance. *Frontiers in Artificial Intelligence, 6*, 1168749.

Vatsavayi, C. (2025). Synthetic data generation: Advancing privacy-conscious AI personalization. *Journal of Computer Science and Technology Studies, 7*(6), 375–384.

Vimbi, V., Shaffi, N., & Mahmud, M. (2024). Interpreting artificial intelligence models: A systematic review on the application of lime and shap in Alzheimer's disease detection. *Brain Informatics, 11*(1), 10.

Vyas, R., & Pandey, R.K. (2025). Image generation with GANS. In *Crafting images with generative adversarial networks (GANs) and models* (pp. 105–130). IGI Global Scientific Publishing.

Wang, A.X., Le, M.Q., Duong, H.-T., Van, B.N., & Nguyen, B.P. (2025). CTVAE: Contrastive tabular variational autoencoder for imbalance data. *Knowledge and Information Systems*, 1–20.

4 Intelligent Educators
From Personalization to Educational Autonomy

Hugo Alberto Álvarez-Pérez

4.1 INTRODUCTION

4.1.1 Background and Context

Over the past two decades, the landscape of educational technology has undergone a profound transformation, moving from rudimentary computer-assisted instruction toward sophisticated, adaptive, and now increasingly autonomous intelligent systems. Early personalization efforts, enabled by adaptive learning algorithms, aimed to tailor instructional content to individual learners' pace, prior knowledge, and preferences (Holmes et al., 2019). However, advances in machine learning, natural language processing, and cognitive modeling have expanded these systems' capabilities to the point where they can make **autonomous pedagogical decisions**—recommending learning paths, assessing comprehension in real time, and adjusting not only the pace but also the epistemological framing of content (Luckin, 2024).

This shift reflects broader trends in AI research that prioritize self-regulating and context-aware agents, capable of moving beyond reactive personalization toward proactive and sometimes self-initiated educational interventions (Zhang & Aslan, 2021). The implications of this evolution are significant: while personalization centers on adapting instruction *to* the learner, autonomy empowers the learning system to set goals *with* or even *for* the learner, blurring the lines between human- and machine-led learning design.

From my vantage point as director of the bachelor's degree in entrepreneurship at Tecnológico de Monterrey, Querétaro Campus, I have observed this shift not merely as a technological trend but as a pedagogical inflection point. In piloting generative AI-powered curricula for entrepreneurship and social innovation, I have seen students respond differently when the system shifts from a passive recommender to an active co-designer of their learning trajectory. This experiential insight reinforces a central argument of this chapter: the move toward educational autonomy demands both theoretical rigor and grounded, context-specific implementation strategies.

4.1.2 Problem Statement and Rationale

Despite the promise of autonomous educational systems, the transition from personalization to autonomy raises complex challenges. Ethical concerns—ranging from bias and transparency to the preservation of learner agency—remain underexplored

DOI: 10.1201/9781003678250-4

in many deployment contexts (A. Nguyen et al., 2023). Moreover, existing frameworks often focus on technological performance rather than pedagogical integration, leaving a gap in understanding how autonomy should be calibrated to complement, rather than replace, human instruction.

From a practical standpoint, my own work designing gamified learning tools and international collaboration programs highlights a recurring tension: while AI can optimize learning sequences for efficiency, this does not inherently guarantee deeper learning or socio-emotional growth. Without deliberate design choices, there is a risk that autonomy in AI educators could inadvertently narrow the learning experience to measurable outputs, sidelining intangible but essential outcomes such as creativity, resilience, and cross-cultural competence.

4.1.3 Objectives of the Chapter

In light of these challenges, this chapter pursues three main objectives (presented in Figure 4.1):

1. **To conceptualize the shift from personalization to autonomy** in AI-driven education, situating it within the historical evolution of intelligent learning systems.

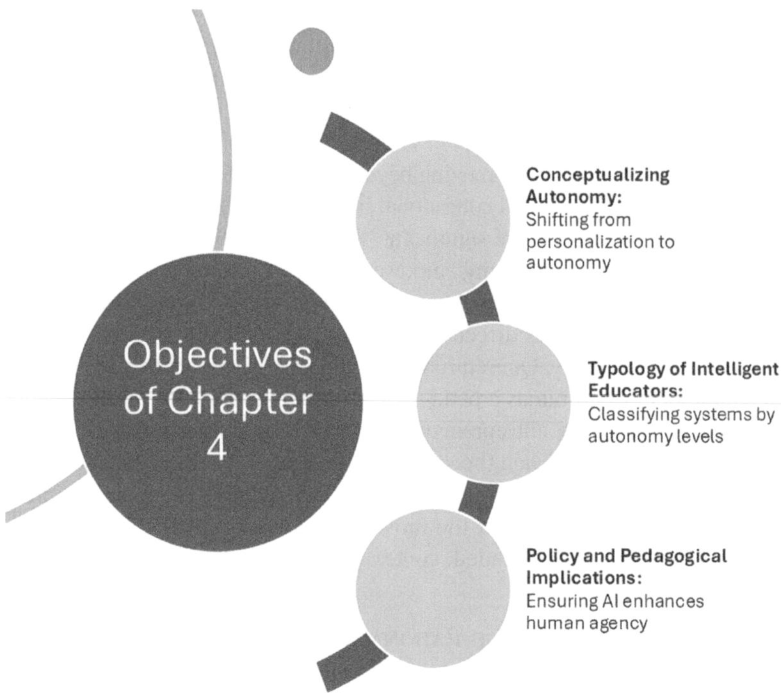

FIGURE 4.1 Objectives of the chapter.

2. **To propose a typology of intelligent educators**, offering a structured framework for classifying systems by their level of reactivity, adaptivity, and decisional autonomy.
3. **To articulate policy and pedagogical implications** that ensure autonomous AI systems enhance rather than diminish human agency, grounded in both empirical literature and practical experience.

These objectives are informed by a belief—developed through my research and practice—that technology should expand the scope of educational possibility without constraining the human dimensions of learning.

4.1.4 Structure of the Chapter

The chapter unfolds in nine sections. Following this introduction, **Section 4.2** examines the trajectory from early adaptive learning toward autonomous educational agents, introducing the concept of *waymorphosis* to describe systemic shifts in pedagogical paradigms. **Section 4.3** develops a typology of intelligent educators, distinguishing reactive, adaptive, and autonomous systems. **Section 4.4** explores human-computer interaction considerations, including emotional, ethical, and cultural factors. **Section 4.5** presents case studies—Squirrel AI Learning, Content Technologies, Inc., and generative AI platforms—providing empirical grounding. **Section 4.6** addresses the design principles for building trust and fostering co-agency between students and AI systems. **Section 4.7** analyzes key risks and challenges, including bias, dependency, and sustainability concerns. **Section 4.8** discusses the pedagogical implications and competencies educators must develop, before **Section 4.9** concludes with research gaps and future directions.

Throughout, I will integrate reflective commentary from my experience leading AI integration in higher education, with particular attention to the entrepreneurial mindset—a perspective that values innovation, adaptability, and ethical responsibility in the face of technological disruption. In doing so, I aim to bridge the theoretical and the practical, providing readers with both scholarly insights and applied strategies for navigating the emerging era of educational autonomy.

4.2 FROM PERSONALIZATION TO AUTONOMY IN LEARNING TECHNOLOGIES

The trajectory from personalized learning to autonomous educational systems reflects both technological maturity and a reimagining of pedagogical agency. While personalization has been a central goal of educational technology since the early 2000s, autonomy marks a more radical shift—one where AI systems are not merely responsive to learners but also self-directing in instructional design and delivery.

4.2.1 Evolution of AI in Education

4.2.1.1 Early Adaptive Learning Systems

The earliest adaptive learning platforms, such as Carnegie Learning's Cognitive Tutor or Knewton, were grounded in rule-based logic and item-response theory.

They excelled at adjusting the *difficulty* and *sequence* of tasks in real time, using learner performance as feedback (Ma et al., 2014). However, these systems remained **reactive**—awaiting student input before making adjustments.

In my early experiments with digital tools at Tecnológico de Monterrey, using the Strategyzer Adaptive Business Model Canvas Tool provided incremental improvements in efficiency and retention. The platform dynamically adjusted guidance on value propositions, customer segments, and revenue models based on each team's inputs and progress, helping students move through business plan development more quickly. However, its limited contextual awareness meant that it could not anticipate learners' motivational or strategic needs—such as recognizing when to pivot, reframing flawed hypotheses, or managing the uncertainty inherent in entrepreneurship. This limitation often required human instructors to step in, facilitating reflective discussions and scenario-based exercises to bridge the gap between procedural mastery and the higher-order strategic thinking essential for entrepreneurial success.

4.2.1.2 Rise of Personalized Learning Environments

Between 2015 and 2020, the rise of data-rich, cloud-based ecosystems—such as DreamBox and Smart Sparrow—ushered in a more nuanced form of personalization, integrating **learning analytics** with **predictive modeling** (Holmes et al., 2019). These systems began to incorporate affective data, capturing indicators like hesitation time, error patterns, and self-reported confidence to offer richer adaptation.

My work integrating gamified entrepreneurship modules for startup valuation into Lovable highlighted a key strength of personalization: it fosters learner engagement by aligning content with individual goals and venture contexts. These modules used simulated investment scenarios, dynamic equity calculations, and interactive market-sizing challenges to keep learners actively applying concepts in real time. Yet personalization remained bounded by predefined instructional objectives, limiting its ability to foster emergent learning paths that respond to unanticipated learner interests, rapidly changing market conditions, or novel strategic opportunities uncovered during the entrepreneurial process.

4.2.2 Conceptualizing Educational Autonomy

4.2.2.1 Defining "Waymorphosis" in Education

The transition to autonomy involves what I describe as *waymorphosis*—a systemic transformation in the pathways through which learning is structured, delivered, and validated. Autonomous systems use reinforcement learning, generative AI, and multi-agent architectures to self-determine instructional goals within broad curricular frameworks (Topali et al., 2025).

This concept is not merely about automation; it signifies a redistribution of pedagogical authority from human educators to hybrid human–machine systems. In practice, this means a platform can, for instance, detect entrepreneurial opportunities in a student's project and suggest pivot strategies without explicit human prompting—a phenomenon I observed during a pilot where AI mentors provided market-entry scenarios to student teams.

4.2.2.2 Distinction Between Personalization and Autonomy

While personalization is learner-centered—adapting to the learner's profile—autonomy is system-centered—granting the platform the capacity to make proactive pedagogical decisions (see Figure 4.2). This distinction has critical implications:

- **Agency:** In personalization, agency remains with the learner; in autonomy, it becomes shared or negotiated between learner and system (Luckin, 2024).
- **Adaptation Scope:** Personalization optimizes for fit within existing curricular bounds; autonomy may redefine the bounds themselves.
- **Complexity:** Autonomous systems engage in multi-objective optimization, balancing academic progress, skill development, and socio-emotional well-being (Zawacki-Richter et al., 2019).

In entrepreneurship education, this distinction is especially salient. A personalized system might tailor case studies to a student's industry interest, whereas an autonomous system could propose entirely new business model frameworks based on real-time market analysis—effectively co-creating knowledge with the learner.

4.2.2.2.1 Reflections From Practice

During a recent cross-campus collaboration, I observed MIT's Orbit platform—an autonomous AI-powered "one-stop shop" for entrepreneurship—operating beyond simple resource recommendation to actively orchestrate interdisciplinary learning sequences. The system integrated design thinking sprints, startup financial modeling tutorials, and sustainability impact assessments into a coherent, optimized learning

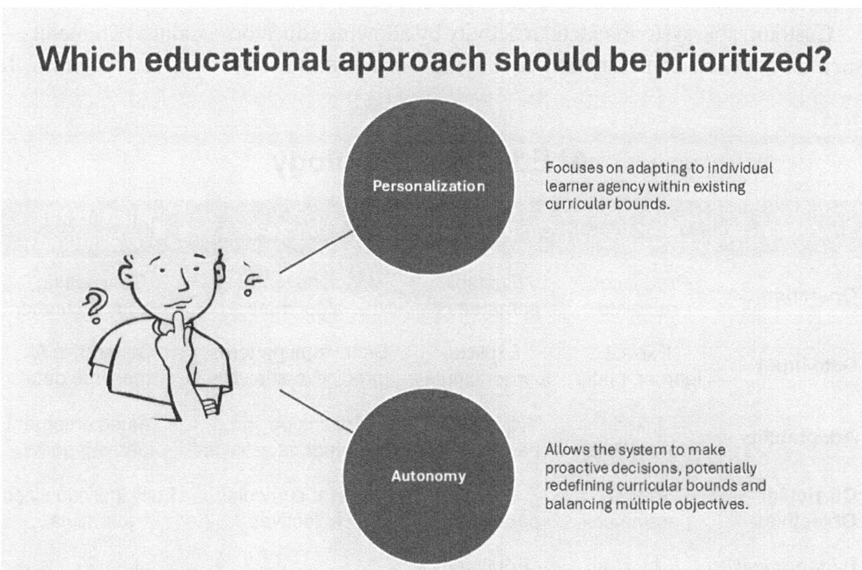

FIGURE 4.2 Differences between personalization and autonomy.

arc tailored to each team's progress. Students consistently described the experience as "**working with a mentor**" rather than "**following a program,**" exemplifying the shift from reactive adaptation to proactive co-agency that defines educational autonomy.

This experience reinforced the importance of intentional pedagogical design in AI integration. Autonomy should not displace human oversight but rather augment educators' capacity to orchestrate complex, context-sensitive learning journeys—an approach that aligns with ethical and inclusive AI adoption principles.

4.3 TYPOLOGY OF INTELLIGENT EDUCATORS

The increasing sophistication of AI in education requires a nuanced classification system to differentiate between levels of intelligence, adaptivity, and autonomy. A **typology of intelligent educators** helps researchers, policymakers, and practitioners align system capabilities with pedagogical goals, ethical considerations, and institutional contexts. Drawing from both literature and my own work integrating AI into higher education, I propose a four-tier framework: **reactive**, **customizable**, **proactive**, and **autonomous-decisional systems** as shown in Figure 4.3.

4.3.1 Reactive and Customizable Systems

Reactive systems operate on predefined rule sets and respond only to explicit learner inputs. These include early intelligent tutoring systems (ITS) and many learning management system (LMS) plug-ins that recommend resources or mark assessments according to fixed parameters (Ma et al., 2014).

Customizable systems extend reactivity by allowing educators to adjust parameters—such as question difficulty or sequencing—without altering the core algorithm. In

AI Educator Typology

Characteristic	Reactive	Customizable	Proactive	Autonomus-Decisional
Operation	Predefined rule sets	Adjustable parameters	Machine learning algorithms	Goal setting, resource curation
Data input	Explicit learner inputs	Explicit learner inputs	Behavioral patterns, predictive analytics	Generative AI, real-time data
Adaptability	Fixed parameters	Adjustable parameters	Adjusts pacing, recommends activities	Creates emergent learning paths
Curricular Objectives	Preset parameters	Preset parameters	Preset curricular objectives	Fully individualized curricula
Pedagogical Agency	Educator primacy	Educator primacy	Co-educators	Lead educators

FIGURE 4.3 AI Educator typology.

my entrepreneurship courses, I have used such tools for market simulation games, where I could modify input variables like demand elasticity or budget constraints, but the platform could not independently alter its simulation logic.

These systems are effective for content mastery and procedural learning, but they lack the capacity to identify unarticulated learner needs or to initiate new learning trajectories without human intervention.

4.3.2 Proactive and Adaptive Systems

Proactive systems employ machine learning algorithms to anticipate learner needs based on behavioral patterns and predictive analytics (Holmes et al., 2019). They can introduce supplemental resources, adjust pacing, or recommend collaborative activities before the learner requests them.

Adaptive systems in this category increasingly leverage multimodal data—including keystroke dynamics, facial expressions, and clickstream analysis—to infer cognitive load or engagement (Zawacki-Richter et al., 2019). In a recent cross-campus entrepreneurship hackathon, a proactive AI system—similar to the engagement analytics embedded in EdTech platforms like Classcraft—monitored team productivity indicators such as collaboration frequency, task completion rates, and message response times. When engagement levels dropped, the system automatically suggested targeted ideation exercises, creative warm-ups, or role-switching activities, effectively functioning as a real-time performance coach. While such proactive systems can enhance personalization and reduce cognitive overload, they remain constrained by preset curricular objectives, limiting their capacity to redefine learning goals or adapt to unexpected shifts in project scope.

While proactive systems can enhance personalization and reduce cognitive overload, they remain constrained by preset curricular objectives, limiting their ability to redefine learning goals.

4.3.3 Autonomous and Decisional Systems

At the highest level of the typology are autonomous-decisional systems—AI platforms capable of goal setting, resource curation, and assessment design without human prompting (Luckin, 2024). These systems integrate generative AI, reinforcement learning, and real-time data synthesis to create emergent learning paths.

An autonomous educational platform for entrepreneurship could integrate market intelligence feeds, sustainability databases, and generative scenario modeling to support ESG-focused startups. Such a system would not only recommend targeted case studies and financial forecasting tools, but also dynamically restructure project timelines when real-time indicators—such as commodity price fluctuations or new regulatory requirements—signal the need for strategic adjustments. In response, it could introduce additional sustainability performance metrics, like carbon footprint reduction or circularity scores, into the evaluation framework.

Such kind of systems introduce profound pedagogical possibilities—ranging from fully individualized curricula to dynamic cross-disciplinary integration—but also heighten ethical and governance concerns, particularly regarding transparency, accountability, and bias (H. T. Nguyen et al., 2024).

4.3.4 Comparative Analysis of Typologies

The transition from reactive to autonomous-decisional systems involves more than technological sophistication; it reflects a redistribution of pedagogical agency. Reactive and customizable systems maintain educator primacy, while proactive and autonomous systems increasingly function as co-educators or even lead instructors in certain contexts.

This progression parallels trends in entrepreneurial ecosystems, where decision-support tools evolve into decision-making partners. Just as in business, the challenge in education is ensuring that decision authority remains aligned with human values, especially in culturally diverse and equity-sensitive contexts (Chan, 2023).

From a governance perspective, institutions must determine where in this typology a given AI system should operate, depending on the maturity of their digital strategy, faculty readiness, and student AI literacy. In my experience, the most successful integrations have been incremental, moving from proactive systems toward semiautonomous modes only after robust human–AI collaboration protocols are established.

4.4 HUMAN-COMPUTER INTERACTION (HCI) IN AUTONOMOUS LEARNING

Human-computer interaction (HCI) in education has traditionally focused on usability, accessibility, and cognitive ergonomics. With the rise of autonomous learning systems, HCI must now account for emotional engagement, ethical responsibility, and co-agency between human and machine actors (Bower, 2019). In the context of intelligent educators, HCI design is not merely about optimizing interface efficiency; it is about shaping the relational experience between learners and AI.

4.4.1 Emotional and Ethical Implications

Autonomous AI educators do not only deliver content; they also simulate empathy, manage feedback tone, and respond to affective cues in ways that influence learner motivation (Calvo et al., 2015). For example, some generative AI tutors adjust their language style to encourage persistence after an incorrect answer, drawing on sentiment analysis of prior interactions.

In my entrepreneurship courses, I have observed how affective alignment—where the AI mirrors the learner's motivational state—can increase persistence in complex problem-solving tasks. However, this also raises ethical questions: should an AI tutor amplify a learner's emotional state (e.g., urgency during deadlines), or should it aim to counterbalance it for well-being? The choice is a pedagogical and ethical decision as much as a technical one (A. Nguyen et al., 2023).

4.4.2 Shifts in Authority and Perceived Care

As AI systems gain autonomy, they begin to occupy positions of authority traditionally reserved for human educators. Learners may defer to the AI's recommendations even when these conflict with their own judgment (Topali et al., 2025). This phenomenon—what I term *algorithmic authority*—requires deliberate HCI design to maintain learner agency.

During an entrepreneurship collaboration project, I saw students adopt AI-generated business pivots without critical review, trusting the system's "expertise" over their own market research. This experience underscores the need for interface cues—such as explainability prompts or alternative scenario options—that encourage reflective decision-making rather than blind compliance.

4.4.3 Student Engagement and Cognitive Load

Effective HCI in autonomous learning systems must manage cognitive load while sustaining deep engagement. Over-personalization risks creating cognitive ease—where learners face too little challenge—while uncalibrated autonomy can overwhelm them with unfiltered choices (Sweller et al., 2019).

In a pilot within an AI-driven innovation lab, students interacted with **VirtualSpeech**, a platform combining immersive simulations with AI-driven feedback for entrepreneurial skill development. The pilot tested tiered interface modes: in *beginner mode*, the system suggested structured responses during activities such as investor Q&A sessions or client negotiations, guiding participants through core project steps with minimal cognitive load. In *advanced mode*, participants were required to generate their own responses in real time, while the system autonomously suggested relevant resources, facilitated interdisciplinary connections, and streamed live market intelligence feeds to inform their decisions. Students in the advanced mode reported a higher perceived challenge–skill balance—a well-established driver of intrinsic motivation—while also noting increased realism and ownership over their learning experience.

4.4.4 Cultural and Contextual Considerations

Autonomous systems often carry cultural biases embedded in their training data (Blodgett et al., 2020). In multicultural classrooms, this can manifest in case study selections, language idioms, or value-laden recommendations that reflect one cultural lens over others.

In my work designing entrepreneurship challenges, I have found that cultural adaptability in HCI is essential—not only in interface language but also in decision-making heuristics. For example, risk tolerance is culturally mediated; an AI suggesting aggressive market entry might align with Silicon Valley norms but clash with collectivist, risk-averse entrepreneurial contexts. Systems must be able to context-switch culturally to maintain relevance and inclusivity.

4.4.4.1 Reflections From Practice

Integrating autonomous AI into education demands an HCI approach that balances authority with empowerment. In my own teaching, I use *negotiated autonomy* interfaces, where the AI proposes but the student must explicitly accept, modify, or reject the suggestion. This design friction is intentional—it keeps learners in an active decision-making role, preserving the co-agency that is critical to both entrepreneurship and lifelong learning.

4.5 CASE STUDIES AND EMERGING APPLICATIONS

Examining concrete examples of intelligent educator systems provides insight into the practical realities, opportunities, and constraints of implementing AI-driven autonomy in education. The following case studies illustrate diverse approaches—ranging from commercial platforms to experimental learning environments—and offer comparative lessons relevant to higher education, entrepreneurship training, and global learning contexts.

4.5.1 Squirrel AI Learning

Squirrel AI Learning is a China-based adaptive learning company that leverages reinforcement learning algorithms to tailor instruction in real time (Knox, 2020). Its architecture enables the system to dynamically assess student mastery at the concept level, adjusting sequencing, difficulty, and review intervals with minimal instructor intervention.

The platform's micro-adaptive granularity allows it to detect knowledge gaps as small as individual procedural steps, a capability particularly relevant to skill-based entrepreneurship courses where competencies build cumulatively. However, my review of Squirrel AI's model reveals limited contextual awareness—the system excels in cognitive skills assessment but does not engage with socio-emotional dimensions, cultural contexts, or open-ended innovation tasks.

In piloting similar adaptive models at Tecnológico de Monterrey for startup valuation literacy modules, I observed that while students mastered technical content faster, creative and collaborative problem-solving required separate interventions beyond the platform's scope.

4.5.2 Content Technologies, Inc.

Content Technologies, Inc. (CTI) specialized in creating AI-generated, customized textbooks and learning materials by using natural language processing to map curricular objectives to tailored resources. Its approach exemplifies the content-autonomy spectrum: the AI could design entirely new instructional materials aligned to specific learning outcomes (Holmes et al., 2019).

When I integrated a CTI-style generative system into an entrepreneurial case study repository, the AI autonomously generated localized market-entry scenarios for student projects. This personalization significantly increased student engagement by mirroring real-world business conditions in Latin American markets. However, it also surfaced data reliability challenges—some generated cases contained outdated or regionally irrelevant information, underscoring the need for human-in-the-loop validation.

4.5.3 Generative AI Platforms in Education

The recent proliferation of large language models (LLMs), such as OpenAI's GPT-4 and Anthropic's Claude, has redefined the boundaries of AI-assisted learning

(Kasneci et al., 2023). Unlike rule-based adaptive systems, LLMs can engage in contextually fluid, multi-turn conversations, co-create learning artifacts, and provide metacognitive prompts.

In 2024, I led an entrepreneurship workshop in the Global Entrepreneurship Summer School (GESS) in Queretaro Chapter, leveraging the AI-powered ideation and validation tools from Board of Innovation, where generative AI acted as both a brainstorming partner and a real-time feedback engine for pitch decks. Students reported that the AI inputs broadened the scope of their ideas, surfacing market niches and sustainability strategies they had not previously considered. However, the pilot also underscored the risk of over-reliance: some teams began to defer critical evaluation of AI-generated suggestions, highlighting the necessity of embedding explicit critical AI literacy into the curriculum to ensure that students remain active evaluators rather than passive recipients of machine-generated insights.

4.5.4 Comparative Evaluation of Impact

Comparing these three models reveals key differences in **pedagogical alignment, autonomy scope, and human oversight needs** (see Figure 4.4):

From my professional perspective, the highest-impact applications arise when autonomy is purposefully bounded—granting the AI decision-making capacity in areas of clear comparative advantage (e.g., data analysis, resource recommendation) while preserving human leadership in ethically complex, culturally sensitive, and creativity-driven tasks. This balance maximizes both efficiency and the human dimensions of learning.

4.6 DESIGNING FOR TRUST AND CO-AGENCY

As AI systems assume greater autonomy in education, trust and co-agency emerge as critical pillars for sustainable integration. Trust determines whether learners and educators will accept AI recommendations, while co-agency ensures that decision-making remains collaborative rather than unilaterally dictated by the machine.

Platform comparison

	Squirrel AI	Content Technologies	Generative AI
Autonomy level	Adaptative	Semi-autonomus	Autonomus
Pedagogical Strengths	Precision micro-skill targeting	Customized content generation	Contextually rich engagement
Limitations	Limited scope	Risk of inaccuracy	Potential for bias

FIGURE 4.4 Platform comparison.

Designing for both requires an alignment of technical transparency, ethical safeguards, and user empowerment strategies.

4.6.1 Transparency and Explainability in AI Systems

Trust in autonomous AI educators depends on explainable AI (XAI)—systems capable of clarifying the rationale behind their decisions (Shin, 2021). Without transparency, even highly accurate recommendations can face resistance or, conversely, lead to uncritical acceptance.

In my entrepreneurship courses, I have integrated AI output explainers that not only provide a recommendation (e.g., a pivot in business strategy) but also present a data-based reasoning trail, such as relevant market signals or historical analogues. Students report that this fosters critical evaluation rather than blind adoption.

However, explainability must also consider cognitive load—overly technical justifications can alienate non-technical learners, reducing trust instead of building it (Long & Magerko, 2020).

4.6.2 Human-in-the-Loop Approaches

The human-in-the-loop (HITL) model keeps final authority with educators or learners, ensuring that AI remains a supporting actor in the pedagogical process (Topali et al., 2025). HITL is particularly important for high-stakes educational decisions, such as progression assessments, skill certifications, and feedback on complex creative work.

In a local hackathon, we implemented an HITL workflow where AI drafted impact evaluation reports, which were then reviewed and contextualized by student teams. This maintained pedagogical ownership while leveraging AI's analytical speed.

4.6.3 Negotiated Autonomy Between Student and System

Negotiated autonomy balances the **initiative of AI systems** with **learner choice**, fostering co-agency. Rather than the system acting unilaterally, it presents options ranked by relevance, accompanied by confidence scores and alternative paths.

In my startup valuation simulator using gamification, I employed this approach in startup types identification exercises. The AI suggested three distinct scenarios (different stages, different industries), each with pros, cons, and trend data, and students chose their preferred trajectory. This design created structured freedom, empowering students to take ownership while benefiting from AI's pattern recognition capabilities.

4.6.4 Metrics for Trust and Effectiveness

Establishing **trust metrics** is essential for evaluating the co-agency model. These may include the following:

- **Perceived reliability** (how often the AI's recommendations align with learner goals)
- **Transparency scores** (student ratings of clarity in AI decision explanations)

- **Agency retention** (measures of whether learners feel in control of their learning path)
- **Engagement indicators** (frequency and depth of learner–AI interactions)

At Tecnológico de Monterrey, I use post-project reflective surveys to gauge these metrics. The feedback informs iterative improvements in AI integration, ensuring that trust remains dynamic and evolves alongside system capabilities.

4.6.4.1 Reflections From Practice

From my perspective, trust in autonomous AI educators is not a static attribute but an earned and maintained quality, dependent on consistent transparency, respect for human agency, and adaptability to diverse learning contexts. The concept of co-agency—rooted in my work designing gamified, culturally inclusive learning tools—is central to ensuring that AI supports rather than supplants the creative, critical, and collaborative dimensions of learning.

4.7 RISKS AND CHALLENGES

The integration of autonomous AI systems into education presents unprecedented opportunities for personalization and efficiency, but it also introduces systemic risks that must be addressed to safeguard equity, learner agency, and institutional integrity. These challenges are technical, ethical, and sociocultural, requiring an interdisciplinary approach to governance and design.

4.7.1 Ethical Dilemmas and Bias

Autonomous AI educators inherit biases embedded in their training data, which can influence the recommendations they generate, the feedback they provide, and the examples they prioritize (Blodgett et al., 2020). In multicultural classrooms, such biases can lead to content misalignment with learners' socio-economic and cultural realities.

In my entrepreneurship courses, I have seen generative AI tools default to U.S.-centric market models, overlooking viable local innovation strategies in Latin America. To mitigate this, I integrate cultural calibration protocols—including localized datasets and manual vetting of AI outputs—into the development pipeline. However, few commercial platforms currently offer this level of regional customization, leaving educators to address bias post hoc.

4.7.2 Dependency and Reduced Human Agency

As AI systems become more capable, there is a risk that learners will over-rely on automated guidance, reducing their capacity for independent problem-solving (Luckin, 2024). This phenomenon is amplified in fully autonomous systems where the AI initiates learning activities and decisions without requiring user engagement in the process.

In a global innovation challenge, I observed student teams accepting AI-generated market forecasts without conducting their own validation. While efficiency increased, critical thinking declined. To counteract this, I now design intentional friction points—such as requiring human approval for AI recommendations—preserving the *reflective loop* that is essential for deep learning.

4.7.3 Privacy and Data Governance Issues

Autonomous systems rely on large volumes of learner data, including behavioral, cognitive, and sometimes biometric inputs, raising significant privacy and compliance concerns (Williamson et al., 2020). These risks are heightened when data is shared across third-party platforms or stored without clear governance policies.

At Tecnológico de Monterrey, I follow institutional guidelines on data minimization—collecting only what is pedagogically necessary and ensuring transparency about storage, use, and sharing. This approach aligns with privacy-by-design principles but requires constant vigilance as AI vendors update their data policies. As part of this framework, the university provides access to **TEC GPT**, its own secure generative AI tool designed to operate within institutional data governance protocols. Faculty and staff, including myself, receive ongoing training on security and responsible AI use, reinforcing both technical safeguards and ethical considerations in the adoption of AI-driven educational tools.

4.7.4 Sustainability and Long-Term Viability

The rapid pace of AI innovation can lead to platform obsolescence and vendor instability. Institutions risk investing in systems that become unsupported or incompatible within a few years (Selwyn, 2021). Additionally, environmental sustainability is an emerging concern, as training and operating large AI models consumes substantial computational and energy resources.

In evaluating AI platforms for our entrepreneurship program, I now include life cycle sustainability audits—assessing not only the vendor's road map but also the ecological footprint of the technology. This is particularly relevant as universities align with ESG commitments and seek to balance educational innovation with responsible resource use.

4.7.4.1 Reflections From Practice

In my experience, proactive risk management is key to sustainable AI integration in education. This means embedding bias detection, agency-preservation mechanisms, privacy safeguards, and sustainability metrics into both the procurement and pedagogical design phases. The future of autonomous learning will be defined not only by technological capabilities but by the ethical frameworks and operational safeguards we build around them.

4.8 PEDAGOGICAL IMPLICATIONS AND FUTURE SKILLS FOR EDUCATORS

The emergence of autonomous AI systems in education requires a redefinition of the educator's role and a recalibration of the competencies needed to thrive in a co-agency learning environment. Rather than diminishing the importance of human educators, AI integration amplifies the need for orchestration, ethical judgment, and meta-pedagogical skills.

4.8.1 Redefining the Role of the Teacher

The shift from personalization to autonomy transforms the teacher's role from content deliverer to learning architect—designing, curating, and regulating human–AI collaboration. As autonomous systems take on administrative and instructional tasks, educators increasingly focus on relationship-building, critical framing, and contextual adaptation (Luckin, 2024).

In my work leading the bachelor's degree in entrepreneurship at Tecnológico de Monterrey, I have found that AI allows faculty to shift their focus toward mentorship and strategic oversight, enabling more nuanced guidance in innovation projects. This transition, however, requires institutional support in redefining job expectations and performance indicators.

4.8.2 New Competencies for Orchestrating Human–AI Interaction

Educators in AI-rich environments must develop skills beyond subject expertise, including the following:

- **AI literacy**: Understanding how AI systems operate, their limitations, and their data requirements (Long & Magerko, 2020).
- **Ethical discernment**: Applying principles of fairness, inclusivity, and accountability in AI-mediated decisions (A. Nguyen et al., 2023).
- **Orchestration skills**: Managing multimodal learning experiences where AI recommendations are one of many inputs.
- **Critical mediation**: Guiding students in evaluating and contextualizing AI-generated insights.

During a multicampus entrepreneurship workshop, students used **VirtualSpeech** in scenario-based simulations to practice high-stakes communication skills such as pitching to investors, negotiating partnerships, and addressing stakeholder concerns. The platform's AI provided real-time feedback on clarity, tone, and persuasion, while I facilitated debrief sessions to address instances of bias or over-reliance on AI-generated suggestions. This simulation-based approach not only enhanced students' communication competencies but also fostered critical reflection on the role of AI as a collaborative partner, helping them balance the benefits of real-time assistance with the need for independent judgment.

4.8.3 Training and Professional Development Needs

Effective integration of autonomous AI requires continuous professional development (CPD) that goes beyond tool training to include design thinking, cultural competence, and adaptive pedagogy (Caena & Redecker, 2019).

At Tecnológico de Monterrey, we continuously receive a kind of **tiered CPD model**:

1. **Foundational workshops** on AI capabilities and risks.
2. **Applied labs** for course-specific integration strategies.
3. **Peer mentoring circles** where educators share implementation experiences and co-develop guidelines.

This layered approach has proven more effective than one-off training, as it fosters communities of practice and allows for iterative refinement of teaching strategies.

4.8.4 Implications for Educational Policy

Educational policy must evolve to support and regulate the integration of autonomous AI in ways that safeguard academic integrity, learner agency, and equity (Selwyn, 2021). Key considerations include the following:

- Establishing **AI integration frameworks** that balance innovation with ethical oversight.
- Creating **credentialing systems** that recognize AI-augmented competencies in both students and educators.
- Funding **research-practice partnerships** to study the impact of AI in varied socio-economic contexts.

In my institution, I have participated for national-level policy dialogues involving educators, technologists, and regulators to ensure that AI adoption in higher education aligns with inclusive innovation goals and ESG commitments.

4.8.4.1 Reflections From Practice

From my perspective, the greatest pedagogical opportunity in the age of autonomous AI lies in **human amplification**—using AI to enhance rather than replace the unique relational, cultural, and ethical dimensions of teaching. Preparing educators for this reality demands visionary leadership, practical upskilling, and policy scaffolding that together enable sustainable, inclusive AI integration.

4.9 CONCLUSIONS AND FUTURE DIRECTIONS

The transition from personalized learning to educational autonomy represents one of the most profound paradigm shifts in contemporary education. Autonomous AI educators, when thoughtfully designed and ethically deployed, have the potential to augment human capabilities, personalize learning pathways at unprecedented granularity, and open new frontiers for creativity and cross-disciplinary integration. Yet as explored in this chapter, these systems also carry significant risks that require deliberate governance, critical pedagogy, and continuous stakeholder engagement.

4.9.1 Summary of Key Insights

Across the chapter, several core themes have emerged (as shown in Figure 4.5):

1. **From personalization to autonomy**—The evolution of AI in education moves from reactive systems toward autonomous decision-making, demanding new frameworks for pedagogical agency and ethical oversight.
2. **Typology of intelligent educators**—A nuanced classification—reactive, customizable, proactive, and autonomous-decisional—helps institutions strategically align AI adoption with readiness and context.
3. **Human–AI co-agency**—Trust, transparency, and negotiated autonomy are essential to maintaining learner engagement and preserving human judgment.
4. **Applied innovation**—Case studies show the benefits and constraints of adaptive, semiautonomous, and generative systems, underscoring the need for purposeful autonomy boundaries.
5. **Risks and governance**—Bias, dependency, data governance, and sustainability remain key challenges, requiring **policy scaffolding** and proactive risk management.
6. **Educator transformation**—The teacher's role evolves into a learning architect and orchestrator, requiring new competencies in AI literacy, ethical mediation, and cultural adaptability.

4.9.2 Research Gaps and Opportunities

While research on AI in education has accelerated, several **gaps** warrant further exploration:

- **Longitudinal impact studies**: Few empirical investigations examine the sustained effects of autonomous AI educators on learner agency, creativity, and critical thinking over multiple years.

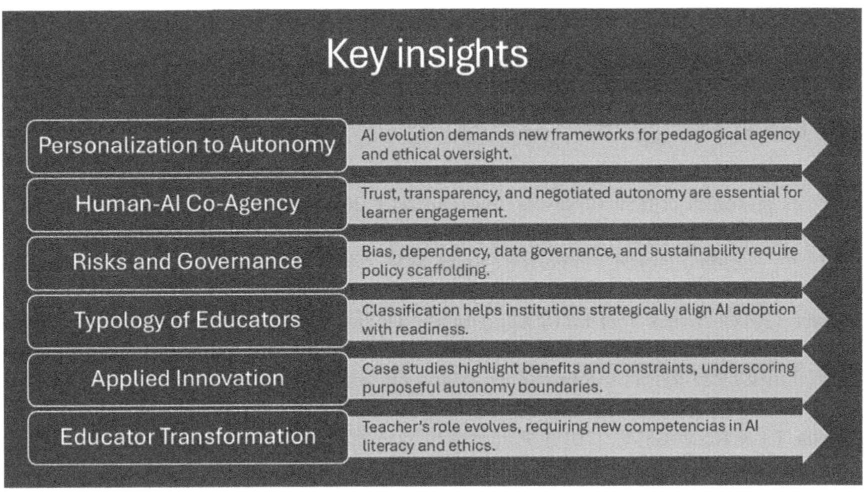

FIGURE 4.5 Core themes from the chapter.

- **Cross-cultural validation**: Most AI learning models are developed in Western or East Asian contexts; Latin American, African, and Indigenous education systems remain underrepresented in training datasets and design processes.
- **Co-agency design metrics**: While conceptual frameworks for human–AI co-agency exist, standardized tools for measuring its effectiveness in varied learning contexts are lacking.
- **Sustainability in AI deployment**: The environmental footprint of large-scale educational AI adoption remains an emerging but urgent area of inquiry.

4.9.3 Final Reflections

From my vantage point as an educator, researcher, and program director, the most compelling potential of autonomous AI lies in its ability to extend the reach of human care, mentorship, and creativity—not to replace them. In leading AI integration initiatives at Tecnológico de Monterrey, I have learned that technology adoption is as much about cultural readiness and ethical commitment as it is about technical capability.

The next decade will demand educators who are both technologically literate and humanistically grounded—professionals who can navigate algorithmic authority without surrendering the values that make education transformative: empathy, curiosity, equity, and social responsibility.

If we design for **trust, co-agency, and inclusivity**, autonomous AI educators can help us move beyond the limits of personalization toward an era of **educational autonomy**—where learners are empowered not only to receive tailored content but to **shape their own learning futures** in partnership with intelligent systems.

4.9.3.1 Declaration of Generative AI Use

Generative AI (GenAI) tools, including institutional platforms such as TEC GPT, were employed as writing and ideation assistants in preparing this chapter. All AI outputs were reviewed, validated, and revised by the author to ensure accuracy, originality, and compliance with academic integrity standards.

REFERENCES

Blodgett, S. L., Barocas, S., Daumé III, H., & Wallach, H. (2020). Language (technology) is power: A critical survey of "bias" in NLP. In D. Jurafsky, J. Chai, N. Schluter, & J. Tetreault (Eds.), *Proceedings of the 58th Annual Meeting of the Association for Computational Linguistics* (pp. 5454–5476). Association for Computational Linguistics. https://doi.org/10.18653/v1/2020.acl-main.485

Bower. (2019). *British Journal of Educational Technology | BERA Journal | Wiley Online Library*. British Educational Research Association. Retrieved August 9, 2025, from https://bera-journals.onlinelibrary.wiley.com/action/showCitFormats?doi=10.1111%2Fbjet.12771&mobileUi=0

Caena, F., & Redecker, C. (2019). Aligning teacher competence frameworks to 21st century challenges: The case for the European Digital Competence Framework for Educators (DigCompEdu). *European Journal of Education*, *54*(3), 356–369. https://doi.org/10.1111/ejed.12345

Calvo, R., D'Mello, S., Gratch, J., Kappas, A., D'Mello, S., & Graesser, A. C. (2015). *Feeling, Thinking, and Computing with Affect-Aware Learning Technologies* (R. Calvo, S. D'Mello, J. Gratch, & A. Kappas, Eds.). Oxford University Press. https://doi.org/10.1093/oxfordhb/9780199942237.013.032

Chan, C. K. Y. (2023). A comprehensive AI policy education framework for university teaching and learning. *International Journal of Educational Technology in Higher Education*, *20*(1), 38. https://doi.org/10.1186/s41239-023-00408-3

Holmes, W., Bialik, M., & Fadel, C. (2019). *Artificial Intelligence in Education Promises and Implications for Teaching and Learning* (1st ed.). Center for Curriculum Redesign. https://circls.org/primers/artificial-intelligence-in-education-promises-and-implications-for-teaching-and-learning

Kasneci, E., Sessler, K., Küchemann, S., Bannert, M., Dementieva, D., Fischer, F., Gasser, U., Groh, G., Günnemann, S., Hüllermeier, E., Krusche, S., Kutyniok, G., Michaeli, T., Nerdel, C., Pfeffer, J., Poquet, O., Sailer, M., Schmidt, A., Seidel, T., . . . & Kasneci, G. (2023). ChatGPT for good? On opportunities and challenges of large language models for education. *Learning and Individual Differences*, *103*, 102274. https://doi.org/10.1016/j.lindif.2023.102274

Knox, J. (2020). Artificial intelligence and education in China. *Learning, Media and Technology*, *45*(3), 298–311. https://doi.org/10.1080/17439884.2020.1754236

Long, D., & Magerko, B. (2020). What is AI literacy? Competencies and design considerations. In *Proceedings of the 2020 CHI Conference on Human Factors in Computing Systems* (pp. 1–16). https://doi.org/10.1145/3313831.3376727

Luckin, R. (2024). Nurturing human intelligence in the age of AI: Rethinking education for the future. *Development and Learning in Organizations: An International Journal*, *39*(1), 1–4. https://doi.org/10.1108/DLO-04-2024-0108

Ma, W., Adesope, O. O., Nesbit, J. C., & Liu, Q. (2014). Intelligent tutoring systems and learning outcomes: A meta-analysis. *Journal of Educational Psychology*, *106*(4), 901–918. https://doi.org/10.1037/a0037123

Nguyen, A., Ngo, H. N., Hong, Y., Dang, B., & Nguyen, B.-P. T. (2023). Ethical principles for artificial intelligence in education. *Education and Information Technologies*, *28*(4), 4221–4241. https://doi.org/10.1007/s10639-022-11316-w

Nguyen, H. T., Vu, T. T. D., Nguyen, H. M., & Nguyen, D. B. P. (2024). SMEs' innovation and government support during the COVID-19 pandemic. *Journal of Asian Business and Economic Studies* (ahead-of-print). https://doi.org/10.1108/JABES-08-2023-0300

Selwyn, N. (2021). Ed-tech within limits: Anticipating educational technology in times of environmental crisis. *E-Learning and Digital Media*, *18*(5), 496–510. https://doi.org/10.26180/14746032.v1

Shin, D. (2021). The effects of explainability and causability on perception, trust, and acceptance: Implications for explainable AI. *International Journal of Human-Computer Studies*, *146*, 102551. https://doi.org/10.1016/j.ijhcs.2020.102551

Sweller, J., van Merriënboer, J. J. G., & Paas, F. (2019). Cognitive architecture and instructional design: 20 years later. *Educational Psychology Review*, *31*(2), 261–292. https://doi.org/10.1007/s10648-019-09465-5

Topali, P., Ortega-Arranz, A., Rodríguez-Triana, M. J., Er, E., Khalil, M., & Akçapınar, G. (2025). Designing human-centered learning analytics and artificial intelligence in education solutions: A systematic literature review. *Behaviour & Information Technology*, *44*(5), 1071–1098. https://doi.org/10.1080/0144929X.2024.2345295

Williamson, B., Bayne, S., & Shay, S. (2020). The datafication of teaching in Higher Education: Critical issues and perspectives. *Teaching in Higher Education*, *25*(4), 351–365. https://doi.org/10.1080/13562517.2020.1748811

Zawacki-Richter, O., Marín, V. I., Bond, M., & Gouverneur, F. (2019). Systematic review of research on artificial intelligence applications in higher education—where are the educators? *International Journal of Educational Technology in Higher Education*, *16*(1), 39. https://doi.org/10.1186/s41239-019-0171-0

Zhang, K., & Aslan, A. B. (2021). AI technologies for education: Recent research & future directions. *Computers and Education: Artificial Intelligence*, *2*, 100025. https://doi.org/10.1016/j.caeai.2021.100025

5 An Augmented Reality–Enhanced Ecosystem for Literacy and Learning in Primary Education

Hector Cardona-Reyes,
Ezra Federico Parra-González,
Carlos Alberto Lara-Álvarez, and
Lizeth Solano-Romo

5.1 INTRODUCTION

Reading comprehension is a fundamental competency for continuous learning and cognitive development in childhood. However, in Latin America, significant gaps persist in this area. The Regional Comparative and Explanatory Study ERCE 2019 (UNESCO Santiago, Oficina Regional de Educación para América Latina y el Caribe (OREALC/UNESCO Santiago), 2021) revealed that in third grade, 44.3% of students were placed at the lowest performance level (Level I), while only 55.7% reached the minimum expected level (Level II). By sixth grade, just 31.2% achieved satisfactory performance in reading comprehension, demonstrating difficulties in making inferences and connecting secondary ideas within a text (UNESCO, 2021, 2023).

These results reflect a broader panorama: according to a joint report by the World Bank and UNICEF, four out of five sixth-grade students in Latin America and the Caribbean are unable to understand a simple text. This not only hinders academic progress but also undermines the future social and economic integration of millions of children (Banco Mundial & UNICEF, 2022). The impact of the COVID-19 pandemic further intensified this situation, widening learning gaps in the most vulnerable sectors.

Beyond structural factors, traditional teaching methods do not always succeed in fostering reading motivation. Recent studies have identified lack of interest and motivation as a widespread issue across the region, limiting the potential for meaningful learning (Prieto-Díaz et al., 2011). Consequently, it is essential to explore innovative pedagogical approaches that not only strengthen comprehension but also prove attractive and motivating for students.

In this regard, it is relevant to propose strategies based on educational ecosystems, understood as complex structures that integrate people, resources,

DOI: 10.1201/9781003678250-5

technologies, institutions, and processes to foster adaptability and lifelong learning in an interconnected environment (Shah et al., 2024). The importance of these ecosystems lies in their ability to respond to the challenges of a constantly changing society, promoting the coevolution and adaptation of their members in the face of emerging technologies and evolving social and economic demands (Nguyen & Tuamsuk, 2022). Learning ecosystems that encompass formal, non-formal, and digital contexts sustain an interdisciplinary perspective of lifelong learning, where interconnection among diverse settings reinforces the continuous development of competencies in individuals and communities (Kodsiri & Kruekamai, 2023; Utkin & Shevchenko, 2022).

Ecosystems also contribute to educational innovation, as they encourage the integration of digital technologies and new methods into the learning process. Moreover, they can adapt to changes in the social, technological, and economic environment (Kicherova & Trifonova, 2023). A key aspect of their implementation lies in integrating technology, digital platforms, learning analytics, and gamification to improve the educational experience (Dmitrieva & Yulmetova, 2021).

Specifically, ecosystems make it possible to promote educational innovation by integrating digital technologies and active methodologies in teaching and learning. In this work, we consider the incorporation of augmented reality (AR) (Wu et al., 2013), an interactive tool with high pedagogical potential. By superimposing digital information onto the physical environment, AR offers immersive experiences that stimulate imagination, attention, and motivation, fostering more active and meaningful learning (Quintero et al., 2019). Although the adoption of these technologies in Latin America faces challenges related to infrastructure and teacher training; various studies highlight their positive impact on motivation and reading comprehension in primary and secondary education, as well as their potential to reduce educational inequalities in rural or low-connectivity contexts through the use of low-cost and accessible devices (Benítez Miranda et al., 2025).

Based on this perspective, this work presents the design of a digital educational ecosystem with AR aimed at promoting reading, accessible via web browsers and aligned with the primary school curriculum. Its main contributions include the following:

1. the development of a virtual library with interactive stories and integrated quizzes that strengthen reading comprehension,
2. the adoption of a user-centered design (UCD) approach (Lowdermilk, 2013) to ensure usability and accessibility,
3. the evaluation of the user experience through standardized usability and satisfaction tests (SUS and PSSUQ) (Vlachogianni & Tselios, 2023), and
4. the generation of empirical evidence on the potential of AR-based ecosystems to enhance motivation, active participation, and equitable access to educational resources for children.

Finally, the AR ecosystem approach can represent an important model for the future of education, promoting cooperation, innovation, and adaptability to changing conditions and ensuring that individuals are prepared to respond effectively and sustainably to global challenges.

This work is organized into eight sections. Section 5.2 reviews related studies on learning ecosystems and the application of augmented reality (AR) in literacy. Section 5.3 details the proposed AR-based ecosystem, describing its components—people, resources, technologies, and environments. Section 5.4 introduces the digital library platform and its interactive AR features. Section 5.5 explains the methodology applied for the evaluation of usability and user experience, while Section 5.6 presents the results of the SUS and PSSUQ tests. Section 5.7 discusses the findings in relation to the existing literature, and Section 5.8 concludes the paper with directions for future work.

5.2 RELATED WORK

Digital learning ecosystems are systems that foster the personalization of educational pathways, improve accessibility, and connect formal and informal learning contexts (Pinto-Llorente & Izquierdo-Álvarez, 2024). However, in the context of literacy in primary education, certain limitations remain, as many digital ecosystems focus primarily on infrastructure and learning management, without systematically integrating immersive technologies such as augmented reality (AR) (Nguyen & Tuamsuk, 2022).

Several studies have highlighted the potential of AR as a tool that generates significant improvements in motivation, active participation, and reading comprehension at both preschool and primary education levels (Basumatary & Maity, 2023). Table 5.1 contrasts different proposals that guide the use of AR in various literacy contexts, ranging from primary education to applications in teaching and health-related topics.

The studies presented in Table 5.1 show that AR has been applied at different levels and areas of literacy. An example of this is early literacy, as in the works of Zilong et al. (2021) and Piatykop et al. (2022), which demonstrate the use of AR in activities involving letter, number, and sound recognition to increase children's motivation, memorization, and self-confidence. Among the reported benefits, AR not only strengthens initial learning but also fosters positive attitudes toward reading and learning. However, these studies still need to further explore the integration of AR into a broader pedagogical ecosystem.

Works such as those by Yeh and Tseng (2020) and Nevrelova et al. (2024) extend the scope of AR to multimodal and digital literacy, showing how this technology enables the integration of text, images, sound, and interactive elements in contexts such as language learning or STEAM teaching in primary education. This perspective highlights the potential of AR to prepare students in key twenty-first-century competencies. Nonetheless, these studies also reveal future challenges, such as the integration of usability mechanisms and curricular alignment, since the presented applications are not fully oriented toward reading comprehension in school contexts.

Finally, the work of Adapa et al. (2020) shifts the focus of literacy to a health-related context, where AR is used as a tool to improve the understanding of complex

TABLE 5.1
Studies on the Use of Augmented Reality in Literacy Across Different Contexts

Title/Reference	Proposal	Technology Used	Results	Conclusions
Zilong et al. (2021)	Introduce AR in preschool classrooms to improve motivation and early literacy skills.	AR application with iPad and augmented books.	Increase in letter-naming speed (6.28% in AR group vs. 3.35% in control). Motivation also increased in both groups.	AR supports early letter learning, enhances motivation, and generates positive perceptions among teachers.
Yeh and Tseng (2020)	Develop multimodal competence in EFL students using AR to create tourism-related content.	Location-based AR app.	Significant improvement in multimodal literacy (integration of visual and auditory modes).	AR fosters the integration of text, image, sound, and video, enhancing multimodal literacy in language learning.
Nevrelova et al. (2024)	Explore how AR apps support digital literacy in primary education.	Mobile AR applications.	Increase in motivation, collaborative communication, and digital competencies.	AR enhances digital literacy and STEAM education, showing strong acceptance among teachers and students.
Piatykop et al. (2022)	Develop a mobile AR app to teach the Ukrainian alphabet, numbers, and animal sounds.	Unity and Vuforia (mobile app with 3D and audio).	Improvement in motivation, attention, and memorization of letters and numbers.	AR fosters early literacy, boosting self-confidence and perceived learning effectiveness.
Adapa et al. (2020)	Map evidence on AR in patient education and health literacy.	Literature review.	Identification of uses in anatomy, rehabilitation, and treatment adherence.	AR can be a key resource for improving health literacy and understanding of complex medical information.

information. In this sense, AR emerges as a resource that can be integrated transversally and adapted to different types of literacy. This work also highlights the challenge of developing ecosystems that articulate content, technologies, and assessment into a unified pedagogical framework.

5.3 LEARNING ECOSYSTEM PROPOSAL

Within the framework of a learning ecosystem approach, this section presents a proposal in which people, resources, technologies, and spaces of interaction converge to enrich educational processes. This perspective integrates both physical and digital dimensions, as well as formal and informal learning, providing flexibility to adapt to diverse educational contexts. Under this vision, Figure 5.1 illustrates the proposed learning ecosystem, oriented toward a virtual library designed to host educational stories and incorporating AR technology to enhance the learning experience and foster student motivation (Islas Torres, 2019; Martí, 2018).

In this way, the articulation of the ecosystem's components—people, resources, technologies, and environments—not only seeks to organize the elements of the virtual library but also to promote interaction, accessibility, and educational inclusion. The following sections describe each of the proposed components.

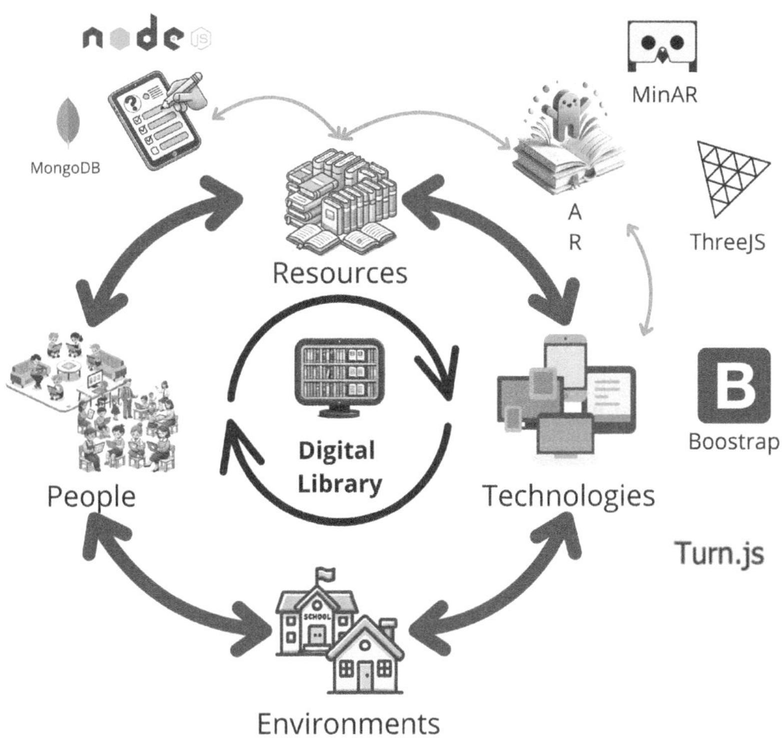

FIGURE 5.1 Elements of the learning ecosystem oriented toward the digital library.

5.3.1 People

The design of the proposed ecosystem focuses on the school community, particularly primary school children and the teaching role of evaluation. In this component, the contents are developed based on curricular themes established by educational authorities, with the aim of ensuring pedagogical relevance. Although students are the primary beneficiaries, the contents designed for the digital library are conceived with an open access approach, allowing their use by the wider society and promoting educational inclusion.

5.3.2 Resources

This component considers two fundamental aspects:

- Educational stories: The narratives were structured following both narrative and pedagogical patterns, incorporating illustrations and assessment activities. These stories function as didactic resources that combine storytelling, imagery, and interactive activities to stimulate students' comprehension and interest.
- Virtual library: Conceived as an online platform, it allows users to access the stories anytime and anywhere. Each story is accompanied by AR experiences that enrich the reading process and create an immersive environment.

5.3.3 Technologies

The technological architecture of the proposed ecosystem integrates both web development and AR tools and is structured around three key aspects:

- Frontend: Built with components such as Bootstrap to design interfaces adaptable to multiple devices, applying usability principles and visual metaphors (Nielsen, 1994). To ensure interactive AR-based reading, the TurnJS library was used to simulate a physical book through a flipbook effect.
- Backend: Developed with NodeJS and MongoDB to manage data and quizzes associated with each story. The use of JavaScript on both client and server sides facilitated smooth integration.
- Augmented Reality: Tools such as Three.js and MindAR were employed to incorporate 3D models and interactive AR experiences. These technologies enable AR directly within browsers, without requiring external applications, thus enhancing both accessibility and the reach of the platform.

5.3.4 Environments

The proposed ecosystem connects the digital environment of the virtual library and AR experiences with the physical environment of the school community. This integration allows students and teachers to interact with AR-enhanced stories both in the classroom and at home, bridging formal and informal learning and fostering continuity in the educational process.

5.4 DIGITAL LIBRARY OF AR STORIES

This section describes the design of the digital platform of AR-based stories, which constitutes the central phase of the proposed educational ecosystem. The purpose of this platform is to provide primary school students with an enriched and immersive reading experience that combines narrative, illustrations, and interactive AR elements. For teachers, it also serves as a support tool for creating content aligned with the current school curriculum. To achieve this, the interface was designed with a focus on simplicity and accessibility, following usability principles specifically oriented toward a child audience (Shneiderman et al., 2016).

5.4.1 Main Interface

The initial interface of the application functions as the Story Library (see Figure 5.2), a space where users can explore the available collection. The interface includes a brief introduction to the purpose of the platform and presents, through a virtual bookshelf, the covers of the stories, which facilitates their visual identification. This graphical resource is especially relevant in child-oriented environments, as it enables intuitive access to the materials without requiring a high level of reading ability (Shneiderman et al., 2016).

To ensure accessibility, a QR code was incorporated into the main page, which can be scanned with a mobile device. This functionality simplifies access to immersive AR experiences by reducing intermediate steps and maintaining a low cognitive load, a key criterion in the design of educational interfaces (Nielsen, 1994).

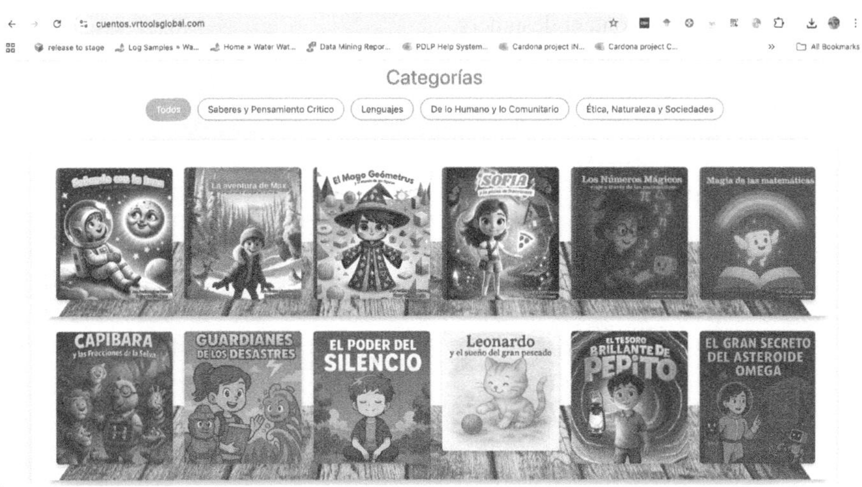

FIGURE 5.2 Digital library main page.

5.4.2 Interactive Navigation

The navigation proposed for the story library is designed to resemble as closely as possible a traditional bookshelf (see Figure 5.3). When a story is selected from the shelf, a digital flipbook developed with TurnJS opens, simulating the turning of pages in a physical book. To optimize the user experience, heuristic principles of usability and accessibility were integrated, as described here:

- Consistency in navigation: Clear forward and backward buttons placed coherently within the interface (Nielsen, 1994).
- Ease of learning: Use of arrows and simple text labels that eliminate the need for additional instructions (Shneiderman et al., 2016).
- Immediate feedback: Visual responses when interacting with buttons, such as color changes or animations.
- Physical accessibility: Large, well-spaced buttons, considering children's motor skills and supported by Fitts's Law (Fitts, 1954).
- Clear and direct language: Easily understandable labels for each action, aligned with WCAG accessibility guidelines (World Wide Web Consortium (W3C), 2018).
- Return to index: Inclusion of a back button to allow users to easily switch to another story.

These criteria ensure that the platform is intuitive, accessible, and child-friendly, fostering autonomous exploration and reducing frustration during navigation.

5.4.3 Learning Resources

Each AR story is accompanied by an interactive quiz. This tool enables the collection and analysis of reading comprehension results, providing valuable information for both teachers and content designers.

FIGURE 5.3 Viewing the flipbook to see the stories created on the bookstore page.

5.4.4 Augmented Reality Experience

Access to AR is enabled through the scanning of a QR code (see Figure 5.4), which directs users to a menu with thumbnail visual representations of each story. This design facilitates selection through visual recognition and minimizes cognitive load. When a story is chosen, the device's camera is activated to scan images of the physical or digital pages, upon which 3D elements and animations created with Three.js and MindAR are superimposed.

This experience does not replace reading but rather complements it by offering an immersive environment that enhances student comprehension and motivation. The design combines consistency, accessibility, and immediate feedback, resulting in an effective and engaging resource that integrates both formal and informal learning.

5.5 METHODOLOGY

This section describes the process followed to evaluate the usability and user experience of the proposed digital library with augmented reality. The objective of the evaluation was to identify the degree of ease of use, accessibility, and perceived satisfaction in order to validate the pedagogical and technological relevance of the proposed ecosystem.

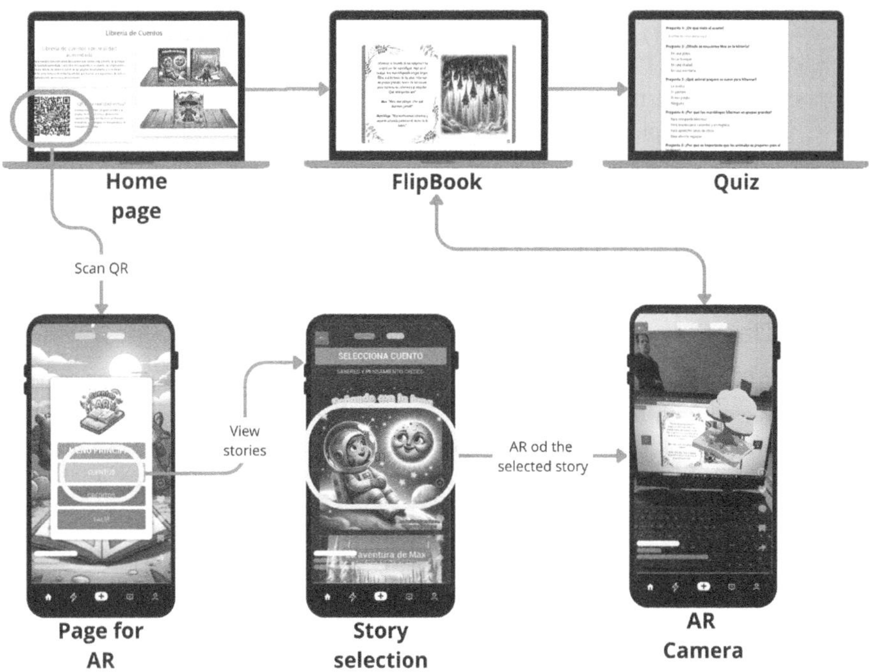

FIGURE 5.4 Application usage flow considering the library and the augmented reality view.

5.5.1 Participants

The sample consisted of ten teachers who voluntarily participated in the study. These users were selected as the target audience because they had experience with learning platforms, digital reading, and AR technologies. No restrictions were established regarding age, gender, or academic level, beyond their belonging to an educational environment (school, university, or training center).

5.5.2 Materials

To analyze usability, two standardized questionnaires were applied:

- System Usability Scale (SUS): An instrument composed of ten items that assess the overall perception of a system's usability. Its purpose is to determine how easy and pleasant the interaction is. The scale uses a 5-point Likert format (1 = Strongly Disagree, 5 = Strongly Agree) (Brooke, 1996).
- Post-Study System Usability Questionnaire (PSSUQ): A questionnaire that measures user experience in three dimensions: system quality, information quality, and interface quality. It consists of 14 questions on a 7-point Likert scale (1–7, where higher scores indicate better usability), complemented by two open-ended questions to gather qualitative feedback (Lewis, 1995).

5.5.3 Measures

- SUS:
  - Odd items (1, 3, 5, 7, 9): score—1.
  - Even items (2, 4, 6, 8, 10): 5—score.
  - The sum of these transformations generates a value from 0 to 40, which when multiplied by 2.5 produces the final score between 0 and 100. A score ≥ 70 is considered an indicator of good usability (Bangor et al., 2009).
- PSSUQ: Responses are grouped into three dimensions (system, information, and interface). The average per dimension is calculated, allowing identification of strengths and areas for improvement in the user experience.

5.5.4 Design

A usability study was conducted under controlled conditions, in which each participant interacted with the platform following a defined flow: selecting a story, reading, exploring the AR features, and finally answering the evaluation questionnaires. Since the purpose was to measure system usability, no control group was included.

5.5.5 Procedure

1. Introduction and consent: Participants were informed about the objective of the study, the procedure, and the voluntary nature of their participation. Informed consent was then obtained.
2. Interaction with the ecosystem: Each teacher accessed the virtual library, selected a story, and explored its AR features without time limits. During the interaction, participants were encouraged to provide spontaneous comments.

3. Questionnaire application: At the end of the experience, participants completed the SUS questionnaire, followed by the PSSUQ, in order to collect both quantitative and qualitative data.
4. Closure: Participants were thanked for their collaboration, and final observations were collected.

5.6 RESULTS

This section presents the findings obtained from the evaluation of the virtual library ecosystem of AR-based stories, carried out through the System Usability Scale (SUS) and the Post-Study System Usability Questionnaire (PSSUQ) with a total of ten participants. The analysis focused on three key aspects: usability, ease of learning, and overall user satisfaction.

5.6.1 SUS Test

The SUS test, designed to measure the overall perception of system usability, yielded the following individual scores: 95, 80, 75, 80, 100, 97.5, 85, 77.5, 95, and 95. As shown in Figure 5.5, the average score was 88/100, which places the virtual library ecosystem in the B range (acceptable usability) according to the standard interpretation of this metric (Bangor et al., 2009).

Ninety percent of participants rated the system as highly usable, highlighting the clarity of the interface and intuitive navigation. However, 10% gave scores below 80, reflecting the need to optimize aspects related to the navigation structure and menu organization. The uniform distribution of scores within a high range indicates consistency in the positive perception of the system and the absence of extreme outliers, reinforcing the robustness of the results.

5.6.2 PSSUQ Test

The PSSUQ assessed user satisfaction after using the system across three main dimensions:

- System quality: Average score of 6.68/7, highlighting system efficiency and reliability.
- Information quality: Average score of 6.38/7, positively rated but the lowest among the three dimensions, indicating a need to improve the accuracy and variety of content.
- Interface quality: Average score of 6.65/7, reflecting satisfaction with visual design and ease of interaction.

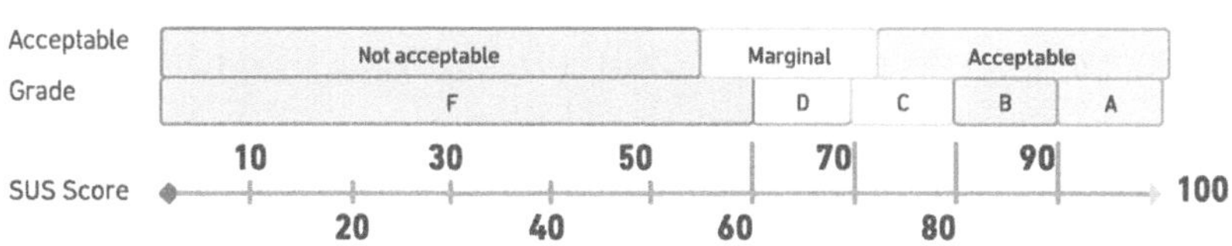

FIGURE 5.5 Application usage flow considering the library and the augmented reality view.

The overall satisfaction average was 6.55/7, indicating a very favorable evaluation of the ecosystem. The low variability (standard deviation < 0.31) suggests consistent responses among participants. Table 5.2 summarizes the individual results and averages obtained for each dimension.

Responses to the open-ended questions reinforced these findings: users highlighted search features, accessibility, and AR-enhanced story images as positive aspects, while areas for improvement focused on simplifying certain texts and expanding the story catalog, with particular attention to age-based classification (3–6 years and 6–9 years).

5.6.3 Friedman Test

To compare the three dimensions evaluated in the PSSUQ, the non-parametric Friedman test was applied (Cleophas & Zwinderman, 2016). The analysis produced a χ^2 value with $p < 0.0001$, indicating statistically significant differences between at least two dimensions. Table 5.3 shows the ranks assigned to each dimension for each user.

TABLE 5.2
Average results by category and overall.

User	System	Information	Interface	Overall
1	7	6	7	6.5
2	6.6	6.3	6	6.4
3	6.2	6	6.5	6.1
4	6.2	6.2	6	6.1
5	7	7	7	7
6	7	6.6	7	6.8
7	6.8	6.8	7	6.8
8	6.2	6	6.5	6.1
9	6.8	6.8	6.5	6.7
10	7	6	7	6.5
Average	6.68	6.38	6.65	6.55

TABLE 5.3
Average Results by Category and Overall

User	System (range)	Information (range)	Interface (range)
1	2.5	1	2.5
2	3	2	1
3	2	1	3
4	2.5	2.5	1
5	2	2	2
6	2.5	1	2.5
7	1.5	1.5	3
8	2	1	3
9	2.5	2.5	1
10	2.5	1	2.5

Post-hoc comparisons revealed the following:

- There were no significant differences between System and Interface ($p \approx 0.1$).
- Information received a significantly lower score than System ($p < 0.01$) and Interface ($p < 0.05$).

These results confirm that, while the system and interface are highly valued, information quality represents the main aspect requiring improvement.

5.7 DISCUSSION

The findings of this study demonstrate that the AR digital library ecosystem not only achieves high levels of usability and satisfaction but also emerges as a valuable pedagogical tool to strengthen reading comprehension and motivation in primary education. The results derived from the evaluations indicate that the average score obtained in the SUS test (88/100) and the consistent results in the PSSUQ (6.38–6.68/7) show that the platform is perceived as intuitive, accessible, and reliable, which constitutes an essential requirement for its integration into school contexts.

A relevant aspect identified through the Friedman test is that, while the system and interface received favorable evaluations, the information dimension scored significantly lower. This highlights the need to improve the quality, relevance, and variety of educational content. Participant feedback suggests clear lines of action: expanding the story catalog (which will grow as the platform is adopted in more schools), simplifying certain texts, and classifying materials by age ranges (e.g., 3–6 and 6–9 years). These improvements not only enhance pedagogical relevance but also foster more meaningful learning and more effective teacher support.

Likewise, the high ratings given to elements such as content search, image attractiveness, and platform accessibility reflect that the user-centered design successfully met the principles established in the literature on educational interfaces. In the school context, these features boost reading motivation, promote inclusion, and ensure that students with different skill levels and technological resources can benefit from the same experience.

The results obtained are consistent with previous research that highlights the positive impact of AR on motivation and reading comprehension in primary levels (Basumatary & Maity, 2023; Nevrelova et al., 2024; Zilong et al., 2021). However, unlike many proposals that require external applications or lack curricular integration, this work focuses on accessibility and availability and is aligned with school objectives, which increases its potential for adoption in real educational settings.

Finally, although the consistency of the results (low standard deviations) suggests stable perceptions among participants, future work will focus on incorporating larger samples and longitudinal studies to analyze the sustained effect of the proposed platform on the development of reading skills and children's motivation. Furthermore, exploring the integration of learning analytics could provide more detailed information on usage patterns, facilitating personalization and the continuous improvement of the ecosystem.

5.8 CONCLUSIONS AND FUTURE WORK

This study presented the design, implementation, and evaluation of a digital learning ecosystem with augmented reality (AR), aimed at improving reading comprehension and motivation in primary education. The results obtained through the SUS and PSSUQ instruments show that the platform achieves high levels of usability and satisfaction, supporting its potential for integration into educational contexts. Positive evaluations of system and interface quality are attributed to the user-centered design approach, while the lower scores in the information dimension highlight challenges such as the need to strengthen the quality, diversity, and pedagogical alignment of digital stories.

From an educational perspective, the proposed platform seeks to contribute to literacy development by combining interactive narratives, immersive AR elements, and integrated assessment quizzes. Teachers and other educational stakeholders can use the system to personalize instruction and encourage active participation, while students gain access to accessible, engaging, and motivating resources. Moreover, being based on accessible technologies, the proposal aims to ensure greater scalability and availability, even in contexts with limited infrastructure.

Although this work has produced valuable results to advance the research line, it presents certain limitations. The platform was evaluated with a small sample of teachers. In addition, the contents of the digital library remain limited in both number and thematic diversity, making it necessary to expand the catalog to include different age levels and curricular contexts. Finally, further studies are required to assess the sustained impact of the ecosystem on the development of reading comprehension and student motivation.

Future work will focus on addressing the identified limitations, such as expanding and diversifying the content catalog. This includes classifying stories by age groups, defining criteria for creating texts for younger readers, and incorporating thematic sections aligned with the school curriculum. Likewise, further studies with larger and more diverse samples are needed to validate the platform's impact across different contexts, along with longitudinal research to evaluate the sustained effect of AR-based ecosystems on reading comprehension and children's motivation.

Finally, the proposed AR ecosystem aspires to establish itself as an alternative to integrate pedagogical innovation, usability principles, and immersive technologies to address one of the most urgent challenges in education: strengthening literacy and reading motivation in primary education. The results obtained serve as a starting point that validates the proposal not only as a viable educational resource but also as a new opportunity to scale similar solutions across diverse learning environments.

REFERENCES

Adapa, K., Jain, S., Kanwar, R., Zaman, T., Taneja, T., Walker, J., & Mazur, L. (2020). Augmented reality in patient education and health literacy: A scoping review protocol. *BMJ Open*, 10(9). https://doi.org/10.1136/bmjopen-2020-038416

Banco Mundial & UNICEF. (2022). *Dos años después: Salvando a una generación*. Banco Mundial y UNICEF. https://www.unicef.org/lac/media/35631/file/Dos-anos-despues-salvando-a-una-generacion.pdf

Bangor, A., Kortum, P., & Miller, J. (2009). Determining what individual SUS scores mean: Adding an adjective rating scale. *Journal of Usability Studies*, 4(3), 114–123.

Basumatary, D., & Maity, R. (2023). Effects of augmented reality in primary education: A literature review. *Human Behavior and Emerging Technologies*, 2023(1), 4695759. https://doi.org/10.1155/2023/4695759

Benítez Miranda, R. S., Cevallos Illicachi, J. R., Pilla Zuñiga, W. I., & Sancho Aguilera, D. (2025). Realidad Aumentada y Realidad Virtual en la Educación en Latinoamérica: Análisis de su Adopción, Desafíos y Oportunidades. *Ciencia Latina Revista Científica Multidisciplinar*, 9(2), 5528–5545. https://doi.org/10.37811/cl_rcm.v9i2.17311

Brooke, J. (1996). SUS: A "quick and dirty" usability scale. In P. W. Jordan, B. Thomas, B. A. Weerdmeester, & I. L. McClelland (Eds.), *Usability evaluation in industry* (pp. 189–194). Taylor & Francis.

Cleophas, T. J., & Zwinderman, A. H. (2016). Non-parametric tests for three or more samples (Friedman and Kruskal-Wallis). In *Clinical data analysis on a pocket calculator: Understanding the scientific methods of statistical reasoning and hypothesis testing* (pp. 193–197). Springer International Publishing. https://doi.org/10.1007/978-3-319-27104-0_34

Dmitrieva, I. A., & Yulmetova, R. F. (2021). Ecosystem approach and innovative educational ecosystems. *IOP Conference Series: Earth and Environmental Science*, 864, 012002. https://doi.org/10.1088/1755-1315/864/1/012002

Fitts, P. M. (1954). The information capacity of the human motor system in controlling the amplitude of movement. *Journal of Experimental Psychology*, 47(6), 381–391. https://doi.org/10.1037/h0055392

Islas Torres, C. (2019). Los ecosistemas de aprendizaje y estudiantes universitarios: Una propuesta de abordaje sistémico. *Revista Argentina de Ciencias Del Comportamiento*, 10(2), 172–186. https://doi.org/10.29059/rpcc.20191126-98

Kicherova, M. N., & Trifonova, I. S. (2023). Principles of the ecosystem approach: Possibilities for modeling educational ecosystems. *Science for Education Today*, 13(3), 45–72. https://doi.org/10.15293/2658-6762.2303.03

Kodsiri, C., & Kruekamai, W. (2023). Learning ecosystems that promote lifelong learning: An interdisciplinary perspective for sustainable development. In *Proceedings of the conference: Four decades of curriculum and instruction: Evolution towards education for the future* (pp. 254–271). https://www.edu.cmu.ac.th/assets/pdf/ci-conf/2567/proceeding-CI-2567-ISBN.pdf

Lewis, J. R. (1995). IBM computer usability satisfaction questionnaires: Psychometric evaluation and instructions for use. *International Journal of Human–Computer Interaction*, 7(1), 57–78. https://doi.org/10.1080/10447319509526110

Lowdermilk, T. (2013). *User-centered design: A developer's guide to building user-friendly applications*. O'Reilly Media, Inc.

Martí, R. (2018). Ecosistemas tecnológicos de aprendizaje y gestión educativa. *Edutec, Revista Electrónica de Tecnología Educativa*, 64, 1–17. https://doi.org/10.21556/edutec.2018.64.1025

Nevrelova, N., Korenova, L., Lavicza, Z., Bruzkova, N., & Schmid, A. (2024). Enhancing digital literacy in primary education through augmented reality. *Frontiers in Education*, 9. https://doi.org/10.3389/feduc.2024.1390491

Nguyen, L. T., & Tuamsuk, K. (2022). Digital learning ecosystem at educational institutions: A content analysis of scholarly discourse. *Cogent Education*, 9(1), 2111033. https://doi.org/10.1080/2331186X.2022.2111033

Nielsen, J. (1994). *Usability engineering*. Morgan Kaufmann.

Piatykop, O. I., Pronina, O. I., Tymofieieva, I. B., & Palii, I. D. (2022). Early literacy with augmented reality. *Educational Dimension*, 6, 131–148. https://doi.org/10.31812/educdim.4491

Pinto-Llorente, A. M., & Izquierdo-Álvarez, V. (2024). Digital learning ecosystem to enhance formative assessment in second language acquisition in higher education. *Sustainability*, 16(11). https://doi.org/10.3390/su16114687

Prieto-Díaz, V., Quiñones-La Rosa, I., Ramírez-Durán, G., Zoe, F.-G., Labranda-Pavón, T., Pérez.Hechavarría, O., & Montero-Valdés, M. (2011). Impacto de las tecnologías de la información y las comunicaciones en la educación y nuevos paradigmas del enfoque educativo. *Eduación Médica Superior*, 25, 95–102.

Quintero, J., Baldiris, S., Rubira, R., Cerón, J., & Velez, G. (2019). Augmented reality in educational inclusion. A systematic review on the last decade. *Frontiers in Psychology*, 10. https://doi.org/10.3389/fpsyg.2019.01835

Shah, R., Cardozo, M. L., & Hjarrand, J. (2024). Learning as ecosystems: Shifting paradigms for more holistic programming in education and displacement. *International Journal of Educational Development*, 104, 102943. https://doi.org/10.1016/j.ijedudev.2023.102943

Shneiderman, B., Plaisant, C., Cohen, M., Jacobs, S., Elmqvist, N., & Diakopoulos, N. (2016). *Designing the user interface: Strategies for effective human-computer interaction* (6th ed.). Pearson.

UNESCO. (2021, December). *Entre 2013 y 2019 México retrocedió en sus logros de aprendizaje, advierte UNESCO*. UNESCO. https://mexico.un.org/es/163801-entre-2013-y-2019-m%C3%A9xico-retrocedi%C3%B3-en-sus-logros-de-aprendizaje-advierte-unesco

UNESCO. (2023, September). *La UNESCO alerta que desde 2013 hay falta de avances en los aprendizajes fundamentales en América Latina y el Caribe*. UNESCO. https://unes.co/pblull

UNESCO Santiago, Oficina Regional de Educación para América Latina y el Caribe (OREALC/UNESCO Santiago). (2021). *Informe de Resultados del Estudio Regional Comparativo y Explicativo (ERCE 2019)*. UNESCO. https://unesdoc.unesco.org/ark:/48223/pf0000378335

Utkin, A., & Shevchenko, K. (2022). Ecosystem approach in education: From metaphor to methodology and practice. *Cherepovets State University Bulletin*, 2, 175–189.

Vlachogianni, P., & Tselios, N. (2023). Perceived usability evaluation of educational technology using the Post-Study System Usability Questionnaire (PSSUQ): A systematic review. *Sustainability*, 15(17). https://doi.org/10.3390/su151712954

World Wide Web Consortium (W3C). (2018). *Web content accessibility guidelines (WCAG) 2.1*. https://www.w3.org/TR/WCAG21/

Wu, H.-K., Lee, S. W.-Y., Chang, H.-Y., & Liang, J.-C. (2013). Current status, opportunities and challenges of augmented reality in education. *Computers & Education*, 62, 41–49. https://doi.org/10.1016/j.compedu.2012.10.024

Yeh, H.-C., & Tseng, S.-S. (2020). Enhancing multimodal literacy using augmented reality. *Language Learning & Technology*, 24(1), 27–37. https://doi.org/10125/44706

Zilong, P., Mary, L., Chenglu, L., & Min, L. (2021). Introducing augmented reality in early childhood literacy learning. *Research in Learning Technology*, 29. https://doi.org/10.25304/rlt.v29.2539

6 Semantic Web and Complex Thinking

The Usefulness of Computational Tools for Achieving Professional Competencies in Health

Luis Clemente Jiménez-Botello,
Iván Miguel García-López,
Francisco J. García-Peñalvo,
and María Soledad Ramírez-Montoya

6.1 INTRODUCTION

In a post-pandemic educational landscape, the accelerated digital transformation demands technological solutions that facilitate personalization and the identification of essential student competencies. This challenge has prompted the exploration of technologies such as the semantic web, ontologies, and learning analytics as means to improve the quality of learning in complex contexts. Several recent studies have shown how these tools strengthen knowledge representation and promote professional development in areas such as healthcare. For example, the educational value of Wikidata as a learning platform based on the semantic web has been explored (Evenstein Sigalov & Nachmias, 2023). Likewise, it has been shown that the semantic web can improve interoperability, information management, and decision support in e-health systems (Haque et al., 2022). This context justifies the purpose of this chapter: to propose a model that integrates the semantic web, learning analytics, and ontologies to assess and develop professional competencies in health. This approach serves as a bridge towards the imminent treatment of the conceptual foundations that support this proposal.

It is a fact that the amount of information available on the web will continue to grow and that better systems for organizing and prioritizing information are necessary. At all times, it must be considered that the process of searching for information on the Internet is a human-computer interaction (HCI) and that the person should always be prioritized over the machine (Liao & Vaughan, 2023). An advance of a web at the service of human beings is WEB 3.0, also known as the semantic web (Suárez Sánchez, 2021), which has significant differences with respect to WEB 2.0,

DOI: 10.1201/9781003678250-6

such as the so-called hyperservice, which in itself defines a much more efficient environment in terms of interoperability and programming of chain codes (blockchain), which significantly increases its security (Liu et al., 2022). When working with this magnitude of complex information, we find ourselves within the field of big data, and when it comes to healthcare information, the field of knowledge is evolving into big healthcare data, which must be based on ontological systems that allow for better analysis and understanding of the information.

6.2 CONCEPTUAL FOUNDATIONS: SEMANTIC WEB, ONTOLOGIES, AND LEARNING ANALYTICS

The semantic web is a proposal that seeks to improve the conventional Web so that information is understandable by machines and can also be processable, using standards (RDF and OWL) that allow the use of metadata, establish relationships, and use concepts in accordance with the W3C within the field of learning analytics. In education, we can define learning analytics as the measurement, collection, and analysis of data derived from learning, with the aim of understanding and subsequently optimizing educational processes, considering the individual and personalized approach, as well as the visualization of students at academic risk through visualization in dashboards. In another aspect, competency ontologies allow us to model in a structured and objective way, the professional competencies that we intend to develop in the student. In this regard, we can mention the COMP2 ontology (Paquette et al., 2021), which was designed so that it can be interpreted by humans and machines, using vocabularies from the Semantic Web.

Ontology is a branch of philosophy related to the nature of "being." In computational science, ontology is a formal and explicit specification of a shared conceptualization. Therefore, to formalize it, standardized ontological languages, such as OWL, and various computational tools that allow the representation of ontologies (Benis et al., 2022), have been developed. This allows for semantic indexing systems based on ontologies and supported by machine learning (ML) (Sharma & Kumar, 2023). One of the most representative semantic systems is SemPryv, which integrates ontology, semantic interrelation, interoperability with other portals, and ML; using standardized vocabulary, ontologies, and taxonomies for the benefit of the user (Calbimonte et al., 2023). Currently, ontology and semantics applied to different areas of knowledge, particularly in health, have taken on great relevance due to their potential benefits for users.

In recent years, ontological systems in healthcare have made significant progress. Examples include SNOMED, MedO, OBI Ontology, GALEN, and Gene Ontology, among others; as well as computational environments such as Resource Description Framework (RDF), Ontology Web Language (OWL), and Open Biomedical Ontology (OBO) (Torres-Ruiz et al., 2022). Likewise, Spanish-language platforms have been developed that integrate the same functionalities in terms of semantic concepts, but considering users from Spain and of course Spanish speakers. The MedLexSp platform uses natural language and recognition of accents and interrelation of concepts in Spanish and English (Campillo-Llanos, 2023). In Mexico, LINDASearch (LINDASearch stands for Linked Data Search), a semantic search system, has been developed with good results but still has room for improvement (Sánchez-Cervantes et al., 2020). Many of the systems that have been developed only function as search engines, but it is important that these ontological systems benefit the user, in particular, allowing them to address and solve problems by achieving complex reasoning skills, especially during their educational process.

Specifically in health education, given the global challenge posed by COVID-19, it was necessary to increase learning about epidemiology, utilizing all available resources. In this regard, public health students have been encouraged to learn about biostatistics and epidemiological data analysis through the use of computational thinking (Zheng, 2022). Applying these advances also requires personnel trained in epidemiology and new technological advances for the study and understanding of public health, genomics, and bioinformatics (Onywera et al., 2024). The integration of knowledge about fundamental areas of medicine, ranging from genetics to the entire human organism and other areas of knowledge such as epidemiology, through computational analysis, gives rise to computational biomedicine and, therefore, computational thinking (Wan & Coveney, 2024). Which allows us to affirm that computational thinking will be fundamental in the analysis of complex information, as well as the understanding and application of knowledge in epidemiology.

Understanding epidemiology and its usefulness can be enhanced through the use of computational thinking. New or re-emerging diseases can be monitored through the use of epidemiological intelligence systems, which can issue early warnings in accordance with World Health Organization guidelines (Menya et al., 2024). In fact, epidemiology has evolved from empirical data and observation to advanced mathematical models that can integrate genomic aspects, increasing the precision and understanding of viral transmission dynamics (Aljabali et al., 2024). Similarly, the importance of having models that predict the spread trajectories of viral diseases such as COVID-19 and its new variants has been emphasized through the analysis of millions of genetic sequences obtained in multiple countries (Levi et al., 2024). These predictive models that integrate complex information are possible through advances in technology and computational thinking applied to epidemiology.

Based on the aforementioned, we can consider that it is possible to develop ontologies of professional competencies, with learning analytics and semantic technologies to methodologically support the conceptual model that will be developed in the following section.

6.3 STATE OF THE ART

Semantic approaches, combined with learning analytics, have been explored to assess competency achievement in educational and healthcare contexts. An example of this is semantic analytics assessment models, which assess explicit and latent competencies in students through the use of semantic representations and activity analysis (Halimi & Seridi-Bouchelaghem, 2021). Furthermore, ontological frameworks have been developed for the analysis of group assessments within collaborative learning environments, using supervised learning, with the aim of predicting performance as accurately as possible (accuracy = 0.92; test = 0.77) (Hadyaoui & Cheniti-Belcadhi, 2023). Similarly, the integration of heterogeneous data has been explored using graphical and ontological databases, with the aim of improving information retrieval and processing in institutional learning analytics (Musa et al., 2024). Within the scope of competencies, the COMP2 ontology was developed, which uses Semantic Web vocabularies to formally describe competencies and profiles, making this ontology human- and machine-readable (Paquette et al., 2021). Finally, we could point out that ontological models focused on competency-based curricula have been generated using semantic techniques (Milosz et al., 2024). The advances discussed here allow us to highlight the importance of combining the Semantic Web, ontologies, and learning analytics in competency assessment processes with innovative perspectives. In this regard, the following section will present a methodology consistent with these advances.

An important application of ontology and semantic web platforms is directly in the area of education. It is precisely in education where the importance of ontological systems for achieving complex thinking skills in higher education students has been identified (Sigahi & Sznelwar, 2022). In this regard, and as far as health education is concerned, evidence has been given of the usefulness of semantic web platforms in health in the training of human resources (Hernandez-Chan et al., 2016) by generating complex reasoning skills in undergraduate students, with their corresponding areas of opportunity and improvement (Toniolo et al., 2022). Therefore, semantic platforms must be continuously perfected so that they can be instruments that truly contribute to fostering complex thinking in students of health careers.

6.4 METHODOLOGICAL PROPOSAL

An integrated methodological model is proposed that combines three axes (Halimi & Seridi-Bouchelaghem, 2021):

- **Ontological model of competencies**, based on COMP2 (Paquette et al., 2021), adapted to the health domain, allowing professional competencies to be represented with semantic precision.
- **Collection and analysis of learning data**, using learning analytics that capture interactions in digital environments and allow the inference of explicit and latent competencies, following previous approaches (Halimi & Seridi-Bouchelaghem, 2021).
- **Prediction and visualization**, using supervised techniques to estimate performance and provide feedback to both educators and learners (Hadyaoui & Cheniti-Belcadhi, 2023).

The methodology would be executed in several phases:

- Phase 1: Design of the ontological model, including classes such as "Competence," "Activity," "Student," relating them semantically (e.g., acquiresCompetence).
- Phase 2: Implementation of a digital educational system that collects behavioral data (participation, activity, responses, comments).
- Phase 3: Application of analytics modules (discourse analysis, topics, etc.) to process learning data and map it to competencies using semantic reasoning.

Fase 4: Entrenamiento de modelos predictivos sobre el rendimiento (área y desempeño) en base a interacciones y estructura ontológica, con evaluación basada en métricas tipo accuracy test.

Phase 5: Visualization, analysis of results and corresponding feedback, to enable pedagogical decision-making.

This proposal will contribute positively to generating academic and, therefore, intellectual value by facilitating the interpretation of real competencies, as well as scaling and applying them within a health education context, allowing for efficient and clear evaluation, thus leading to the next case study.

6.5 CASE STUDY IN HEALTH EDUCATION

6.5.1 Context and Participants

The study analyzed was conducted in a Latin American health sciences faculty and included 126 medical and nursing students, ranging in age from 19 to 26 years, as well as eight faculty members responsible for clinical subjects. Participants were selected using purposive probability sampling, focusing on students taking subjects with a significant practical component. This approach allowed data collection in both real-life and clinical simulation scenarios, taking into account the recommendations found in previous studies on learning analytics in medical education (Bokolo, 2021). This allowed for a better assessment of students' clinical competencies.

6.5.2 Implementation of Tools and Platforms

With the objective of mapping the clinical skills acquired in the practical sessions, a platform based on the semantic web and another based on competency ontologies were combined, adapting the COMP2 model to the healthcare context. Specific relationships such as diagnose, prescribe, evaluate, and educate the patient were also included (Paquette et al., 2021). Learning analytics were implemented through an engine that processed interaction data (response time, number of interventions, and diagnostic accuracy) and likewise semantically linked them to competencies, both explicit and latent (Halimi & Seridi-Bouchelaghem, 2021). This is a major advance in the combined use of ontological and semantic resources in favor of professional healthcare competencies.

6.5.3 Evaluation of Acquired Professional Skills

To assess the competencies, two complementary methods were used: (1) traditional rubric-based teacher assessment and (2) automatic assessment using ontological reasoning and data analysis. The results showed a high correlation ($r = 0.87$) between both assessments, which supports previous findings on the reliability of semantic assessment models (Hadyaoui & Cheniti-Belcadhi, 2023). Furthermore, the system identified competencies not declared in the rubrics, such as communication skills in the delivery of diagnoses, in line with studies on transversal competencies in health (Aggarwal et al., 2023).

6.5.4 Results and Discussion

The results showed that the integration of the Semantic Web and learning analytics not only facilitates the monitoring of explicit competencies but also the detection of emerging skills. This highlights the ability of ontological models to integrate and analyze heterogeneous data in real time (Musa et al., 2024). The feedback generated in the form of graphs and concept maps was positively valued by teachers and students, as it allowed progress and areas for improvement to be clearly visualized.

6.6 DISCUSSION

The integration of the semantic web, ontologies, and learning analytics in healthcare education demonstrates a high potential to transform the assessment and development of professional competencies. First, the findings of this study confirm what was reported by Halimi and Seridi-Bouchelaghem (2021), where the semantic representation of competencies allows for more accurate and consistent tracking than traditional methods. Second, the incorporation of automatic metrics derived from student interaction data coincides with what Hadyaoui and Cheniti-Belcadhi (2023) proposed, demonstrating that predictive analytics complements teacher evaluation with a high correlation. Additionally, the model's ability to identify non-explicit competencies, such as communication and ethical reasoning skills, reinforces what (Aggarwal et al., 2023) suggested about the importance of capturing transversal competencies in clinical settings. This suggests that ontology-based systems can overcome the limitations of static rubrics by dynamically adapting to the complexity of real-life interactions. Similarly, using conceptual maps and visualization systems to provide feedback to students and teachers is aligned with the approach of Musa et al. (2024), since the visual representation of results contributes to better understanding and, likewise, to decision-making within the pedagogical context. An important consideration is that semantic systems depend on high-capacity technological equipment and institutional regulations that guarantee data protection and equity in access to information.

In summary, the reviewed study provides evidence of the usefulness of the combined use of technologies, semantic systems, and information analytics, which positively contributes to professional training in the health field. It also presents ethical and logistical challenges that must be overcome for effective implementation on a larger scale.

6.7 CONCLUSIONS AND RECOMMENDATIONS

This chapter has shown that the integration of the Semantic Web, ontologies, and learning analytics constitutes an effective strategy for assessing and developing professional competencies in health education, combining technical precision, adaptability, and the ability to detect emerging skills. Documented experience supports the view that semantic models not only replicate traditional assessments but also enhance them by identifying transversal competencies and generating personalized feedback.

Educational institutions are recommended to:

- Adopt ontological models adapted to their domain to ensure accurate representation of competencies.
- Integrate real-time learning analytics to capture skill development and generate immediate learning interventions.
- Form multidisciplinary teams that include experts in educational technology, pedagogy, and disciplinary expertise.
- Ensure transparency and ethics in data processing, complying with international privacy regulations.

Finally, future research is encouraged to explore the scalability of this approach to other areas of knowledge and to evaluate the longitudinal impact of these technologies on professional practice.

REFERENCES

Aggarwal, A., Tam, C. C., Wu, D., Li, X., & Qiao, S. (2023). Artificial intelligence-based chatbots for promoting health behavioral changes: Systematic review. *Journal of Medical Internet Research*, *25*, e40789. https://doi.org/10.2196/40789

Aljabali, A. A. A., Obeid, M. A., El-Tanani, M., Mishra, V., Mishra, Y., & Tambuwala, M. M. (2024). Precision epidemiology at the nexus of mathematics and nanotechnology: Unraveling the dance of viral dynamics. *Gene*, *905*, 148174. https://doi.org/10.1016/j.gene.2024.148174

Benis, A., Grosjean, J., Billey, K., Montanha, G., Dornauer, V., Crişan-Vida, M., Hackl, W. O., Stoicu-Tivadar, L., & Darmoni, S. J. (2022). Medical informatics and digital health multilingual ontology (MIMO): A tool to improve international collaborations. *International Journal of Medical Informatics*, *167*, 104860. https://doi.org/10.1016/j.ijmedinf.2022.104860

Bokolo, A. J. (2021). Exploring the adoption of telemedicine and virtual software for care of outpatients during and after COVID-19 pandemic. *Heliyon*, *7*(7), e06014.

Calbimonte, J. P., Aidonopoulos, O., Dubosson, F., Pocklington, B., Kebets, I., Legris, P. M., & Schumacher, M. (2023). Decentralized semantic provision of personal health streams. *Journal of Web Semantics*, *76*, 100774. https://doi.org/10.1016/j.websem.2023.100774

Campillos-Llanos, L. (2023). *Journal of Biomedical Semantics*, *14*, 2. https://doi.org/10.1186/s13326-022-00281-5

Evenstein Sigalov, S., & Nachmias, R. (2023). Investigating the potential of the semantic web for education: Exploring Wikidata as a learning platform. *Education and Information Technologies*, *28*(10), 12565–12614. https://doi.org/10.1007/s10639-023-11664-1

Hadyaoui, A., & Cheniti-Belcadhi, L. (2023). Ontology-based group assessment analytics framework for performances prediction in project-based collaborative learning. *Smart Learning Environments*, *10*(1), 43. https://doi.org/10.1186/s40561-023-00262-w

Halimi, K., & Seridi-Bouchelaghem, H. (2021). Students' competencies discovery and assessment using learning analytics and semantic web. In *Proceedings of the International Conference on Advanced Learning Technologies* (pp. 77–97). Springer.

Haque, A. K. M. B., Arifuzzaman, B. M., Siddik, S. A. N., Kalam, A., Shahjahan, T. S., Saleena, T. S., Alam, M., Islam, Md. R., Ahmmed, F., & Hossain, Md. J. (2022). Semantic web in healthcare: A systematic literature review of application, research gap, and future research avenues. *International Journal of Clinical Practice*, *2022*(1), 6807484. https://doi.org/10.1155/2022/6807484

Hernandez-Chan, G. S., Ceh-Varela, E. E., Cervera-Evia, G., & Quijano-Aban, V. (2016). Using semantic technologies for an intelligent medical trainer. In A. Martin-Gonzalez & V. Uc-Cetina (Eds.), *Intelligent Computing Systems* (Vol. 597, pp. 74–82). Springer International Publishing. https://doi.org/10.1007/978-3-319-30447-2_6

Levi, R., Zerhouni, E. G., & Altuvia, S. (2024). Predicting the spread of SARS-CoV-2 variants: An artificial intelligence enabled early detection. *PNAS Nexus*, *3*(1), 424. https://doi.org/10.1093/pnasnexus/pgad424

Liu, Z., Xiang, Y., Shi, J., Gao, P., Wang, H., Xiao, X., Wen, B., Li, Q., & Hu, Y.-C. (2022). Make Web3.0 connected. *IEEE Transactions on Dependable and Secure Computing*, *19*(5), 2965–2981. https://doi.org/10.1109/TDSC.2021.3079315

Lu, S., Tazin, A., Chen, Y., et al. (2023). Detection of inconsistencies in SysML/OCL models using OWL reasoning. *SN Computer Science*, *4*, 175. https://doi.org/10.1007/s42979-022-01577-0

Menya, E., Interdonato, R., Owuor, D., & Roche, M. (2024). Explainable epidemiological thematic features for event based disease surveillance. *Expert Systems with Applications*, *250*, 123894. https://doi.org/10.1016/j.eswa.2024.123894

Milosz, M., Nazyrova, A., Mukanova, A., Bekmanova, G., Kuzin, D., & Aimicheva, G. (2024). Ontological approach for competency-based curriculum analysis. *Heliyon*, *10*(7), e29046. https://doi.org/10.1016/j.heliyon.2024.e29046

Musa, A., Omoregbe, N., & Kehinde, L. O. (2024). Leveraging knowledge graph and semantic web technologies for student performance analytics in higher education. *Procedia Computer Science*, *227*, 156–164.

Onywera, H., Ondoa, P., Nfii, F., Ogwell, A., Kebede, Y., Christoffels, A., & Tessema, S. K. (2024). Boosting pathogen genomics and bioinformatics workforce in Africa. *The Lancet Infectious Diseases*, *24*(2), e106–e112. https://doi.org/10.1016/S1473-3099(23)00394-8

Paquette, G., Marino, O., & Bejaoui, R. (2021). A new competency ontology for learning environments personalization. *Smart Learning Environments*, *8*(1), 16. https://doi.org/10.1186/s40561-021-00160-z

Sánchez-Cervantes, J. L., Colombo-Mendoza, L. O., Alor-Hernández, G., García-Alcaráz, J. L., Álvarez-Rodríguez, J. M., & Rodríguez-González, A. (2020). LINDASearch: A faceted search system for linked open datasets. *Wireless Networks*, *26*(8), 5645–5663. https://doi.org/10.1007/s11276-019-02029-z

Sharma, A., & Kumar, S. (2023). Machine learning and ontology-based novel semantic document indexing for information retrieval. *Computers & Industrial Engineering*, *176*, 108940. https://doi.org/10.1016/j.cie.2022.108940

Sigahi, T. F. A. C., & Sznelwar, L. I. (2022). Exploring applications of complexity theory in engineering education research: A systematic literature review. *Journal of Engineering Education*, *111*(1), 232–260. https://doi.org/10.1002/jee.20438

Suárez Sánchez, A. (2021). *Web vs web semántica: métodos distintos de organización de información en la red*. Instituto de Investigaciones Bibliotecológicas y de la Información, UNAM. Recuperado de: https://repositorio.unam.mx/contenidos/5042526

Toniolo, R. M. M., Peres, A. M., & Montezeli, J. H. (2022). Approaches of the systematization of nursing care, complexity and ontology in the professional practice of nurses. *Revista Gaúcha de Enfermagem*, *43*, e20210213. https://doi.org/10.1590/1983-1447.2022.20210213.en

Torres-Ruiz, M., Quintero, R., Guzman, G., & Chui, K. T. (2022). Healthcare recommender system based on medical specialties, patient profiles, and geospatial information. *Sustainability*, *15*(1), 499. https://doi.org/10.3390/su15010499

Wan, S., & Coveney, P. V. (2024). Introduction to computational biomedicine. In A. Heifetz (Eds.), *High Performance Computing for Drug Discovery and Biomedicine. Methods in Molecular Biology* (Vol. 2716). Humana. https://doi.org/10.1007/978-1-0716-3449-3

Zheng, Q. (2022). Integrating computational thinking into a longitudinal data analysis course for public health students. *Discover Education, 1*(1), 15. https://doi.org/10.1007/s44217-022-00015-w

2. **From religious to individual**: the "religious" or "individualistic-religious" dimension evolved into "individual," understood as the pursuit of personal autonomy, self-realization, and a sense of meaning, not necessarily tied to institutional religiosity.
3. **Emergence of regulatory**: subsequent psychometric developments introduced a "regulatory" dimension, associated with a preference for rules, structures, and external order, capturing motivations that in the original model were diffused between political and religious domains.

The result is a seven-dimensional motivational structure that incorporates Spranger's classical legacy while aligning with more recent instruments used to diagnose values and motivations [11, 12].

In this study, we adopt this seven-dimension framework because it more accurately reflects the way modern instruments capture motivational profiles and allows integration of motivations oriented toward self-realization and knowledge (aesthetic, theoretical, individual) as well as those connected to power and utility (political, economic), alongside two dimensions with strong social components (altruistic, and regulatory).

Accordingly, the model used in our analysis includes the following seven motivational dimensions:

Aesthetic: valuing form, beauty, and harmony; striving for creative self-realization.
Economic: interest in utility, efficiency, and tangible returns on resources.
Political: motivation for power, influence, and capacity to affect others.
Altruistic: orientation toward care for others, solidarity, and service.
Theoretical: interest in knowledge, understanding, and rational analysis.
Individual: pursuit of independence, identity, and personal meaning.
Regulatory: preference for rules, norms, and external structures that provide order.

This updated framework provides a more refined lens to examine the diversity of motivational orientations among LTP students, while maintaining a clear link to Spranger's original conceptual foundation.

7.2.2 DISC Model

Another important construct for understanding personality is the *DISC* model, proposed by William M. Marston in *Emotions of Normal People* in 1928 [9]. Unlike Spranger, who focuses on internal values, the DISC framework emphasizes observable behavioral patterns and styles of everyday interaction.

Decades later, John Geier operationalized the model through the *Personal Profile System*, which allowed its application in educational, organizational, and personal development contexts [13]. The model distinguishes four fundamental dimensions:

Dominance (D): result-oriented, assertive, and inclined to control.
Influence (I): associated with persuasion, communication, and social interaction.

Steadiness (S): characterized by patience, loyalty, and cooperation.
Conscientiousness (C): linked to precision, analysis, and adherence to rules.

No style is superior; rather, everyone combines these dimensions in varying degrees, forming a unique interaction profile in relation to others and to challenges.

7.3 BACKGROUND AND RELATED WORK

7.3.1 The Leaders of Tomorrow Program

The Leaders of Tomorrow (LTP) program at Tecnologico de Monterrey was established in 2014 to support academically outstanding students from low-income backgrounds. Applicants must demonstrate a minimum high school GPA of 90/100, leadership potential, entrepreneurial spirit, and commitment to community well-being. Scholarship benefits include full tuition, health insurance, and educational materials allowances for the duration of the degree, conditional on maintaining a minimum GPA of 85/100 and fulfilling some service requirements. By 2024, more than 2,100 students had benefited from the program, with participants representing all 32 Mexican states. Retention rates have consistently exceeded 97% after the first year, and nearly half of graduates have engaged in international experiences [7]. These outcomes highlight the program's role in fostering equity and transformative leadership in higher education.

7.3.2 Scholarship Impact and Student Success

A growing body of research has examined how scholarships affect student performance and persistence. Meta-analyses covering millions of students suggest that financial aid reliably increases enrollment, credit accumulation, and degree completion, while effects on GPA and post-college outcomes remain less consistent [14]. Other studies emphasize the mediating role of renewal requirements, showing that merit aid improves retention when conditions such as GPA thresholds and full-time status are accessible and attainable [15]. Evidence from Latin America reinforces these findings: programs in Colombia and Peru demonstrate that targeted scholarships for talented but disadvantaged students enhance academic outcomes and narrow socioeconomic gaps [16, 17].

7.3.3 Prior Studies on LTP Cohorts

Previous analyses of LTP students at Tecnológico de Monterrey have shown that co-curricular participation, such as involvement in student groups, international activities, and community service, correlates with higher academic performance. Demographic factors, including gender, urban origin, and first-generation status, have also been linked to differences in cumulative GPA [18]. A complementary study explored the motivational architecture of LTP students, identifying clusters along altruistic, theoretical, and aesthetic-individual dimensions [19]. These studies underscore the value of combining academic, motivational, and contextual perspectives, laying the groundwork for the present chapter's broader learning analytics approach.

7.4 DATA AND METHODOLOGY

7.4.1 Dataset Description

The whole analytic dataset comprises 22,718 longitudinal records corresponding to 1,796 unique students who participated in the *Líderes del Mañana* scholarship program, hereafter LTP until 2022. Each student contributes multiple entries reflecting the different academic terms enrolled, which enables longitudinal tracking of academic performance and co-curricular engagement. The present analysis focuses on a subgroup of $N = 826$ students belonging mainly to the Tec21 Educational Model, across six entry cohorts (2017–2022), with the largest cohorts corresponding to 2019 (236 students), 2020 (191), 2021 (187), and 2022 (199). The early cohorts of 2017 and 2018 are much smaller, with only 2 and 11 students, respectively.

The dataset integrates four main dimensions of student information: (a) academic performance indicators, such as high-school GPA, term GPA, final GPA, and full-time equivalent (FTE) load; (b) demographic attributes, such as gender, age band, geographic origin, first-generation status; (c) psychosocial constructs defining personality traits measured through the DISC model and value indices, such as altruistic, theoretical, and economic orientations; and (d) co-curricular participation, such as leadership, community service, sports, cultural, academic, and international activities. A descriptive statistical summary for the Tec21 cohorts is presented in Table 7.1.

The data reveal a student population with strong academic preparation with mean high school GPA = 96.0 and high performance at the undergraduate level, with mean final GPA = 93.8. Term GPA exhibits a bimodal distribution, with most observations concentrated above 90/100, but also a secondary cluster near zero, which likely reflects non-enrollment or administrative placeholders rather than genuine academic outcomes. The academic load is predominantly full-time, with mean FTE = 0.84 (where FTE = 1 correspond to full academic load), with slight variation across terms. Demographically, students are mostly in the 19–21 age band, near gender parity, and primarily of urban origin. Psychosocial variables show substantial heterogeneity, consistent with the diversity of motivational and personality profiles. Co-curricular participation is characterized by high levels of leadership involvement but limited international exposure.

In higher education research, a persistent challenge lies in moving beyond descriptive indicators of student success to uncover the heterogeneity of learning trajectories. Aggregate measures such as GPA averages, completion rates, or retention percentages provide useful but partial insights, often obscuring students' progress through diverse pathways shaped by academic, social, motivational, and contextual factors. For scholarship programs like LTP, whose mission extends beyond academic performance to social leadership and holistic development, this limitation is particularly critical. To address this issue, we employ analytical techniques that probe deeper structures within the data. Correlation analysis serves as a first step, highlighting coherent associations among academic, psychosocial, and co-curricular variables. These associations not only validate the richness of the dataset but also provide a basis for grouping students in meaningful ways. Building on this foundation, clustering methods allow us to delineate distinct profiles that make visible the

TABLE 7.1
Summary Statistics for 2017–2022 Cohort

Dimension	Indicator	Value (Tec21 only)
Population	Unique students	826
	Longitudinal records	9,274
	Cohorts (2017–2022)	2, 11, 236, 191, 187, 199
Academic	High-school GPA, mean (SD)	96.0 (2.8)
	Final GPA, mean (SD)	93.8 (5.4)
	Term GPA, mean (SD)	83.7 (30.0)
	FTE load, mean (SD)	0.84 (0.30)
Demographic	Age band	Predominantly 19–21
	Gender	Female ~52%, Male ~48%
	Zone of origin	Mostly urban; small semi-rural/rural shares
Psychosocial	DISC traits	Mid/upper ranges, multimodal distributions
	Values indices	Altruistic 67.2 (17.7); Theoretical 68.8 (18.6); Aesthetic 43.4 (15.1); Economic 38.9 (23.5); Individual 40.7 (12.9); Political 55.4 (14.2); Regulatory 39.7 (12.7)
Co-curricular	Leadership	High involvement
	International exposure	Minimal (majority at baseline level)
Academic structure	Top Tec schools	EIC (Engineering; largest), EN (Business), ECSG (Social Science and Government), EHE (Humanities and Education), EAAD (Architecture, Art and Design)
	Top majors	Business (NEG), Biotechnology (IBT), Biomedical Engineering (IBQ), Computer Science and Technology (ITC), Chemical Engineering (IQ), among others

different patterns through which students sustain achievement, assume leadership, or engage in social impact, thereby revealing student trajectories to the success that would remain hidden under conventional descriptive statistics.

7.4.2 Exploratory Factor Analysis

To explore the latent motivational structure of Leaders of Tomorrow (LTP) students, we applied Exploratory Factor Analysis (EFA) to the seven motivational dimensions derived from Spranger's updated framework (aesthetic, economic, political, altruistic, theoretical, individual, and regulatory). EFA is a multivariate statistical technique that identifies underlying factors by examining the interrelationships among observed variables and grouping them into latent constructs [20].

Prior to extraction, the suitability of the dataset for factor analysis was assessed using standard diagnostics. The Kaiser-Meyer-Olkin (KMO) measure of sampling adequacy exceeded the recommended threshold of 0.6, and Bartlett's test of sphericity was statistically significant, confirming that correlations among variables were sufficiently strong to justify factor analysis. Factor retention was guided by Kaiser's criterion (eigenvalues > 1) combined with visual inspection of the *scree plot*, which pointed to a three-factor solution.

To enhance interpretability, factor loadings were rotated using the varimax orthogonal rotation method. This procedure facilitated the reduction of the multidimensional set of motivational variables into a smaller number of latent characteristics, each capturing coherent orientations that summarize students' underlying motivations. In addition, for visualization purposes, we also explored a two-factor solution, which provided a clearer representation of the main motivations and their relative positioning on a factorial plane. The retained three-factor model, which explained 54.4% of the variance, was subsequently interpreted and related to descriptive statistics and academic outcomes, as discussed in the following sections.

7.4.3 Ethical Considerations

The data used in this study were obtained from the Institute for the Future of Education (IFE) Data Hub at Tecnologico de Monterrey, through a competitive call for research projects. Access was granted under a signed terms-of-use agreement and coordinated by the institutional custodian of the dataset. Only de-identified and aggregated records were available to the research team; no personally identifiable information, such as student names, ID numbers, or class groups, was accessed at any stage. The confidentiality of individual participants was therefore fully preserved. Responsibility for the protection of personal data remains with the institutional custodian, while the authors ensured that all analyses and results were reported exclusively at an aggregate level.

> The data that support the findings of this study are available from the Institute for the Future of Education (IFE)'s Educational Innovation collection of the Tecnologico de Monterrey's Research Data Hub but restrictions apply to the availability of these data, which were used under a signed "Terms and Conditions of Data Use" document for the current study, and are not publicly available. Data are, however, available from the IFE Data Hub upon reasonable request at https://doi.org/10.57687/FK2/UFM2QH [21].

7.5 RESULTS AND ANALYSIS

This section presents the main findings of the study, structured in two complementary parts. First, we analyze student profiles within the Tec21 cohorts through clustering techniques, identifying coherent groupings that reflect diverse academic, motivational, and co-curricular trajectories (Section 7.5.1). Second, we examine the motivational landscape of Leaders of Tomorrow students in greater depth, exploring both descriptive distributions and latent structures derived from factor analysis (Section 7.5.2).

Taken together, these results provide a comprehensive picture of how scholarship recipients sustain academic achievement, engage in co-curricular activities, and articulate their underlying motivations. The findings not only reveal plural forms of excellence but also highlight structural tensions, such as the balance between academic performance and social engagement, that are critical for understanding the pathways of high-achieving students from disadvantaged backgrounds.

7.5.1 Tec21 Student Profiles

Defining student profiles is not just a technical task; it directly influences institutional decision-making, enabling the program to recognize diverse forms of excellence, anticipate risks, and create tailored interventions. To achieve this, we used clustering techniques to identify hidden groups among students who share similar patterns across academic, psychosocial, and co-curricular areas.

7.5.1.1 Correlational Landscape as an Analytical Primer

Before applying clustering, it was necessary to verify whether the dataset contained meaningful relationships that justified segmentation. A Spearman correlation heat map (Figure 7.1) revealed several consistent patterns. As expected, term GPA is highly correlated with final GPA, indicating that steady performance across semesters is a key factor in overall success. DISC dimensions showed internal consistency, with notable correlations between influence and conscientiousness, while motivational values tended to cluster into understandable groups (e.g., aesthetic with political, economic with altruistic).

These relationships show that the variables are far from random, supporting the pursuit of student profiles through clustering.

7.5.1.2 From Correlations to Clusters

Using aggregated student data, we applied the *k*-means algorithm to a set of enrollment-aware variables that reflect academic, psychosocial, and co-curricular traits. We tested values of *k* between three and eight and evaluated solutions using the *silhouette* coefficient.

The three-cluster solution was the most balanced, avoiding unnecessary micro-clusters while maintaining meaningful interpretation. Although the silhouette value was modest (0.060), which is common in complex educational datasets, the clusters were distinct enough to represent meaningful profiles.

Principal component analysis (PCA) was used for visualization (Figure 7.2). The three clusters occupy partially separate regions in the factorial plane, confirming they reflect true structural differences rather than random divisions. The names of the clusters were adapted after the characteristics identified in Table 7.3.

7.5.1.3 Profiles of Tec21 Students

Figure 7.3 provides a visual overview of the three clusters across academic, motivational, and co-curricular dimensions, while Table 7.2 complements this by synthesizing their main characteristics in comparative form. Taken together, these two elements highlight the distinct academic momentum, value orientations, and activity patterns that define each profile, setting the stage for a more detailed narrative interpretation.

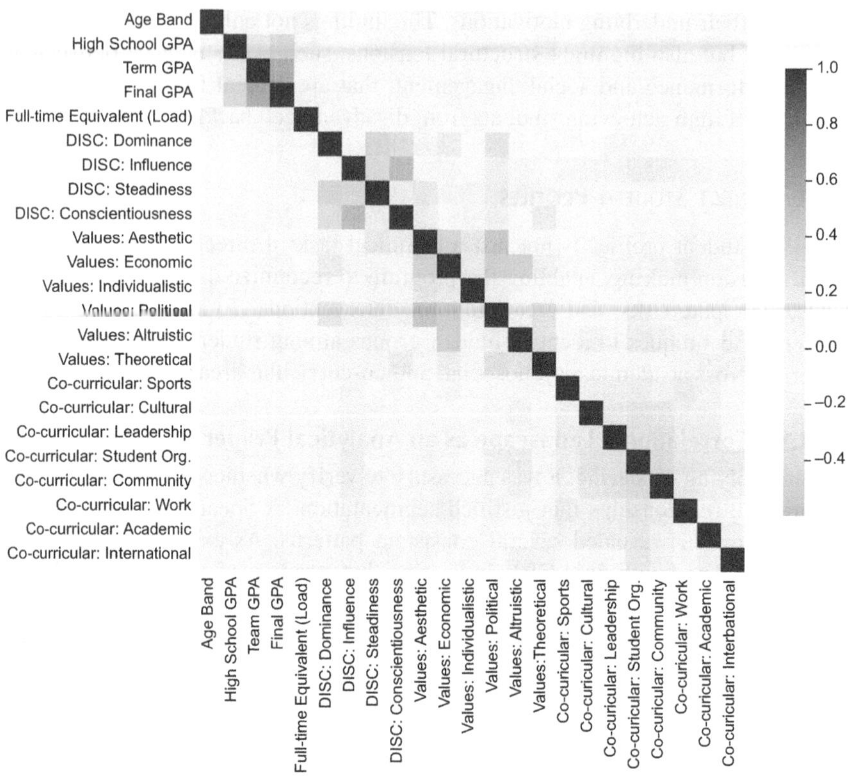

FIGURE 7.1 Spearman correlation heat map of Tec21 student variables.

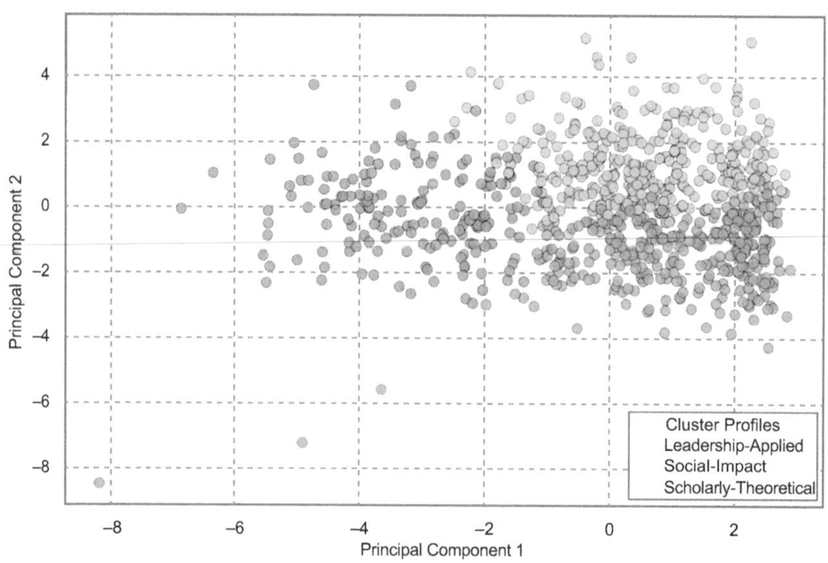

FIGURE 7.2 PCA projection of Tec21 students colored by cluster (k = 3).

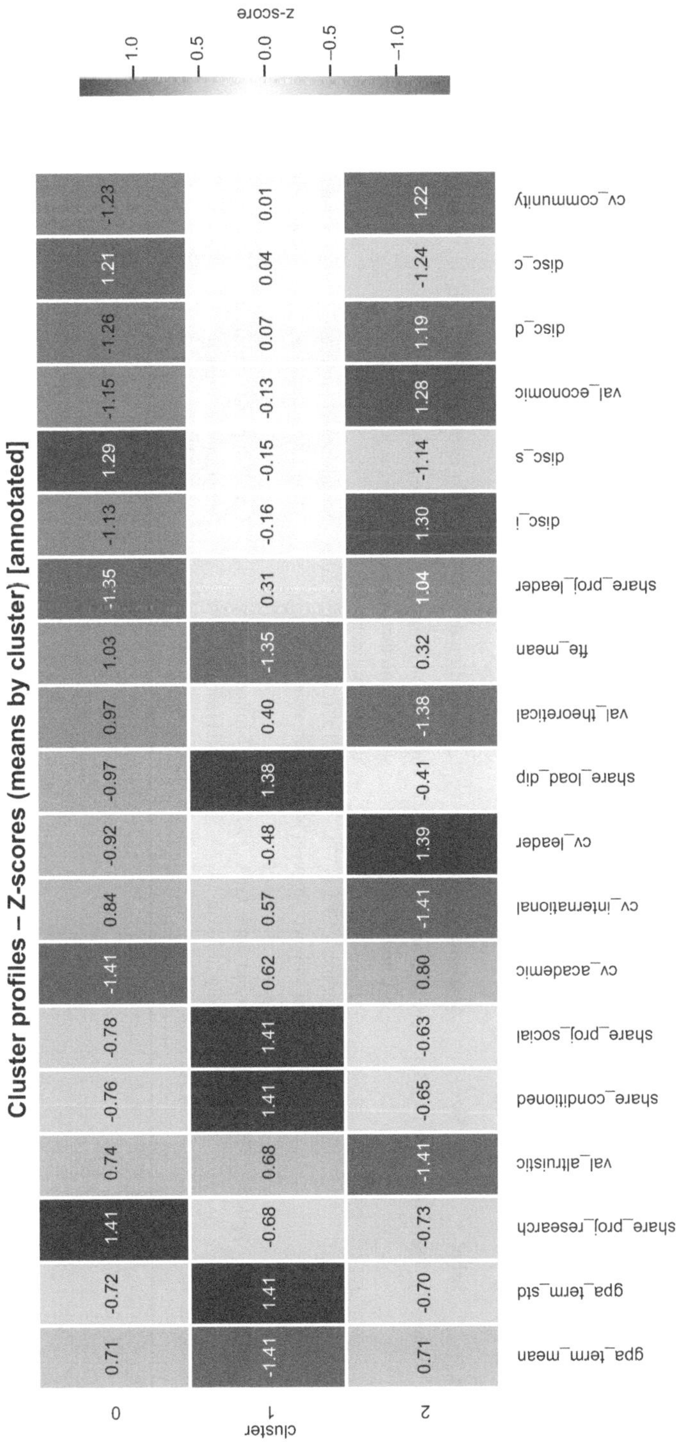

FIGURE 7.3 Profiles of Tec21 students across academic, motivational, and co-curricular dimensions.

TABLE 7.2
Summary Comparison of Tec21 Student Profiles (k = 3).

Cluster	Label	Size	Academic Momentum	Motivational Traits	Co-curricular Emphasis	Contextual Concentration
1	Scholarly–Theoretical	316 (~38%)	Very high and stable GPA (~94), minimal dips.	High Conscientiousness; strong theoretical, elevated altruistic & Economic.	Research/technology projects; modest leadership.	Concentrated in EIC, EAAD, EHE; majors IBT, ITC, IIT.
2	Social-Impact	174 (~21%)	Lower mean GPA (~77), high variance, frequent load dips.	High altruistic values; other traits near mean.	Social-impact projects; moderate leadership	Over-represented in EMCS; majors MC, IBQ, NEG.
3	Leadership–Applied	336 (~41%)	High and stable GPA (~94), steady full load.	High influence & dominance; lower conscientiousness.	Leadership and community engagement; limited research.	Concentrated in EN, ECSG; majors NEG and other applied programs.

Scholarly–Theoretical (38%): Students in this group exhibit very high and stable academic performance (average GPA ≈ 94) with minimal fluctuations in coursework. Their motivational profile shows high conscientiousness, strong theoretical values, and above-average altruistic and economic orientations. Their co-curricular activities focus on research and technology projects, with modest involvement in leadership roles.

Social-Impact (21%): This group has the most vulnerable trajectory, with significantly lower average GPA (≈ 77), high variability, and frequent drops in enrollment. These students score high on altruistic values and are actively involved in social-impact projects. However, their mission-driven focus can conflict with maintaining academic momentum, leading to instability.

Leadership–Applied (41%): The largest group maintains high and consistent GPAs (≈ 94) and steady full-time enrollment. Their motivational profile features high influence and dominance but lower conscientiousness. They excel in leadership positions, community initiatives, and applied projects, though their research participation is relatively limited.

The three profiles are further detailed by comparing their main academic, motivational, and co-curricular traits, as summarized in Table 7.2.

7.5.2 Diversity of Motivations: What Drives Leaders of Tomorrow Scholarship Recipients

The motivational orientations of Leaders of Tomorrow (LTP) scholarship recipients display remarkable heterogeneity, reflecting plural aspirations, interests, and priorities rather than a single dominant pattern. To better understand this diversity, we first examine the descriptive distributions of each value dimension and then move toward their latent structure through exploratory factor analysis (EFA).

7.5.2.1 Descriptive Landscape of Motivations

Although histograms were generated for all seven motivational dimensions, Figure 7.4 presents only three representative cases to illustrate the main patterns observed. Altruistic and theoretical values exhibit a pronounced concentration at elevated levels, suggesting that many students place solidarity and knowledge at the center of their academic and personal development. Economic values, by contrast, are skewed toward lower levels, indicating that utility and financial considerations are a priority for only a minority of students. The remaining four dimensions (aesthetic, political, individual, and regulatory) show more balanced and symmetric distributions around intermediate levels, reflecting plural and moderate orientations across the cohort.

7.5.2.2 From the Visible to the Latent: Factor Extraction

To identify the underlying structure of these values, an EFA was applied to the seven motivational dimensions (see Section 7.4.2 for methodological details). The scree

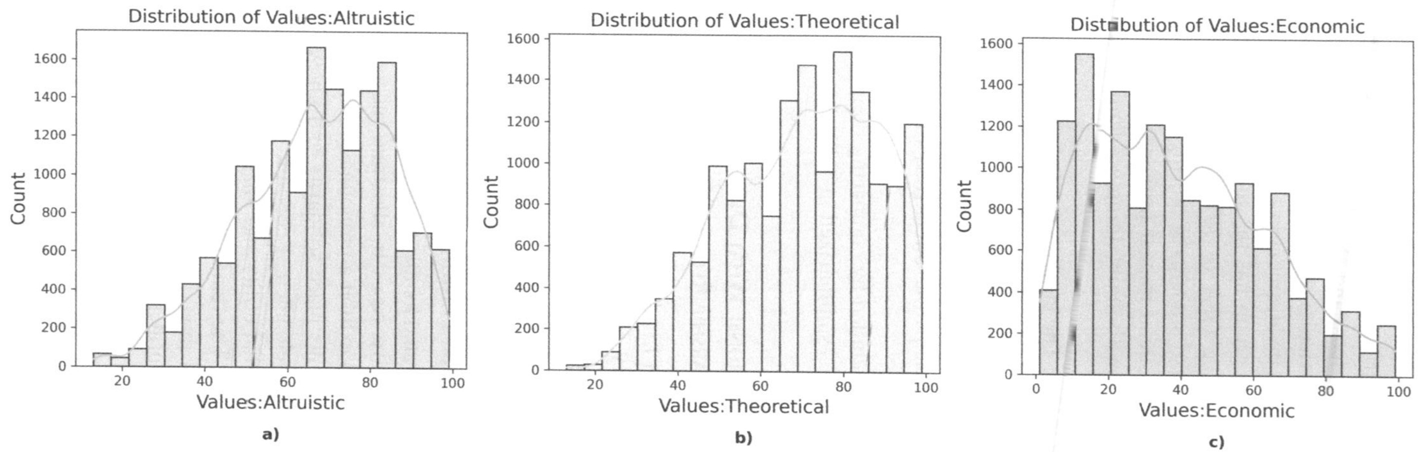

FIGURE 7.4 Representative distributions of three motivational dimensions among LTP students (altruistic, theoretical, and economic). The other four values showed symmetric distributions at intermediate levels and are therefore described in the text rather than displayed graphically.

plot (Figure 7.5) shows a clear inflection after the third component, supporting a three-factor solution based on Kaiser's criterion (eigenvalue > 1). Together, these three factors account for 54.4% of the total variance, which is considered satisfactory for exploratory social science research.

7.5.2.3 A Two-Dimensional View: Pragmatism vs. Idealism

To facilitate interpretation, a factorial plane was constructed using the first two extracted factors (Figure 7.6). The horizontal axis contrasts economic and political values with aesthetic, theoretical, and individual values, reflecting a **pragmatic-material orientation** versus an **intellectual-cultural one**. The vertical axis is largely defined by altruistic values, with regulatory values occupying an intermediate position. This two-dimensional view highlights the motivational tensions faced by LTP students, oscillating between pragmatic pursuits of achievement and an idealism grounded in solidarity and knowledge.

7.5.2.4 The Motivational Triangle: Three Latent Dimensions

The three-factor rotated solution (Table 7.3, Table 7.4) provides a richer structure that we describe as a motivational triangle:

1. **Aesthetic–Altruistic–Individual vs. Pragmatic (Economic–Political)**: contrasts orientations focused on harmony, solidarity, and autonomy against those emphasizing utility and influence.

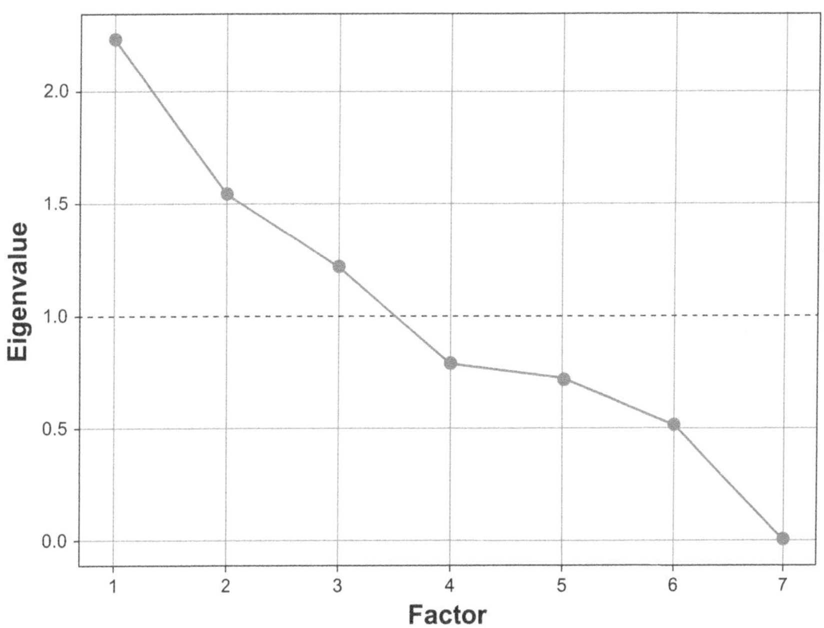

FIGURE 7.5 Scree plot of exploratory factor analysis for motivational values.

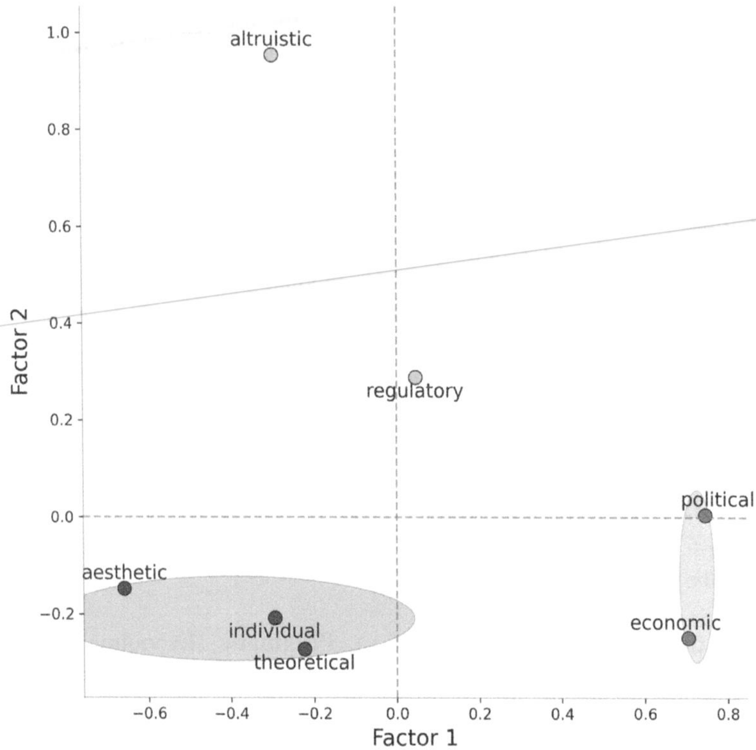

FIGURE 7.6 Factorial plane of motivational values (two-factor solution).

TABLE 7.3 Factor loadings of motivational values

Variable	Factor 1	Factor 2	Factor 3	Communalities
Aesthetic	**0.61**	−0.05	0.29	0.46
Economic	**−0.8**	−0.05	0.19	0.68
Individual	**0.3**	−0.16	**0.53**	0.4
Political	**−0.69**	−0.17	−0.05	0.5
Altruistic	**0.41**	−0.3	**−0.47**	0.48
Regulatory	0.04	−0.08	**−0.49**	0.25
Theoretical	0.17	**1**	0.05	1.03

(varimax rotation, three-factor solution).

2. **Theoretical**: defined almost exclusively by theoretical value, underscoring the independent weight of intellectual pursuit.
3. **Autonomy vs. Regulation** captures the tension between individual independence and external normative structures, with altruism also contributing to this axis.

TABLE 7.4
Explained Variance by the Three Main Motivational Factors.

Factor	Ratio	Cumulative variance
Factor 1	0.253	0.253
Factor 2	0.166	0.419
Factor 3	0.125	0.544

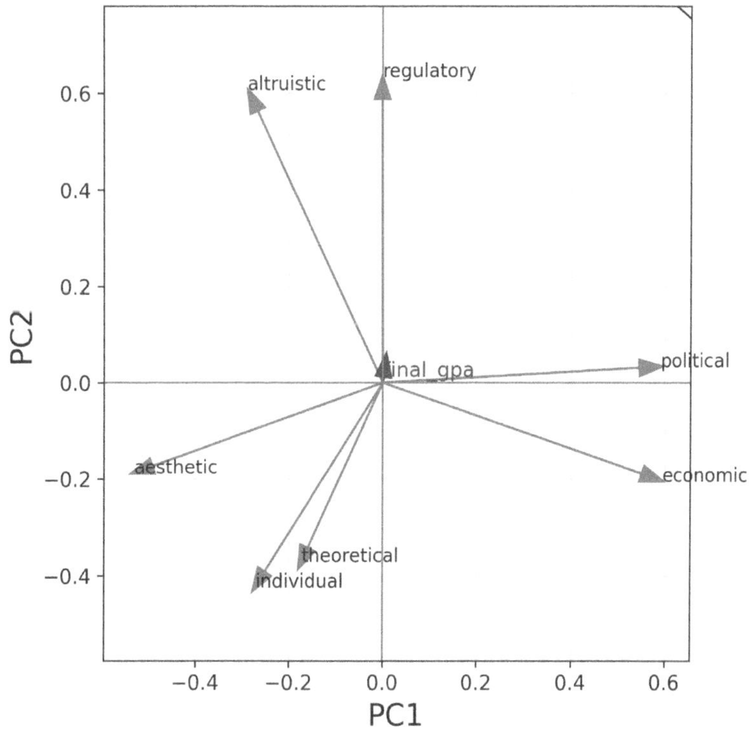

FIGURE 7.7 Correlation circle of motivational values and academic performance (final GPA).

This threefold structure organizes the diverse motivational profiles of LTP students into coherent latent dimensions that articulate solidarity, intellectual pursuit, and pragmatism.

7.5.2.5 Motivational Profiles and Academic Performance

Finally, we examined whether motivational orientations are associated with academic outcomes. Figure 7.7 presents the PCA correlation circle of the seven motivational dimensions together with final GPA. Three coherent bundles emerge: (i) economic–political, (ii) aesthetic–theoretical–individual, and (iii) altruistic–regulatory.

The position of the *final GPA* close to the center indicates only a weak association with motivational axes. This finding suggests that, although motivations are diverse and structured, they are not strong predictors of academic performance. LTP students appear capable of achieving high academic outcomes regardless of their underlying motivational profiles.

7.6 DISCUSSION

The findings of this study provide new insights into the academic and motivational pathways of Leaders of Tomorrow students. Rather than reiterating descriptive results, this section interprets their meaning, situates them in the literature, and outlines institutional implications.

7.6.1 Plural Pathways to Academic Success

The clustering analysis shows that excellence among scholarship recipients is plural. Some sustain high performance through theoretical rigor and conscientiousness, others through leadership and applied engagement, while a third group faces fragility due to competing social-impact commitments. This diversity challenges the idea of a single archetype of success and highlights the need for differentiated support strategies.

These findings align with evidence that scholarships improve persistence and credit accumulation but do not uniformly affect GPA [14]. They also reflect Johnson's (2022) insight that retention effects are mediated by continuity in full-time status and GPA thresholds [15]. In our case, course-load stability was the strongest differentiator between stable and fragile pathways.

7.6.2 Structural Tensions in Scholarship Pathways

The most altruistic students illustrate a tension: community engagement may compete with academic momentum. Without proper scaffolding, mission-driven commitments can increase volatility in GPA and enrollment. Similar dynamics have been observed in Latin American programs, where aid improved performance only when paired with mentoring and support [16, 17]. International exposure was uniformly low, suggesting structural rather than motivational barriers. Expanding such opportunities remains an equity challenge.

7.6.3 Implications for Institutional Practice

Three implications stand out: (i) prioritize volatility indicators over GPA in early-warning systems, (ii) provide differentiated mentoring to balance external commitments, and (iii) expand equitable access to high-impact practices such as international experiences through low-cost, embedded formats.

7.6.4 Relation to Broader Scholarship Literature

Our results confirm that financial aid reliably reduces attrition and supports progression [14], while also highlighting diverse forms of excellence. Evidence from

Colombia and Peru shows that rigorous placement and continuity enhance durable gains [16, 17]. Our study extends this by demonstrating how motivational diversity interacts with institutional conditions to produce distinct, valid success pathways.

7.6.5 Motivational Structures

The exploratory factor analysis revealed a three-factor "motivational triangle": (i) altruism versus pragmatism, (ii) theoretical pursuit, and (iii) autonomy versus regulation. These axes highlight tensions between solidarity, knowledge, and utility, but also confirm that no single motivational profile predicts academic achievement. This supports the program's recognition of multiple forms of excellence and suggests motivations may be more useful for designing tailored co-curricular opportunities than for predicting GPA.

7.7 CONCLUSION AND FUTURE DIRECTIONS

This study analyzed the academic, motivational, and co-curricular trajectories of Leaders of Tomorrow (LTP) students through a learning analytics approach. The evidence confirms that success within the program is not monolithic but plural, expressed through distinct yet equally valid pathways. Three clusters of student profiles illustrate this plurality: one characterized by high academic rigor and conscientiousness, another by leadership and applied engagement, and a third defined by strong social-impact involvement but greater academic fragility. Beyond clustering, the exploratory factor analysis of motivational values revealed a latent "motivational triangle" contrasting altruism and pragmatism, highlighting theoretical pursuit as an autonomous dimension, and balancing autonomy against regulation. Together, these findings show that motivations are diverse but structured, and that high achievement is attainable through multiple orientations. Importantly, academic stability—measured as continuity in enrollment and credit load—proved a stronger predictor of success than GPA averages, reinforcing the idea that volatility, rather than grades alone, is the key risk marker for scholarship recipients.

The contributions of this work extend beyond descriptive insights. By combining clustering and factor analysis, the study demonstrates how learning analytics can uncover hidden structures in student data, providing institutions with tools to identify fragile trajectories and to recognize plural excellence. For practice, the results suggest three main implications. First, early-warning systems should prioritize volatility indicators, such as sudden drops in credit load or repeated enrollment interruptions, which are more reliable predictors of risk than GPA. Second, differentiated mentoring is required for students with strong leadership or social orientations, whose external commitments may compete with academic progress; tailored advising and coaching could help balance mission-driven activities with degree requirements. Third, equitable access to high-impact practices, especially international experiences, should be expanded through curriculum-embedded and low-cost formats such as short exchanges, virtual collaborations, or joint projects, ensuring that financial barriers do not limit opportunities for global exposure.

Like any study, this work is not without limitations. The clustering solution, while interpretable, achieved modest silhouette values, reflecting the complexity of educational datasets. Motivational measures were based on self-report instruments, which are subject to bias. In addition, the analysis focused on a single institution and program, which may constrain generalizability. These limitations point to several promising directions for future research. Longitudinal tracking of post-graduation outcomes could clarify how plural academic and motivational pathways translate into labor-market performance, civic engagement, and social impact. Integrating behavioral data from digital learning environments, such as LMS activity or course-level engagement, could enrich the analysis of volatility and reveal more granular patterns of persistence. Intervention studies would be particularly valuable: testing the effectiveness of mentoring models, scaffolding strategies for students with strong social-impact commitments, or the use of volatility indices in early warning dashboards. Finally, validating the motivational triangle across diverse institutions and cultural contexts would strengthen its explanatory power and confirm whether the structure observed in LTP cohorts is consistent more broadly.

In conclusion, the chapter underscores that scholarship recipients achieve excellence through multiple trajectories shaped by diverse motivations, and that institutional support must be sensitive to this heterogeneity. By shifting attention from averages to trajectories, and from static indicators to volatility and structure, learning analytics can help scholarship programs move from reactive remediation to proactive trajectory management. Such an approach not only safeguards academic performance but also enhances the equity and transformative potential of higher education.

ACKNOWLEDGMENTS

The authors thank the Data Hub of the Institute for the Future of Education, Tecnologico de Monterrey, Mexico, for the data used in this work, and for providing us with such data through the Call "Encouraging Research on Higher Education Students' Profiles with Social Commitment." AI tools were used for drafting support and editing under the supervision of the authors.

REFERENCES

[1] United Nations. (2025). *Sustainable Development Goals*. United Nations Regional Information Centre for Western Europe. Retrieved August 15, 2025, from https://unric.org/en/united-nations-sustainable-development-goals/

[2] Banco Santander. (2025). Retrieved August 15, 2025. https://www.bancosantander.es/universidades/educacion/becas

[3] Fundación BBVA. (2025). *Educación*. Retrieved August 15, 2025, from https://www.fundacionbbva.mx/

[4] Fundación Telmex. (2025). *Becas Telmex Telcel*. Retrieved August 15, 2025, from https://www.fundaciontelmextelcel.org/becas

[5] Fundación Carlos Slim. (2025). *Educación*. Retrieved August 15, 2025, from https://fundacioncarlosslim.org/educacion-2/

[6] Tecnológico de Monterrey. (2025). *Líderes del Mañana*. Retrieved August 15, 2025, from https://lideresdelmanana.tec.mx/#programa/1

[7] Tecnológico de Monterrey. (2024). *Reporte de resultados Líderes del Mañana 2023–2024*. Retrieved August 15, 2025, from https://lideresdelmanana.tec.mx/noticia/reporte-de-resultados-ldm-2023-2024

[8] Spranger, E. (1928). *Types of Men* (P. J. W. Pigors, Trans.). G. E. Stechert Company. (Original work published 1914).
[9] Marston, W. M. (1928). *Emotions of Normal People*. Kegan Paul, Trench, Trubner & Co.
[10] Allport, G. W., Vernon, P. E., & Lindzey, G. (1960). *Study of Values* (3rd ed.). Houghton Mifflin.
[11] Stewart, D. J. (1998). Spranger's dimensions of value. *The Psychology Institute*. Retrieved September 12, 2025, from https://thepsychology.institute/theories-of-personality/sprangers-value-oriented-personality-types-overview/
[12] Brown, D., & Crace, R. K. (1996). Values in life role choices and outcomes: A conceptual model. *The Career Development Quarterly*, *44*(3), 211–223. https://doi.org/10.1002/j.2161-0045.1996.tb00439.x
[13] Geier, J. G. (2001). *DISC Personality Testing and the Personal Profile System*. Inscape Publishing.
[14] LaSota, R. R., Polanin, J. R., Perna, L. W., Rodgers, M. A., & Austin, M. J. (2024). Does aid matter? A systematic review and meta-analysis of the effects of grant aid on college student outcomes. *Review of Educational Research*, *95*(3), 464–504. https://doi.org/10.3102/00346543241239955
[15] Johnson, I. (2022). Merit aid and retention: Mediation and moderation. *Research in Higher Education*, *63*(5), 713–739. https://doi.org/10.1007/s11162-021-09661-9
[16] Londoño-Vélez, J., Rodríguez, C., Sánchez, F., & Álvarez-Arango, M. (2023). *The Long-Term Impacts of "Ser Pilo Paga"*. NBER Working Paper No. 31737. https://doi.org/10.3386/w31737
[17] Cristóbal Velásquez, D. H., Dávila Rivera, J. M., Maggi Poisetti, G., Morey Lezama, O. J., Susanibar Arévalo, J. P., & Virgilio, G. P. M. (2024). Causal performance of scholarship students: A case study of a Peruvian university. *Journal of Hispanic Higher Education*, *24*(3), 235–259. https://doi.org/10.1177/15381927241265765
[18] González-Nucamendi, A., Neri, L., García-Castelán, R. M. G., Robledo-Rella, V., Valverde-Rebaza, J., & Noguez, J. (2024a). Impact of demographic and co-curricular factors on the academic success of students from low-income families: A scholarship program study. In *2024 IEEE Frontiers in Education Conference (FIE)* (pp. 1–8). IEEE. https://doi.org/10.1109/FIE61694.2024.10893057
[19] González-Nucamendi, A., Neri-Vitela, L. J., Robledo-Rella, V., García-Castelán, R. M. G., Noguez, J., & Valverde-Rebaza, J. C. (2024b). A factor analysis of student motivations of the Tecnologico de Monterrey Leaders of Tomorrow Scholarship. In *ICERI 2024 Proceedings* (pp. 2886–2893). IATED. https://doi.org/10.21125/iceri.2024.0752
[20] Hair, J., Babin, B., Anderson, R., & Black, W. (2018). *Multivariate Data Analysis* (8th ed.). Cengage Learning.
[21] Institute for the Future of Education [IFE]. (2024). *Dataset on Higher Education Students' Profiles with Social Commitment (Version 1)*. Tecnológico de Monterrey. https://doi.org/10.57687/FK2/UFM2QH

8 Accessible Human Computer Interaction (HCI) for Inclusive Education

Designing Educational Tools for Diverse Learners

Amjad Kamal, Mohd. Faiz, Imran, Saim Atique, Mohd Anas Wajid, and Claudia Camacho-Zuñiga

8.1 INTRODUCTION

The global pursuit of inclusive education, as championed by the United Nations Sustainable Development Goal 4 (SDG-4), underscores the imperative to provide equitable, high-quality learning opportunities for all, irrespective of ability, identity, or socio-economic context (UNESCO, 2016). As educational systems increasingly integrate digital technologies such as learning management systems (LMS), virtual classrooms, and artificial intelligence-driven platforms ensuring accessibility for diverse learners becomes both a critical opportunity and a complex challenge. Human-computer interaction (HCI) offers a robust framework for designing educational tools that accommodate varied cognitive, sensory, physical, and sociocultural needs, thereby fostering inclusivity. However, many existing digital learning environments fall short of accessibility standards, disproportionately marginalizing learners with disabilities, neurodiverse profiles, or those from multilingual and low-resource settings (Alotaibi, 2024; Lazar et al., 2015). This study explores the role of accessible HCI in bridging the gap between technological innovation and educational equity, drawing on principles of universal design for learning (UDL) and participatory design. Through an analysis of theoretical frameworks, global case studies, and strategic recommendations, this research advocates for a paradigm shift in educational technology design, prioritizing inclusivity as a core principle to ensure no learner is excluded in the digital era. Recent advancements, such as AI-driven assistive technologies, further highlight HCI's potential to enhance inclusivity by enabling adaptive interactions for diverse learners (e.g., gesture-based systems for students with physical impairments) (Kimmons & Veletsianos, 2016). By reimagining design processes, this study contributes to the discourse on creating equitable digital learning ecosystems that empower all learners (Figure 8.1).

 DOI: 10.1201/9781003678250-8

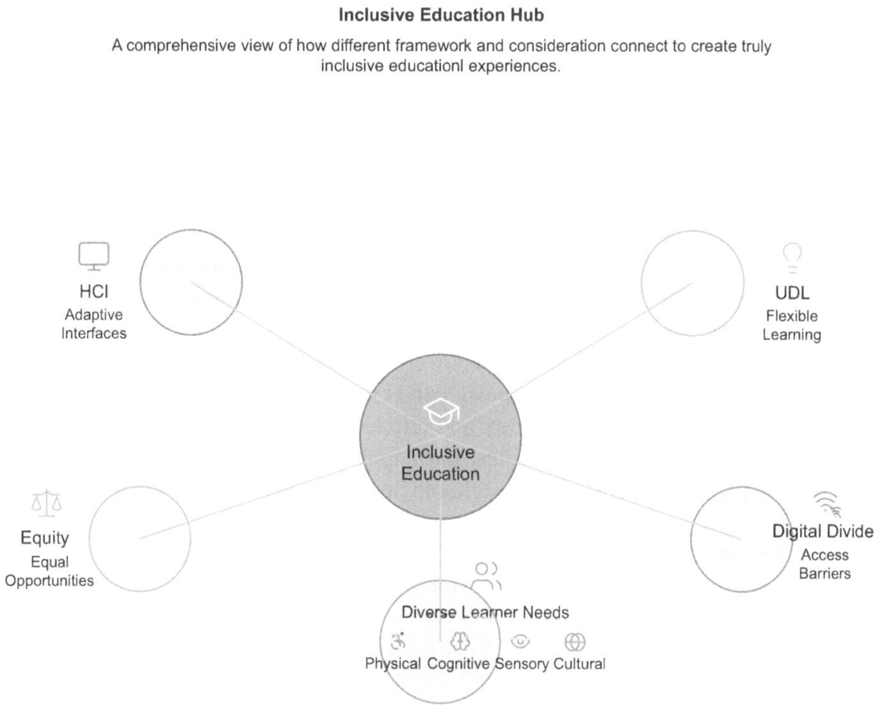

FIGURE 8.1 Intersection of HCI and inclusive education.

8.2 BACKGROUND AND RATIONALE

In the twenty-first century, inclusive education has become a key goal in global educational reform, emphasizing principles of equity, social justice, and human rights. The United Nations Sustainable Development Goal 4 (SDG-4) specifically calls for "inclusive and equitable quality education and lifelong learning opportunities for all," encouraging education systems to eliminate structural barriers that prevent marginalized and underrepresented groups from participating (UNESCO, 2016). Inclusion is no longer just about the physical presence of learners with disabilities in mainstream classrooms; it also involves pedagogical methods, curriculum design and, importantly, the digital tools that support learning experiences. At the same time, education is experiencing a rapid digital transformation. Technologies such as learning management systems (LMS), virtual classrooms, mobile apps, AI-powered personalized learning environments, and immersive platforms like augmented reality (AR) and virtual reality (VR) have become essential in both formal and informal learning settings (Selwyn, 2016; Holmes et al., 2019). Although these innovations have the potential to boost learner engagement and scalability, they often fail to serve learners with diverse needs unless accessibility is built in from the beginning.

Despite international commitments and the growth of ed-tech solutions, accessibility remains a significant challenge. Many educational technologies are not designed with diversity in mind, leading to the marginalization of students with visual, auditory, cognitive, motor, or linguistic impairments (Al-Azawei et al., 2017; Lazar et al., 2015). For example, students with visual impairments often face incompatible screen readers, while learners with dyslexia may struggle with text-heavy, unstructured digital content. In multilingual settings, monolingual digital interfaces further exclude non-native speakers, reinforcing systemic inequalities (Kimmons & Veletsianos, 2018). These challenges are worsened by the digital divide, especially in low-resource environments where technological infrastructure, connectivity, and device access are unevenly distributed (OECD, 2021). Against this backdrop, human-computer interaction (HCI) provides a powerful framework to tackle these inequalities by emphasizing the user in the design and evaluation of digital tools. Traditional HCI methods often focus on usability and efficiency, but an inclusive HCI approach integrates universal design principles, participatory design strategies, and contextual awareness to make educational technologies adaptable and responsive to diverse user needs (Shneiderman et al., 2017; Burgstahler, 2015). Incorporating accessibility early in the design process rather than as an afterthought facilitates the creation of tools that are not only usable by everyone but also empowering for marginalized learners (Akcil, 2017).

Therefore, this study highlights the urgent need to rethink educational technology from the perspective of accessible HCI. It argues that inclusive education in the digital age requires more than just adopting new tools; it calls for a shift in design thinking that prioritizes learner diversity as essential to educational quality. By presenting theoretical frameworks, design methodologies, case studies, and policy recommendations, this study seeks to contribute to the conversation on how accessible HCI can bridge the gap between technological innovation and educational equity.

8.3 ROLE OF HUMAN-COMPUTER INTERACTION (HCI)

8.3.1 Defining HCI in Educational Contexts

Human-computer interaction (HCI) is an interdisciplinary field that explores the design, evaluation, and development of interactive computing systems for human use, along with the key phenomena related to them (Dix et al., 2004; Rogers et al., 2011). In education, HCI plays a crucial role in shaping the interface between learners and digital learning environments. This includes software applications (e.g., learning management systems), hardware tools (e.g., interactive whiteboards, tablets), and emerging technologies (e.g., virtual reality, AI tutors, eye-tracking tools) that enhance educational experiences. Educational HCI not only focuses on interaction efficiency and performance but also explores how learners cognitively, emotionally, and socially engage with technology during the learning process (Soloway et al., 1994). It considers user traits such as age, cognitive skills, learning preferences, prior knowledge, and cultural background. Significantly, it aims to understand and enhance the user experience (UX) in learning settings, ensuring that technology serves as a facilitator rather than a barrier to gaining knowledge (Sharples, 2013).

While traditional HCI in educational settings focused on usability, navigation flow, and interface aesthetics, current discussions increasingly support inclusive, learner-centered, and adaptive systems. The shift of HCI from a usability-focused field to one grounded in accessibility, equity, and participatory design signifies a major change.

8.3.2 Shift From Usability to Accessibility and Inclusivity

The early development of HCI systems emphasized usability, aiming to make systems effective, efficient, and satisfying for the typical user (Nielsen, 1993). However, as digital learning environments grew more central to education, it became evident that designing for the average user often excluded those with unique needs, such as learners with disabilities, neurodiverse learners, and individuals from non-dominant linguistic or cultural backgrounds (Shneiderman et al., 2017; Lazar et al., 2015). In response, a growing movement within HCI has emphasized accessibility, ensuring that people with diverse abilities and preferences can use systems. This shift has been supported by international standards, such as the Web Content Accessibility Guidelines (WCAG), which set benchmarks for creating inclusive digital content (W3C, 2018). Accessibility, however, is not just about compliance; it is about creating meaningful, barrier-free interactions that enable all learners to participate fully in digital education.

Furthermore, there is growing recognition that accessibility must be integrated into broader ideas of inclusivity. Inclusive HCI extends beyond technical specs to include social, cultural, linguistic, and emotional factors in the design process (Burgstahler, 2015). It supports universal design for learning (UDL), a framework that encourages flexible teaching methods and technology use, catering to the diverse needs of learners instead of retrofitting systems for specific user groups after they are deployed (Rose & Meyer, 2002). A key driver of this change is the participatory design approach, where diverse users, including students with disabilities, teachers, and caregivers, actively contribute to developing educational tools. This approach democratizes the creation process and makes sure tools reflect real-world usage and needs (Frauenberger et al., 2015).

The role of HCI in education is no longer limited to enhancing usability metrics; it is increasingly responsible for promoting equity, representation, and empowerment through thoughtful, inclusive design. This shift positions HCI as a key driver in the pursuit of educational justice in a digitally connected world.

8.4 THEORETICAL AND CONCEPTUAL FRAMEWORK

8.4.1 Inclusive Education Paradigms

As education becomes more digital, the need to base technological design on inclusive educational theory has become more important. Inclusive education frameworks supply the philosophical and practical foundation necessary for accessible human-computer interaction (HCI), moving beyond physical presence to address social and digital construction of barriers (Goggin & Newell, 2003). This study examines three main paradigms guiding the development of inclusive educational technologies:

universal design for learning (UDL), the social model of disability (Oliver, 1996), and the difference between equity and equality in digital education.

8.4.2 Universal Design for Learning (UDL)

Universal design for learning (UDL) is a research-based framework that promotes flexible learning environments to accommodate individual differences (Rose, Meyer, & Gordon, 2013). Rooted in universal design principles from architecture, UDL emphasizes proactive design to support all learners, including those with disabilities, neurodiverse profiles, and diverse linguistic or cultural backgrounds. The framework is built on three core principles: engagement (providing varied ways to motivate and engage learners), representation (offering content in diverse formats, e.g., text, audio, video to suit different learning preferences), action and expression (allowing learners to demonstrate knowledge through varied methods, e.g., writing, speaking, or interactive tasks). In HCI, UDL guides the creation of adaptable interfaces that enhance accessibility and learner autonomy. For example, a learning management system (LMS) might offer text-to-speech options, customizable interfaces, or gamified elements to cater to diverse needs.

The UDL framework's design is shown in the Figure 8.2.

This diagram illustrates how UDL's principles converge to create inclusive HCI systems, ensuring that educational tools are flexible and accessible to all learners, from those with sensory impairments to those in multilingual settings (Rose et al., 2014). UDL's universalist approach benefits not only learners with disabilities but also gifted students, second-language learners, and those in underserved contexts

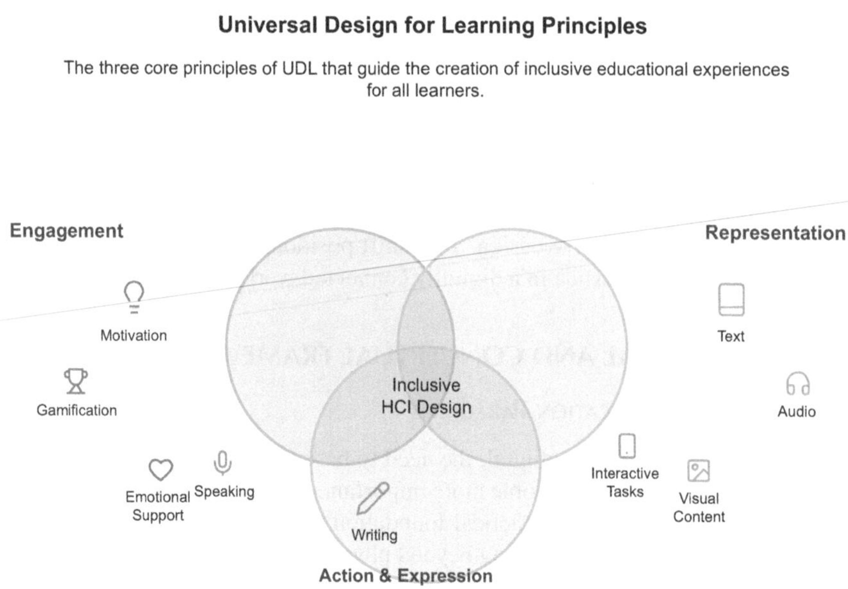

FIGURE 8.2 UDL framework.

(Hall, Meyer, & Rose, 2012). UDL shifts the responsibility from the learner to adapt to the system onto the system adapting to the learner, a core principle of inclusive HCI.

Moreover, UDL is not just a disability framework; it is a flexible design strategy that benefits all learners, including those who are gifted, second-language learners, or in underserved settings (Hall, Meyer, & Rose, 2012). Its universalist philosophy aligns with current demands for educational equity in technology-rich learning environments.

8.4.3 Equity vs. Equality in Educational Technology

A key difference in inclusive education is between equality, which means giving the same resources to all learners, and equity, which involves distributing resources to meet different needs, contexts, and abilities (OECD, 2018). While educational technology often aims to democratize learning through scaling, equal access to tools does not ensure equitable results (Eynon, 2015). In accessible HCI, this shift from equality to equity is crucial. An interface designed for average users might overlook the needs of learners with low digital literacy, limited internet access, or different cognitive processing styles. For example, while an online assessment platform may be technically accessible to all students, without alternative formats, language support, or adaptive feedback, it remains inequitable in practice.

The following Figure 8.3 visualizes the difference between equality and equity in the context of educational technology design.

Figure 8.3 visualizes the distinction between equality and equity in educational technology, illustrating how equal access (uniform resources) contrasts with equitable outcomes (customized support, e.g., screen readers, offline modes). By integrating cultural responsiveness and localized pedagogies, equity-driven HCI ensures fair, inclusive learning experiences that align with diverse sociocultural and infrastructural contexts (Roy & Gandhimathi, 2024).

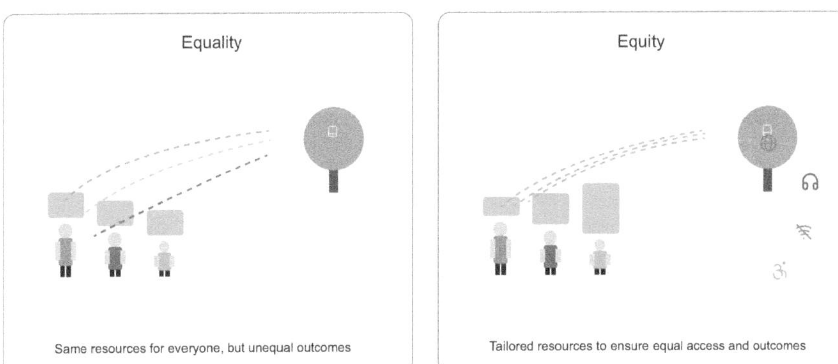

FIGURE 8.3 Difference between equal access and equitable outcomes, emphasizing HCI's role in achieving equity.

8.5 PRINCIPLES OF ACCESSIBLE HCI

As human-computer interaction (HCI) develops within the educational field, accessibility has become a key principle of ethical and inclusive technology design. Accessible HCI aims to develop interactive systems that accommodate the broadest possible range of human abilities and situations. HCI in inclusive education outlines two main sets of principles supporting accessible HCI in education: (1) formal accessibility guidelines and compliance frameworks, and (2) cognitive and affective design theories that foster learner engagement and inclusion through multimodal interaction.

8.5.1 Accessibility Guidelines

Formal accessibility standards form the core infrastructure for creating inclusive digital technologies. Among the most impactful is the Web Content Accessibility Guidelines (WCAG) created by the World Wide Web Consortium (W3C). The most recent version, WCAG 2.1, outlines success criteria based on four key principles: perceivable, operable, understandable, and robust (POUR) (W3C, 2018) (Figure 8.4).

The infographic "WCAG POUR Principles in Educational HCI" visually represents the four core principles of the Web Content Accessibility Guidelines (WCAG 2.1) perceivable, operable, understandable, and robust in the context of educational human-computer interaction (HCI). Each quadrant of the infographic illustrates a

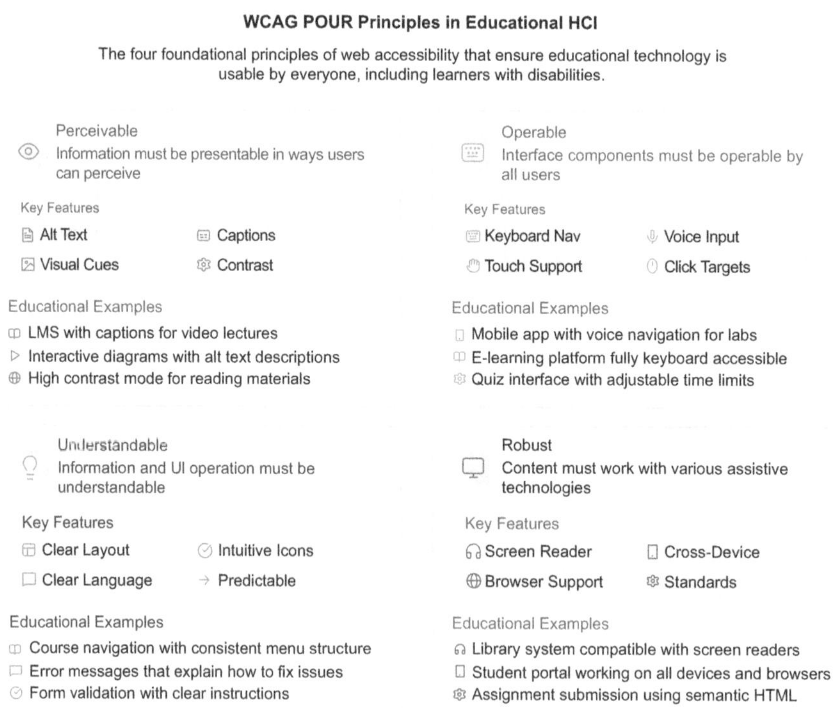

FIGURE 8.4 Relevance of WCAG POUR principles in education.

principle with relevant icons and examples: perceivable includes text alternatives and captions (e.g., subtitles for videos); operable features keyboard navigation and voice input (e.g., for motor-impaired learners); understandable emphasizes clear, consistent UI design (e.g., intuitive icons for cognitive accessibility); and robust ensures compatibility with assistive technologies (e.g., screen readers for LMS platforms). This infographic highlights how these principles guide the design of inclusive educational technologies, ensuring accessibility for diverse learners, such as those with sensory, motor, or cognitive impairments, in alignment with the paper's focus on equitable education.

Meanwhile, Section 508 of the U.S. Rehabilitation Act requires that all federal electronic and information technology be accessible to people with disabilities (U.S. General Services Administration, 2017). These standards have shaped policies worldwide and are frequently adopted or modified by educational institutions to ensure their digital learning environments meet basic accessibility standards. However, compliance alone does not guarantee true usability or inclusion. Critics argue that although WCAG and Section 508 offer essential checklists, they risk turning accessibility into a technocratic or checkbox task if not incorporated into broader user-centered design (UCD) and inclusive pedagogical approaches (Kelly, Phipps, & Swift, 2004). Therefore, while these guidelines provide important support, accessible HCI must extend beyond mere compliance to include understanding the context and experiences of learners.

8.5.2 Cognitive Load Theory, Affective Computing, and Multimodal Interaction

Beyond technical compliance, accessible HCI also relies on cognitive and emotional theories of learning. Recognizing how learners process information, manage emotions, and engage across different modes is key to developing inclusive educational tools.

Cognitive load theory (CLT), developed by Sweller (1988), indicates that effective learning occurs when instructional materials are designed to accommodate the limited capacity of working memory. User-friendly interfaces should therefore minimize unnecessary cognitive load, such as cluttered layouts, confusing navigation, or excessive animations, which can disproportionately affect learners with attention deficits or learning disorders (Mayer, 2009). For example, breaking information into segments, using intuitive icons, and reducing distractions are strategies that align with CLT principles and enhance accessibility. Affective computing, a part of HCI, examines how systems can recognize, interpret, and respond to human emotions (Picard, 1997). In educational settings, affective computing enables emotion-aware interfaces that adjust to learners' feelings of frustration, confusion, or engagement. These systems can enhance accessibility by providing real-time support, scaffolding, or encouragement, particularly for students who may struggle with motivation or confidence in traditional learning environments (D'Mello & Graesser, 2012).

Furthermore, multimodal interaction, which utilizes multiple input and output methods such as speech, gesture, touch, and visual cues, provides flexible interaction options for users with diverse abilities. For example, combining voice commands with visual feedback can assist learners with motor impairments or low literacy (Oviatt, 2003). Similarly, sign language avatars, haptic feedback, or eye-tracking systems can improve digital learning environments for users with specific accessibility needs. Multimodal design also tackles the "one-size-fits-none" problem by allowing learners to interact with content in ways that suit their preferences and situations. This closely aligns with universal design for learning (UDL), which encourages providing multiple means of engagement, representation, and expression (CAST, 2018).

8.6 LEARNER DIVERSITY AND EDUCATIONAL NEEDS

One of the main challenges in designing educational technologies for inclusive learning environments is managing learner diversity. Educational systems are increasingly aware that learners differ not only in ability but also in how they perceive, process, and interact with content, influenced by various biological, psychological, cultural, and contextual factors. Accessible HCI must thus address a wide range of learner needs through adaptive, flexible, and inclusive design principles. This explores key types of learners' differences and emphasizes the importance of integrating intersectionality as a fundamental concept in educational technology design.

8.6.1 Typologies of Learner Differences: Physical, Cognitive, Sensory, Sociocultural

Learner diversity involves a range of functional, cognitive, and sociocultural traits that influence how students engage with educational technologies. Developing accessible HCI requires a clear understanding of these categories to ensure that educational tools do not unintentionally exclude or disadvantage certain user groups. These differences could be physical, cognitive, sensory, and sociocultural etc.

8.7 CASE FOR INTERSECTIONALITY IN DESIGN

While addressing individual learner types is important, intersectionality offers a more comprehensive perspective by exploring how multiple, overlapping identities influence learners' interactions with educational technology. Intersectionality emphasizes how social categories such as race, disability, gender, and class interconnect to create unique forms of discrimination or marginalization (Crenshaw, 1989).

In accessible HCI, intersectionality encourages designers to go beyond single-factor approaches, such as focusing only on visual impairments or physical disabilities, and instead consider how complex, overlapping factors shape user needs and interactions. For example, a low-income learner with a physical disability living in a rural area may face combined barriers like limited device access, unreliable connectivity, and inaccessible platforms, which are not fully addressed by solutions that target only one of these issues. Designing for intersectionality involves engaging with diverse users during co-design, applying context-aware design principles, and

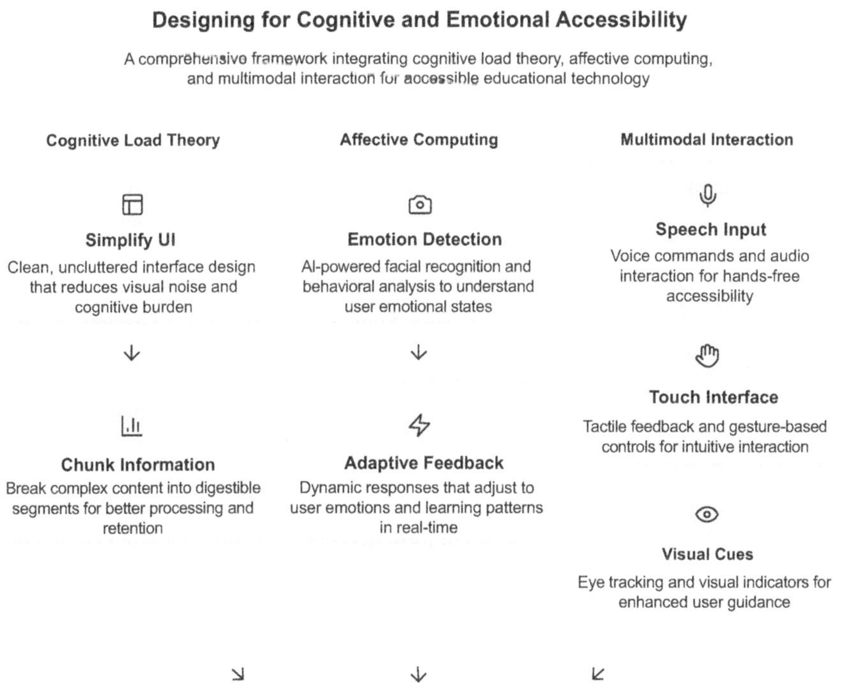

FIGURE 8.5 Factors affecting intersectionality in ed-tech design.

testing tools in real-world, culturally varied settings. It also calls for inclusive data collection and ethical research practices that reflect the lived realities of users from multiple marginalized groups (Costanza-Chock, 2020).

Importantly, intersectional design is not about creating tailored solutions for every individual user variation but rather about incorporating flexibility, empathy, and adaptability into the core principles of educational technologies. This shifts the focus from building universally accessible systems to designing systems that are inclusively responsive and capable of addressing diverse and changing user needs across different contexts (Figure 8.5).

8.8 DESIGNING FOR ACCESSIBILITY AND INCLUSION

Inclusive educational technologies are not accidental by-products of innovation but result from intentional, ethically grounded design processes. Designing for accessibility and inclusion requires a paradigm shift from creating tools for learners to developing solutions with and by the communities they serve. This section details the core strategies and features that support accessible HCI in educational settings: participatory design methodologies, inclusive design elements, and the contextual integration of technologies within learning environments.

8.8.1 Participatory and Co-Design Methodologies

8.8.1.1 Involving Learners, Educators, and Caregivers in the Design Process

Participatory design (PD) and co-design are methods that actively involve end-users such as students, teachers, caregivers, and community members throughout the entire development process of educational technologies. Originating from Scandinavian democratic design traditions (Bodker, 1996), these approaches focus on sharing power, working together, and mutual learning between designers and users.

In educational contexts, participatory design supports the development of technologies that reflect the lived experiences, contextual challenges, and real needs of diverse learners. For example, involving visually impaired students in the prototyping of screen-reader-compatible interfaces ensures that the tools are not only technically accessible but also pedagogically and emotionally usable (Frauenberger et al., 2011). Similarly, engaging caregivers in the design of home-based learning apps helps surface sociocultural norms, usability constraints, and linguistic preferences that shape tool adoption and engagement. Participatory methodologies also challenge the deficit model often linked with disability and marginalization by framing learners as agents of change instead of passive recipients of help. This change helps create technologies that are empowering, respectful, and relevant to the context (Ladner, 2015) (Figure 8.6).

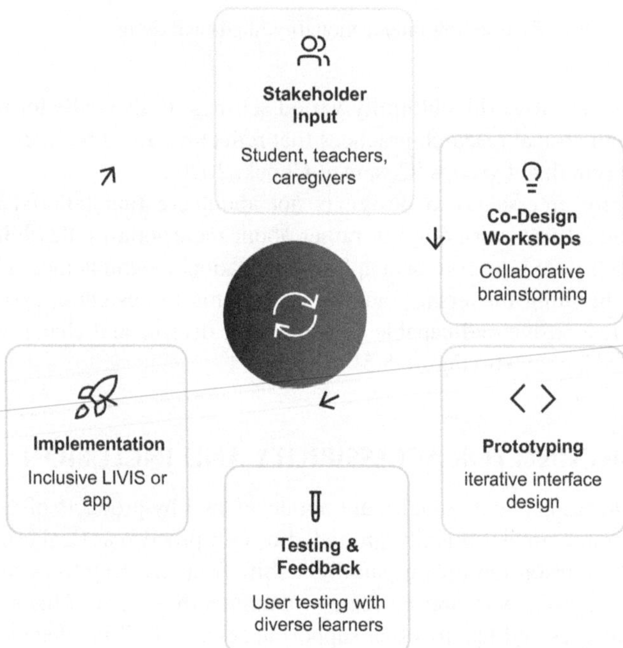

FIGURE 8.6 Iterative stages of inclusive educational technology design.

8.8.1.2 Ethical and Methodological Considerations

Despite their democratic ethos, participatory approaches are not without ethical and methodological complexities. Power imbalances between researchers and participants, tokenistic participation, and challenges in ensuring informed consent, particularly with children or individuals with cognitive impairments, demand careful ethical scaffolding (Simonsen & Robertson, 2013).

Furthermore, the methodological validity of participatory findings can be affected by diverse perspectives and the non-linear nature of the design process. Therefore, inclusive co-design should include iterative reflection, culturally sensitive facilitation, and context-aware engagement strategies to ensure meaningful participation. Researchers also need to focus on accessibility during the design process by using plain language, alternative communication formats, and multi-sensory facilitation to ensure all voices are heard.

8.8.2 Design Features for Diverse Needs

Creating accessible educational technologies involves incorporating specific design features that meet the needs of users with various physical, cognitive, sensory, and cultural differences. This emphasizes key inclusive features that should be considered essential, not optional, in educational software and platforms.

8.8.2.1 Screen Readers, Text-to-Speech, and Alternative Navigation

Support for screen readers is essential for blind or visually impaired learners. Interfaces should follow semantic markup standards (such as ARIA roles), avoid visual-only instructions, and support logical tab ordering. Text-to-speech (TTS) functionality can benefit not only learners with visual impairments but also those with dyslexia, low literacy, or second-language acquisition needs (Sosa Neira et al., 2017). Alternative navigation strategies, such as keyboard-only access, gesture controls, and voice commands, are crucial for users with motor impairments. For example, learners who use assistive switches or eye-tracking devices require interfaces that minimize complexity and support time-flexible inputs (Lazar et al., 2015).

8.8.2.2 Multilingual Interfaces, Low-Bandwidth Compatibility, and Gamification

In multilingual and multicultural learning contexts, language accessibility is a core dimension of inclusion. Interfaces should support local language options, simple vocabulary, and culturally appropriate metaphors and icons. Moreover, systems should allow for customizable text translation and voiceovers, particularly in regions with limited access to formal language learning support.

In low-resource settings, bandwidth constraints pose significant barriers. Tools optimized for offline access, low-data modes, or SMS/USSD-based interaction can widen access for rural and underserved learners (UNESCO, 2021). Additionally, features like adaptive file compression, text-first interfaces, and progressive content loading can improve accessibility for users with limited connectivity. Gamification, the use of game mechanics such as points, levels, and avatars, can enhance engagement, especially for neurodiverse learners or those who struggle with traditional instructional models. When carefully designed, gamified features can support self-regulation, motivation, and differentiated learning pathways (Deterding et al., 2011).

8.8.2.3 Culturally Responsive UI/UX

Cultural dimensions, including power distance, time orientation, and collectivism vs. individualism, influence how learners interact with technology (Hofstede, 2001). Culturally responsive UI/UX design ensures that visual elements, interaction patterns, content presentation, and feedback mechanisms resonate with the learner's identity and social context (Gay, 2018). For example, color symbolism, iconography, and gesture norms may vary significantly across cultures; a thumbs-up icon may indicate approval in one culture and offense in another. Interface localization should go beyond translation to incorporate cultural symbolism, narrative structures, and user metaphors. Engaging local designers and educators in UI/UX testing further ensures contextual relevance.

8.8.3 Technology Integration in Learning Environments

8.8.3.1 Classroom vs. Remote Learning Contexts

Accessibility in educational technology must be considered in relation to its deployment environment. In classroom settings, tools can utilize teacher mediation, peer support, and physical infrastructure, enabling more complex multimodal interactions. However, classroom integration requires compatibility with existing ICT infrastructure, professional development for educators, and alignment with curricula (Selwyn, 2016). In contrast, remote or hybrid learning environments increase challenges related to device access, digital literacy, self-directed learning, and home learning setups. Accessibility features must therefore support asynchronous learning, cross-device compatibility, and easy user on-boarding. In both settings, focusing on universal design and reducing cognitive load improves usability for all learners, especially those with disabilities or learning difficulties.

8.8.3.2 Assistive Technology and Mainstream Ed-Tech Convergence

Traditionally, assistive technologies such as screen magnifiers, alternative input devices, and speech generating systems have been kept separate from mainstream educational tools. However, recent trends show a convergence, with mainstream tools now including inclusive features as standard. For example, Microsoft's Immersive Reader, Google's voice typing, and iPad's built-in switch control are now commonly available across general platforms. This convergence has both practical and ideological importance; it normalizes inclusion, reduces stigma, and promotes design equity (Al-Azawei et al., 2016). However, this integration must avoid superficial accessibility where features exist but are poorly implemented or seldom used. Genuine convergence requires collaboration among assistive tech experts, educators, and developers to ensure that inclusive features are integrated, user-friendly, and effective.

8.9 CASE STUDIES AND BEST PRACTICES

While theoretical frameworks and design principles lay the groundwork for accessible educational technologies, practical applications and real-world testing are crucial to assess their effectiveness and scalability. This section offers global case studies demonstrating inclusive HCI in practice and explores methods for evaluating design results, focusing on both user experience and educational impact.

8.9.1 Global Case Studies

Case studies from various geopolitical, cultural, and economic settings provide valuable insights into how inclusive HCI principles are understood, adapted, and applied in different educational environments. The following examples demonstrate how context-aware design and user-focused development can create meaningful educational technologies.

8.9.1.1 Example 1: Designing E-Learning Tools for Neurodiverse Students in the UK

In the United Kingdom, increasing focus has been placed on neurodiversity in education, especially supporting students with autism spectrum conditions (ASC), ADHD, and dyslexia. A notable example is the development of the "Brain in Hand" app, a personalized digital support system initially created for college students experiencing anxiety or executive functioning challenges (Morris et al., 2015).

This system incorporates routine management tools, self-monitoring features, real-time human support access. The design process included co-creating with neurodiverse students to ensure the interface prevented cognitive overload and sensory overstimulation. For example, a minimalistic visual design and customizable reminders helped lessen anxiety triggers. Evaluation showed improvements in self-regulation, academic retention, and reduced demand on in-person support services (Musaray & Muskaj, 2022). This case illustrates how inclusive HCI can extend beyond content delivery to support mental health and self-management—critical elements for neurodiverse learners.

8.9.1.2 Example 2: Low-Cost Accessible Platforms in Rural India

In rural areas of India, where infrastructure and language barriers overlap with digital inequality, projects like Diksha (Digital Infrastructure for Knowledge Sharing) have become scalable, inclusive platforms. Created by the Indian Ministry of Education, Diksha provides multilingual learning content, offline access, and QR code integration in textbooks to make learning materials easily accessible on low-end smartphones (Nedungadi et al., 2014).

Key features include support for over 30 Indian languages, offline functionality for low-bandwidth areas, text-to-speech, and visual content adaptations.

The interface was co-designed with teachers and tested in low-resource classroom environments, emphasizing cultural relevance, linguistic accessibility, and device compatibility. The platform has reportedly improved student engagement and teacher satisfaction, especially in underserved tribal and remote areas (Sharma, 2021). This case exemplifies how inclusive ed-tech does not always require high-end innovation, but rather context-sensitive design rooted in equity and multilingualism.

8.9.1.3 Example 3: Mobile Learning for Visually Impaired (VI) Students in Sub-Saharan Africa

In Sub-Saharan Africa, visually impaired learners face significant barriers due to limited infrastructure, costly assistive devices, and inadequate teacher training. The "VI-Learn" mobile platform, developed through collaboration between NGOs and educational institutions in Kenya and Uganda, addresses these challenges with a mobile-first, accessible design optimized for screen readers and offline use (Al-Azawei et al., 2016). Key features include audio-based curriculum delivery, voice navigation, and compatibility with Braille devices, co-designed with blind students, teachers, and rehabilitation specialists to ensure cultural and pedagogical relevance. Pilot evaluations demonstrated increased academic engagement, improved literacy rates, and enhanced learner autonomy compared to traditional print-based methods. This case underscores the impact of mobile-inclusive HCI and participatory design in low-resource settings, highlighting scalable, community-driven solutions for equitable education.

8.9.2 Evaluation of Design Outcomes

Designing accessible educational technology requires strong methods to evaluate its effectiveness, usability, and impact on learners. Assessment should go beyond basic metrics to include pedagogical relevance, user satisfaction, accessibility effectiveness, and social equity results.

8.9.3 Qualitative and Quantitative Assessment Methods

A mixed-methods approach is recommended to evaluate inclusive HCI solutions, combining the statistical robustness of quantitative data with the contextual depth of qualitative insights (Creswell & Plano Clark, 2017). Common quantitative tools include pre- and post-**tests** to assess learning gains, usability scales (e.g., system usability scale), engagement analytics (e.g., time-on-task, dropout rates). These are often supplemented by qualitative methods such as user interviews, cognitive walk-throughs, focus groups, and ethnographic observations. Participatory evaluation, where learners and educators co-analyze outcomes, adds another dimension by democratizing the feedback process and uncovering emergent needs that may escape traditional data collection.

8.9.3.1 User Satisfaction, Learning Outcomes, and Engagement Metrics

To evaluate the effectiveness of inclusive educational technologies, three key dimensions are considered: user satisfaction, learning outcomes, and engagement metrics. User satisfaction captures learners' perceptions of a tool's ease of use, usefulness, and emotional resonance, often measured through tools like the AttrakDiff questionnaire or Likert-scale surveys (Hassenzahl et al., 2003). Learning outcomes focus on tangible academic achievements, such as improved test scores and assignment completion, while also valuing self-efficacy and independence for neurodiverse learners or those with disabilities. Engagement metrics track interaction frequency, session duration, and module completion, reflecting a tool's relevance and accessibility when paired with qualitative insights. Additionally, emerging inclusion impact indicators highlight the reduction of systemic barriers, such as increased enrollment for girls with disabilities or enhanced participation among linguistically diverse learners, aligning with global equity goals (UNESCO, 2020). These dimensions collectively ensure that educational tools foster equitable, meaningful learning experiences.

8.10 CHALLENGES AND ETHICAL CONSIDERATIONS

Despite promising advances in inclusive HCI, the journey toward widespread adoption and long-term viability faces technological, institutional, and ethical hurdles. These barriers often hinder the implementation and expansion of accessible educational tools, especially in under-resourced or structurally disadvantaged settings.

8.10.1 Technological and Infrastructural Barriers

One of the most pressing issues is the persistent digital divide. Access to reliable hardware, software, and internet connectivity remains unequal across geographic and socioeconomic lines, particularly in the Global South (Robinson et al., 2015). Even where devices are available, their specifications may be insufficient to run advanced accessibility features such as screen readers or AI-based tutoring systems.

Affordability is another critical barrier. While some tools are open-source or subsidized, the majority of assistive technologies and inclusive platforms remain cost-prohibitive for many learners, especially those from marginalized communities (UNESCO, 2020). Additionally, the lack of energy infrastructure in certain rural or conflict-affected regions limits the feasibility of deploying even low-bandwidth solutions. These barriers highlight the need for low-tech, high-impact solutions, such as mobile-first platforms, SMS-based learning tools, and community-supported ICT hubs that prioritize universal design principles within constrained environments (Selwyn, 2016).

8.10.2 Institutional and Policy Limitations

Institutional inertia poses significant hurdles to the integration of accessible HCI into mainstream educational systems. Despite international frameworks like the UN's Convention on the Rights of Persons with Disabilities (CRPD), many countries lack enforceable national accessibility standards for educational technologies (European Agency for Special Needs and Inclusive Education, 2022).

Furthermore, teacher training programs seldom include modules on digital accessibility, universal design for learning (UDL), or inclusive pedagogy, creating a gap between technology and classroom use (Florian & Black-Hawkins, 2011). Without support from administration, teachers might see accessibility tools as extra work instead of helpful, transformative resources. A related issue is the fragmented implementation of policies, where accessibility mandates exist on paper but lack technical guidance, monitoring mechanisms, or funding to ensure scaling effective operation.

8.10.3 Ethical Dilemmas in Accessibility Design

As educational technologies become more inclusive and integrate AI, machine learning, and user analytics, new ethical issues arise. One major concern is data privacy, especially with tools that gather sensitive information from learners with disabilities or in vulnerable situations. Insufficient consent procedures or vague data policies risk infringing on the rights of already marginalized groups (Costanza-Chock, 2020). Algorithmic bias is another critical problem. AI-powered personalization systems might reproduce or deepen social biases, whether in language models, recommendation engines, or assessment algorithms, if datasets lack diverse user experiences (Noble, 2018). This could worsen educational inequality even as they claim to provide personalized solutions.

Finally, exporting Western-designed educational tools to non-Western contexts raises concerns about cultural dominance. Universal design should not lead to cultural erasure; instead, it must incorporate local epistemologies, languages, and values to promote genuinely inclusive learning.

8.11 STRATEGIC RECOMMENDATIONS

To bridge the gap between intention and impact in inclusive HCI, a multi-tiered strategy is required. This includes policy-level reform, pedagogical innovation, and research advancement, all grounded in equity and inclusivity.

8.11.1 Policy-Level Interventions

To advance inclusive human-computer interaction (HCI) in education, governments, NGOs, and multilateral organizations must adopt a proactive, coordinated approach to policy reform. This involves enforcing and monitoring rigorous digital accessibility standards for all state-funded educational technology procurements, ensuring compliance with frameworks like WCAG 2.1 to prioritize diverse learner needs. Additionally, strategic investments in infrastructure, such as expanding broadband access and providing affordable devices in underserved regions, are critical to bridging the digital divide and enabling equitable access to inclusive tools. To spur innovation, policymakers should incentivize the development of accessible technologies through grants, tax benefits, and public-private partnerships that prioritize equity-driven solutions. Leveraging international platforms like UNESCO's Global Education Coalition or G3ict can further promote collaborative frameworks, capacity-building initiatives, and policy alignment across borders, fostering a global commitment to inclusive educational technologies that empower all learners, regardless of ability or context.

8.11.2 Pedagogical Strategies

To ensure the effective integration of inclusive educational technologies, pedagogical strategies must position educators as key agents of change. This involves embedding training on digital accessibility and universal design for learning (UDL) within teacher education programs to equip educators with the skills to implement inclusive tools effectively. Collaborative co-teaching models, where general and special educators work together, can facilitate the seamless integration of accessible technologies into diverse classroom settings, enhancing support for all learners. Furthermore, curriculum diversification is essential, incorporating locally relevant content, languages, and culturally responsive examples to resonate with students' identities and contexts. Promoting open educational resources (OERs) is also critical, as their cost-effectiveness and adaptability allow educators to tailor materials to meet varied learner needs, fostering equity and inclusion across educational environments (OECD, 2021).

8.11.3 Research and Innovation Pathways

To advance inclusive human-computer interaction (HCI) in education, future research must prioritize interdisciplinary collaboration, ethical innovation, and long-term impact assessment. This involves fostering partnerships among HCI experts, educators, disability rights advocates, and cultural theorists to develop technologies that address diverse learner needs holistically. Research should focus on ethically aligned AI-driven personalization, ensuring adaptive systems are culturally contextualized and free from biases that could exacerbate inequities (Noble, 2018). Additionally, longitudinal studies are essential to evaluate not only academic outcomes but also learner identity, confidence, and social integration, providing a comprehensive understanding of inclusive technology's impact. Emerging fields like affective computing, haptic interaction, and immersive reality hold transformative potential, but their development must be guided by equity-first principles to ensure accessibility and relevance across diverse educational contexts (OECD, 2021).

8.11.4 Conclusion

This study argues that accessible HCI is a core part of inclusive education, not just an extra feature. Using frameworks like UDL, participatory design, and multimodal interaction, we can develop educational tools that meet the diverse needs of learners. But technological innovation alone isn't enough. The success of inclusive HCI relies on being responsive to the context, practicing ethical stewardship, reforming institutions, and maintaining ongoing collaboration across sectors and regions. As educational systems become more digitized, the need to prioritize equity, empathy, and accessibility becomes even more critical. The goal for inclusive education in a digital future isn't about everyone being the same but about tailored inclusivity creating a future where every learner, regardless of ability, identity, or location, can succeed.

REFERENCES

Akcil, U. (2017). The use of mobile learning for visually impaired learners school in tolerance education contents. *Quality & Quantity*, *52*. https://doi.org/10.1007/s11135-017-0552-1.

Al-Azawei, A., Parslow, P., & Lundqvist, K. (2017). The effect of universal design for learning (UDL) application on e-learning acceptance: A structural equation model. *International Review of Research in Open and Distributed Learning*, *18*(6), 54–87. https://doi.org/10.19173/irrodl.v18i6.2880

Al-Azawei, A., Serenelli, F., & Lundqvist, K. (2016). Universal Design for Learning (UDL): A content analysis of peer-reviewed journal papers from 2012 to 2015. *Journal of the Scholarship of Teaching and Learning*, *17*(3), 67–84. https://doi.org/10.14434/josotl.v17i3.22102.

Alotaibi, N. (2024). The impact of AI and LMS integration on the future of higher education: Opportunities, challenges, and strategies for transformation. *Sustainability*, *16*, 10357. https://doi.org/10.3390/su162310357.

Bodker, S. (1996). Creating conditions for participation: Conflicts and resources in systems design. *Human-Computer Interaction*, *11*(3), 215–236. https://doi.org/10.1207/s15327051hci1103_2.

Burgstahler, S. (2015). *Universal design in higher education: From principles to practice* (2nd ed.). Harvard Education Press.

CAST. (2018). *Universal Design for Learning Guidelines version 2.2*. http://udlguidelines.cast.org.

Costanza-Chock, S. (2020). *Design justice: Community-led practices to build the worlds we need*. MIT Press.

Crenshaw, K. (1989). Demarginalizing the intersection of race and sex: A black feminist critique of antidiscrimination doctrine, feminist theory and antiracist politics. *University of Chicago Legal Forum*, *1989*(1), 139–167.

Creswell, J. W., & Plano Clark, V. L. (2017). *Designing and conducting mixed methods research* (3rd ed.). Sage.

Deterding, S., Dixon, D., Khaled, R., & Nacke, L. (2011). From game design elements to gamefulness: Defining "gamification". In *Proceedings of the 15th international academic MindTrek conference* (pp. 9–15). https://doi.org/10.1145/2181037.2181040.

Dix, A., Finlay, J., Abowd, G., & Beale, R. (2004). *Human-computer interaction* (3rd ed.). Pearson Education.

D'Mello, S., & Graesser, A. (2012). AutoTutor and affective autoTutor: Learning by talking with cognitively and emotionally intelligent computers that talk back. *ACM Transactions on Interactive Intelligent Systems*, 2(4), 1–39. https://doi.org/10.1145/2395123.2395128.

European Agency for Special Needs and Inclusive Education. (2022). *Inclusive digital education: Guidelines for policy and practice*. https://www.european-agency.org

Eynon, R. (2015). The quantified self for learning: Critical questions for education. *Learning, Media and Technology*, *40*(4), 407–411. https://doi.org/10.1080/17439884.2015.1064461.

Florian, L., & Black-Hawkins, K. (2011). Exploring inclusive pedagogy. *British Educational Research Journal*, *37*(5), 813–828. https://doi.org/10.1080/01411926.2010.501096.

Frauenberger, C., Good, J., Fitzpatrick, G., & Iversen, O. S. (2015). In pursuit of rigour and accountability in participatory design. *International Journal of Human-Computer Studies*, *74*, 93–106. https://doi.org/10.1016/j.ijhcs.2014.09.004

Frauenberger, C., Good, J., & Keay-Bright, W. (2011). Designing technology for children with special needs—bridging perspectives through participatory design. *CoDesign: International Journal of Co-Creation in Design and the Arts*, *7*, 1–28. https://doi.org/10.1080/15710882.2011.587013.

Gay, G. (2018). *Culturally responsive teaching: Theory, research, and practice* (3rd ed.). Teachers College Press.
Goggin, G., & Newell, C. (2003). *Digital disability: The social construction of disability in new media*. Rowman & Littlefield.
Hall, T. E., Meyer, A., & Rose, D. H. (Eds.). (2012). *Universal design for learning in the classroom: Practical applications*. Guilford Press.
Hassenzahl, M., Burmester, M., & Koller, F. (2003). AttrakDiff: A method for measuring perceived hedonic and pragmatic quality. In *Human-computer interaction: Theory and practice* (pp. 291–296). Lawrence Erlbaum Associates.
Hofstede, G. (2001). *Culture's consequences: Comparing values, behaviors, institutions and organizations across nations* (2nd ed.). Sage.
Holmes, W., Bialik, M., & Fadel, C. (2019). *Artificial intelligence in education: Promises and implications for teaching and learning*. Center for Curriculum Redesign. https://curriculumredesign.org/our-work/artificial-intelligence-in-education/
Kelly, B., Phipps, L., & Swift, E. (2004). Developing a holistic approach for e-learning accessibility. *Canadian Journal of Learning and Technology*, *30*(3), 1–14.
Kimmons, R., & Veletsianos, G. (2016). Education scholars' evolving uses of Twitter as a conference backchannel and social commentary platform. *British Journal of Educational Technology*, *47*(3), 445–464. https://doi.org/10.1111/bjet.12428
Kimmons, R., & Veletsianos, G. (2018). Public internet data mining methods in instructional design, educational technology, and online learning research. *TechTrends*, *62*(7), 626–635. https://doi.org/10.1007/s11528-018-0307-4
Ladner, R. E. (2015). Design for user empowerment. *Interactions*, *22*(2), 24–29. https://doi.org/10.1145/2723869
Lazar, J., Goldstein, D. F., & Taylor, A. (2015). *Ensuring digital accessibility through process and policy*. Morgan Kaufmann. https://lib.ugent.be/catalog/ebk01:2670000000619284
Mayer, R. E. (2009). *Multimedia learning* (2nd ed.). Cambridge University Press. https://doi.org/10.1017/CBO9780511811678
Morris, M. R., Begel, A., & Wiedermann, B. (2015). Understanding the challenges faced by neurodiverse software engineering employees: Towards a more inclusive and productive technical workforce. In *Proceedings of the 17th international ACM SIGACCESS conference on computers & accessibility (ASSETS '15)* (pp. 173–184). Association for Computing Machinery. https://doi.org/10.1145/2700648.2809841
Musaray, J., & Muskaj, B. (2022). Technology as a learning tool. Access of autistic children to e-learning. *International Journal of Special Education (IJSE)*, *37*, 129–139. https://doi.org/10.52291/ijse.2022.37.46.
Nedungadi, P., Jayakumar, A., & Raman, R. (2014). Low cost tablet enhanced pedagogy for early grade reading: Indian context. In *2014 IEEE region 10 humanitarian technology conference (R10-HTC)* (pp. 35–39). IEEE. https://doi.org/10.1109/R10-HTC.2014.7026322
Nielsen, J. (1993). *Usability engineering*. Morgan Kaufmann.
Noble, S. U. (2018). *Algorithms of oppression: How search engines reinforce racism*. NYU Press.
Oliver, M. (1996). *Understanding disability: From theory to practice*. Macmillan.
Organisation for Economic Co-operation and Development. (2018). *Equity in education: Breaking down barriers to social mobility*. OECD Publishing. https://doi.org/10.1787/9789264073234-en
Organisation for Economic Co-operation and Development. (2021). *Education at a glance 2021: OECD indicators*. OECD Publishing. https://doi.org/10.1787/b35a14e5-en
Oviatt, S. L. (2003). Multimodal interfaces. In J. A. Jacko & A. Sears (Eds.), *The human–computer interaction handbook: Fundamentals, evolving technologies, and emerging applications* (pp. 286–304). CRC Press. https://doi.org/10.1007/0-387-30038-4_171

Picard, R. W. (1997). *Affective computing*. MIT Press.

Robinson, L., Cotten, S. R., Ono, H., Quan-Haase, A., Mesch, G., Chen, W., . . . & Stern, M. J. (2015). Digital inequalities and why they matter. *Information, Communication & Society, 18*(5), 569–582. https://doi.org/10.1080/1369118X.2015.1012532

Rogers, Y., Sharp, H., & Preece, J. (2011). *Interaction design: Beyond human-computer interaction* (3rd ed.). John Wiley & Sons.

Rose, D. H., Gravel, J. W., & Garden, D. T. (2014). Universal design for learning. In P. Peterson, E. Baker, & B. McGaw (Eds.), *International encyclopedia of education* (3rd ed., pp. 119–124). Elsevier.

Rose, D. H., & Meyer, A. (2002). *Teaching every student in the digital age: Universal Design for Learning*. Association for Supervision and Curriculum Development (ASCD). Retrieved December 5, 2024, from CAST website: https://www.cast.org/resources/tips-articles/teaching-every-student-in-the-digital-age-universal-design-for-learning/

Rose, D. H., Meyer, A., & Gordon, D. (2013). *Universal design for learning: Theory and practice*. CAST Professional Publishing. https://udltheorypractice.cast.org

Roy, S. S., & Gandhimathi, S. N. S. (2024). Self-directed learning for optimizing sustainable language learning via mobile assisted language learning: A systematic review. *Frontiers in Education, 9*. https://doi.org/10.3389/feduc.2024.1463721

Selwyn, N. (2016). *Education and technology: Key issues and debates* (2nd ed.). Bloomsbury Academic.

Sharma, A. (2021). *DIKSHA: Learnings from India experience* (CSD Working Paper No. 50). Center for Sustainable Development.

Sharples, M. (2013). Mobile learning: Research, practice and challenges. *Distance Education in China, 3*, 5–11.

Shneiderman, B., Plaisant, C., Cohen, M., Jacobs, S., Elmqvist, N., & Diakopoulos, N. (2017). *Designing the user interface: Strategies for effective human-computer interaction* (6th ed.). Pearson.

Simonsen, J., & Robertson, T. (Eds.). (2013). *Routledge international handbook of participatory design*. Routledge. https://doi.org/10.4324/9780203108543

Soloway, E., Guzdial, M., & Hay, K. E. (1994). Learner-centered design: The challenge for HCI in the 21st century. *Interactions, 1*(2), 36–48.

Sosa Neira, E. A., Salinas, J., & De Benito, B. (2017). Emerging Technologies (ETs) in education: A systematic review of the literature published between 2006 and 2016. *International Journal of Emerging Technologies in Learning (iJET), 12*(5), 128–149. https://doi.org/10.3991/ijet.v12i05.6939

Sweller, J. (1988). Cognitive load during problem solving: Effects on learning. *Cognitive Science, 12*(2), 257–285. https://doi.org/10.1207/s15516709cog1202_4

UNESCO. (2016). *Education 2030: Incheon declaration and framework for action*. UNESCO. https://unesdoc.unesco.org/ark:/48223/pf0000245656

UNESCO. (2020). *Global education monitoring report: Inclusion and education—All means all*. https://unesdoc.unesco.org/ark:/48223/pf0000373718

UNESCO. (2021). *Reimagining our futures together: A new social contract for education*. https://unesdoc.unesco.org/ark:/48223/pf0000379707

U.S. General Services Administration. (2017). *Section 508 standards and guidelines*. https://www.section508.gov/manage/laws-and-policies/

W3C. (2018). *Web content accessibility guidelines (WCAG) 2.1*. https://www.w3.org/TR/WCAG21/

9 Emerging Technologies and Regenerative Pedagogies in the Era of Education 6.0

José Manuel Nieto Jalil

9.1 INTRODUCTION: FROM THE EXHAUSTION OF THE MODEL TO A NEW PEDAGOGICAL CONTRACT

The evolution of educational models has been shaped by the interplay between technology, culture, and the pursuit of cognitive justice. In recent years, post-humanist perspectives and the field of digital humanities have called for a reconfiguration of the relationship between knowledge, technology, and humanity, projecting education as a space for sustainability and regeneration [1]. At the same time, the challenge of closing digital divides and designing systems that are genuinely inclusive for all learners has gained critical ethical and practical relevance, particularly in a society increasingly mediated by algorithms and automation [2]. This dual horizon, the evolution toward post-humanist thinking and the urgency of true digital inclusion, forms the foundation upon which the emerging paradigm of Education 6.0 is built.

The classroom we inherited was designed for a world of linear causes and closed problems [3]. Today we educate within an ecosystem marked by the climate crisis, epistemic inequality, and technological acceleration that reshapes how we perceive, model, and act upon reality [4]. In that context, teaching is no longer the transmission of content: it is the building of judgment, character, and the capacity to intervene with evidence and within explicit ethical bounds. This chapter proposes a deliberate pivot: moving from instructional efficiency to educational regeneration, where learning also means repairing what sustains us. Put differently, learning is conceived as a public practice that leaves a verifiable trace inside and beyond the classroom.

We call Education 6.0 a new pedagogical contract that articulates technology with ethics and cognitive justice. It is not about collecting gadgets but integrating capabilities: generative AI as an instructional mediator with human verification; explainable analytics that guide real-time decisions with minimal data capture; XR and digital twins to practice without risk and transfer to the physical world; digital provenance to safeguard academic integrity; verifiable micro-credentials to recognize stackable competencies; and neurotechnologies governed by informed consent and neurorights. In this framework, the educator does not disappear; they are

DOI: 10.1201/9781003678250-9

amplified as a designer of experiences, mentor, and custodian of student agency, with an explicit role in orchestrating AI agents, data, and authentic tasks [5, 6].

The central thesis is operational: perceive–model–act with evidence and a regenerative purpose. To that end, Education 6.0 combines evidence-based instructional design, short hypothesis–test–reflection cycles, bioregional living labs, and authentic assessment through impact portfolios. The expected result transcends academic performance: we seek verifiable improvements in water, energy, mobility, health, or well-being, achieved without sacrificing dignity, privacy, or equity. To ensure this promise is auditable rather than rhetorical, we make explicit two instructional mechanisms often omitted in the literature:

a) Data didactic contracts: clear agreements—between faculty and students—on what data are collected, for what purpose, for how long, with granular rights of revocation and equivalent low-tech pathways.
b) Per-course energy budgets: planning accounts for the computational cost of AI-mediated activities and favors small, local models when objectives allow, thereby integrating Green AI into teaching practice.

These two elements turn sustainability and data ethics into instructional decisions, not appendices.

The dominant educational model has reached its historical limit. It optimizes coverage and control, yet offers little traction for reasoning under uncertainty, deliberating with evidence, and designing interventions in complex systems. In a world marked by the climate crisis, epistemic inequality, and accelerated technological disruption, it is no longer enough to produce functional graduates or to deliver decontextualized content. We must reimagine education as a regenerative process that forms citizens capable of acting with intelligence, ethics, and planetary responsibility. Thus, this chapter presents Education 6.0 not as a technological fashion, but as a new pedagogical contract in which artificial intelligence, sustainability, and cognitive justice redefine the very purpose of learning.

We will refer to Education 6.0, in continuity with the aforementioned, as a hyper-personalized, ethical, and regenerative learning ecosystem that integrates algorithmic literacy and digital provenance; general-purpose AI and explainable analytics to steer instructional decision-making in real time; XR and digital twins for safe, transferable practice; educational neurotechnologies under neurorights and informed consent; verifiable micro-credentials and impact portfolios; and data governance aligned with Green AI principles (measurement and minimization of footprint). This operational definition avoids technological fetishism and sets a bar: technology is valuable insofar as it improves learning with less harm (to privacy, attention, the planet, and dignity) [7–9].

To situate the scope of this proposal, it is useful to make explicit its technological horizon and current limits. Education 6.0 is conceived as a qualitative leap in the evolution of learning, with adaptive hyper-personalization enabled by frontier technologies: artificial general intelligence (AGI), quantum computing, neurotechnologies, and immersive realities. Unlike prior transitions, many of these capabilities have not yet reached full maturity; consequently, the debate concerns not only what is, but what could be—and its ethical, equity, and pedagogical implications. This recognition obliges three safeguarding practices:

a) Local explainability and authorship traceability (provenance) for every artifact.
b) Subgroup algorithmic audits to prevent averages from masking distributional harm.
c) Pedagogically equivalent pathways without connectivity or without biological data capture, so as not to reproduce the 6.0 divide.

Thus, the vision does not displace the educator; it redefines their role, freeing them from administrative tasks to focus on the irreplaceable work of cultivating judgment, character, and citizenship. At the same time, it requires addressing the digital divide and establishing regulatory frameworks that protect privacy and dignity in an era of symbiotic human–machine interaction. With this framing, we move from horizon to operational architecture in the present, where every decision is measurable, justifiable, and revocable.

By way of a brief trajectory, education has evolved from 1.0 (one-way transmission and standardization), through 2.0/3.0 (digitization of formats without transforming our relationship to knowledge), to 5.0 (a humanistic emphasis on well-being, creativity, and sustainability). Education 6.0 emerges as a horizon rather than an accomplished state: it projects hyper-personalized, adaptive learning enabled by general-scope AI, quantum computing, neurotechnologies, and immersive realities, and in parallel, demands an ethical and equity-centered debate on privacy, the digital divide, and governance. Far from replacing the educator, it reconfigures the role: automation handles data engineering and repetitive tasks; teaching concentrates on the irreplaceable—diagnosing real needs, designing scaffolds, posing questions that open problems, and safeguarding agency. This shift also installs a competency rarely addressed in manuals: the critical reading of algorithmic trust, which requires calling for counterfactual explanations, evidence anchors (what we later term Retrieval-Augmented Teaching, RAT), and transparent energy budgets for every course [5, 10, 11].

Building upon this conceptual framework, the chapter is organized to progressively articulate the technological, pedagogical, and ethical dimensions of Education 6.0. Section 2 examines the emerging capabilities—from generative AI to explainable analytics and neurotechnologies—highlighting both their formative potential and epistemic boundaries. Section 3 introduces regenerative pedagogies and impact evaluation models grounded in equity, sustainability, and environmental repair. Section 4 proposes an operational architecture supported by theories of change, measurement systems, and didactic data-and-energy contracts. Section 5 develops governance mechanisms and principles of algorithmic justice that enable responsible and auditable implementation. Finally, Section 6 presents the conclusions, reflecting on Education 6.0 as a new pedagogical contract between human intelligence, artificial systems, and the planet that sustains them.

9.2 TECHNOLOGICAL CAPABILITIES WITH PEDAGOGICAL VALUE (AND THEIR LIMITS)

In the era of Education 6.0, learning stops resembling a conveyor belt and behaves like a living system that perceives, models, and acts. It perceives with situated data—interaction traces, sensors, qualitative observations, reflective journals; it models with instruments capable of representing complexity—learning analytics, generative AI, digital twins; and it acts through pedagogical decisions validated by evidence of impact, not only by grades. This transition repositions the university: it ceases to be a container of courses and operates as cognitive and ethical infrastructure in service of human and planetary well-being. To sustain this didactically, instructional design aligns explicitly (constructive alignment) across outcomes, activities, and assessment, and adopts frequent feedback cycles that reduce the temporal gap between performance and support [12, 13].

Within that frame, generative AI ceases to be a shortcut and becomes a metacognitive mediator. Its value does not lie in "answering" but in sustaining processes: adjusting challenge to the zone of proximal development, producing graduated hints, proposing alternative solution paths and, above all, making its uncertainty explicit. Teaching students to read a system's confidence, when the model is certain and why, is a competency largely absent from the literature and essential for exercising judgment in algorithmic environments. Therefore, instead of accepting closed answers, we request counterfactual explanations (what would need to change in the problem for your recommendation to fail?) and edge cases that reveal assumptions. We also propose a practical principle: Retrieval-Augmented Teaching (RAT). Every AI-generated explanation must be anchored in cited passages from course texts, data, or standards. Thus, AI stops being oracular and becomes auditable; students do not merely consume answers, they learn to locate knowledge and justify it. To avoid dependence, guided-practice phases are combined with scaffold withdrawal (fading) and far-transfer assessments that verify generalization beyond seen examples [14, 15].

Next-generation analytics, in turn, avoids data maximalism: it captures the minimum necessary, operates with differential privacy and federated learning, and deploys dashboards with local explanations that indicate why an alert fired and what support routes are suggested. Rather than "measuring for measurement's sake," data didactic contracts are agreed between faculty and students: what is captured, for what purpose, for how long, and with what granular right of revocation. Evidence guides; pedagogical judgment decides. To add rigor, alert models are validated with comprehensible metrics (sensitivity, specificity, AUROC) and audited by subgroups (first-generation students, gender, employment status) to prevent average improvements from hiding harm.

Digital twins and XR are not technological fireworks; they are scientific instruments with purpose. One course can model a constructed wetland and its effect on turbidity/BOD before installing prototypes; another can simulate ventilation and shading policies to flatten electricity demand peaks; urban planning can evaluate optimal biofilter placement before digging. When simulation demands embodiment, XR and haptics provide embodied experience: exploring a 3D electric field at human scale, executing safety maneuvers on turbomachinery without risk, practicing virtual dissections with tactile feedback. Authentic assessment, in this approach, ceases to be an exam and becomes the observation of performance, the quality of decisions, and the depth of reflection. Fidelity of implementation is monitored with checklists and peer-calibrated rubrics (inter-rater reliability ≥ 0.70) to distinguish the effect of technology from the effect of design [16, 17].

Recognition of learning is materialized in verifiable micro-credentials that are not digital stickers but evidence contracts: they specify what one can do, to what standard, under what validity criteria, and to which reproducible evidence they point. Digital provenance (C2PA) adds a verifiable chain of authorship and editing: who did what, when, with which tools, and what changed. This traceability, with informed consent and equivalent low-tech pathways, allows, for example, an oral defense to be not just a speech but a transparent reconstruction of decisions with proofs in hand. In low-connectivity contexts, the standard operates with offline flows and soft binding that preserve the signature and history upon synchronization. To raise rigor, each micro-credential declares expiration or update criteria and requires replication packages (data, code, lab notes) where applicable.

Educational neurotechnology occupies a delimited, clear place. It does not read minds: it estimates proxies of attention, load, and effort to adjust didactics without labeling people. Pilots with non-invasive EEG have helped dose exposure times and personalize scaffolds; in some profiles, transcranial random noise stimulation (tRNS) has shown improvements when implemented under rigorous protocols [18]. The operational frame is unambiguous: opt-in participation with no penalty, strictly educational (non-clinical) use, reinforced cybersecurity, protection of sensitive data, and pedagogically equivalent routes without biological capture. Teaching with neurotechnologies is, in truth, teaching neurorights. In addition, cognitive load is monitored with validated instruments (brief self-report and, if appropriate, aggregated physiological indicators) to adjust pace and information density without invading privacy.

An underexplored opportunity is teacher–AI orchestration. Rather than depending on a single "large model" that monopolizes decisions, the instructor conducts a team of agents with specific roles: a Socratic tutor that asks questions, a reasoning verifier that detects logical leaps, an assessor that suggests initial feedback with rubrics, a curator that retrieves materials with marked provenance. This algorithmic diversity makes visible that there is no single computational view of a problem and trains students to compare perspectives critically. Didactically, participation modes alternate under ICAP (constructive and interactive) to maximize deep learning, and delayed post-tests (4–6 weeks) are scheduled to measure true retention.

Another infrequent angle in education is the energy footprint. We propose per-course energy budgets and computational-cost reports per activity (local vs. cloud inference, model size, call frequency). Designing compact prompts, batching inferences, and preferring small edge models when possible is not mere technical efficiency: it is Green AI literacy. Sustainability enters the classroom not as discourse but as measurable practice: students learn to optimize requests, evaluate cost/benefit, and justify the use of large models only when they provide clear marginal pedagogical value.

Accessibility demands the same intentionality. An anti-dopamine-by-design approach protects deep attention with distraction-light interfaces, scheduled pauses, on-demand audio summaries, captions and descriptions, dyslexia-friendly typefaces, and pace personalization. Universal Design for Learning ceases to be an appendix and becomes the norm: AI not only explains but also accompanies and regulates, listening to differences rather than homogenizing experiences. In practice, parallel routes are offered (text, audio, interactive visualization), and their use is documented to identify combinations that improve understanding without increasing load.

Education 6.0 also cannot depend on perfect connectivity. Minimal computing and offline-first strategies guarantee essential functionality without internet and deferred synchronization. In remote labs, spectrophotometers, fluid benches, cobots with safety cells, rich process traces are stored locally and uploaded when a network is available. This aesthetics of low-spectacle technology is, in many contexts, the frontier between promise and possibility. It also reduces exposure to systemic failures and strengthens the resilience of the teaching–learning process.

As important as capabilities are their failure modes. Teaching with technology requires teaching how to doubt: high-confidence hallucinations, automation bias, model drift with local data, privacy inferences by correlation, cognitive fatigue from poorly calibrated alerts. Turning these failures into objects of study, algorithmic-error clinics, fortifies critical thinking: What did the model see? What did it miss? How do we measure uncertainty, and when is it preferable to switch to manual? Operational guardrails respond to that spirit: evidence or silence (if AI cannot anchor with RAT, it does not justify), assessment decoupling (no high-stakes task is graded solely by AI), equity checklists with pedagogical red-teaming, explicit energy limits, and interruption protocols when ethical or technical doubts arise. As a closing rule, every innovation is subjected to exit criteria: clear conditions to pause, correct, or withdraw—communicated to students and the community.

Two vignettes set the scene. In the first semester, a student models an SIR system: the reasoning verifier flags two logical leaps; the Socratic tutor redirects with questions; the curator anchors the explanation in a scholarly article and open data; the twin simulates three intervention policies with different energy costs; the microcredential requires an oral defense with provenance for every figure. To increase rigor, the exercise incorporates RAT (every recommendation cites sources) and a parallel pre–post on conceptual understanding and transfer. The defense is graded with a rubric weighting: (i) model justification and assumptions; (ii) treatment of uncertainty (intervals, parameter sensitivity); (iii) decisions under energy constraints (reported compute budget); (iv) C2PA traceability of artifacts and lab logs. A delayed post-test at 4–6 weeks is included to measure retention, along with a brief "error clinic" in which the student explains why the first model version failed and what changed after feedback. In this way, the grade ceases to be a number and becomes a history of auditable decisions, with reproducible evidence and explicit quality criteria.

In another course, a team designs a thermal corridor to mitigate urban heat islands: analytics detects low self-regulation in a subgroup and suggests micro-interventions (study pairs, active breaks, audio summaries). The instructional protocol adds a two-week baseline, low-cost sensors (fixed points and mobile transects), and a quasi-experimental difference-in-differences design with a comparable segment as control. To reduce confounders (cloud cover, wind), time windows and day fixed effects are used; data and scripts are published as a replication package. Decision-making incorporates equity criteria (shade during school waiting hours, pedestrian accessibility for older adults), the project's energy budget, and an offline-first route to ensure continuity when there is no connectivity. The outcome is not a visual before–after, but a technical–ethical argument that documents trade-offs, risks, and maintenance responsibilities, and can be audited by peers and the community.

The state of the art supports this direction, with necessary nuance: well-designed AI tutors can outperform active-learning classes in certain contexts; AI-generated hints have achieved performance comparable to human hints in algebra/statistics; and a recent meta-analysis reports positive effects on performance, motivation, and some forms of higher-order thinking, with heterogeneity by discipline and design. To strengthen validity, it is advisable to report moderators (education level, domain, task type, dosage, fidelity of implementation), use transparent metrics (Cohen's d/Hedges' g, 95% CI), and conduct subgroup analyses to detect distributional effects. Ecological validity also matters: replicate in authentic contexts, avoid control contamination, and record opportunity costs (teaching time, cognitive load, energy footprint). We also know that without instructional guardrails (scaffolding that privileges reasoning over answer-giving, human verification for high-stakes tasks, RAT, authentic assessment) results can suffer; with safeguards, they tend to hold or improve. The practical call is clear: instructional design + guardrails + evaluation with retention and far-transfer measures beyond immediate accuracy, and transparency about costs (computational, energy, and implementation) to decide when to scale and when to rethink.

In sum, pedagogically valuable technology is that which enables better learning with less harm: less harm to privacy, attention, the planet, and dignity. To achieve this, we anchor AI, analytics, twins, and XR in clear purposes, auditable evidence, revocable consent, and equivalent non-tech routes. Only then does Education 6.0 transcend device fascination and become a responsible practice that truly engages: it returns to education its boldest promise, cultivating judgment to design preferable futures, while prudently and rigorously repairing the world we share. As a closing operational commitment, any technological incorporation must demonstrate a learning or equity gain and measurable harm reduction; failing that, it is re-scoped or retired. That standard turns innovation into discipline, and the university into a living system that learns from its own decisions.

Figure 9.1 synthesizes the operational architecture of Education 6.0, articulating its core pedagogical, technological, ethical, and governance components and their interdependencies.

Table 9.1 organizes illustrative references aligned with the key dimensions of the Education 6.0 framework discussed in this section.

Research Gaps Identified:

- Insufficient longitudinal studies that connect the use of generative and explainable AI with measurable and sustained learning outcomes.
- Limited empirical evidence regarding the ethical integration of neurotechnologies and the protection of neurorights in higher education.

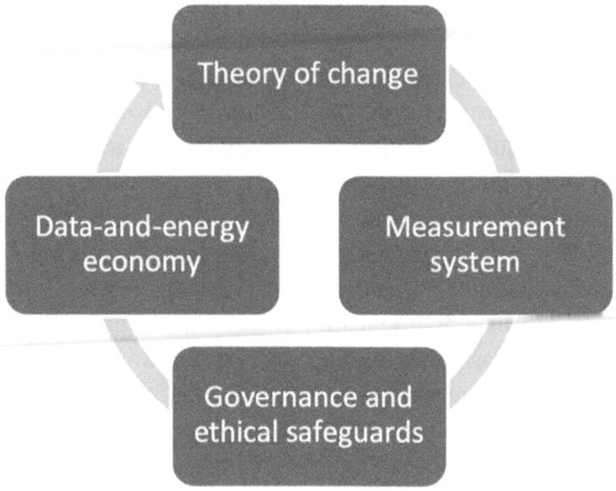

FIGURE 9.1 Operational Architecture of Education 6.0

TABLE 9.1
Selected References Supporting Education 6.0 Framework

Focus Area	Reference	Key Contribution
Generative and Explainable AI in learning	Moleka (2023) [5]	Highlights adaptive and personalized learning through AI mediation.
Regenerative and Restorative Pedagogies	Damus (2024) [19]	Emphasizes education as ecological and social repair.
Green AI and Sustainability Metrics	Toktaş (2025) [1]	Introduces Green AI principles for low-energy digital education.
Authentic Assessment in Engineering Contexts	Nieto-Jalil et al. (2023) [13]	Demonstrates challenge-based learning as an evidence-driven assessment model.

- Lack of standardized frameworks to evaluate the energy efficiency and environmental footprint of AI-driven educational systems.
- Absence of validated models linking data contracts and revocable consent to students' sense of agency and cognitive justice.
- Scarcity of comparative analyses assessing how hybrid human–AI teaching models reshape instructional roles and pedagogical decision-making.

9.3 REGENERATIVE PEDAGOGIES AND IMPACT EVALUATION

Speaking of regenerative pedagogies means shifting the axis: moving beyond a do no harm ethic to assuming responsibility for restoring socio-environmental systems while we learn [19, 20]. It is not about adding a green project to a traditional course, but about reordering the formative logic: real problems, agreed upon with the community, are the raw material; the university contributes method, ethical safeguards, and rigor; technology amplifies perception and modeling; and public evidence attests to what was learned and transformed. Within this frame, the curriculum stops operating as a sequence of topics and becomes an architecture of decisions in which every pedagogical action responds to an explicit hypothesis about how to improve a living system, a river, a neighborhood, a classroom, a supply chain, with justice criteria and well-defined verification routes.

The regenerative experience begins before the classroom, with collaboration agreements that recognize local actors as co-authors of knowledge: free, prior, and informed consent; shared benefits; and clear rules for intellectual property and data provenance to avoid academic extractivism. Epistemic justice is not decorative rhetoric: it changes the method. Indigenous and community knowledges do not merely "illustrate" a topic; they deliberate with frontier science, define success criteria, and modulate the scale of intervention. Thus, an engineering course stops optimizing an abstract objective function to negotiate with situated realities: seasonal flows, social arrangements, histories of dispossession, and practices that have conserved ecosystems for generations. This co-authorship is documented in data agreements (who decides, where data reside, for how long, under which licenses) and in participation logs that ensure social traceability, not only technical.

Instructional design adopts short, cyclical rhythms, hypothesis, test, reflection, with questions that go beyond technical efficacy: Who gains and who loses with this solution? What externalities appear when it scales? How will we know whether improvement holds once the semester ends? A theory of change guides each cycle and requires distinguishing leading indicators—self-regulation, quality of argumentation, time to useful feedback, density of local collaborations, from lagging indicators, changes in turbidity and BOD, reductions in surface temperature, energy savings, user satisfaction, institutional adoption. Where randomized trials are not viable, we turn to realist evaluation and contribution analysis, to quasi-experimental designs with baseline and comparison group, and even to interrupted time series and falsification (placebo) tests to sustain inferences without betraying context. Mixed-methods triangulation is made explicit with joint displays that integrate quantitative and qualitative findings in a single interpretive matrix.

Evaluation stops viewing the student in isolation and advances toward impact portfolios that combine technical evidence (models, sampling protocols, sensitivity analyses), justified decisions (reflective logs, assumptions, limits, ethical dilemmas), and public proof (oral defenses, field demonstrations, open data with quality metadata). Integrity is protected through digital provenance and reproducibility practices (versioning, replication packages, preregistration where applicable). This does not turn the classroom into an audit office: it restores its intellectual density and social responsibility. Learning is no longer "knowing about" the world; it is learning with the world and being accountable for what we do in it. To strengthen comparability across cohorts, we report effect sizes and thresholds of educationally meaningful change, not only averages [21, 22].

Regenerative pedagogy is also a pedagogy of care. There is no sustainable transformation without attention to bodies and rhythms. Designing for neurodiversity means enabling multiple avenues of representation and expression, fostering deep attention (low-noise interfaces, active pauses, text-to-speech, captions and enhanced descriptions, dyslexia-friendly typefaces), and recognizing that cognitive and emotional overload is not an individual weakness but a design parameter. Rather than measuring engagement as time on screen, we observe belonging and flourishing: who feels part of the community, who takes the floor, who learns to ask for help and to offer it. Digital tools do more than deliver content; they accompany learners so that rigor is compatible with life, with workload protocols that distribute effort and avoid unnecessary peaks.

A seldom-explored dimension is the temporality of learning. Educational innovation sometimes suffers from accelerationism: everything must happen now. Regenerative practices introduce the right to slowness: time for field observation, silence to think, iterations under controlled pressure, and rest windows that allow synaptic and social connections to consolidate. This ethics of tempo is not romantic; it is neuroscientifically sensible and politically necessary. Learning to defer decisions until sufficient evidence is available is a civic competency in times of anxious algorithms. The academic calendar, therefore, is understood as a pedagogical instrument, not merely a logistical constraint.

Dialogue with technology is deliberately instrumental. AI helps plan sampling, estimate uncertainty, and compare policies; digital twins rehearse scenarios; XR trains skills; analytics detects early risk and suggests supports; micro-credentials record what is demonstrable and portable; content provenance protects authorship in a hybrid ecosystem of human and synthetic artifacts. But no tool alone decides what matters. In fact, the energy footprint becomes a pedagogical criterion: per-course energy budgets are set, and small, local models are preferred when the task allows. Sustainability enters the curriculum through the front door: as a design decision with explicit opportunity costs and scaling criteria tied to verifiable pedagogical benefits.

To avoid technosolutionism and pilotitis, pilots that dazzle and do not persist, academic governance establishes committees with student and community voice, consent protocols, algorithmic audits by subgroups, and equity checklists applied before releasing a tutor or an analytic. When connectivity fails or infrastructure is absent, equivalent low-tech routes are activated, paper protocols, physical simulations, mobile labs, that preserve the learning objective without excluding anyone. Inclusion is not an appendix; it is the validity criterion of innovation. And in terms of institutional sustainability, implementation costs, teaching time, and maintenance are reported so decision-making is informed and responsible.

Two scenes help visualize the promise. In an interdisciplinary workshop, a team co-designs a thermal corridor with the municipality: they map heat islands with low-cost sensors, model scenarios for tree planting and permeable pavements, estimate the energy costs of each alternative, and deliberate with residents about maintenance and shade. The portfolio ends up containing not only a before–after, but assumptions, trade-offs, risks, and commitments. In a course on water and health, another team prototypes a constructed wetland; AI suggests parameters, the hydrologic twin tests combinations, and the community defines the success threshold ("drink without fear," not merely "meet the standard"). The public defense judges not only model accuracy, but methodological honesty and social pertinence. Both cases include transfer plans and post-course monitoring to evaluate the sustainability of changes.

Fertile lines remain open for research and practice. We need better frameworks to attribute impact when multiple actors converge; to measure medium-term transfer without oversimplification; to teach uncertainty as algorithmic citizenship; to formalize data contracts that are legible and revocable; to document pedagogical failure modes of technology and turn them into content; to integrate economies of care, time, energy, attention, into rubrics; to design micro-credentials that certify not only skills but judgment and responsibility. We also urgently need to study governance models with student-held data, educational data cooperatives, and community peer-review circuits that complement academic committees. Another frontier is cultural validity: adapting instruments and metrics so they measure what matters where it matters, avoiding uncritical transplantation.

In the end, the promise of regenerative pedagogies is not that every problem is solved in a semester, but that each cohort leaves the ground better than it found it and learns to be accountable for that. The most beautiful educational transformation is not seen on a dashboard; it is recognized in the quality of the questions and in the ethical steadiness with which we decide to act—or not. If Education 6.0 achieves this, judgment with evidence, imagination with prudence, technological power with care, then the university will have returned to its highest vocation: cultivating the judgment that makes it possible to design preferable futures while repairing the world we share.

Regenerative pedagogies turn innovation into public discipline: every intervention begins with a legitimate question, unfolds with an auditable method, is evaluated with triangulated evidence, and is sustained by participatory governance. When learning is conceived in this way, as situated action that improves systems and protects dignities, the university stops administering content and recognizes itself as a living system that perceives, models, and acts responsibly.

9.4 OPERATIONAL ARCHITECTURE: THEORY OF CHANGE, CASES, AND EVIDENCE

Operating Education 6.0 requires moving from horizon to routine: turning principles into auditable everyday decisions. The operational architecture rests on four interdependent supports:

a) an explicit, verifiable theory of change, formalized with "if–then–because" assumptions and causal diagrams (DAGs) that make confounders and enabling conditions explicit;
b) a measurement system that separates processes from results, defines primary/secondary outcomes, includes parallel pre/post-tests, delayed retention, and inter-rater reliability;
c) a data-and-energy economy with didactic data contracts (minimization, purpose, limited retention, revocation), C2PA provenance, and energy budgets (kWh/gCO_2e) per course and per activity;
d) governance that legitimizes the project (syllabus policies, model/data cards, algorithmic impact assessment, appeal pathways, and equivalent low-tech routes).

In practice, before designing activities we pre-specify the analytic plan (metrics, moderators, effect thresholds, and subgroup equity thresholds), set phase gates with public criteria for scaling and kill criteria for pausing; we measure before, during, and after; we record fine-grained traceability (tools, versions, prompts, cognitive/social/energy costs); and we publish replication packages and an adverse events log. Every result is open to scrutiny and to the possibility of stopping or redesigning when evidence demands it: here, innovation is discipline, not spectacle.

The theory of change organizes learning in a causal chain that does not pretend to be linear: inputs, activities, outputs, and impacts coexist with feedback loops and enabling conditions. Inputs are no longer just content and credits; they include public problems prioritized with the community, contextual data and local knowledge, as well as ethical frameworks and energy budgets. Activities combine evidence-based instructional design, short hypothesis–test–reflection cycles, and teacher–AI orchestration with retrieval-augmented knowledge to anchor recommendations. To strengthen inference, we sketch DAGs that make possible confounders and mediation pathways explicit, and we fix a pre-specified analysis plan (primary/secondary outcomes, expected moderators, metrics, and thresholds). Outputs are demonstrable learning and validated prototypes in living labs; impacts are observed on two planes: deep competencies (critical thinking, modeling, ethical judgment) and verifiable improvements in the bioregion (water quality, thermal comfort, energy efficiency, data governance with participation). The chain is made explicit as conditional propositions ("if the team does X with safeguards Y, then we expect Z"), with assumptions and risks noted in the margins, this avoids the illusion of simple causality and helps decide when to scale, pause, or abandon.

Measurement rigorously distinguishes leading from lagging. For processes, we track self-regulation, density and quality of argumentation, time to useful feedback, belonging, and well-being. For outcomes, we observe changes in environmental/urban indicators (turbidity/BOD, surface temperature, kWh saved), quality of decisions in novel situations, and transfer to different contexts. When randomization is not viable or would be unjust, we use quasi-experimental designs with baseline and comparison groups, realist evaluation and contribution analysis; we triangulate quantitative methods (parallel pre/post-tests, blind grading with inter-rater reliability, subgroup effects) with qualitative ones (interviews, observations, journals). Robustness is explored via multiverse analysis (reasonable analytic variants) and sensitivity to assumptions. We report effect sizes (d/g) with 95% CIs and model calibration; when pertinent, we estimate CATE (conditional average treatment effect) to identify heterogeneity and distributional risks. Reproducibility is not outsourced: computational notebooks, replication packages, and authorship manifests, with C2PA provenance, allow auditing versions of data, decisions, and code, and enable another cohort or an external reviewer to replicate results without rebuilding the history from scratch.

The differential equations case illustrates the assembly. In a ten-week course with five sections (≈108 students), the intervention anchored real phenomena, SIR epidemics, mixing and water contaminants, heat transfer, forced oscillations, and integrated simulation, scenario validation, and ethical reflection (article in press). AI functioned as a cognitive tutor with graduated hints and human verification; XR was reserved for high-risk practice; the regenerative portfolio required mathematical justifications, evidence-based decisions, and traceability of changes. Analyses showed significant improvements in conceptual understanding, modeling, and applied reasoning, with moderate–large effect sizes and normalized gains around $g \approx 0.48–0.50$; student perception was very positive, and oral defenses revealed transfer beyond the trained problem. Learning was not a spike in immediate accuracy but a gain in judgment: teams learned to explain why one method was preferable to another, to estimate uncertainty, and to declare validity limits, habits scarce in early engineering courses.

A second example involved second-semester engineering and business students tackling an authentic challenge proposed by Labopat (clinical diagnostics): design and model an EPS (polystyrene) cooler capable of maintaining +2 to +10 °C for five days, while in parallel formulating a prevention-oriented business model. Instructional design combined project-based learning and cooperative learning, with coordinated multidisciplinary blocks (each with its Canvas space), sub-competency assessment, direct observation, and team-based argumentative exams. The study adopted a quasi-experimental design to compare the interdisciplinary approach with a traditional course. Results report +9.5 pp in student participation (80.7% control vs. 90.2% experimental) and improvements in transversal competencies of +9.9% (engineering) and +5.8% (business), suggesting that early industry integration accelerates theory-to-practice transfer and strengthens interdisciplinary collaboration [22].

Methodologically, the theory of change was made explicit in if–then–because propositions; teams constructed an energy balance (conduction–convection–radiation), instrumented tests with data loggers, and defended decisions with sensitivity analyses and RAT (every recommendation anchored to sources). Teacher–AI orchestration used a Socratic tutor (questions), a reasoning verifier (logical leaps), and a regulatory curator (cold chain), without delivering final answers. Evaluation combined parallel pre/post, blind grading with inter-rater reliability, and a delayed post-test for retention and transfer; artifacts (drawings, tables, reports) carried provenance to trace authorship and versions.

The project incorporated energy budgets (computational cost of simulations), life cycle analysis (insulating material, refrigerant recovery, reverse logistics), and zero-waste goals in prototyping; local/small models and recyclable materials were prioritized, and kWh/gCO_2e were reported alongside thermal performance. Thus, from the earliest semesters, Education 6.0 weaves applied science, business, and environmental responsibility, cultivating the judgment needed to achieve the cold chain with less harm to people and planet.

A third vignette is set in online Differential Equations courses. Engineering teams turned the smartphone into a personal lab, accelerometer, gyroscope, microphone, and barometer via Physics Toolbox, and modeled ODEs (damped/forced mass–spring, physical pendulum, acoustic attenuation, pressure gradients) in MATLAB with parameter estimation and sensitivity analysis. Measurement combined parallel pre/post-tests, participation and performance, at-home replication to validate assumptions, and residual analysis; artifacts (scripts, figures, tables) carried provenance and were released as replication packages for external audit. AI played a bounded role (regulatory curation, graduated hints under RAT), while didactic data contracts and local compute minimized footprint and dependencies (BYOD, deferred synchronization). Impact was measured on two fronts: learning (significant increases in motivation, participation, understanding, and transfer) and operations (expanded access without specialized hardware, lower cost, and lower energy footprint by avoiding energy-intensive physical labs). Here the operative principle of Education 6.0 is clear: learn better with less harm, digitally and environmentally alike [23].

These experiences work because the data-and-energy economy becomes part of the method. Signals are not captured "just in case"; didactic data contracts are agreed with purpose, limited retention, and granular revocation rights. Analytics is explainable and contained; dashboards show not only alerts but local reasons for each signal and support routes that the instructor validates. Every course plans an energy budget: small, local models are preferred when the task allows; inferences are batched; the computational cost of intensive activities is reported. Sustainability is not a separate chapter; it is a didactic design criterion that leaves a trace in how we request, evaluate, and scale.

These experiences work because data and energy are part of the method. Before measuring, a didactic data contract is signed that answers four questions: what is captured, who uses it, how long it is kept, and for what purpose (with revocation and an equivalent low-tech route). Analytics is explainable: dashboards show local reasons, thresholds, and support actions; subgroup bias audits are also conducted. Each course operates with an energy budget: small/local models, batched inference, and edge compute are prioritized; kWh and gCO_2e of intensive activities are reported. Scaling depends on learning gain per footprint: if it does not improve, it is refactored or stopped. Thus, sustainability is not an annex: it guides how we request, evaluate, and scale.

Governance ties the pieces together. Syllabi make explicit permitted AI uses, citation criteria, limits for assessments, and appeal pathways; ethics committees with student and community voice are established; subgroup performance is audited to detect biases and inequities; an equivalent low-tech route is guaranteed for any practice requiring biological signal capture or constant connection. Transparency in critical decisions—for example, why a pilot was halted or why it was scaled to the whole school—is indispensable for legitimacy. The architecture also includes phase-graduation criteria: evidence and equity thresholds for moving from pilot to expansion, and kill criteria to pause or close initiatives that do not meet the standard (even if popular or flashy). Complementarily, model/data cards, algorithmic impact evaluations, and exit/portability plans are required to avoid technological lock-in.

No less important is learning from failure modes. Documentation of systematic errors, high-confidence hallucinations, automation bias in grading, model drift with local data, fatigue from poorly calibrated alerts, unintended risk shifting, feeds algorithmic error clinics where students develop a rare literacy: knowing when to distrust and how to fall back to manual procedures. This culture of pedagogical and technological safety turns novelty into prudent habit and prepares interruption protocols that prioritize low-risk routes.

The result of this architecture is not merely a set of modern courses, but an institution that thinks in public: it publishes replication packages, opens data (when ethically appropriate), signs deliverables with content credentials, accounts for its footprint, and evaluates its success not by the number of licenses or dashboards but by the quality of judgment it cultivates and by verifiable impact in its bioregion. Education 6.0 stabilizes when actors can precisely describe what problem they are solving, what evidence supports them, what trade-offs they accepted, what they learned from what did not work, and how they safeguarded people and planet in the process. With that standard, the transition from horizon to practice ceases to be a promise and becomes a shared discipline.

When theory of change, measurement, the data-energy economy, and governance become routine, Education 6.0 stops being a promise and becomes institutional capability. Operating this way implies a simple, demanding pact: we only scale what demonstrates learning and equity, and we only sustain what reduces footprint and harm. Everything else is paused, corrected, or archived with transparency. This architecture does not aim to dazzle, but to provide public reasons: what problem we addressed, with what evidence, at what cost, for whom it worked, and what we would do differently next time. By also documenting failure modes and keeping low-tech routes and exit plans open, the university recognizes itself as a living system that perceives, models, and acts with evidence and care. That is the standard that legitimizes innovation before students, faculty, and community, and the threshold that allows us to move from pilot to public good: learn better, with less harm, and be accountable for it.

9.5 RESPONSIBLE IMPLEMENTATION: GOVERNANCE, EQUITY, AND A PHASED PATH

Rolling out Education 6.0 is neither a software sprint nor a cosmetic reform; it is a sustained institutional practice that combines public ethics, instructional engineering, and care for people. Responsible implementation requires three foundational decisions: precisely naming which problem we are solving and for whom; agreeing on how we will know it works without causing harm; and declaring in advance when we will stop or redesign, even if the solution is popular. Everything else, technology, contracts, metrics, follows from there. To harden this logic, each initiative begins with a premortem (foreseeable risks and mitigations), defines its harm surface (privacy, attention, footprint, equity), and records success and exit criteria that any actor can audit.

Governance begins in the syllabus, not in the licensing contract. Every course should make explicit policies for AI and analytics use, citation and traceability criteria, limits for evaluative activities, appeal pathways, low-tech alternatives, and data retention times. That micro-pact anchors to institutional frameworks: ethics committees with student and community voice; revocable informed-consent protocols; algorithmic subgroup audits to detect bias and unintended effects; and a lean data economy that applies minimization, specific purpose, and automatic expiry. An innovation is legitimate only if it can be explained in plain language and if it anticipates equivalent routes without biological signal capture and without dependence on continuous connectivity.

Relationships with vendors and internal developments require a cultural shift. We do not buy black boxes; we contract for transparency. We request model and data cards, clear training and retention policies, energy and footprint reports, evidence of subgroup evaluations, an exit and portability plan (export to open formats), and compliance with interoperability standards (LTI, xAPI, IMS/1EdTech). Any tutor or analytics panel that cannot explain locally why it suggests something, or that disallows audit and change traceability, is not fit for education. In parallel, we create an inventory of legacy systems and a responsible decommissioning plan: fewer tools but better integrated, with living contracts that reward pedagogical performance and security practices, not merely technical uptime.

Security is pedagogical: we threat-model learning activities, not only servers. We rehearse prompt injection, didactic red-teaming, rubric overfitting, leakage by correlation, and alert fatigue. We document failure modes and activate interruption protocols: when ethical or technical doubt arises, automation is halted, a low-tech route is used, and students are informed about what happened and why. We also maintain incident logs and review them in open forums with improvement actions and assigned owners. Transparency builds trust more than any slogan.

Equity is a validity requirement, not an appendix. Before scaling, we simulate subgroup impacts; we set explicit thresholds (no intervention is released if baseline suggests net harm to any group, even if the average improves); and we activate compensatory measures: device lending and maintenance, connectivity spaces, offline-first design, materials in multiple formats, and academic/economic recognition for community co-authorships [24, 25]. The so-called 6.0 divide is not merely lack of devices; it is unequal time, energy, mental health, and support networks. Hence workload policy and the academic calendar are part of the reform: scheduled rest windows, less unproductive bureaucracy, course releases or protected time for those leading redesigns, and funded professional development via faculty micro-credentials aligned to the model (AI-assisted instructional design, authentic assessment, data ethics, Green AI).

Energy is constitutive. Each course works with an energy budget per credit/week and reports the computational cost of intensive activities. We favor small, edge models where the task allows, batch inferences, and modulate analysis frequencies. Students learn to optimize prompts, batching, and pipelines: sustainability becomes technical literacy. For scaling decisions, we use a practical indicator: learning gain per unit footprint (kWh or gCO_2e per 0.1σ improvement); if the ratio is poor, we redesign or stop.

A phased path avoids technosolutionism and pilotitis. In the pilot phase, we work with two or three courses of high potential and low risk, with a clear baseline, parallel pre/post instruments, process metrics (time to useful feedback, self-regulation, collaboration density) and impact metrics (an environmental/urban/organizational indicator agreed with the community). The output includes a didactic replication package (plans, rubrics, feedback examples, AI scripts with RAT anchors, assumptions and limits), plus an energy report and a failure-mode registry. The decision to move to expansion uses public criteria: minimum improvement threshold, no subgroup harms, ethical and logistical acceptability, and energy viability. If unmet, we stop without blame: failing with dignity is also innovation.

Expansion consolidates infrastructure and practice: standardizes consent and provenance, creates evidence repositories, offers workshops and peer mentoring, and establishes cross-cutting communities of practice. The learning engineer/instructional designer role is professionalized (stable, not volunteer). We negotiate framework contracts with sandboxes and no-penalty exit clauses. We integrate evidence dashboards with two layers: a public one (impacts and processes in plain language) and one for research and continuous improvement (with anonymized or synthetic data, as appropriate). External evaluation, academic peers and community representatives, accompanies the phase with rapid reviews and course-level recommendations. We also monitor fidelity of implementation to distinguish design failure from execution failure.

Institutionalization is less glamorous and more decisive: it makes good practices boringly normal. Elements become standard: all syllabi include AI and data policies; oral defenses with traceability are routine; analytics are explainable by design; data contracts are legible and revocable; subgroup audits are scheduled into the academic cycle; energy budgets are integrated into course costing; kill criteria are written and applied when warranted; and achievements are recognized in career progression and incentives, not only in press releases. A mature Education 6.0 university does not look futuristic; it looks trustworthy.

None of this works without honest communication. Instead of selling promises and hiding costs, we communicate uncertainties, assumptions, and trade-offs; we explain why a technology was chosen or discarded; we acknowledge what we learned from what did not work. That tone builds a culture of care and critical thinking, turning students, families, and partners into informed, and demanding, allies. Public transparency also fuels research and transfer: what is learned in one classroom improves the next.

A delicate point remains: mental rights when considering neurotechnologies. The rule is simple and strict: voluntary participation without penalty; operational separation between clinical and pedagogical protocols; reinforced cybersecurity with independent evaluation; scope limited to aggregated, non-clinical measures; and equivalent pedagogical routes without biological capture [26]. Public deliberation is also required regarding acceptable uses, storage and destruction periods, and governance that includes those most affected, children and adolescents, whose power asymmetry is greater. Teaching neurorights is not an ethical appendix: it is core content of algorithmic citizenship.

To sustain change over time, incentives must update. We recognize community co-authorship, design time, and rigorous evaluation; we reward evidence quality and verifiable improvements over the number of tools adopted; and we value care practices, reduced overload, emotional-support structures, as conditions for deep learning. Innovation that burns its people is not innovation; it is extraction.

The operational close is simple to state and hard to uphold: each technological decision must improve learning and reduce harm, less harm to privacy, attention, the planet, and dignity. If such improvement cannot be shown with evidence, and such reduction with metrics, it is postponed or abandoned. With that bar, Education 6.0 becomes credible: an everyday public policy anyone can audit. The university then stops chasing fashions and embraces its most demanding vocation: think in public, be accountable, and cultivate the judgment capable of designing preferable futures while repairing, prudently and rigorously, the world we share.

Figure 9.1 synthesizes the operational architecture of Education 6.0, articulating its core pedagogical, technological, ethical, and governance components and their interdependencies.

A schematic representation integrating the four foundational pillars of Education 6.0: (1) theory of change, which links pedagogical actions to measurable learning outcomes; (2) measurement system, which ensures validity through pre/post designs, inter-rater reliability, and retention indicators; (3) data-and-energy economy, emphasizing didactic data contracts and course-level energy budgets; and (4) governance and ethical safeguards, which guarantee explainability, equity, and transparency.

Together, these components form a self-auditable and regenerative educational ecosystem that aligns technological innovation with human and planetary well-being.

9.6 CONCLUSION

Education 6.0 is an auditable public discipline: we scale only what demonstrates learning and equity, and we sustain only what reduces footprint and harm. The novelty is not the devices but the ethics and evidence of their use: legible, revocable data contracts, explicit energy budgets, instructional safeguards, verifiable provenance, and impact evaluation with subgroup analyses. The rule is simple and demanding: learn better with less harm—to privacy, attention, the planet, and dignity, and be able to demonstrate it with evidence.

The invitation is operational and starts tomorrow: rewrite the syllabus with AI and data policies in plain language; agree to a four-question didactic data contract (what, for what purpose, for how long, and with what right of revocation); set an energy budget per activity; require RAT in every AI-generated explanation; define exit criteria to stop what does not work or that harms a group. If each course tells an auditable story of decisions and each credential verifies competence with purpose, we will stop chasing fashions to build public trust: a university that accounts for its actions, cares for its people, and cultivates the judgment capable of designing preferable futures while repairing, prudently and rigorously, the world we share.

REFERENCES

[1] Toktas, E. (2025). Future scenarios of digital humanities and post-humanist education. *Journal of Foresight and Health Governance*, 2(1), 21–31.

[2] Newell, A. F. (2011). *Design and the Digital Divide: Insights from 40 Years in Computer Support for Older and Disabled People*. Morgan & Claypool Publishers.

[3] Lin, M. J. (2020). The social and genetic inheritance of educational attainment: Genes, parental education, and educational expansion. *Social Science Research*, 86, 102387.

[4] Kotzee, B. (2017). Education and epistemic injustice. In *The Routledge Handbook of Epistemic Injustice* (pp. 324–335). Routledge.

[5] Moleka, P. (2023). Exploring the role of artificial intelligence in education 6.0: Enhancing personalized learning and adaptive pedagogy.

[6] Moleka, P. (2025). Education 6.0: Advancing the frontiers of learning in the digital era.

[7] Kiiskilä, P., Kukkonen, A., & Pirkkalainen, H. (2023). Are micro-credentials valuable for students? Perspective on verifiable digital credentials. *SN Computer Science*, 4(4), 366.

[8] Johnson, R. S., Mims-Cox, J. S., & Doyle-Nichols, A. (2009). *Developing Portfolios in Education: A Guide to Reflection, Inquiry, and Assessment*. Sage.

[9] Privitera, A. J., & Du, H. (2022). Educational neurotechnology: Where do we go from here? *Trends in Neuroscience and Education*, 29, 100195.

[10] Shahidi Hamedani, S., Aslam, S., Mundher Oraibi, B. A., Wah, Y. B., & Shahidi Hamedani, S. (2024). Transitioning towards tomorrow's workforce: Education 5.0 in the landscape of society 5.0: A systematic literature review. *Education Sciences*, 14(10), 1041.

[11] Lantada, A. D. (2020). Engineering education 5.0: Continuously evolving engineering education. *International Journal of Engineering Education*, 36(6), 1814–1832.

[12] Félix-Herrán, L. C., Rendon-Nava, A. E., & Nieto Jalil, J. M. (2019). Challenge-based learning: An I-semester for experiential learning in Mechatronics Engineering. *International Journal on Interactive Design and Manufacturing (IJIDeM)*, 13(4), 1367–1383.

[13] Nieto-Jalil, J. M., Seuret-Jiménez, D., Gutiérrez-Cruz, I., Tec-Chim, A. I., & Kinto-Ramírez, H. (2023, May). Challenge-based learning applied to engineering modelling classes using dynamic systems. In *2023 IEEE Global Engineering Education Conference (EDUCON)* (pp. 1–7). IEEE.

[14] Nieto-Jalil, J. M., Chim, A. I. T., Seuret-Jimenez, D., & Huerta, J. M. M. (2025, March). The impact of GPT, experiential learning, and reinforcement methods on complex problem solving. In *2025 IEEE Engineering Education World Conference (EDUNINE)* (pp. 1–6). IEEE.

[15] Dimitriadou, E., & Lanitis, A. (2023). A critical evaluation, challenges, and future perspectives of using artificial intelligence and emerging technologies in smart classrooms. *Smart Learning Environments*, 10(1), 12.

[16] Menezes, C., França, B., & Lopes, Y. (2024). A survey on extended reality, digital twins, and metaverse applications in power systems. *IEEE Internet of Things Journal*.

[17] Jalil, J. M. N., Bazua, A. C., Herrán, L. C. F., Castillo, F. I. G., Katase, D. O., & Valenzuela, O. A. G. (2022, March). The virtual reality as a flexible resource to improve engineering education. In *2022 IEEE Global Engineering Education Conference (EDUCON)* (pp. 579–585). IEEE.

[18] Privitera, A. J., & Du, H. (2022). Educational neurotechnology: Where do we go from here? *Trends in Neuroscience and Education*, 29, 100195.

[19] Damus, O. (2024). Regenerative and restorative pedagogy: The foundation of a new contract for cognitive justice. *Prospects*, 54(2), 441–449.

[20] Yates, A., Pedersen Zari, M., Bloomfield, S., Burgess, A., Walker, C., Waghorn, K., . . . & Palmer, F. (2022). A transformative architectural pedagogy and tool for a time of converging crises. *Urban Science*, 7(1), 1.

[21] Morris, R., Perry, T., & Wardle, L. (2021). Formative assessment and feedback for learning in higher education: A systematic review. *Review of Education*, 9(3), e3292.

[22] Nieto-Jalil, J. M., Jimenez, D. S., Serrano, Y. M., Romero, M. A. P., Moranchel, N. A., Mena, C. H., . . . & Cruz, I. G. (2024, May). From theory to practice: Enhancing competencies in an interdisciplinary collaborative approach between Business and Engineering. In *2024 IEEE Global Engineering Education Conference (EDUCON)* (pp. 1–7). IEEE.

[23] Chim, A. I. T., Nieto-Jalil, J. M., Huerta, J. M. M., & Crúz, I. G. (2025, January). Breaking barriers: Smartphone sensors, mobile technology in online teaching of differential equations. In *2025 Institute for the Future of Education Conference (IFE)* (pp. 1–7). IEEE.

[24] Alam, A., & Mohanty, A. (2023). Cultural beliefs and equity in educational institutions: Exploring the social and philosophical notions of ability groupings in teaching and learning of mathematics. *International Journal of Adolescence and Youth*, 28(1), 2270662.

[25] Pittman, J., Severino, L., DeCarlo-Tecce, M. J., & Kiosoglous, C. (2021). An action research case study: Digital equity and educational inclusion during an emergent COVID-19 divide. *Journal for Multicultural Education*, 15(1), 68–84.

[26] Alipoor, J., & Pourrashidi, H. (2025). A critical study on the researches about the application of neurotechnology in education. *International Journal of Neuroscience*, 135(4), 496–503.

10 Measuring Educational Initiatives Through Student Engagement

A Data-Driven Evaluation Framework in Engineering Education

Aldo A. Cortes, Jenaro Nosedal-Sanchez, and Camilo Lozoya

10.1 INTRODUCTION

10.1.1 Context of Engineering Education

In recent years, engineering education has undergone a profound transformation, driven by advances in digital technologies, society demands and the global push for sustainability. These changes have led to a shift towards a more student-centered model, emphasizing active learning approaches that prioritize hands-on situations, real-world problem-solving, and collaborative work environments [1]. Traditional pedagogies, based solely on content delivery, are being conceived by new generations as disengaging or outdated. As a result, the educator's role is evolving to give students the opportunity to play a leading role in constructing their own knowledge.

Some of the most well-known approaches to new education are project-based learning (PjBL), problem-based learning (PBL), and other situational approach methods which can be seen extensively implemented in engineering programs across the globe. These models not only foster technical competences and soft skills but also promote higher levels of student engagement, creativity, and collaboration among peers [2]. Although across academic institutions, these innovations are encouraged, most educators still lack consistent evidence-based methods to evaluate the true impact of these strategies.

Recent research highlights that passive forms of instruction are insufficient in today's technology-filled world, especially in science education. Students' engagement should be placed at the center of curricular design, emphasizing the importance of participation, reflection, and practice over memorization or isolated knowledge. Only students who are truly engaged in their studies, those who can be challenged to

DOI: 10.1201/9781003678250-10

solve problems critically, communicate effectively, and apply their knowledge to real situations, are more likely to achieve long-term academic and professional growth [3].

In this context, gamification has emerged as popular complementary strategy to support active learning. There are systematic reviews that demonstrated its potential to positively influence emotional and cognitive engagement, especially when applied aligned to learning objectives. Gamified experiences not only increase motivation but also support the development of persistence and problem-solving skills in engineering contexts [4].

Together, these examples of new ways of education illustrate a common goal: to foster meaningful, lasting engagement in students by transforming how technical disciplines are taught. Yet despite the diversity of innovative practices, what is often missing is a clear way to measure the true impact of these innovations, especially from the perspective of the student. This gap highlights the need for structured, replicable evaluation methods that connect student engagement with the actual effectiveness of educational innovations.

10.1.2 The Need for Tools to Evaluate Educational Innovation

Despite the growing investment in educational innovation across education programs, most institutions continue to rely on traditional assessment metrics, such as final grades. While these indicators offer standardized measures of performance, they often fail to capture deeper dimensions of learning, such as student motivation, emotional involvement, or sustained engagement. As previous studies have shown, students may succeed academically without being genuinely engaged, and disaffection may remain hidden behind good grades [5, 6]. This gap underscores the need for validated instruments capable of reflecting how students truly experience the learning process. One such tool is the Utrecht Work Engagement Scale for students (UWES-9S), which measures vigor, dedication, and absorption and has been successfully applied worldwide. This chapter builds on these foundations to explore engagement as a meaningful way to evaluate educational innovations in engineering education and its impact on students' motivation.

10.1.3 Objectives and Scope of This Chapter

This chapter explores how student engagement can offer a deeper and more meaningful way to evaluate educational innovations, especially in engineering education. While grades and completion rates are still commonly used, they often overlook how students feel and respond to what they are learning. Engagement-based evaluation brings attention to aspects like motivation, focus, and emotional involvement; factors that can greatly influence the learning process.

The chapter presents three educational experiences implement in a Mechatronics Engineering program in Mexico during 2003–2004:

1. A full semester class of robotics-based learning environments using gamification and Edu tools to increase interest in STEM education.

2. A one-week intensive design challenge (Hackathon), to boost engineering abilities and foster a sense of community among students.
3. A one-time educational innovation intervention designed to search for strengthen abilities on an engineering curriculum.

Unlike previous studies reported in the literature, this chapter not only collects engagement data using UWES-9S survey but also compares these results with students' academic performance to explore possible correlations between engagement levels and final grades.

Finally, this chapter aims to provide practical guidance for educators interested in evaluating the real impact of their teaching strategies. By using student engagement as a tool for analysis, teachers can obtain insight into which innovations connect with students and promote deeper learning. The proposed framework seeks to support more informed decision-making, helping educators direct their efforts where they can have the greatest effect, both in terms of academic performance and the overall student experience.

As described in Figure 10.1 a conceptual flowchart illustrates the evaluation of impact on educational innovations. The process begins with the implementation of an innovation, followed by an assessment of its impact on student engagement across three experimental cases (A, B, C). Data is collected through UWES-9S, cluster statistical analysis and qualitative feedback, leading to a comparative analysis.

10.2 THEORETICAL BACKGROUND

10.2.1 Defining Student Engagement

Originally framed in occupational health psychology, engagement was introduced as a response to the dominant focus on negative outcomes of work in the early 2000s.

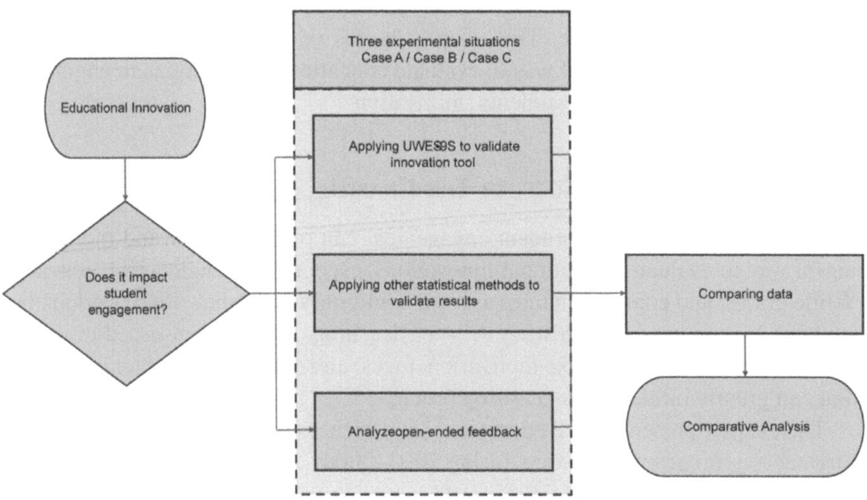

FIGURE 10.1 Framework for evaluating educational innovations through student engagement and complementary data.

At that time, most research examined diseases, injuries, and burnout, while very few studies explored positive states such as motivation or satisfaction. Engagement was thus defined as the positive counterpart to burnout: while individuals experiencing burnout report exhaustion, detachment, and cynicism, those with high engagement feel energized and enthusiastic about their activities [7].

According to Schaufeli et al. (2002), engagement is a positive, fulfilling state of mind characterized by three dimensions: vigor, dedication, and absorption. It is not an elusive emotion but a more enduring affective-cognitive state that reflects a person's sustained connection to their activities [8]. These three-factor structure was empirically validated through a factor analysis in samples of both students and employees, reinforcing its robustness across contexts [9]. These dimensions are summarized in Table 10.1

To measure engagement, Schaufeli and collaborators developed the Utrecht Work Engagement Scale (UWES), a psychometric instrument originally consisting of 17 items and later refined to a shorter (UWES-9) for practical application [7]. A student-specific version (UWES-9S) retained the same three dimensions but adapted items to the academic environment. The instrument has been validated in multiple countries, providing reliable data on how students connect with new educational experiences.

Understanding engagement as an evaluation tool allows educators to move beyond intuition or end-of-semester surveys. It enables the early detection of motivational difficulties, supports targeted strategies tailored to students' needs, and fosters student-centered curriculum design. In this sense, engagement becomes a powerful tool for enhancing the effectiveness of educational innovations.

10.2.2 Related Work in Engineering

Recent research in engineering education has increasingly adopted the UWES-9S to evaluate the impact of innovative teaching strategies. Studies in Latin America have confirmed its factorial validity in this region, [10] reinforcing its applicability to local student populations. Similarly, studies in 2022 showed that gamification raised motivation and engagement among engineering students, even when academic

TABLE 10.1
Definitions of Vigor, Dedication, and Absorption

Dimension	Definition
Vigor	High levels of energy and persistence while studying, even when facing difficulties.
Dedication	A strong sense of involvement, feeling inspired, enthusiastic, proud, and challenged by academic tasks.
Absorption	Deep concentration and immersion in study activities, often losing track of time.

(adapted from Schaufeli et al., 2002).

performance remained unchanged, underscoring the need to complement grades with engagement measures [11].

Other international studies converge on this idea: in Greece on 2020 reported that online response systems (Kahoot, Mentimeter) improved engagement through active participation [12]; same year in Australia, studies demonstrated that continuous measurement of engagement using UWES yielded richer insights than grades alone [13]; Italy, 2024 linked resilience and psychological well-being with vigor and dedication [14]; and in Peru, Domínguez-Lara et al. (2020) found that engagement correlated with satisfaction and perceived success [15]. Together, these works highlight UWES-9S as a reliable instrument to capture dimensions of learning often invisible in traditional evaluation.

Beyond survey-based measures, earlier research illustrates how innovations in education such as technological integration can reinforce engagement in engineering education. One example is the use of Cyber-Physical Labs (CPLs) as cost-effective environments that bring industrial ambiances to the classroom showed that the use of new technologies enhanced student motivation and performance, with more than 80% of participants reporting that emulations significantly supported learning [16].

10.3 METHODOLOGY

10.3.1 Instrument Selection and Evaluation Protocol

The main instrument used to assess student engagement in this study was the Utrecht Work Engagement Scale for Students (UWES-9S) [7], previously described in Section 10.2. This survey evaluates engagement across three dimensions: vigor, dedication, and absorption, and has been validated internationally, including in Latin American contexts.

The UWES-9S survey was applied on a 0–6 Likert scale. The Spanish version was used without modification in our classes, ensuring comparability with prior Latin American studies and preserving the instrument's reliability. Before each application, students were reminded to answer with reference only to the course where their educational innovation will be held ensuring contextual accuracy. In some cases, the UWES-9S was complemented by an optional open-ended question, allowing students to share qualitative feedback on the innovation. These responses provided additional context to the numerical data and supported interpretation of student perceptions beyond quantitative results.

10.3.2 Description of the Educational Intervention

Three different interventions were analyzed to explore how educational innovations influenced student engagement. In each case, the UWES-9S survey was administered before and after the activity to capture changes in vigor, dedication, and absorption. The interventions differed in duration, number of participants, and date of application. All experiences were carried out at the undergraduate level in the Mechatronics Engineering program at Tecnológico de Monterrey University, Chihuahua, Mexico.

10.3.2.1 Full Semester Course: Gamifying the Classroom

This first intervention was conducted from August to November 2023 with a total of 18 students (7 women, 11 men). The aim was to foster student motivation into STEM and mechatronics topics by integrating gamified strategies and digital tools into the curriculum. The course included elements such as leaderboards, missions, and digital badges to enhance motivation and sustain active participation. Engagement was measured five times: once at the beginning and after each gamified intervention. The pedagogical goal was to foster sustained engagement by embedding game mechanics and digital tools into the learning environment. This experience is detailed in the publication *Gamifying the classroom: Bringing video games to life through innovation in education to increase student engagement in STEM subjects* [17].

10.3.2.2 One-Week Experience: Mechatronics Hackathon

The second intervention took place during a one-week intensive hackathon held from 6–10 May 2024 as part of a disciplinary *TEC Week*, an institutional initiative, at *Tecnológico de Monterrey*, in which students engage in elective activities to strengthen soft or hard skills. For this edition, the Mechatronics Department organized a disciplinary week focused on "Mechatronics in the food industry," supported by female leaders form the local food sector. A total of 44 Mechatronics students (9 women, 35 men) participated in the challenge, which encouraged them to develop technological solutions for real-world problems related to the food industry. Engagement was measured at the beginning and at the end of the event using UWES-9S. The pedagogical goal was to develop both technical skills and soft skills, such as resilience, teamwork, and self-learning, within a compressed time frame.

10.3.2.3 Educational Tool: Physical-Digital Robotic System

The third case involved the integration of a didactic SCARA robotic arm as a learning tool within a robotics course. Rather than being a standalone intervention, the activity was embedded in regular class sessions to support the understanding of specific concepts. A total of 16 students (2 women, 14 men) engaged first in simulation activities using MATLAB and then transferred their solutions to the physical robot. The pedagogical goal was to strengthen the comprehension of abstract mathematical concepts through direct interaction with hybrid physical-digital systems. Engagement was measured before and after the activity using UWES-9S. This intervention is described in detail in the paper "*Impact of Using Physical-Digital Systems in STEM Education: A Case Study with a Didactic Robot*" presented at IFE Conference 2025 [18].

As comparative analysis, Table 10.2 provides a summary of the three educational interventions, including their duration, number of participants, and pedagogical objectives.

10.3.3 Data Sources and Analysis Approach

In addition to the UWES-9S results, the study incorporated complementary data such as students' final grades, institutional perception surveys, and optional open-ended comments. These data points enabled comparisons between engagement scores, academic performance, and subjective perceptions.

TABLE 10.2
Comparative Description of the Three Educational Interventions

ID	Name of Intervention	When Applied	Participants Undergraduates (aged 18–23)	Objective of the Intervention
A	Full Semester Course: Gamifying the Classroom	August–November 2023	18 students (7 women, 11 men)	To foster motivation in STEM and mechatronics through gamified strategies and digital tools.
B	One-Week Experience: Mechatronics Hackathon	6–10 May 2024	44 students (9 women, 35 men)	To boost engineering abilities and soft skills (resilience, teamwork, self-learning) by addressing real-world problems in the food industry.
C	Physical-Digital Robotic System Implementation	May 2024	16 students (2 women, 14 men)	To deepen understanding of abstract mathematical concepts by applying simulations and transferring solutions to a physical robotic arm.

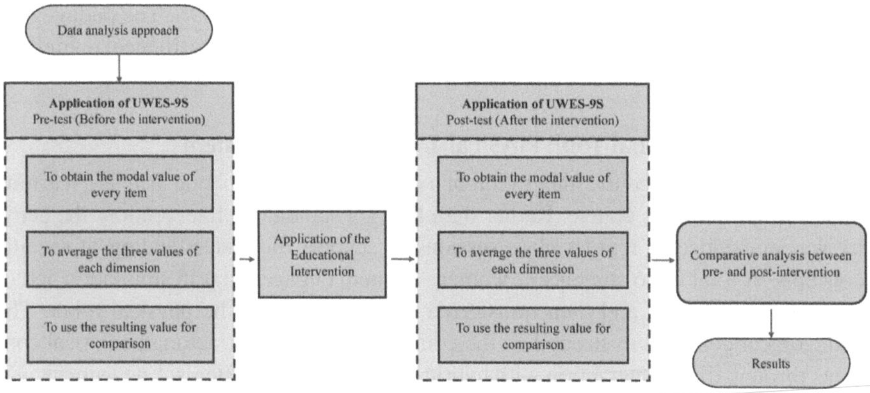

FIGURE 10.2 Data analysis procedure for UWES-9S results.

For the first stage of analysis, the UWES-9S data was processed in several steps. For each case, the modal value of every item was calculated, and then the three values corresponding to each dimension (vigor, dedication, and absorption) were averaged, following the instrument's official guidelines [7]. These values were used to compare pre- and post-intervention results in each case. To verify robustness, additional descriptive statistics (standard deviation and standard error) were also examined to identify patterns or discrepancies. Pre- and post-intervention results were then contrasted across the three case studies to assess growth as illustrated in Figure 10.2, which outlines the data analysis procedure for UWES-9S results.

After this test, hierarchical cluster analysis was applied to group students according to similarities in their engagement profiles, allowing us to observe how individuals with low, medium, or high initial engagement migrated across clusters after each intervention. This spatial analysis, represented in three dimensional figures, provided insights into how interventions influenced not only average scores but also subgroup dynamics.

Finally, the qualitative comments collected through the open-ended questions were analyzed thematically and categorized into positive perceptions, challenges, or instructor-related aspects. These qualitative findings were integrated with quantitative results to enrich the interpretation of engagement outcomes.

10.4 CASE STUDIES AND RESULTS

10.4.1 Case Study: Full Semester Course: Gamifying the Classroom

10.4.1.1 UWES-9S Results by Dimension

As the longest of the three interventions, this case provides the most comprehensive information. Engagement was assessed at five points during the semester: once at the beginning and after each new gamified intervention. Results shown in Table 10.3 along with their corresponding statistical values illustrate how engagement values gain an upward trend across all three dimensions over time.

Vigor increased from a moderate level (M = 2.67) at the start to a moderately high level (M = 4.67) at the end, reflecting greater energy and persistence in completing their activities and assignments. **Dedication**, which began at a high level (M = 5.67), slightly decreased after the initial novelty effect but stabilized at consistently high values (M = 5.00–5.67). **Absorption** showed the most remarkable change, rising from a very low level (M = 1.00) at the beginning to a high level (M = 5.00) by the end of the course, indicating that students felt increasingly immersed in their learning. For extra clarification, the distribution of scores across the five measurement points is summarized in Figure 10.3. Using the categorization rages provided in the UWES-9S manual [7] (Table 10.4), the study was able to interpret and compare engagement scores obtained.

TABLE 10.3
Descriptive Statistics for Vigor, Dedication, and Absorption across Five Measurement Points

	Vigor			Dedication			Absorption		
Date	M	St Dv	St E	M	St Dv	St E	M	St Dv	St E
07-ago	2.67	2.31	0.54	4.67	0.58	0.14	1.00	1.73	0.41
16-ago	4.00	0.00	0.00	4.67	0.58	0.14	4.67	0.58	0.14
06-sep	3.67	0.58	0.14	4.67	0.58	0.14	4.33	1.15	0.27
04-oct	4.67	0.58	0.14	5.00	0.00	0.00	5.00	0.00	0.00
03-nov	4.67	0.58	0.14	5.67	0.58	0.14	5.00	0.00	0.00

(means, standard deviations, and standard errors).

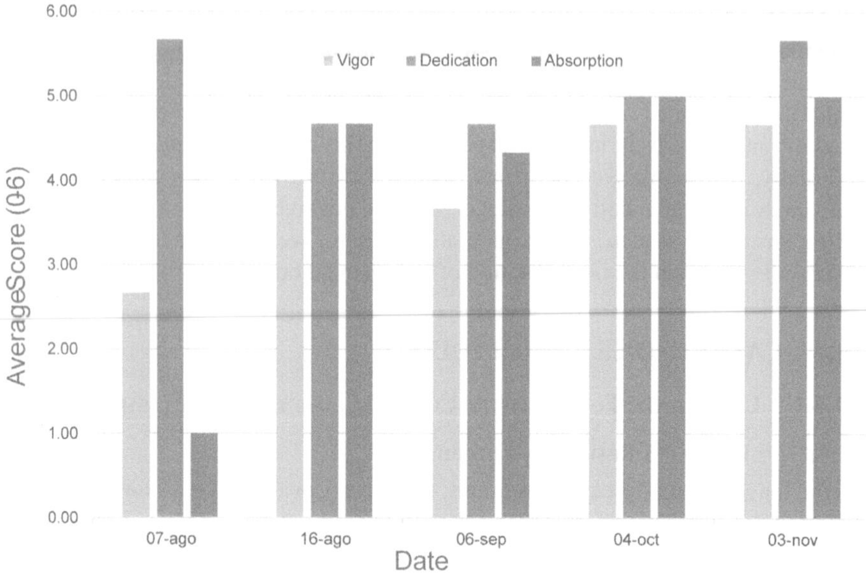

FIGURE 10.3 Evolution of vigor, dedication, and absorption.
(Semester-Long Course)

TABLE 10.4
Categorization of Vigor, Dedication, and Absorption Values According to the UWES-9S Manual

	Reference Values Table		
	Vigor	**Dedication**	**Absorption**
Very low	≤ 2.0	≤ 1.33	≤ 1.77
Low	2.01–3.25	1.34–2.90	1.18–2.33
Average	3.26–4.80	2.91–4.70	2.34–4.2
High	4.81–5.65	4.71–5.69	4.21–5.33
Very high	≥5.66	≥5.70	≥5.34

(very low to very high).

10.4.1.2 Perception of the Course and Teacher Observations

Overall, student perception of the gamified course was highly positive when compared with other college courses. Final grades were strong, with most students scored between 94 and 98 out of 100, with only five cases falling outside this range. Institutional surveys reflected high satisfaction: on a 1–10 scale the average rating for "Would you recommend this professor?" was 9.33, and for "Recommendation based on the pedagogy" it reached 9.66. The few open-ended comments highlighted the professor's patience and the enjoyable nature of the class. From the instructor's perspective, gamification transformed the classroom dynamics, increasing student persistence and collaboration during competitive activities (Socrative or Kahoot). However, it also required substantial preparation time to align game scenarios with academic content. A key challenge was ensuring that the playful elements supported rather than overshadowed education, since some students risked perceiving learning as "just a game."

10.4.2 Case Study: One-Week Experience: Mechatronics Hackathon

10.4.2.1 UWES-9S Results by Dimension

Engagement was also assessed pre- and post-hackathon. Results showed a substantial increase across all three dimensions. Vigor rose from a high (M = 4.33) to very high (M = 6.00). Dedication, already high at the beginning (M = 5.67), reached the maximum score (M = 6.00) after the event. Absorption also showed a significant increase, from high (M = 4.67) to very high (M = 6.00). These findings suggest that the hackathon format, with its intensive workload and collaborative dynamic, fostered immediate and strong engagement among students. Figure 10.4 illustrates these changes, showing the comparative pre and post test results across engagement's three dimensions.

10.4.2.2 Perception of the Course and Teacher Observations

Student perception of the hackathon was very positive. Although final grades were only pass/fail, all participants successfully completed the event. The institutional

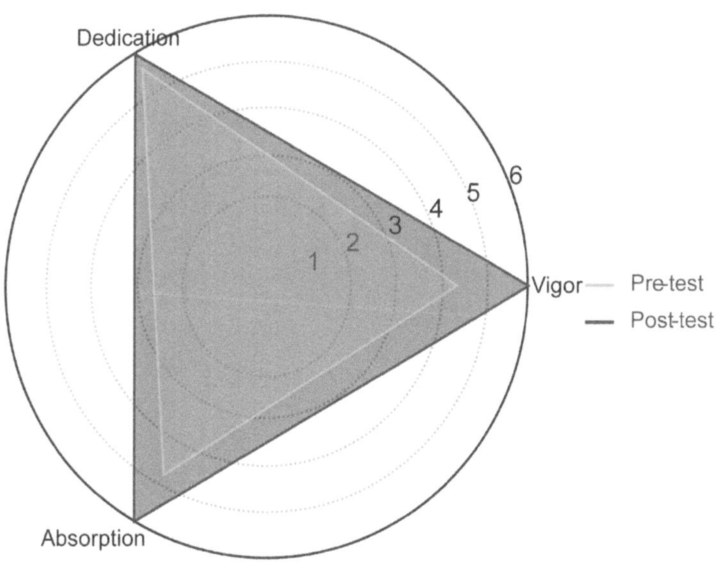

FIGURE 10.4 Hackathon—pre vs post.

(Radar Chart)

survey showed high satisfaction, with an average recommendation score of 9.73/10. In the open-ended questions following the UWES-9S, 39 responses highlighted collaboration with peers, the challenge of working under time constraints, and the acquisition of new skills as the most valuable aspects. Students especially valued designing prototypes that connected mechatronic systems with real-world applications. From the instructor's perspective, the hackathon provided an engaging space for resilience and teamwork, allowing students to step outside their regular coursework. However, its compressed duration limited opportunities for sustained impact, and further data would be needed to assess long-term influence on engagement.

10.4.3 Case Study: Physical-Digital Robotic System

10.4.3.1 UWES-9S Results by Dimension

Engagement was measured before and after the single-day intervention using the UWES-9S. Results showed a moderate improvement across all three dimensions. Vigor increased slightly from an average level (M = 3.67) to a higher but still moderate level (M = 4.00). Dedication rose from high (M = 5.33) to very high (M = 5.67). Absorption showed the most substantial change, moving from average (M = 3.67) to high (M = 5.67). These results suggest that the use of a physical-digital system that can show the theoretical results applied into a physical robotic arm can generate a boost in student engagement, particularly in terms of immersion. Figure 10.5 illustrates these findings, comparing the pre and post-test values across engagement's three dimensions.

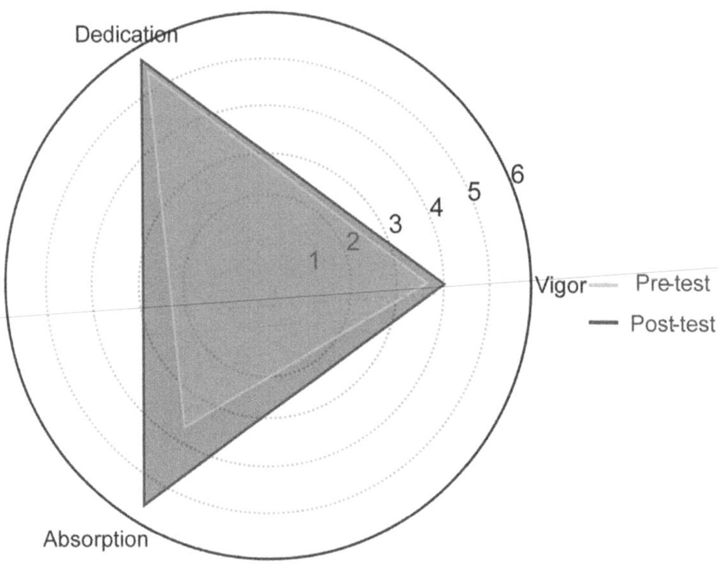

FIGURE 10.5 Physical-digital robotic system—pre Vs post.
(Radar Chart)

10.4.3.2 Perception of the Course and Teacher Observations

The physical-digital robotics activity also received very high scores in institutional surveys: 9.86/10 for overall satisfaction and 9.93/10 for pedagogy. Although open comments were limited, students emphasized the instructor's teaching quality and the relevance of the activity; both factors were reinforced by students' perception using an educational innovation. Final grades averaged above 95/100, reinforcing the alignment between engagement and performance. From the teacher's perspective, the use of a physical robot effectively closed the gap between abstract math concepts with real-world problems, offering students an "eye-opening" experience. The activity allowed sufficient time for reflection and problem-solving, creating a balanced combination of novelty and depth that fostered immersion without overwhelming the course structure.

10.4.4 Comparative Analysis of Engagement Results

To enable cross case comparison, the UWES-9S results are presented in Table 10.5 which reports initial and final values for vigor, dedication, and absorption, as well as observed growth and categorical shifts (values were obtained by calculating the mode of each item and averaging the three modal values per dimension).

Identification of Patterns

- **The hackathon (Case B)** achieved the highest overall engagement values, with all dimensions reaching very high levels. Growth was smaller than in other interventions, but this was due to high starting points rather than lack of impact.
- **The semester long gamified course (Case A)** showed the most dramatic improvements, especially in absorption (+4.00, from very low to high). Vigor also rose notably, while dedication remained stable at a consistently high level. Our hypothesis is that this was because of the introduction of video game dynamics that encouraged students to return to the classroom.

TABLE 10.5
Comparative UWES-9S Results Across Interventions

Case	Dimension	Initial → Final (Growth)	Category Shift	
A. Semester-long Gamification	Vigor	2.67 → 4.67 (+2.00)	Moderate → High	✓
	Dedication	5.67 → 5.67 (0.00)	High → High	→
	Absorption	1.00 → 5.00 (+4.00)	Very Low → High	✓
B. One week Hackathon	Vigor	5.43 → 6.00 (+1.67)	High → Very High	✓
	Dedication	5.67 → 6.00 (+0.33)	High → Very High	✓
	Absorption	4.67 → 6.00 (+1.33)	High → Very High	✓
C. Physical-Digital System	Vigor	3.67 → 4.00 (+0.33)	Average → Average	→
	Dedication	5.33 → 5.67 (+0.34)	High → High	→
	Absorption	3.67 → 5.67 (+2.00)	Average → High	✓

- **The physical-digital system (Case C)** yielded moderate gains, particularly in absorption (+2.00, average to high). Vigor grew only slightly, while dedication stayed high throughout.

These results indicate that different interventions foster engagement in distinct ways. The hackathon generated intense but short-lived peak engagement, the gamified course sustained immersion over time, and the physical-digital system strengthened cognitive involvement by linking theory to practice. Comparative evidence suggests that intensity, duration, and focus each shape engagement outcomes, as observed when students in the hackathon reported fatigue by the third day, compared to the semester-long course where energy had to be sustained week after week. Overall, the findings highlight complementary rather than hierarchical effects, with broader implications discussed in Section 5.

10.4.5 Additional Statistical Analysis Through Clustering

In addition to the descriptive comparisons presented previously, a complementary analysis was performed using hierarchical cluster analysis, which is an unsupervised learning approach. Unlike supervised learning methods, clustering aims to uncover hidden patterns within the data. In this case, clustering students according to similarities across the three UWES-9S dimensions allows us to explore how engagement distributions shifted across subgroups, which allows a more specific understanding.

The method applied was hierarchical clustering with three classes, which enabled the observation of how participants with low, medium, and high engagement levels before the intervention migrated across clusters after completing the activity. To ease the visualization of these patterns, the analysis incorporated a 3D representation of the spatial distribution among the three UWES-9S dimensions. This three-axis perspective allowed a more precise understanding of how engagement levels shifted, making it possible to identify not only average changes but also the composition and relocation of clusters before and after the intervention.

10.4.5.1 Clustering Analysis—Case Study A: Semester-Long Course

The clustering analysis divided the data into three groups, each reflecting students with low, medium, or high engagement profiles. As shown in Table 10.6, the cluster characteristics before and after the intervention confirm these groupings. The post-intervention results showed a mixed pattern of migration across clusters. On the one hand, a contraction was observed in the maximum values of vigor and dedication, suggesting that students who began at high levels in these dimensions slightly decreased after the intervention. On the other hand, a notable increase appeared in absorption, as the group shifted toward higher levels of immersion and focus on the academic activities. Figure 10.6 illustrates this migration, showing the special distribution of clusters begore and after the course.

Despite these contrasting movements, Cluster 1 displayed greater homogeneity in the post-intervention stage. The reduction in distances within this cluster suggests that students with initially lower or medium engagement became more aligned after the course. This indicates that the semester-long gamification approach was effective

TABLE 10.6
Clusters' Characteristics for Semester-Long Course Pre (left) and Post (right) Dataset

	Pre-analysis					Post-analysis			
	Observation	Within cluster sum of squares	Avg Distance from centroid	Max Distance from centroid		Observation	Within cluster sum of squares	Avg Distance from centroid	Max Distance from centroid
Cluster1	12	544.58	3.25	6.64	Cluster1	11	92.73	2.82	4.38
Cluster2	1	0.00	0.00	0.00	Cluster2	6	149.50	4.75	6.72
Cluster3	5	64.40	3.54	4.19	Cluster3	1	0.00	0.00	0.00

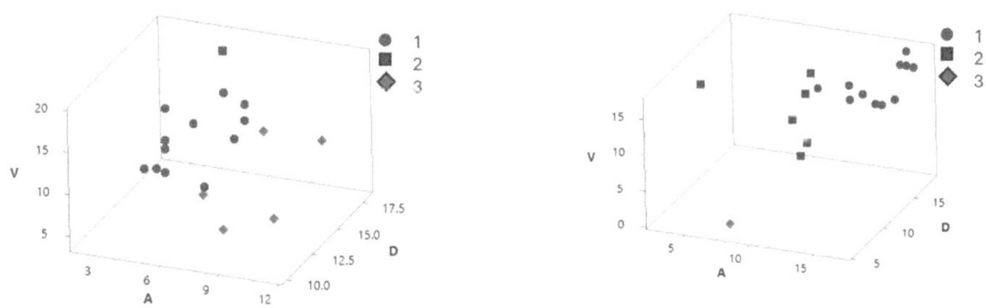

FIGURE 10.6 Clusters' spatial distribution for semester-long course pre (left) and post (right) dataset.

in strengthening engagement for students starting at lower levels, even though it did not maintain the same momentum among those who were already highly engaged.

Overall, the semester course appears most effective at increasing absorption, providing students with deeper immersion in learning tasks. However, the slight decreases in vigor and dedication highlight the challenge of sustaining energy and enthusiasm over an extended period. This suggests that while gamification strategies can successfully foster cognitive engagement, their long-term design must carefully balance novelty and rigor to prevent declines in persistence and dedication among highly engaged students.

10.4.5.2 Clustering Analysis—Case Study B: Mechatronics Hackathon

The post-intervention results revealed a clear migration toward higher values of vigor at the group level. As shown in Table 10.7 the cluster characteristics before and after the hackathon confirm these changes. Students who initially belonged to clusters with low or medium engagement tended to move into denser post-intervention clusters located in the upper region of the 3D space. Figure 10.7 show a 3D vision of this migration, displaying the spatial distribution of clusters before and after the

TABLE 10.7
Clusters' Characteristics for Hackathon Pre (left) and Post (right) Dataset

Pre-analysis					Post-analysis				
	Observation	Within cluster sum of squares	Avg Distance from centroid	Max Distance from centroid		Observation	Within cluster sum of squares	Avg Distance from centroid	Max Distance from centroid
Cluster1	30	569.00	4.07	6.10	Cluster1	39	360.82	2.87	5.52
Cluster2	13	130.00	2.85	5.25	Cluster2	4	49.50	3.42	4.37
Cluster3	1	0.00	0.00	0.00	Cluster3	1	0.00	0.00	0.00

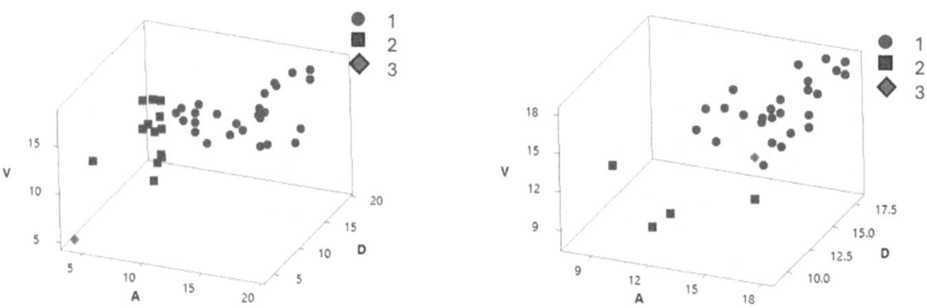

FIGURE 10.7 Clusters' spatial distribution for hackathon pre (left) and post (right) dataset.

hackathon. This indicates that the hackathon format was effective in energizing students and promoting persistence, especially among those who were not strongly engaged at the outset.

At the same time, some participants in clusters 2 and 3 exhibited relocation without substantial changes in their overall scores (sum of V, D, and A). For these individuals it can be said that the total impact of the innovation was neutral, suggesting that the hackathon did not significantly alter their engagement profile.

Cluster 1 displayed the most notable transformation. Its relocation toward the corner of the plot, together with reduced distances between subclusters, this reflects a more homogeneous group. This suggests that the hackathon aligned participants' engagement levels, raising the baseline for those with initially lower scores.

Overall, the most strongly affected dimension was vigor, which increased consistently among most participants. Dedication and absorption remained stable at high levels, though with a slight contraction at the upper extremes. This reinforces the conclusion that the hackathon's primary effect lies in energizing and motivating students with low or moderate initial engagement, while its influence is less pronounced for those who were already highly engaged.

10.4.5.3 Clustering Analysis—Case Study C: Digital-Robotics System

The results revealed a clear upward shift across all three engagement dimensions. As shown in Table 10.8, the cluster characteristics before and after the intervention confirm this trend. Both spatial distribution and relocation of clusters indicated that students moved toward higher values of vigor, dedication, and absorption after the intervention. Figure 10.8 illustrates these shifts, displaying the 3D distribution of clusters in the pre and post analysis. This confirms that the integration of a physical-digital robotic system generated a strong overall impact on student engagement.

For the subgroup of students who began with high engagement, the results showed a relocation toward even higher levels of absorption and vigor, reinforcing the immersive quality of this learning approach. Meanwhile, students with medium engagement exhibited denser and more homogeneous post-intervention clusters. This reduction in variability suggests that robotics activity not only raised engagement but also aligned the group more consistently.

Overall, the use of a digital-robotics system during a class demonstrated a positive and generalized effect, benefiting students regardless of their initial engagement levels. Its strongest influence appears in deepening cognitive immersion (absorption) and energizing persistence (vigor), highlighting the value of combining theoretical problem-solving with hands-on robotic implementation in fostering engagement.

TABLE 10.8
Clusters' Characteristics for Robotics Pre (left) and Post (right) Dataset

Pre-analysis					Post-analysis				
	Observation	Within cluster sum of squares	Avg Distance from centroid	Max Distance from centroid		Observation	Within cluster sum of squares	Avg Distance from centroid	Max Distance from centroid
Cluster1	30	569.00	4.07	6.10	Cluster1	39	360.82	2.87	5.52
Cluster2	13	130.00	2.85	5.25	Cluster2	4	49.50	3.42	4.37
Cluster3	1	0.00	0.00	0.00	Cluster3	1	0.00	0.00	0.00

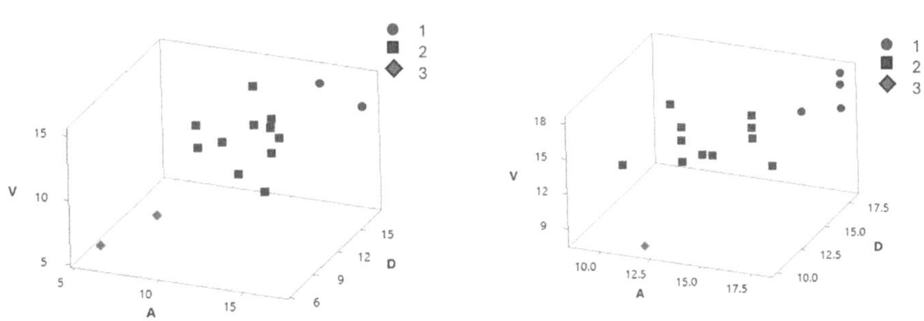

FIGURE 10.8 Clusters' spatial distribution for robotics pre (left) and post (right) dataset.

10.4.5.4 Appraisal of the Relative Effect and Influence Quantified Among the Three Educational Approaches

The summary of the positive effects observed in terms of the enhancement of the engagement dimensions analyzed, based on the classification and analysis of the spatial distribution of the obtained clusters for each innovation, is provided in Table 10.9.

10.5 DISCUSSIONS

10.5.1 Interpreting Engagement Patterns

The combined descriptive, clustering, and qualitative analyses highlight how each educational innovation fostered engagement in distinct ways. Case A (semester-long gamified course) produced gradual gains, most notably in absorption, where students reported becoming more immersed as new game-like elements were introduced. Institutional surveys confirmed strong satisfaction, with ratings above 9/10 for both pedagogy and professor recommendation, highlighting the positive impact of gamification on the learning experience. Teacher observations added the negative aspects of gamification, noting that although gamification encouraged enthusiasm, the heavy workload of designing game scenarios was a limitation, and some students risked losing the connection between classroom activities and real-world engineering applications. This duality can also be seen in the clustering results: increased absorption for students starting at low and medium levels, but slight declines in vigor and dedication among those who began highly engaged.

In Case B (Hackathon), UWES-9S results indicated sharp increases in vigor dimension, with clustering showing denser post-intervention groups at higher engagement levels. This was consistent with open-ended student comments, which emphasized collaboration, challenge, and skill acquisition as the most valuable aspects. Teachers also observed that students were deeply engaged in building resilience and tackling complex tasks under time pressure. However, both survey data and instructor commentaries pointed out that the brevity of the intervention was a weak point of the innovation. This could also be observed on the quantitative analysis: while

TABLE 10.9
Appraisal Summary of the Impact Observed

Innovation	Effect on Students With Low Engagement Before	Effect on Students With Medium Engagement Before	Effect on Students With High Engagement Before
Semester	High on Absorption dimension only	High on Absorption dimension only	Not observed
Hackathon	Moderate on all three dimensions	Moderate on all three dimensions	Moderate on Vigor dimension only
Robotics	High on all three dimensions	High on all three dimensions	High on Absorption and Vigor dimensions

enthusiasm peaked, the format's short duration limited opportunities for sustained impact, particularly for students who were already highly dedicated.

The robotics activity yielded a broad and generalized positive effect, with clustering showing upward shifts across all three dimensions and especially strong improvements in absorption and vigor. Student surveys rated both satisfaction and pedagogy close to 10/10, reinforcing the impact of the intervention. While open comments were limited, they underlined the quality of instruction and the relevance of applying theory in practice. Teacher observations confirmed these impressions: the physical-digital system effectively bridged abstract mathematical concepts with real-world applications, providing an "eye-opening" experience for students. Among the three cases, this activity offered the most balanced combination of depth, novelty, and engagement, fostering immersion without overwhelming the course structure.

10.5.2 Lessons Learned for Educational Innovation

Taken together, these findings suggest that quantitative patterns, student perceptions, and teacher insights converge to show that each innovation promotes engagement differently: the hackathon drives immediate enthusiasm and teamwork, the semester-long course builds sustained immersion but requires careful design to maintain energy, and the robotics activity fosters a strong sense of relevance and cognitive involvement through hands-on application.

Several lessons emerge from this comparative and experimental analysis. In practice, short and intensive formats such as hackathons are particularly effective at mobilizing energy and social collaboration. Students valued the challenge of building prototypes in a limited time, and teachers observed how resilience and problem-solving emerged naturally under pressure. However, the intensity of the format also highlights its limitations, as the gains in vigor may not translate into long-term engagement without follow-up activities.

Long-term gamification can sustain student immersion, as reflected in the gradual rise of absorption throughout the semester. Surveys and teacher reports confirmed that game-like elements motivated participation and persistence, but they also revealed the challenge of maintaining dedication and vigor at high levels. The key lesson is that gamification must be carefully balanced with meaningful real-world applications to prevent the perception of learning as "just a game."

On the other hand, the implementation of real problems like a physical-digital system proved to be a powerful tool for deepening engagement across all dimensions. Students appreciated seeing abstract concepts applied to a real robot, while teachers highlighted the "eye-opening" effect of bridging theory and practice. The homogeneity observed in the clustering analysis suggests that this format benefits students regardless of their initial engagement levels, acting as a leveling mechanism that aligns the group toward higher immersion.

In summary, across all cases, the strongest improvements were observed among students with initially low or medium engagement, showing that well-designed innovations can reduce disparities and create more inclusive learning environments. By lifting the baseline, these interventions allow less motivated students to catch up with their peers and find important implications for designing equitable educational strategies

10.5.3 Challenges and Limitations

Although each intervention enhanced engagement, specific challenges were observed. In the hackathon, the short duration generated enthusiasm but also caused workload pressure and limited long-term impact. The semester-long gamified course increased immersion, yet sustaining dedication and vigor was difficult, and some students perceived activities as detached from real-world applications. The robotics activity produced broad gains but required specialized equipment and preparation, which may limit scalability. These findings suggest that duration, workload, and resource availability are critical factors when designing educational innovations.

Beyond these contextual aspects, methodological limitations must also be acknowledged. The UWES-9S results are summarized using the modal value of each item to represent group tendencies. While this approach captures the most frequent response, it may not always reflect the variability or full distribution of the group, potentially leading to conclusions that are less representative of the entire cohort. A practical challenge was ensuring that all students completed the survey simultaneously, since delays or staggered responses could affect comparability, especially on small samples. Recent studies have highlighted that although the UWES-9 demonstrates good reliability, persistent debates remain about its factorial validity and dimensionality, suggesting the importance of complementing *Classical Test Theory* with *Item Response Theory* approaches for a more precise psychometric evaluation [19]. In terms of extra work, ensuring anonymity through alphanumeric identifiers requires additional effort to securely link pre- and post-responses without compromising confidentiality. Together, these factors emphasize both the potential and the boundaries of survey-based engagement measures, highlighting the need for strict protocols in data collection, analysis, and ethical oversight.

10.6 ETHICAL AND METHODOLOGICAL CONSIDERATIONS

All procedures in this study followed institutional guidelines for research ethics. Prior to data collection, students were asked to sign an informed consent form, in which the objectives, procedures, and conditions of participation were explained. In cases where participants were under 18 years old, consent was requested from their parents to be signed up. Every signed form is then stored for five years since its recollection.

To protect confidentiality, no personal identifiers such as names or student IDs were used in the datasets. Instead, anonymized alphanumeric codes were assigned to each participant. This ensured that individual responses could not be traced back to specific students. All data are stored securely by the research team, and it has only been reported in aggregate form.

Additionally, students were informed that participation was voluntary and that they could withdraw at any time without any academic consequence. The consent form explicitly states that the information collected would be used exclusively for academic purposes, including publications and presentations, and that participants' privacy would be always safeguarded.

These measures were implemented to minimize risks, ensure informed participation, and uphold ethical standards in the handling and interpretation of student data.

10.7 CONCLUSIONS

This study demonstrated that student engagement, measured through the UWES-9S and complemented with perception surveys, teacher observations, and clustering analysis, provides a robust framework for evaluating educational innovations in engineering. The three interventions analyzed—a semester-long gamified course, a one-week hackathon, and a one-day robotics activity—showed that engagement outcomes vary depending on the intensity, duration, and nature of the learning experience. The semester course fostered gradual increases in absorption but highlighted the difficulty of sustaining dedication and vigor across a long period; the hackathon generated immediate enthusiasm and teamwork but with limited long-term impact; and the robotics activity produced broad and consistent improvements, particularly in bridging abstract theory with practical application. Together, these cases confirm that engagement is a multidimensional construct that can act as a meaningful indicator of the effectiveness of educational strategies. The findings also underscore that the greatest benefits were consistently observed among students with initially low or medium engagement, suggesting that well-designed innovations can act as leveling mechanisms that reduce disparities and foster inclusivity. At the same time, the study revealed important methodological and practical limitations, such as the challenges of coordinating survey completion, the reliance on modal values that may not fully represent group variability, and the complexity of safeguarding student identifiers and data privacy. Despite these constraints, the integration of quantitative and qualitative perspectives offers a replicable approach for educators in engineering, seeking to refine their teaching practices. The conclusions reinforce the importance of designing interventions that balance novelty, workload, and authenticity, while also adopting rigorous and ethical methods of evaluation. By doing so, educators can ensure that innovation not only enriches student experiences but also provides reliable evidence of its real impact on learning.

ACKNOWLEDGMENTS

The authors would like to acknowledge the financial support of Novus (ID 692002) and (ID 417827) Institute for the Future of Education, Tecnologico de Monterrey, Mexico, in the production of this work.

REFERENCES

[1] C. Rodríguez-Sabiote, Á. M. Úbeda-Sánchez, J. Álvarez-Rodríguez and D. Álvarez-Ferrándiz, “Active Learning in an Environment of Innovative Training and Sustainability. Mapping of the Conceptual Structure of Research Fronts through a Bibliometric Analysis. Sustainability,” *Sustainability*, vol. 12, no. 19, p. 8012, 2020.

[2] V. Sukackė, A. O. P. D. C. Guerra, D. Ellinger, V. Carlos, S. Petronienė, L. Gaižiūnienė, S. Blanch, A. Marbà-Tallada and A. Brose, “Towards Active Evidence-Based Learning in Engineering Education: A Systematic Literature Review of PBL, PjBL, and CBL,” *Sustainability*, vol. 14, no. 21, p. 13955, 2022.

[3] B. Wright, P. Alonzi and A. Rivera, “The Future of Data Science Education,” *arXiv*, School of Data Science, University of Virginia, 2024.

[4] N. Zeybek and E. Saygı, "Gamification in Education: Why, Where, When, and How?—A Systematic Review. Games and Culture," *Games and Culture*, vol. 19, no. 2, pp. 237–264, 2023.
[5] E. Skinner, T. Kindermann and C. Furrer, "Classroom, A Motivational Perspective on Engagement and Disaffection: Conceptualization and Assessment of Children's Behavioral and Emotional Participation in Academic Activities in the," *Educational and Psychological Measurement*, no. 3, pp. 493–525, 2009.
[6] M. A. Carmona-Halty, W. Schaufeli and M. Salanova, "The Utrecht Work Engagement Scale for Students (UWES-9S): Factorial Validity, Reliability, and Measurement Invariance in a Chilean Sample of Undergraduate University Students," *Frontiers in Psychology*, vol. 10, p. 1017, 2019.
[7] W. B. Schaufeli, A. B. Bakker and M. Salanova, "The Measurement of Work Engagement with a Short Questionnaire: A Cross-National Study," *Educational and Psychological Measurement*, vol. 66, no. 4, pp. 701–716, 2006. https://doi.org/10.1177/0013164405282471
[8] W. Schaufeli, M. Salanova, V. González-Romá and A. B. Bakker, "The Measurement of Engagement and Burnout: A Confirmatory Analytic Approach," *Journal of Happiness Studies*, vol. 3, no. 1, pp. 71–92, 2002.
[9] M. Salanova, W. B. Schaufeli and V. Gonzalez, "The Measurement of Engagement and Burnout: A Two Sample Confirmatory Factor Analytic Approach," *Journal of Happiness Studies*, pp. 71–92, 2004.
[10] S. Domínguez-Lara, M. Trógolo and J. Moreta-Herrera, "Resolving Dimensionality Issues of the Utrecht Work Engagement Scale for Students Using an Integrative Data-Analytic Framework.," *Journal of Psychoeducational Assessment*, pp. 36–60, 2025.
[11] I. Silva, I., A. Wong, B. Auria, D. Zambrano and V. Echeverria, "Gamification in Engineering Education: Exploring Students' Performance, Motivation, and Engagement," in *2022 IEEE Sixth Ecuador Technical Chapters Meeting (ETCM)*, Quito, Ecuador, 2022.
[12] S. Dimitriadou, K. Lavidas, T. Karalis and K. Ravanis, "Study Engagement in University Students: A Confirmatory Factor Analysis of the Utrecht Work Engagement Scale with Greek Students," *Journal of Well-Being Assessment*, vol. 4, pp. 291–307, 2020.
[13] S. Muir, L. Tirlea, B. Elphinstone and M. Huynh, "Promoting Classroom Engagement Through the Use of an Online Student Response System: A Mixed Methods Analysis," *Journal of Statistics Education*, vol. 28, no. 1, pp. 25–31, 2020.
[14] C. Dumitru, M. M. Stan and G. Dumitru, "Academic Support Through Tutoring, Guided Learning, and Learning Diaries in the Context of the COVID-19 Pandemic: An Experimental Model for Master's Students," *Frontiers in Education*, vol. 9, 2024.
[15] S. Dominguez-Lara, A. R. Sánchez-Villena and M. Fernández-Arata, "Psychometric Properties of the UWES-9S in Peruvian College Students," *Acta Colombiana de Psicología,* vol. 23, no. 2, pp. 24–39, 2020.
[16] M. Macías, A. Cortés and A. Izaguirre, "Cyber-Physical Labs to Enhance Engineering Training and Education," *International Journal on Interactive Design and Manufacturing (IJIDeM)*, vol. 14, pp. 1253–1269, 2020.
[17] A. A. Cortés, "Gamifing the Classroom: Bringing Videogames to Life Through Innovation in Education to Increase Student Engagement in STEM Subjects," in *2024 IEEE Gaming, Entertainment, and Media Conference (GEM)*, Turin, Italy, 2024.
[18] M. Valencia, A. A. Cortés and L. M. Orona, "Impacto del uso de sistemas físico-digitales en el aprendizaje STEM: Caso de estudio con robot didáctico," in *IFE Conference 2025: 11ª edición—Ponencia de Innovación*, Monterrey, 2025.
[19] B. Um and J. Ji, "Psychometric Properties of the Utrecht Work Engagement Scale-9 in a School Counselor Sample Using Classical Test Theory and Item Response Theory," *Measurement and Evaluation in Counseling and Development*, vol. 57, no. 1, pp. 336–350, 2024.

11 Teacher-in-the-Loop Learning Analytics for LLM-Enhanced Intelligent Tutoring Systems

Oleksiy Levchuk, Ariana Espinoza Salinas, Isabel Lopez Hurtado, and Jesus Favela

11.1 INTRODUCTION

The rapid emergence of Generative AI (GenAI), which gained momentum following the introduction of transformer architecture by Vaswani et al. (2017), has expanded the scope of what learning analytics (LA) can achieve. Traditional approaches to LA have emphasized the importance of understanding learners and their surrounding contexts (Ferguson, 2012). Yet in an increasingly AI-mediated world, there is a growing need to examine not only learners themselves but the dynamic context of student-AI interactions (Noy & Zhang, 2023). Insights about how students appropriate, resist, or adapt to GenAI-based agents are integral to their continued learning process, particularly as we see the GenAI become increasingly integrated into educational tools such as intelligent tutoring systems (ITS) (Schmucker et al., 2023). Consequently, this opens an opportunity for LA to evolve beyond tracking traditional learning behaviors, toward analyzing how students seek support and construct meaning through interactions with GenAI-driven ITS.

Just as the evolving contexts of student learning pose new challenges for LA, they also create opportunities to harness the capabilities of GenAI. Large language models' (LLMs) ability to analyze vast and diverse datasets allows them to construct detailed learner profiles, providing a holistic view of learning trajectories and transforming conventional LA dashboards. Beyond pattern recognition, they enable new forms of insight and content generation (Ochoa et al., 2025). Early work in the field primarily focused on using AI for predictive modeling and early-warning systems (Turner & Patrick, 2008; Hattie & Timperley, 2007). More recently, contributions have framed GenAI as a collaborator capable of shaping data collection, analysis, and intervention simultaneously while also reinforcing the importance of human-centered, ethical, and privacy principles (Khosravi et al., 2025).

Yet this transition raises fundamental concerns about learner agency and the roles of educators. Promising directions emphasize student-centered approaches that focus on learner experience and engagement (Alfredo et al., 2024; Topali et al.,

DOI: 10.1201/9781003678250-11

2024). These perspectives are enriched by insights from human-computer interaction, educational design, and software engineering, which advocate for collaborative approaches that involve both students and educators acknowledging challenges in user expertise (Martinez-Maldonado, 2023; Dollinger & Lodge, 2018). This trajectory underscores the need for rethinking the role of LA in mediating such partnerships (Cukurova, 2024).

As Hernández-Leo (2023) argues, analytics must clearly distinguish between AI assistance, human intelligence, and AI complementarity to align outputs with pedagogical intentions. Ethical considerations (i.e., fairness of access, mitigating digital divide, and ensuring environmental sustainability) must also guide implementation. In response, scholars are increasingly calling for hybrid approaches that combine the scalability and adaptability of GenAI with rigorous human oversight, thereby laying the groundwork for human-in-the-loop architecture. Within classrooms, this shift entails a re-examination of the interplay among students, teachers, and AI systems. It further requires rethinking teachers' roles, particularly their capacity and autonomy to interpret data, make pedagogical decisions, and shape the learning environment. By deliberately designing opportunities for teachers to explore, learn, and exercise control in AI-mediated classrooms, LA can ensure teacher's judgements continue to be central in classrooms.

This chapter makes the following contributions:

- **Human–AI integration:** We introduce a teacher-in-the-loop LA approach that combines expert-coded interaction traces with scalable LLM-based analytics.
- **Empirical validation:** We report findings from a two-phase study that (i) develops and validates a taxonomy of student–ITS interaction intents and (ii) evaluates six LLMs under three different prompting strategies for automated classification.
- **Dashboard design:** We propose a proof-of-concept LA dashboard that operationalizes these analytics to enhance teachers' situational awareness and enable timely pedagogical intervention.
- **Responsible adoption:** We articulate design implications for ensuring that LLM-powered analytics remain interpretable, ethically aligned, and supportive of teacher agency in AI-mediated classrooms.

To achieve these contributions, we address the following research questions:

- **RQ1:** What conversational characteristics do students display when interacting with a trained conversational agent in the context of solving mathematical exercises?
- **RQ2:** To what extent can LLMs achieve accuracy comparable to human coders when automatically classifying student intents in ITS interactions?

The remainder of this chapter is organized as follows. Section 2 reviews related work on GenAI in LA, conversational agents, and teacher agency. Section 3 outlines our two-phase study design. Section 4 details the human coding process of student–ITS interactions. Section 5 reports the automated classification results using six LLMs. Section 6 presents the design of the teacher-in-the-loop dashboard. Section 7 discusses conclusions and future research directions.

11.2 RELATED WORK

11.2.1 GenAI in LA and Educational Data Mining

Recent reviews synthesize the growing applications of GenAI across the LA and educational data mining (EDM) pipeline. Misiejuk et al. (2025) review 41 studies to map the use of GenAI across different stages of the LA/EDM cycle, highlighting applications such as data augmentation to improve predictive performance, automated scoring, and automated text summarization. They also note that while LA has traditionally relied heavily on LMS log data, text data remains crucial yet highly labor-intensive to process. To address this, researchers have begun experimenting with BERT and GPT models to automatically code discourse data, often as part of the preprocessing stage to feed dashboards or generate feedback. Nonetheless, the evidence indicates that GenAI cannot yet be relied upon to code text data without rigorous human validation, as human evaluators remain more reliable. However, with a human-in-the-loop approach, GenAI may still provide valuable preprocessing support, provided that human oversight is maintained (Misiejuk et al., 2025).

Complementing this, Rodríguez-Ortiz et al. (2025), in a PRISMA-based review of 9,590 records resulting in 101 empirical studies, found that, compared to traditional machine learning techniques, GenAI-based LA systems were applied in areas such as personalized feedback, cognitive engagement modeling through sentiment or discourse analysis, ITS, and real-time content scaffolding. These implementations were typically experimental and text-focused, often relying on adjusting the employed LLMs via prompt engineering or fine-tuning.

Taken together, these reviews suggest that while GenAI demonstrates a range of promising applications in LA, particularly in processing and interpreting text data, it remains experimental, requires careful tuning, and necessitates human validation. This opens opportunities for LA to rely on GenAI to analyze discourse data, such as that of chatbot-student interactions, but not without human oversight.

11.2.2 Chatbots as Pedagogical Agents

In parallel, research on conversational agents in ITS have positioned student-chatbot interactions as a valuable means for learning. Consequently, emerging literature has focused on the design and training of conversational agents to support student learning. For example, recent pedagogical frameworks describe using conversational agents to guide students' learning through dialogue using conversation agents trained in Socratic questioning (Orynbassarova & Porta, 2024). Similarly, other pedagogical approaches have focused on training conversational agents in motivational theories to foster positive motivational behaviors in students (Handa et al., 2023).

11.2.3 Student-Chatbot Interaction Patterns

Despite this growing design literature, less is known about how students interact with chatbots and what constitutes effective interaction. Several studies have begun to address that gap. Lai et al. (2025) found that higher-scoring students engage more in reflective and evaluative activities when interacting with chatbots, whereas lower-scoring students primarily seek answers. Usher and Amzalag (2025) examined graduate students' academic writing interactions, identifying distinct patterns of assistance-seeking such as verification, content generation, and concept clarification. They extended this analysis by categorizing seven types of writing assistance, communication styles, and tones. These findings suggest that while students actively employ chatbots, they often rely on them for lower-order or surface-level tasks, underutilizing them for higher-order processes such as synthesis and argument development. Similarly, Lin et al. (2025) created a map of interaction pathways in peer feedback contexts. They found that students frequently overestimated their understanding, resulting in ineffective chatbot use, and proposed analytic frameworks to better capture process-level dynamics. This underscores the need to go beyond categorization of assistance types toward understanding the mechanisms by which interaction shapes learning.

11.2.4 Teacher Agency in Student-Chatbot Interactions

LA provides powerful tools to support teachers in the iterative process of improving course effectiveness and enhancing student performance. In the context of student-chatbot interactions, teachers are uniquely situated to provide pedagogical interpretation and contextualization of the patterns emerging from these exchanges. They can determine which behaviors reflect meaningful learning, superficial engagement, or misconceptions that warrant intervention. Studies have already demonstrated the impact of teacher presence on student learning when chatbots are integrated, showing that outcomes differ significantly depending on whether teachers are actively involved. For example, Li et al. (2025) found that teacher presence in GenAI-supported learning environments significantly improved students' emotional and agentic engagement, even when cognitive and behavioral engagement levels remained constant. They identified six distinct teacher roles in chatbot-mediated learning, demonstrating how teachers can shape productive student–chatbot interactions. Tarun et al. (2025) extend this perspective by showing how feedback mechanisms can adapt LLM responses in real time, emphasizing that teacher judgment must remain central. Applied to LA, this highlights the need for teacher-facing systems that do more than automate classification but also summarize interpretable patterns of student–chatbot interaction that teachers can use to adapt their instruction and guide student learning even within chatbot-mediated environments.

In summary, existing research demonstrates the potential for GenAI to process discourse data, design pedagogically oriented chatbots, and categorize student interaction patterns, while also emphasizing the role of teacher judgment. However, few studies have translated these findings into teacher-facing LA tools capable of automatically characterizing student–ITS exchanges in ways that inform actionable instructional decisions—a theme that our work seeks to address.

11.3 OVERVIEW OF STUDIES

Transforming raw student–ITS exchange messages into actionable LA requires going beyond gradebooks, as these interactions reveal help-seeking, misconceptions, off-task drift, and reasoning otherwise invisible to teachers. In a teacher-in-the-loop architecture, such traces must be consistently interpreted so teachers can detect difficulties, understand causes, and intervene effectively.

To operationalize this, we used a two-phase approach. **Phase I** involved three experts creating and refining a qualitative codebook to capture recurrent behaviors (e.g., assistance requests, conceptual queries, confirmations, incomprehension, off-task drift). Consensus resolution and inter-rater reliability ensured validity, and the resulting codes served as both analytic vocabulary and ground-truth data. **Phase II** used this coded corpus in classification experiments with six LLMs under zero-shot, few-shot, and zero-shot + interaction history prompting. Given dataset size, we emphasized prompt-engineering over fine-tuning, embedding all models into an R pipeline that logged predictions and token costs.

This design shows how teacher-in-the-loop LA can work in practice: human coders define a valid framework, and LLMs scale it into real-time analytics for instructor dashboards. The subsequent sections detail the coding process (**Section 4**) and report the results of the automated classification experiment (**Section 5**), highlighting their implications for real-time instructor dashboards (**Section 6**).

11.4 HUMAN CODING OF STUDENT-ITS INTERACTIONS

11.4.1 Context and Purpose

As part of a broader investigation into factors influencing students' motivation when engaging with LLM-powered ITS, we developed "Grow Together," an LLM-enhanced math tutoring environment designed to foster STEM interest through problem-solving. Mathematics was selected given its curricular relevance across educational levels and its frequent perception as a challenging subject. Within this environment, the system guided students without directly providing answers, instead offering growth-oriented feedback (Dweck & Yeager, 2019) to sustain engagement. Both student responses and full interaction logs were systematically stored for later analysis.

The objective of this phase was to identify the conversational characteristics students displayed when interacting with the tutor, and to determine whether the agent's motivational approach contributed to task completion. By coding these interactions, we aimed to capture both productive dimensions (e.g., requests for guidance or conceptual inquiries) and unproductive dimensions (e.g., interactions that do not contribute to the learning process, such as confusion or frustration).

11.4.2 Methodology

We applied conventional content analysis (Hsieh & Shannon, 2005) to student–ITS interaction logs, a method well suited to explore communication patterns where the text itself is the primary source of evidence. Our approach was also informed by recent studies that employed similar coding schemes for chatbot interactions, enhancing validity and comparability (e.g., Usher & Amzalag, 2025).

11.4.3 Participants and Data Collection

The study was conducted in collaboration with three high schools in Ensenada, Baja California, Mexico, involving four classrooms across grades 11 and 12. Of the 112 students invited, 93 provided informed consent and 88 participated. Data collection occurred during regular school hours. Each intervention lasted about 50 minutes. Students first watched a tutorial video introducing the system and then completed a mathematical knowledge pre-test. They next interacted with "Grow Together" for approximately 20 minutes, during which they solved problems with the system's support, consulting the agent when (if) needed. Finally, students completed a post-test survey to evaluate their experience.

The sample included 47 males (54%), 37 females (42%), two non-binary (2%), and two who preferred not to disclose gender, with an average age of 17.2 years (SD = 0.7). The dataset included 814 interactions, with each entry recording conversation ID, student ID, problem ID, user message, agent response, and timestamp. For each entry, an expert-assigned code was added later.

11.4.4 Coding Procedure

To avoid bias, participant IDs were masked, and coders agreed not to consult agent responses or student utterances from other exercises beyond the one to which the analyzed row belonged. The process unfolded in four stages (see Figure 11.1):

1. Data extraction and cleaning.
2. Initial coding of a randomly sampled 20% subset of entries.

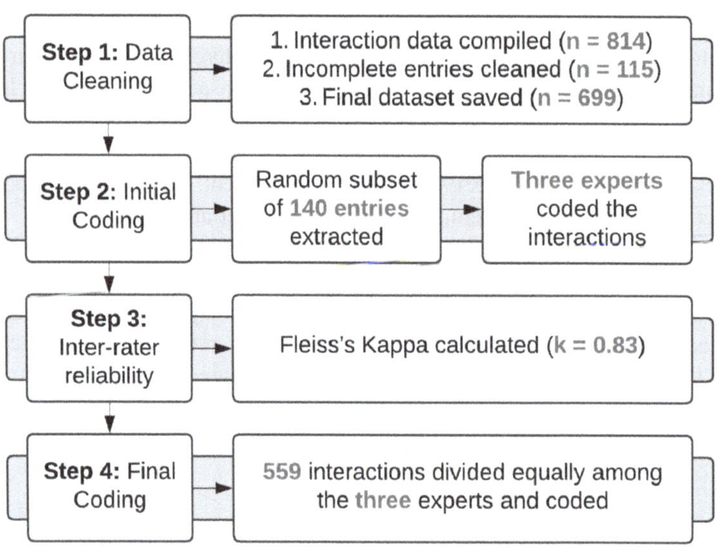

FIGURE 11.1 Coding process illustrating data cleaning, initial coding, inter-rater reliability (Fleiss's Kappa), and final coding of student–LLM interactions.

3. Inter-rater reliability check, resolving disagreements through discussion.
4. Final coding of the remaining 80% of entries using the agreed-upon scheme.

Each turn was treated as a unit of analysis and received exactly one intent label to support single-label classification and subsequent sequence modeling. In cases where a turn could plausibly fit multiple categories, coders assigned the one that best reflected its primary purpose within the interaction.

11.4.5 Codebook Development

An initial set of 22 fine-grained codes (including both productive and unproductive dimensions) was consolidated into 12 mutually exclusive categories aligned with instructional decision-making needs. Table 11.1 summarizes the final codes with definitions and examples.

TABLE 11.1
Final coding scheme with 12 categories of student–LLM interactions.

Code	Description	Example	Dimension
Call for Assistance	Petition for general help or step-by-step guidance on how to solve a problem or to move forward	"Could you help me?"/"How do I solve this?"	productive
Demand for Direct Answer	Explicit request for the answer without showing intent to understand the procedure	"Give me the answer"/"I need you to solve this exercise for me"	unproductive
Conceptual Query	Questions about basic concepts or mathematical formulas needed to solve an exercise	"What are the prime factors?"/"Formula for an area of a circle"	productive
Expression of Incomprehension	Expressions that show a lack of understanding or frustration about not being able to solve the exercise or follow the agent's explanation	"I don't understand"/"Forget it then, better nothing"	unproductive
Confirmation of Reasoning	The user provides an answer or procedure and seeks validation from the agent	"The greatest divisor is 18"/"I got that it's 9"	productive
Request for Example	Petition for a worked example to understand how to apply a procedure or solve a similar exercise	"Show me an example"/"Illustrate it with some examples"	productive
Negative Expression	Use of sarcastic, aggressive, or derogatory language toward the agent	"It's 9, genius"/"Stupid, you don't know anything"	unproductive
Formal Expression	Greeting or expressing thanks as part of the interaction, unrelated to the exercise content	"Hello"/"Thanks"	productive

(Continued)

TABLE 11.1 (*Continued*)
Final coding scheme with 12 categories of student–LLM interactions.

Code	Description	Example	Dimension
Problem Transcription	Copying or transcribing the full statement of the math problem without explicitly requesting help or asking to solve it	"A rectangle height is three times the base . . ."/"Pedro had 5 apples and Juan had . . ."	productive
Calculation or Operation	The user asks the agent to perform a specific mathematical operation	"63 divided by 3"/"square root of 124 multiplied by 12"	productive
Off-Topic	Message unrelated to the educational content or contains colloquial language	"yarbis"/"I have problems with my gf"	unproductive
Response to the Agent	Affirmative or negative response to an agent's question	"Yes"/"No"	productive

11.4.6 Results of Human Coding

The interaction dataset comprises 88 students working on up to 17 math exercises. Students interacted with the tutor a mean of ≈3 times per exercise (maximum 19 interactions on a single exercise). Interaction volume was concentrated in early tasks—Exercise 1 (175 interactions), Exercise 2 (162), and Exercise 5 (139)—with later items (10–17) showing very low counts (≤ 8 each), suggesting a drop-off in progression/engagement after the first five exercises. Many interaction turns were brief clarifications (≈7–10 seconds), while others extended to 2–3 minutes; a few students accumulated 4–6 minutes in total. Overall, the average time spent interacting with "Grow Together" was 332s (SD = 248s), which represented about one-quarter of the total time dedicated to solving the math exercises. The mean of student utterances per exercise was 3.01 (SD = 2.8), and the average time per exercise was 107s (SD = 97s).

The coding process revealed that the tutor was primarily used for learning purposes: most interactions were classified as productive, while only 130 entries (19%) were identified as unproductive. Importantly, frustration did not occur randomly but often followed otherwise constructive exchanges. In fact, in about two-thirds of the frustration cases (41 out of 63), an initial request for guidance, a conceptual inquiry, or confirmation of reasoning was followed by an expression of incomprehension. This pattern suggests that breakdowns were frequently triggered when seemingly helpful responses failed to meet students' expectations, which in some instances escalated into disengagement. These distributions and sequential patterns directly informed the design of the dashboard presented in *Section 6*, where they were incorporated into the automated LA pipeline to flag early signs of unproductive interaction loops.

11.5 AUTOMATED CLASSIFICATION OF STUDENT INTENTS USING LLMS

11.5.1 Context and Purpose

Having established a validated codebook through expert analysis, the next step was to examine whether LLMs could approximate this classification at scale. The objective was not limited to technical feasibility but extended to assessing whether automated coding could generate interpretable insights for teachers. By doing so, we sought to operationalize a teacher-in-the-loop approach where LLMs augment instructor awareness by surfacing patterns of student intent, such as help-seeking or off-task behavior.

11.5.2 Methodology

Dataset: The final dataset after cleaning missing/incomplete entries comprised 699 student–ITS interactions, with each containing a conversation ID, student ID, problem ID, user message, agent response, timestamp, and an expert-assigned code, which served as the ground truth for classification.

Taxonomy: Twelve discrete categories obtained from the human coding were consolidated into eleven after merging "Negative Expression" with "Off-Topic" due to the first having very few entries. They were used to annotate each message along two dimensions: (i) productive versus unproductive contribution to learning and (ii) the specific intent expressed by the student.

Model selection: Six LLMs were evaluated (Table 11.2), representing a mix of commercial and open-source options: GPT-3.5-Turbo, GPT-4-Turbo, GPT-4o, LlaMA-3.3 (70B), Mistral-Small (24B), and DeepSeek-V3. All models were accessed through their respective APIs and integrated into a unified R-based classification pipeline. Configuration was done by controlling temperature (0.2) and top_p (1.0) parameters. LLMs were constrained to output only the selected category label.

TABLE 11.2
Specifications of the LLMs Used in This Study

LLM name	Provider	Cost per 1M Tokens (Input/Output) as of July 2025	Size	Context Window
GPT-3.5-turbo	OpenAI	\$0.50/\$1.50	~6–20B (undisclosed)	16k
GPT-4-turbo	OpenAI	\$10/\$30	~1T MoE (~55B active)	128k
GPT-4o	OpenAI	\$2.5/\$10	~1T MoE (~55B active)	128k
LLaMA 3.3 70B	Meta	\$0.10/\$0.25	70B dense	128k
Mistral S 3.2 24B	Mistral	\$0.10/\$0.30	24B dense	128k
DeepSeek-V3	DeepSeek	\$0.07/\$1.68	671B MoE (37B active)	128k

TABLE 11.3
Prompting Conditions Evaluated

		Zero-shot prompting	Few-shot prompting	Zero-shot + history
Instruction	"Act as a classifier of student queries according to . . ."	✓	✓	✓
Taxonomy	[Code 1 + description] . . . [Code 11 + description]	✓		✓
Taxonomy + examples	[Code 1 + description + 5 examples] . . . [Code 11 + description + 5 examples]		✓	
User message	"I need help with . . ."	✓	✓	
User message + past interaction	"I need help with . . ." + The last system message before this utterance			✓
Mean (SD) token cost		523 ± 6.7	1077 ± 6.5	702 ± 34

(zero-shot, few-shot, and zero-shot + history).

Prompting strategies: To assess how input structuring influenced performance, we evaluated three prompting conditions (Table 11.3). *Zero-shot prompting:* classifier instructions and taxonomy only; *Few-shot prompting:* taxonomy plus 5 labeled examples per category; *Zero-shot + history:* classifier instructions, taxonomy, and the immediate prior system message to provide conversational context.

11.5.3 Performance

General performance: Across top-performing models, precision ranged between 51–61%, with the highest performance achieved by Mistral zero-shot + history—424 matches (60.6%), GPT-4o few-shot—418 matches (59.7%), GPT-4-turbo few-shot—386 matches (55.2%), Llama few-shot—375 matches (53.6%), and GPT-4o zero-shot + history—361 matches (51.6%). Here, performance was computed as the ratio of total correct matches produced by the model to the total number of ground truth codes. Although absolute precision was modest, these results demonstrate the feasibility of approximating expert coding, particularly when examples or conversational context are provided.

Category-level insights: Figure 11.2 presents the highest accuracy obtained for each category across the 18 possible model configurations. Few-shot prompting consistently outperformed other strategies for most categories, mirroring how human coders are trained with examples. Models were identified as top performers based on the mean precision across the 11

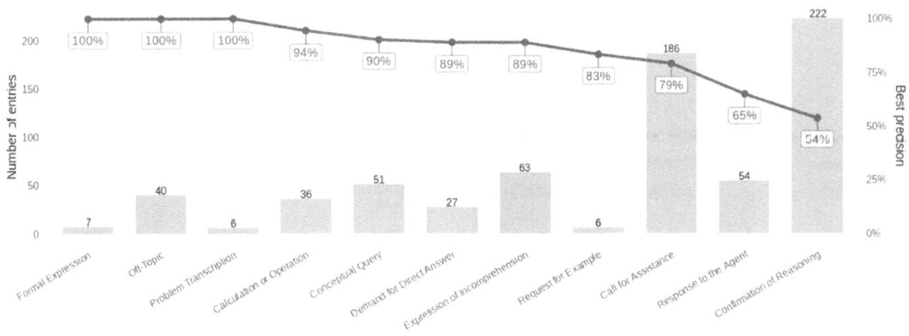

FIGURE 11.2 Distribution of coded entries across categories (bars, left axis) and the highest precision achieved by LLMs for each category (line, right axis).

categories, rather than weighted by the raw frequency of each category, ensuring that less frequent but pedagogically important categories were not overshadowed by high-volume ones. According to this criterion, the best-performing models were Llama few-shot (83.3%), GPT-4-turbo few-shot (82.5%), Mistral few-shot (79%), GPT-3.5-turbo few-shot (77.8%), and GPT-4o few-shot (77.8%).

For instance, *Request for Assistance* and *Conceptual Query* were reliably identified under few-shot conditions. By contrast, *Confirmation of Reasoning* was the most challenging category: even the best-performing model (Mistral zero-shot + history) achieved only 54% precision. Notably, four of the five best-performing models for this category came from the zero-shot + history condition, suggesting that additional conversational context may help compensate for the subtle interpretive demands. This also points toward the potential for fine-tuning when larger datasets become available. The second most frequent category, *Call for Assistance*, was dominated by few-shot models, though two zero-shot + history configurations also appeared among the top five. In contrast, *Calculation or Operation* was unique in that zero-shot models outperformed few-shot, likely due to the formulaic nature of the queries.

11.5.4 Results of Automated Classification

Few-shot prompting offered the best balance between accuracy and interpretability, albeit with higher token costs. Zero-shot prompting proved lightweight but less reliable, while zero-shot + history improved performance on context-dependent categories but introduced variability in token usage. Among zero-shot configurations, GPT-o showed the best results. Few-shot configurations were dominated by Llama, while zero-shot + history showed best results under Mistral LLM.

These findings suggest that LLMs, when appropriately prompted, can complement human coders by classifying student intents with moderate reliability. While far from perfect, such automation can still provide valuable early-warning signals in real time. For example, high-precision detection of off-topic conversations or frustration episodes can alert teachers to intervene, even if subtler categories like confirmation of reasoning remain better handled by human oversight.

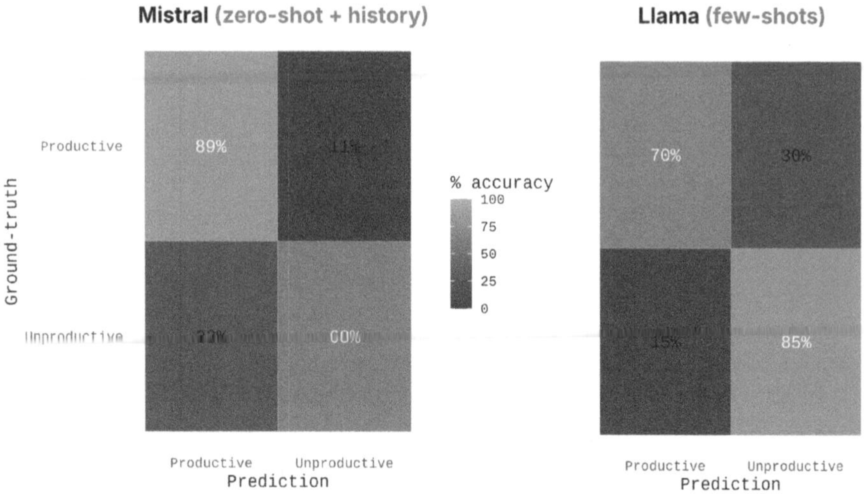

FIGURE 11.3 Comparison of the best general model (Mistral, zero-shot + history) and the best category-focused model (Llama, few-shot) in classifying productive versus unproductive interactions.

We found that the models exhibit a clear precision–recall trade-off (Figure 11.3). Mistral zero-shot + history minimizes Type-I errors (false alarms), labeling only ~11% of productive turns as unproductive, but misses more true at-risk cases (Type-II ≈ 32%). In contrast, Llama few-shot reduces Type-II errors (misses ≈ 15%) at the cost of more false alarms (Type-I ≈ 30%).

From an LA perspective, the most promising outcome is not replacing expert coding but scaling it: enabling dashboards to continuously flag at-risk patterns without requiring teachers to manually inspect every interaction. Importantly, the pedagogical implications are twofold. First, categories that align with visible behavioral markers (assistance requests, conceptual queries) can be semi-automated to free teacher attention. Second, categories requiring nuanced interpretation (reasoning confirmation, frustration loops) highlight where human judgment remains indispensable.

11.6 DESIGN OF A TEACHER-IN-THE-LOOP DASHBOARD

11.6.1 LA-Powered Teacher-in-the-Loop Approach

ITS are typically structured around four core modules—**Interface, Student, Pedagogical,** and **Domain**—each responsible for a distinct aspect of system functionality. Recent studies have shown that LLMs can not only enhance these modules (Liu et al., 2024; Gao et al., 2024), but in some cases may even replicate their functions (Schmucker et al., 2023; Levchuk et al., 2024). Within this context, we design a dashboard that strengthens the teacher-in-the-loop paradigm for managing LLM-powered ITS by employing LLMs to generate LA derived from student interactions with the system. This information is then presented in the form of interactive dashboards that enable instructors to dynamically adjust and control key parameters responsible for student-ITS quality of interaction, as shown in Figure 11.4. This form

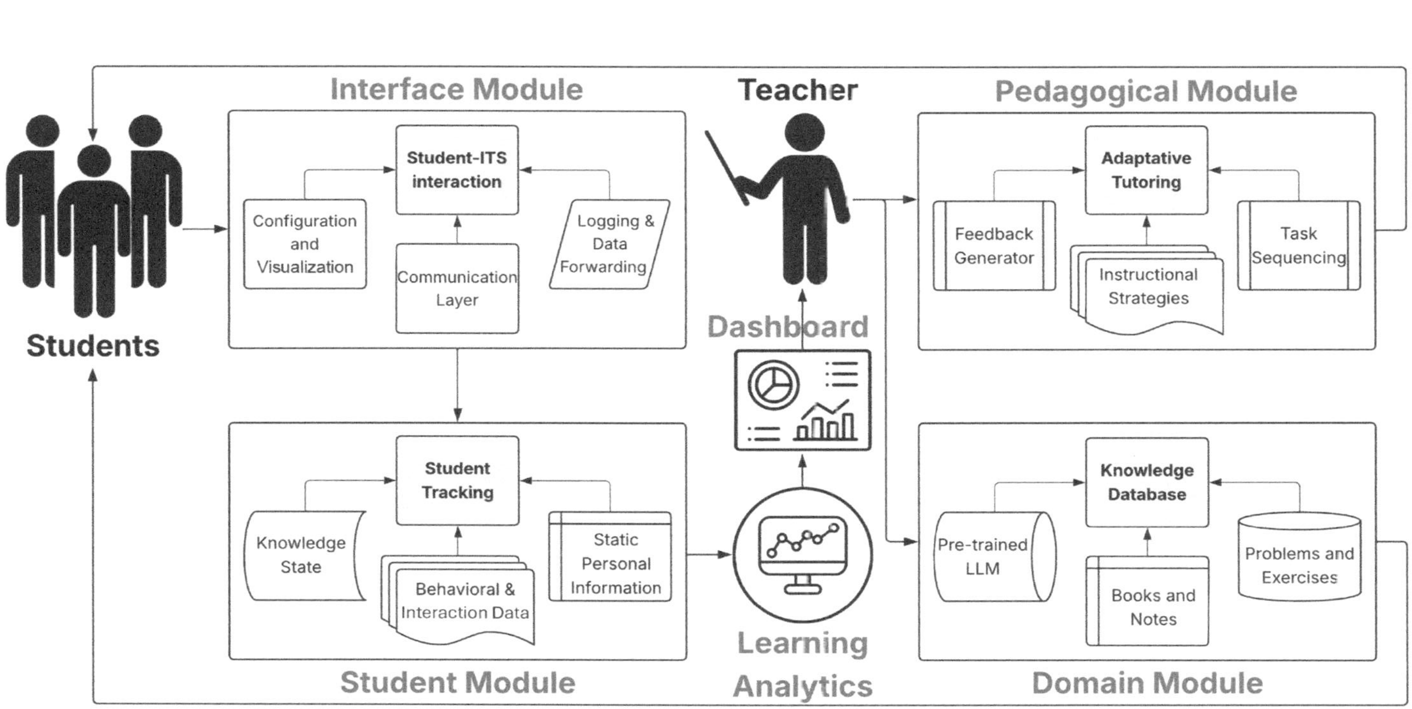

FIGURE 11.4 Teacher-in-the-loop ITS architecture integrating LA. The proposed architecture illustrates how the four fundamental modules of an ITS interact with both students and teachers. The dashboard acts as a mediator, channeling LA derived from student–ITS interactions toward the teacher, enabling instructors to adjust pedagogical strategies or domain-level resources while monitoring students in real time.

of intermediary oversight might counterbalance the inherent reliability risks associated with non-deterministic systems, like LLMs (Bommasani et al., 2021; Song et al., 2024).

For instance, the student module records information such as problems completion rate, number of attempts, sequence position, knowledge state, and behavioral patterns during problem-solving. These data are complemented by the interface module, which tracks time on task (both cumulative and per exercise), idle time, and interaction recency. Accuracy and performance metrics—when available—are also incorporated, including correctness rates and the number of incorrect attempts. Furthermore, student-ITS interaction logs register the frequency of exchanges (e.g., turns per minute or per problem), types of help requested, and recurrence of specific requests such as conceptual explanations or direct answers. Together, these variables enable teachers to refine instructional strategies, adjust task sequencing, recalibrate feedback mechanisms, or shift emphasis toward underdeveloped domain concepts. By aligning rich, multidimensional learning analytics with teacher oversight, such a system can foster more precise and personalized academic support for each learner, while simultaneously mitigating risks associated with fully automated LLM-driven tutoring.

11.6.2 Automating LA With LLMs

As indicated in Section 5, the best category-level classification accuracy was slightly above 80%, while the overall precision barely surpassed 60%. Such performance remains insufficient for an ITS to autonomously make decisions regarding students' cognitive engagement level or to personalize/adapt the course content accordingly. However, when interactions are aggregated into productive versus unproductive categories, the resulting patterns—despite some classification errors—can still provide teachers with useful insights for deciding whether to intervene or monitor a student more closely. Importantly, the decision to flag a potentially struggling student should be based not on the classification of a single interaction, but on a sequence of interactions within the broader problem-solving context that can provide a better picture of each student's struggle.

With this in mind, we propose an initial dashboard design that transforms raw student–ITS exchanges into actionable signals, enabling teachers to notice, interpret, and respond effectively. The dashboard combines a cohort-level overview for rapid triage with seamless drill-downs for individual diagnosis, offering the following key affordances: **at-a-glance situational awareness** (identify which students are progressing, potentially stuck, struggling, or disengaged); **fast drill-down** (move directly from an alert to the specific interaction snippets or student turns that triggered it); **human override** (allow teachers to add comments, annotate student interactions, or filter agent replies before they are delivered); **configurable thresholds** (enable teachers to set individualized thresholds for status changes—for instance, deciding to monitor new students more closely).

11.6.3 Traffic-Light Semantics

To provide situational awareness of student progress, we implemented a status model based on traffic-light semantics. Statuses are designed as **heuristics** that guide teacher attention rather than final judgments. Each status is computed over a sliding window (default: **10 minutes or the last 12 turns**, whichever is shorter) and allows teachers to identify potentially struggling students quickly. Table 11.4 summarizes the heuristics derived from the dataset described in Section 4. An "on track" status indicates steady progress in exercises with a low error rate and predominantly productive exchanges. A "potentially stuck" status reflects limited progress and/or repeated expressions of incomprehension (e.g., confusion or frustration), with up to 89% classification accuracy based on our top-model performance. A "struggling" status is triggered by requests for direct answers (89% accuracy) or when an expression in inappropriate language is detected (100% accuracy). Finally, a "disengaged" status corresponds to more than five minutes of inactivity within the ITS, provided that the problem being worked on has not been solved.

Figure 11.5 illustrates the dashboard design. Each student is represented as a tile displaying their status, problem progress, and time on task. By selecting a tile, the teacher can access a detailed interaction history (both actual exchanges and coded interaction categories), a more granular view of recent progress, and the option to send targeted comments with hints, clarifications, or encouragement. The dashboard also includes performance metrics such as time on task for recent problems and interaction frequency within the last 30 minutes, providing teachers with additional situational awareness.

Table 11.5 illustrates an interaction from our dataset that begins with the student requesting help but gradually escalates to verbal aggression toward the ITS. Before this point, the student explicitly demanded a direct answer to the problem. Such a pattern would have been successfully flagged by the LA dashboard as a "red" alert, enabling the instructor to intervene before the student escalates the conflict and loses interest in solving the exercise with the support of the ITS. It is also interesting to note that in this example there appears to be one classification error (second

TABLE 11.4
Progress Status Based on Type of Interaction, Frequency and Activity

Status (Color)	Type of Interaction	Related Frequency	Related Activity
On track (● Green)	Call for Assistance Conceptual Query Confirmation of Reasoning Request for Example Calculation or Operation	As long as no other status color is activated	The student is advancing in exercise completion even though some errors can be present
Potentially stuck (○ Yellow)	Expression of Incomprehension Off-Topic	≥ 3 of these interaction types in the last 5 minutes	Little to no progress for ≥ 5 minutes or off-topic conversations
Struggling (● Red)	Demand for Direct Answer Negative Expression	≥ 1 verbal aggression ≥ 1 intent to obtain direct solution	The student is trying to cheat his way out or is using inappropriate language
Disengaged (● Purple)	Long period of inactivity	0 interactions in the last 5 minutes	No activity detected for ≥ 5 minutes

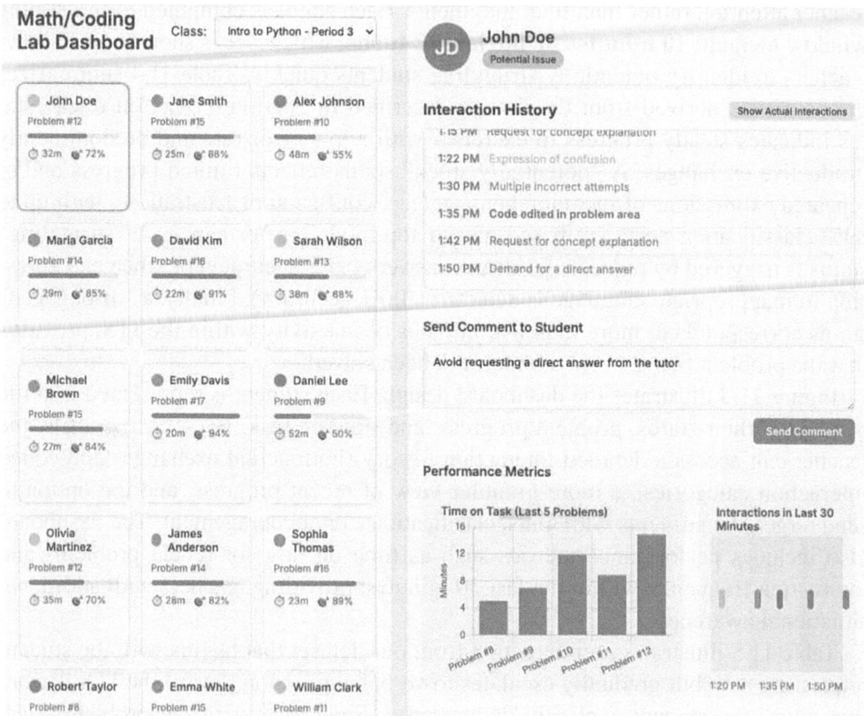

FIGURE 11.5 Dashboard design for situational awareness and teacher intervention.

TABLE 11.5
Example of Escalating Student–ITS Interaction with LLM and Expert Coding

Time Spent	Student's Message	LLM-Assigned Code	Expert-Assigned Code
0	Can you help me?	Call for Assistance	Call for Assistance
0:01:47	it has a height 3 times the length of the base . . .	Problem Transcription	Confirmation of Reasoning
0:02:10	yes	Response to the Agent	Response to the Agent
0:02:49	give me the value of the base and height	Demand for Direct Answer	Demand for Direct Answer
0:03:20	stupid, you don't know anything	Negative Expression	Negative Expression

exchange) made by LLM. Yet under further review one expert coder agreed that it was indeed a direct problem transcription from the student, which could potentially be interpreted as a demand for guidance or a direct response.

Beyond classroom monitoring, this integration establishes a foundation for adaptive orchestration: teachers can combine LA-driven signals with contextual knowledge (e.g., prior student performance, motivational states) to adjust both the pacing of instruction and the focus of automated feedback. In doing so, the dashboard operationalizes the principle of human-centered AI, ensuring that scalable LLM-powered analytics remain aligned with pedagogical goals and ethical constraints.

11.7 CONCLUSION AND FUTURE WORK

11.7.1 Conclusion

In Experiment 1, three human experts developed and validated a codebook to capture the conversational characteristics of student–ITS interactions within a mathematics tutoring environment. The resulting taxonomy of 12 categories distinguished between productive behaviors (e.g., calls for assistance, conceptual queries, confirmations, and example requests) and unproductive ones (e.g., demands for direct answers, incomprehension, or off-topic drift). This process not only revealed patterns of engagement but also highlighted how sequences of interactions can escalate from constructive exchanges into frustration or disengagement, providing a foundation for pedagogically relevant LA.

In Experiment 2, six LLMs were evaluated under three prompting strategies (zero-shot, few-shot, and zero-shot with conversational history) to assess their capacity to automate student interactions classification. Results indicated moderate precision overall (≈60%), with category-level accuracies exceeding 80% for certain intents under few-shot conditions. Importantly, aggregated distinctions between productive and unproductive behaviors proved reliable enough to generate actionable early-warning signals. While subtler categories such as confirmation of reasoning remain best interpreted by humans, these findings suggest that LLMs can serve as effective preprocessing engines to scale qualitative insights into real-time actionable analytics.

Building on these insights, we designed a teacher-facing dashboard that converts interaction data into actionable LA. The dashboard employs traffic-light semantics to flag at-risk learners, provides drill-down access to coded interactions, and enables human override, annotation, and threshold configuration. By operationalizing teacher oversight, it ensures that LLM-powered LA does not replace but rather augment pedagogical decision-making, counterbalancing risks like hallucinations or context drift.

11.7.2 Future Work

Fine-tuning and hybrid modeling: Expanding the dataset of coded interactions would enable model fine-tuning and the development of hybrid pipelines that combine rule-based heuristics with LLM predictions. This is particularly relevant for subtle categories where current models struggle. The main rationale for pursuing this line of research lies in our findings that few-shot prompting achieved the highest category-level accuracy, suggesting that a larger corpus of coded student–ITS interactions is needed to extend the representational window of each category, thereby improving coverage and reducing misclassification of outliers that previously fell into incorrect categories.

Real-time classroom deployment: Evaluating the dashboard in authentic classroom contexts is critical. Beyond measuring technical performance, such trials are useful to examine how teachers interpret alerts, how they act upon them, and what effects such teacher interventions have on student outcomes. Classroom deployment will also reveal practical usability issues, since users tend to express their preferences and needs more clearly after experiencing real-life scenarios. Iterative evaluation of the UI will thus be paramount to ensure alignment with teacher workflows and classroom constraints.

Adaptive orchestration: A promising direction is to explore how LA-driven insights can be combined with contextual data such as prior achievements, motivational profiles, or engagement histories. Such integration would strengthen the reliability of the ITS personalization sub-processes, leading to tutoring responses that are not only technically accurate but also cognitively and pedagogically meaningful. By supporting dynamic adaptation of both Pedagogical and Domain Modules, adaptive orchestration can transform dashboards from monitoring tools into intelligent orchestration systems.

Ethical and trust dimensions: Any use of AI in education inevitably raises questions of transparency, fairness, and trust. For dashboards to be adopted sustainably, they must present analytics in interpretable ways that empower teachers rather than overwhelm them. Moreover, issues such as bias in classification and equitable access to AI-enhanced learning tools must be addressed explicitly. Future research should therefore focus on co-designing dashboards with teachers to ensure usability, clarify the boundaries of AI versus human judgment, and implement safeguards that make trustworthiness an integral design feature rather than an afterthought.

Teacher reliance and behavioral evolution: An additional consideration is how teachers' behavior evolves once they begin to rely on such tools. Recent evidence from the medical field shows that physicians using AI systems can experience performance declines when they become over-dependent on the technology, potentially overlooking their own expertise and judgment (Budzyń et al., 2025). A similar risk could emerge in education if teachers defer excessively to dashboards rather than engaging critically with their own professional insights. Investigating how reliance patterns develop over time and designing mechanisms that reinforce teachers' agency while preventing over-trust, will therefore be essential to ensure long-term, responsible adoption.

Cross-domain generalization: Finally, while this study was situated in the domain of mathematics, replicating the approach in other areas such as programming, academic writing, or language learning will help test the generalizability of the framework. Such extensions would refine the taxonomy of student intents, reveal domain-specific interaction patterns, and assess whether the proposed teacher-in-the-loop architecture remains robust across diverse curricular contexts.

In conclusion, this chapter provides empirical and design evidence that human-in-the-loop LA can scale qualitative insight through LLM automation while keeping teachers at the center of instructional orchestration. By advancing toward real-time, interpretable, and ethically aligned dashboards, we take an important step toward more trustworthy and effective ITS in the era of generative AI.

11.7.2.1 Compliance Statement

The authors affirm strict compliance with the ethical and publication integrity standards established by the target journal. GenAI tools were employed exclusively for language polishing, structuring drafts, and improving clarity, while all conceptual contributions, methodological designs, data analyses, and interpretations are the sole responsibility of the authors. Failure to comply with these guidelines may result in academic penalties, and the authors accept full responsibility for any issues arising from non-compliance.

REFERENCES

Alfredo, R., Echeverria, V., Jin, Y., Yan, L., Swiecki, Z., Gašević, D., & Martinez-Maldonado, R. (2024). Human-centred learning analytics and AI in education: A systematic literature review. *Computers and Education Artificial Intelligence*, 6, 100215. https://doi.org/10.1016/j.caeai.2024.100215

Bommasani, R., Hudson, D. A., Adeli, E., Altman, R., Arora, S., von Arx, S., . . . & Liang, P. (2021). On the opportunities and risks of foundation models. *arXiv preprint*. https://doi.org/10.48550/arXiv.2108.07258

Budzyń, K., Romańczyk, M., Kitala, D., . . . Mori, Y. (2025). Endoscopist deskilling risk after exposure to artificial intelligence in colonoscopy: A multicentre, observational study. *The Lancet. Gastroenterology & Hepatology*. https://doi.org/10.1016/s2468-1253(25)00133-5

Cukurova, M. (2024). The interplay of learning, analytics and artificial intelligence in education: A vision for hybrid intelligence. *British Journal of Educational Technology*. https://doi.org/10.1111/bjet.13514

Dollinger, M., & Lodge, J. M. (2018). Co-creation strategies for learning analytics. In *Proceedings of the 8th International Conference on Learning Analytics and Knowledge* (pp. 97–101). Association for Computing Machinery. https://doi.org/10.1145/3170358.3170372

Dweck, C. S., & Yeager, D. S. (2019). Mindsets: A view from two eras. *Perspectives on Psychological Science*, 14(3), 481–496. https://doi.org/10.1177/1745691618804166

Ferguson, R. (2012). Learning analytics: Drivers, developments and challenges. *International Journal of Technology Enhanced Learning*, 4(5), 304–317. https://doi.org/10.1504/IJTEL.2012.051816

Gao, L., Lu, J., Shao, Z., Lin, Z., Yue, S., Ieong, C., . . . & Chen, S. (2024). Fine-tuned large language model for visualization system: A study on self-regulated learning in education. *IEEE Transactions on Visualization and Computer Graphics*. http://doi.org/10.1109/TVCG.2024.3456145

Handa, K., Clapper, M., Boyle, J., Wang, R. E., Yang, D., Yeager, D. S., & Demszky, D. (2023). "Mistakes help us grow": Facilitating and evaluating growth mindset supportive language in classrooms. In *Proceedings of EMNLP* (pp. 8877–8897). https://doi.org/10.18653/v1/2023.emnlp-main.549

Hattie, J., & Timperley, H. (2007). The power of feedback. *Review of Educational Research*, 77(1), 81–112. https://doi.org/10.3102/003465430298487

Hernández-Leo, D. (2023). ChatGPT and generative AI in higher education: User-centered perspectives and implications for learning analytics. In *Proceedings of LASI Spain 2023* (pp. 1–10). CEUR Workshop Proceedings. https://ceur-ws.org/Vol-3542/paper2.pdf

Hsieh, H. F., & Shannon, S. E. (2005). Three approaches to qualitative content analysis. *Qualitative Health Research*, 15(9), 1277–1288. https://doi.org/10.1177/1049732305276687

Khosravi, H., Shibani, A., Jovanovic, J., Pardos, Z. A., & Yan, L. (2025). Generative AI and learning analytics. *Journal of Learning Analytics*, 12(1), 1–11. https://doi.org/10.18608/jla.2025.8961

Lai, J. W., Qiu, W., Thway, M., Zhang, L., Jamil, N. B., Su, C. L., Ng, S. S. H., & Lim, F. S. (2025). Leveraging process-action epistemic network analysis to illuminate student self-regulated learning with a Socratic chatbot. *Journal of Learning Analytics*, 1–19. https://doi.org/10.18608/jla.2025.8549

Levchuk, O., Sánchez, C., Pacheco, N., López, I., & Favela, J. (2024). Interaction design (IxD) of an intelligent tutor for programming learning based on LLM. *Avances En Interacción Humano-Computadora*, 9(1), 1–10. https://doi.org/10.47756/aihc.y9i1.137

Li, Y., Wu, Y., & Chiu, T. K. F. (2025). How teacher presence affects student engagement with a generative artificial intelligence chatbot in learning designed with first principles of instruction. *Journal of Research on Technology in Education*, 1–17. https://doi.org/10.1080/15391523.2025.2493942

Lin, C., Chang, K. E., & Winne, P. H. (2025). Analyzing student–chatbot interaction patterns to scaffold peer feedback: A methodological framework. *Journal of the Learning Sciences*. https://doi.org/10.1007/s11423-024-10408-3

Liu, H., Zhang, Y., & Jia, J. (2024). The design of guiding and adaptive prompts for intelligent tutoring systems and its effect on students' mathematics learning. *IEEE Transactions on Learning Technologies*, 17, 1379–1389. https://doi.org/10.1109/TLT.2024.3382000

Martinez-Maldonado, R. (2023). Human-centred learning analytics: Four challenges in realising the potential. *Learning Letters*, 1, 6. https://doi.org/10.59453/FIZJ7007

Misiejuk, K., López-Pernas, S., Kaliisa, R., & Saqr, M. (2025). Mapping the landscape of generative artificial intelligence in learning analytics. *Journal of Learning Analytics*, 1–20. https://doi.org/10.18608/jla.2025.8591

Noy, S., & Zhang, W. (2023). Experimental evidence on the productivity effects of generative artificial intelligence. *Science*, 381(6654), 187–192. https://doi.org/10.1126/science.adh2586

Ochoa, X., Huang, X., & Shao, Y. (2025). Exploring the potential of generative AI to support non-experts in learning analytics practice. *Journal of Learning Analytics*, 12(1), 65–90. https://doi.org/10.18608/jla.2025.8615

Orynbassarova, D., & Porta, S. D. L. (2024). Implementing the Socratic Method with AI: Opportunities and challenges of integrating ChatGPT into teaching pedagogy. In *2024 ICETA* (pp. 526–532). IEEE.

Rodríguez-Ortiz, M. Á., Santana-Mancilla, P. C., & Anido-Rifón, L. E. (2025). Machine learning and generative AI in learning analytics for higher education: A systematic review of models, trends, and challenges. *Applied Sciences*, 15(15), 8679. https://doi.org/10.3390/app15158679

Schmucker, R., Xia, M., Azaria, A., & Mitchell, T. (2023). Ruffle&riley: Towards the automated induction of conversational tutoring systems. *arXiv preprint*. https://doi.org/10.48550/arXiv.2310.01420

Song, Y., Wang, G., Li, S., & Lin, B. Y. (2024). The good, the bad, and the greedy: Evaluation of llms should not ignore non-determinism. *arXiv preprint*. https://doi.org/10.48550/arXiv.2407.10457

Tarun, B., Du, H., Kannan, D., & Gehringer, E. F. (2025). Human-in-the-loop systems for adaptive learning using generative AI. *arXiv preprint*. https://doi.org/10.48550/arXiv.2508.11062

Topali, P., Ortega-Arranz, A., Rodríguez-Triana, M. J., Er, E., Khalil, M., & Akçapınar, G. (2024). Designing human-centered learning analytics and artificial intelligence in education solutions: A systematic literature review. *Behaviour And Information Technology*, 1–28. https://doi.org/10.1080/0144929x.2024.2345295

Turner, J. C., & Patrick, H. (2008). How does motivation develop and why does it change? Reframing motivation research. *Educational Psychologist*, 43(3), 119–131. https://doi.org/10.1080/00461520802178441

Usher, M., & Amzalag, M. (2025). From prompt to polished: Exploring student–chatbot interactions for academic writing assistance. *Education Sciences*, 15(3), 329. https://doi.org/10.3390/educsci15030329

Vaswani, A., Shazeer, N., Parmar, N., Uszkoreit, J., Jones, L., Gomez, A. N., . . . & Polosukhin, I. (2017). Attention is all you need. *Advances in Neural Information Processing Systems*, 30. https://doi.org/10.48550/arXiv.1706.03762

12 Multimodal Learning Analytics in Practice

Lessons From the 1st IFE Experiential Classroom Call

Jessica Alejandra Ruiz-Ramírez, Cynthia Karyna López-Botello, Luis Fernando Morán-Mirabal, and Dayannis Tamayo-Preval

12.1 INTRODUCTION

The constant development and availability of new educational technology platforms (EdTechs), together with the evolution of educational models and the growing need to assess the development of students skills and abilities, have reinforced the importance of studying and analyzing the learning dynamics that occur inside and outside classrooms in higher education institutions (Bygstad et al., 2022). One discipline that has been positioned to address this challenge is multimodal learning analytics (MMLA), in which diverse technologies are integrated to collect and analyze multiple attributes of teaching and learning scenarios (Blikstein & Worsley, 2016).

Through MMLA, factors such as engagement, concentration, collaborative work, and communication can be examined by combining data from portable EEGs, smart bracelets, eye trackers, and depth cameras with demographic information, self-perception surveys, and performance assessment instruments (Guerrero-Sosa et al., 2025). The purpose of MMLA is the provision of actionable feedback for teachers and students, with the aim of improving educational practices (Worsley et al., 2021).

The concept of *multimodality* is frequently referenced in communication theory, where it is defined as the ability to convey meaning through different media. These media may include videos, books, films, websites, social networks, and emerging technologies such as artificial intelligence. In this framework, communication is not limited to verbal language but is also considered to involve non-verbal, visual, auditory, and digital elements. When this concept is applied to MMLA, the scope is broadened to include the multiple ways in which individuals communicate and learn. The discipline is characterized by the analysis of interactions between learners, content, and environments, using technologies that collect information from video, audio, gestures, login records, and biosensors, among others (Ochoa et al., 2022).

 DOI: 10.1201/9781003678250-12

12.1.1 Mapping and Execution as Core Phases of Multimodal Learning Analytics

In the first phase, *mapping*, a logical connection is established between the theoretical construct of learning under analysis and the multimodal data that can be observed during the learning process. This stage is carried out through four fundamental steps. First, the construct of interest is defined, understood as the specific aspect of learning to be examined. This definition is guided by the priorities of those responsible for the educational process, including teachers, researchers, or instructional designers. Once this conceptual map between learning and potential data sources has been created, the second phase begins.

The second phase, *execution*, is developed in an inverse order. The process begins with the collection and analysis of multimodal data in order to assess the desired learning outcomes. In this stage, multimedia signals such as video, audio, movement, or physiological data are recorded and subsequently processed to extract low-level features, for example, including gestures, facial expressions, or voice patterns. These features are then analyzed and integrated to produce high-level representations that allow the inference of behaviors, attitudes, or levels of understanding (Yurum, 2025). The resulting high-level information is used to detect relevant behavioral patterns and to provide more accurate assessments of learner progress or learning states. In this way, MMLA is recognized as a discipline that provides a more comprehensive view of the educational process while supporting pedagogical decision-making with greater precision (Ochoa et al., 2022).

Among the main advantages of this approach is the possibility of obtaining richer and more precise data about teaching and learning processes. Such data enable a more detailed analysis of student progress and allow assessments of the learning environment to be conducted in a more natural and authentic manner. Furthermore, the information obtained can be applied by educators to design more personalized content, better aligned with learners needs, thereby enhancing the overall educational experience.

Nevertheless, the implementation of these methodologies involves significant ethical concerns. The collection, reproduction, and dissemination of sensitive multimodal data raise critical issues related to privacy, consent, and responsible use. These concerns have frequently been described as the elephant in the room, since their existence is widely acknowledged yet often overlooked. In the context of rapidly advancing educational technologies, it is considered essential to establish robust and transparent regulations that guarantee the protection of user rights and ensure the ethical application of multimodal analytics (Yurum, 2025).

12.1.2 Innovation and Co-Creation Through Multimodal Learning Analytics

The implementation of multimodal learning analytics (MMLA) has been described as an opportunity not only for methodological advancement but also for innovation in collaborative educational research. In recent years, initiatives have emphasized that the added value of MMLA lies in the possibility of designing research frameworks that integrate multiple perspectives, enabling co-creation processes among teachers, students, researchers, and technologists. The involvement of different stakeholders has been recognized as essential to ensure that multimodal data are not interpreted exclusively from a technical standpoint, but rather from an educationally meaningful perspective (Dollinger et al., 2019).

The perspective of commitments has been introduced as a way to guide the growth of MMLA as a discipline. Worsley et al. (2021) proposed twelve commitments that highlight the importance of intentionality in data collection, ethical standards, participatory interpretation, and transparency in dissemination. These commitments underline that innovation in MMLA requires not only technological development but also co-responsibility with the educational community in order to ensure that analyses remain contextualized, ethical, and pedagogically relevant. From this standpoint, the process of innovation through MMLA is conceived as a shared construction that demands both methodological rigor and collaborative engagement.

Several empirical studies have shown that MMLA deployments can be effective only when participatory and co-designed approaches are adopted. Martinez-Maldonado et al. (2023) documented lessons learned from a large-scale implementation, identifying ethical, technical, and collaborative challenges, and highlighting the importance of involving teachers as co-designers of analytic systems. Similarly, Ouhaichi et al. (2024) emphasized that system design must be carried out with a human-centered approach, in which the needs of end users guide the construction of tools and interfaces. Finally, innovation and co-creation in MMLA have also been framed as part of the broader role of higher education institutions in promoting social and educational innovation. Universities are expected to act not only as spaces for the development of knowledge but also as facilitators of collaborative ecosystems in which teachers and students actively contribute to the design and evaluation of new practices (Kumari et al., 2020).

In order to deepen the understanding of experiences and interactions in real learning scenarios mediated by technology, a specialized laboratory named IFE Experiential Classroom—Learning Lab (IFE EC-LL) was established by the Living Lab of the Institute for the Future of Education (IFE Living Lab). This laboratory was designed to conduct MMLA studies with the objective of promoting the evidence-based use of educational technologies (Morán-Mirabal et al., 2025). The laboratory is equipped with more than 40 devices and sensors designed to collect, process, and analyze multimodal data. These devices include posture (depth cameras), facial gestures (RGB cameras), eye gaze (eye trackers), oral interactions (microphones), neural activity (portable EEGs), and digital biomarkers (smart bracelets). This infrastructure has allowed the study of teaching and learning processes with up to 30 participants simultaneously.

To initiate the operations of IFE EC-LL, collaboration was established between the IFE Living Lab and the IFE Novus initiative, which is oriented toward the promotion of educational innovation and research within the Tecnológico de Monterrey academic community. Through this collaboration, the first *Experiential Classroom Call* for proposals (ECC) was launched, in which faculty members were invited to submit MMLA-based research projects to investigate classroom methodologies and dynamics. A total of 13 proposals were received and subsequently reviewed by a committee of experts from educational institutions in Spain, Finland, Chile, and Mexico. Six proposals were selected to be implemented at IFE EC-LL during the first semester of 2025. The methodology applied in these projects, together with their main findings, challenges, and limitations, is described in the following sections.

These findings reinforce the argument that institutional models of innovation, such as the ECC, acquire value precisely because they promote collaboration across disciplinary and geographic boundaries. In this sense, the ECC is positioned as an example of how institutional calls can lower barriers to access, provide shared infrastructure, and enable collaborative experimentation. By aligning with international commitments for the responsible growth of MMLA, such initiatives illustrate the potential of universities to drive transformative educational practices that are co-created with their academic communities.

12.2 METHODOLOGY

The methodology of the ECC was conceived as a co-creation process aimed at fostering educational innovation through the application of MMLA. This approach was designed to reduce barriers for faculty interested in conducting experimental research by providing access to infrastructure, methodological guidance, and international evaluation. The framework was structured to balance methodological rigor with the flexibility required to address diverse disciplinary contexts. As a result, the call functioned not only as a mechanism for funding and project selection but also as a collaborative model that promoted innovation, cross-disciplinary exchange, and the systematic use of data-driven practices in higher education. Selection was based on criteria of methodological rigor, disciplinary relevance, and potential impact on students learning. Once selected, projects were implemented during the first academic semester of 2025, supported by institutional infrastructure and methodological guidance provided by the IFE Living Lab and Novus initiatives.

12.2.1 Institutional and Methodological Protocol (IFE Novus Framework)

Proposals were submitted by faculty members and reviewed by an international committee composed of experts from Spain, Finland, Chile, and Mexico. Once selected, projects were implemented during the first academic semester of 2025, supported by institutional infrastructure and methodological guidance provided by the IFE Novus initiative.

The documentation of the project proposals and progress across their different stages was recorded on the Novus digital platform. In this way, three main phases are considered (Figure 12.1):

1. Reception of proposals: A total of 13 applications were submitted for evaluation by the expert committee.

2. Experimental protocol: The experimentation protocols are included and reviewed by the Novus team for approval and/or identification of areas for improvement based on three general dimensions:
   - Problem to be addressed and selection of variables
   - Description of procedures
   - Ethical considerations in the implementation of the projects
3. Project management and results reporting: This phase includes the completion of the corresponding information for project closure in three dimensions:
   - General project information (including any emerging changes during implementation, previously reported to the faculty research team who managed, monitored, and mentored the projects)
   - Results and impact of the experimentation
   - Comments on educational innovation

12.2.2 Variables and Instruments

Specifically, IFE Novus requests measurement of two key variables: engagement and technological acceptance. To measure these variables, the Novus team provides two validated instruments to ensure the reliability and validity of the measurements.

Particularly, academic engagement is described as students involvement in academic learning and achievement (Assunção et al., 2020). According to Schaufeli et al. (2002), engagement is a positive, fulfilling, work-related, or study-related state of mind that is characterized by vigor, dedication, and absorption. It refers to a more persistent and pervasive affective-cognitive state that is not focused on any specific object, event, individual, or behavior.

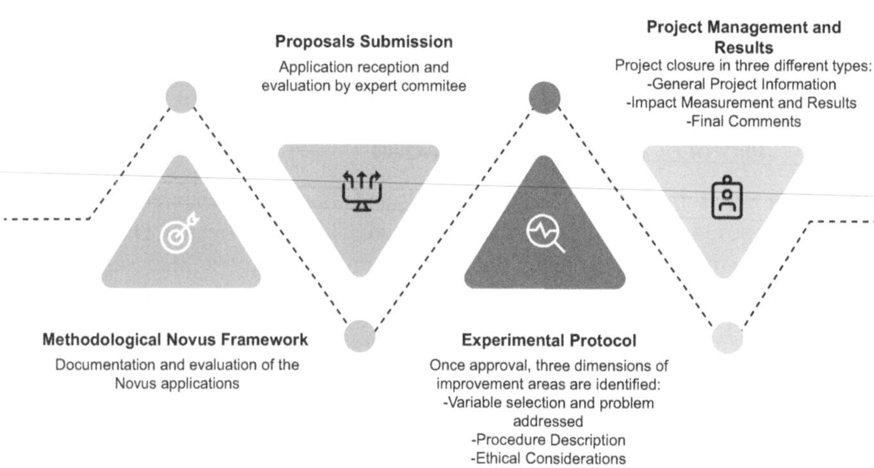

FIGURE 12.1 Methodology for documentation and evaluation: Novus Framework.

The instrument developed by Schaufeli et al. (2006) is known as the Utrecht Work Engagement Scale (UWES). The original version of the instrument consists of 24 items, distributed across the following three dimensions:

- Vigor: The willingness of students to engage in current activities, dedicating effort and perseverance in facing course challenges.
- Dedication: The degree to which students feel committed to the course content and activities.
- Absorption: The level of concentration and satisfaction that students experience with the course activities.

A short version of the instrument includes nine items, maintaining the same three dimensions, with three items per dimension. The Cronbach's alpha for the entire instrument was 0.93, indicating high internal consistency. The alpha values for the individual dimensions were as follows: vigor: 0.82, dedication: 0.90, and absorption: 0.84. This short version is shared with the professors for its application during the implementation phase.

On the other hand, the variable of technological acceptance or user experience allows for the evaluation of how students perceive the use of biometric technology as part of their learning process—an essential aspect for its future implementation. The instrument reported Cronbach's alpha values ranging from 0.85 to 0.91, indicating high internal consistency. The components of the instrument include the following:

- Perceived ease of use
- Perceived usefulness
- Intention to use
- Enjoyment

12.2.3 Experimental Protocols (IFE Living Lab Framework)

The theoretical foundations of the mapping and execution phases of multimodal learning analytics were introduced in Section 1.1. In the present section, these phases are revisited exclusively from an applied perspective, illustrating how they were operationalized through the shared framework of the IFE Living Lab. Rather than re-describing their conceptual underpinnings, the emphasis here is placed on the concrete procedures, instruments, and adaptations that guided the implementation of the six selected projects. This distinction ensures continuity with the theoretical model while avoiding unnecessary repetition, highlighting instead the methodological coherence achieved across diverse disciplinary contexts.

12.2.4 Purpose of the Shared Framework

The establishment of a shared methodological framework was intended to provide coherence across the projects developed in the IFE EC-LL. By defining a common structure, the initiative ensured that diverse disciplinary approaches could be aligned under comparable methodological conditions. This framework was conceived as a means to balance the need for consistency with the flexibility required to accommodate the particularities of each academic field (Zhao & Xu, 2024).

The primary purpose of this shared framework was to create a foundation that enabled the systematic integration of MMLA into teaching and learning contexts. Sufficient adaptability was maintained to allow disciplinary variations in constructs, instruments, and pedagogical strategies (Eradze et al., 2020). In this way, the shared framework served not only as a methodological guideline but also as an institutional mechanism for fostering collaboration, comparability, and scalability across projects.

Through the adoption of standardized stages for project design, implementation, and evaluation, the framework guaranteed that multimodal data collected in different disciplines could be analyzed in a coherent and replicable manner. These phases provided a sequential process that guided all projects, ensuring both methodological coherence and adaptability to diverse disciplinary contexts. The framework was inspired by the conceptual model of the multimodal data value chain (M-DVC), which emphasizes the systematic transformation of raw multimodal evidence into actionable insights for pedagogical decision-making (Ruiz-Ramírez & Glasserman-Morales, 2021). By grounding the framework in the principles of the M-DVC, the methodology ensured that multimodal data were not only collected but also transformed into reliable and pedagogically relevant information. The stages of the framework are summarized in Figure 12.2.

The design phase was initiated with the identification of experiential needs and the subsequent formulation of project proposals. The project objectives were defined and systematically translated into specific technological requirements. This phase culminated in the development of an experimental protocol, in which learning constructs were explicitly aligned with multimodal data sources. In this manner, theoretical definitions were operationalized through observable measures, ensuring methodological rigor and internal coherence.

In the implementation phase, experimental scenarios were deployed within the IFE EC-LL, enabling the collection of multimodal data in real time. Portable EEGs, physiological wristbands, eye trackers, depth cameras, and additional devices were employed to capture diverse dimensions of student behavior. These data were systematically integrated into a shared database, allowing cross-project comparability and synthesis. This phase reflected the execution dimension of MMLA, emphasizing the capture, synchronization, and fusion of multimodal signals to support subsequent analyses.

The evaluation phase was oriented toward the transformation of multimodal data into pedagogically meaningful insights. Analytical models, including machine learning and artificial intelligence techniques, were applied to the integrated datasets. Findings were disseminated through visualizations, facilitating the communication of results to both teachers and students. This phase prioritized the generation of actionable feedback, ensuring that the insights produced could inform pedagogical practices and guide iterative improvements. In this way, the framework established a systematic pathway from conceptualization to applied evaluation, providing the consistency required for comparability while preserving the flexibility necessary for disciplinary adaptation. This methodological framework ensured the consistency

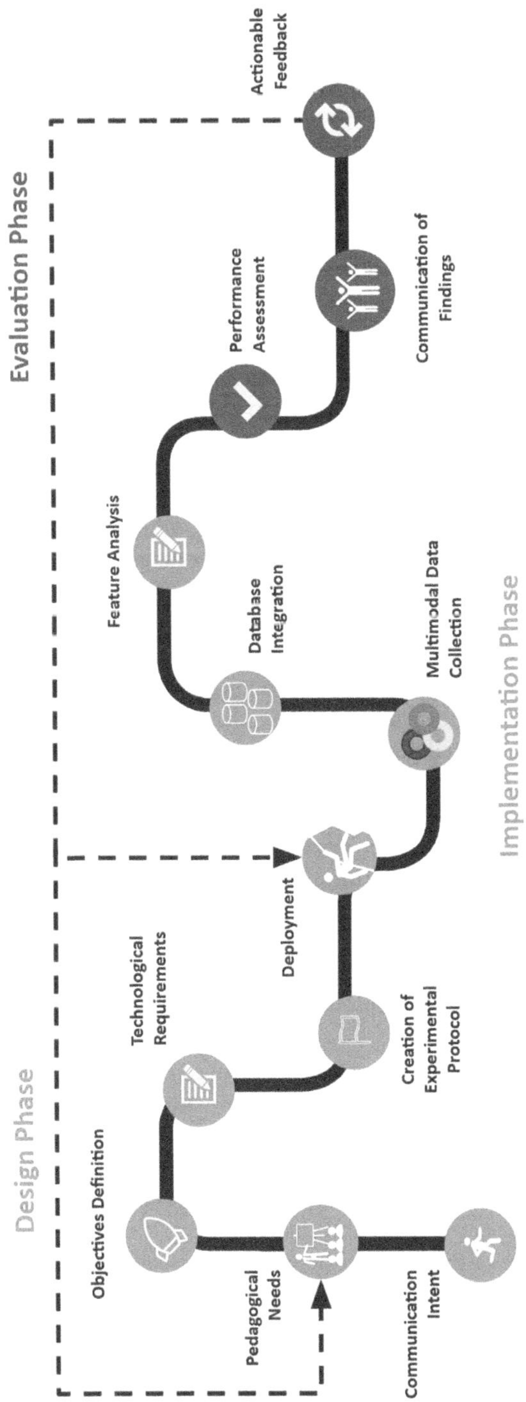

FIGURE 12.2 Conceptual model of the methodological framework applied in the IFE EC-LL.

required for comparability while preserving the flexibility necessary for disciplinary adaptation, thereby setting the stage for the subsequent analysis of project outcomes.

12.3 RESULTS

The implementation of the six selected projects in the IFE EC-LL during the first academic semester of 2025 produced a robust set of findings across diverse educational disciplines. While each project generated specific results and applied unique analytical models, detailed details of which will be presented in forthcoming scientific publications, this chapter offers a cross-case synthesis that highlights shared trends, methodological contributions, and pedagogical insights

12.3.1 From Design to Deployment: Implementing Experimental Protocols in the IFE EC-LL

The six selected projects implemented within the IFE EC-LL during the first semester of 2025 reflected a diverse set of disciplinary objectives, yet all adhered to a shared methodological structure. This structure ensured coherence in experimental design, data collection, and outcome reporting, while allowing for context-specific adaptations aligned with each field of study.

Each project was framed by a design protocol in which learning constructs were mapped to multimodal data sources, allowing theoretical variables such as self-regulation, decision-making, and oral communication to be operationalized through physiological, behavioral, and interactional indicators. During implementation, faculty teams deployed tailored pedagogical scenarios within the IFE EC-LL, leveraging devices such as EEG headbands, physiological wristbands, eye-tracking glasses, and high-definition cameras to capture students' cognitive and emotional states.

Across projects, data collection protocols followed the execution phase of the MMLA framework, emphasizing the real-time recording of multimodal evidence in naturalistic learning environments. Despite the diversity of academic domains—ranging from entrepreneurship and negotiation to behavioral self-regulation and public speaking—common patterns emerged. These included elevated student engagement, increased self-perception of learning gains, and positive responses to technology-mediated feedback.

Each project also reported on specific challenges encountered during implementation, including students' initial unfamiliarity with biometric devices, logistical complexity in sensor calibration, and the need for iterative adjustments in data capture protocols. Nonetheless, faculty participants consistently highlighted the added value of experimental learning environments for fostering reflection, motivation, and contextualized practice.

Overall, this phase of the initiative confirmed the feasibility of embedding multimodal experimentation into real-world educational practice. It also underscored the value of institutional support, methodological alignment, and shared infrastructure in fostering high-impact, evidence-based innovation in higher education. A summary of the six selected projects, including their academic focus, core objective, and deployed technologies, is provided in Table 12.1.

TABLE 12.1
Summary of Projects Implemented in the IFE EC-LL (2025)

No.	Project Title	Academic Focus	Objective	Devices Used
1	Biometric Recognition in Engineering Labs Using Quanser® Systems	Control Engineering/ Quality Evaluation	To assess student engagement and learning quality using multimodal data during practical lab sessions with Quanser® stations.	EEG headbands and physiological wristbands
2	The Classroom of the Future: Anticipatory Thinking and Experimental Practice	Business, Architecture, Talent Dev.	To explore students' anticipatory visions and scenario construction using immersive technologies and physiological data.	EEG headbands, physiological wristbands, and XR headsets
3	Neurofeedback for Entrepreneurs: Decoding Entrepreneurship with Technology	Entrepreneurship	To enhance innovation and decision-making through EEG and multimodal feedback during a 3-block project-based course.	EEG headbands, physiological wristbands, eye-tracking glasses, and microphones
4	Immersive Learning in Thermal Systems Through VR	Chemical Engineering/ Thermodynamics	To improve learning and engagement in thermal systems via immersive simulations of industrial plants.	Physiological wristbands and VR headsets
5	Emotional Impact in Negotiation: A Data-Driven Perspective	Business, Negotiation	To optimize emotional regulation and communication strategies in high-pressure negotiation scenarios.	EEG headbands and physiological wristbands
6	Human-Computer Feedback System for Public Speaking	Neuroscience/ Humanities	To design a real-time feedback system to improve public speaking, stress management, and persuasive communication.	EEG headbands and physiological wristbands

Although the shared methodological framework ensured coherence across projects, disciplinary adaptations were introduced to address the specific constructs, instruments, and pedagogical strategies of each academic field. These adaptations illustrate the versatility of the framework, as well as its capacity to support diverse lines of inquiry within the IFE EC-LL.

In this way, the adaptability of the framework was demonstrated through its application to diverse educational disciplines. While the methodological core remained constant, each project was able to contextualize the framework to address its specific objectives, thereby ensuring both comparability and disciplinary relevance.

12.3.2 Methodological and Infrastructural Contributions

The IFE EC-LL infrastructure proved effective for the synchronization and fusion of multimodal signals from up to 30 participants simultaneously. Projects demonstrated feasibility in integrating heterogeneous data streams—including physiological, neural, visual, and audio signals—into centralized dashboards for subsequent analysis.

A total of 29 structured data collection sessions were carried out between February and July 2025, distributed across pre- and post-intervention phases of the six projects. These sessions involved more than 750 students from undergraduate and postgraduate programs, representing one of the largest coordinated deployments of multimodal technologies in higher education settings to date. The sessions varied in format, ranging from small-group experimental activities (10–15 participants) to large-scale immersive simulations with more than 70 students per session. Each deployment demanded precise logistical planning, from device calibration and battery management to the synchronization of physiological and audiovisual streams.

The systematic recording of biometric and behavioral evidence enabled the generation of rich multimodal datasets, which were subsequently visualized and discussed with instructors and students during debriefing sessions. This process reinforced reflective learning practices while also providing faculty with unprecedented insights into classroom dynamics. Importantly, the capacity of the IFE EC-LL to sustain intensive cycles of data acquisition without compromising instructional flow validated its role as a scalable and reliable research infrastructure.

12.3.3 Multimodal Contributions to Teaching and Learning Processes

Beyond the methodological and infrastructural achievements, the projects also highlighted the value of multimodal data as a source of pedagogically meaningful insights. Two specific lines of analysis exemplify these contributions: conversational pattern analysis for collaborative work and psychophysiological monitoring during instructional activities.

12.3.3.1 Conversational Patterns and Collaborative Work

The study of collaborative work relied on the systematic analysis of conversation patterns extracted from audio-recordings of group interactions. This approach focused on a series of quantitative metrics, such as turn-taking frequency (Total Turns), turn-length (Words per Turn), lexical diversity, and a key predictor of balanced participation: Communication Equality. The interpretation of these metrics revealed that a high volume of communication is not necessarily conducive to effective collaboration but may be a signal of dysfunctional dynamics. The results uncovered two qualitatively different profiles of imbalance: while some groups were hindered by "Interruptions," in the form of brisk and frequent turns by a few dominant individuals and discouraging wider participation, others were slowed down by "Monologues," long discourses by an individual member that dominated the conversation. Figure 12.3 illustrates the variation in Communication Equality within the groups and thus offers a clear visual representation of these disparate modes of collaboration. This visualization helped professors to identify the dynamics of groups, allowing them to determine if imbalances stemmed from dominant leaders or unequal allocation of conversational floor time and to understand the varying logics underlying the interactivity of each group.

12.3.3.2 Psychophysiological Data in Instructional Scenarios

Physiological monitoring using a medical-grade wristband (Empatica Embraceplus) focused on three key variables: electrodermal activity (EDA), skin temperature (T), and heart rate estimated from systolic peaks (BVP). These measures allowed students to understand their physiological activation across different phases of the session. Interpretations were grounded in psychophysiological literature, which associates EDA with arousal and emotional engagement (Boucsein, 2012; Healey & Picard, 2005). For instance, low baseline EDA and stable temperature reflected calm states during information reception, whereas increases in EDA during performance and feedback phases indicated higher emotional activation, often linked to stress or anticipation. Figure 12.4 provides an example of the psychophysiological reports generated with the wristbands data, illustrating the temporal evolution of electrodermal activity (EDA), skin temperature, and heart rate across three phases of a

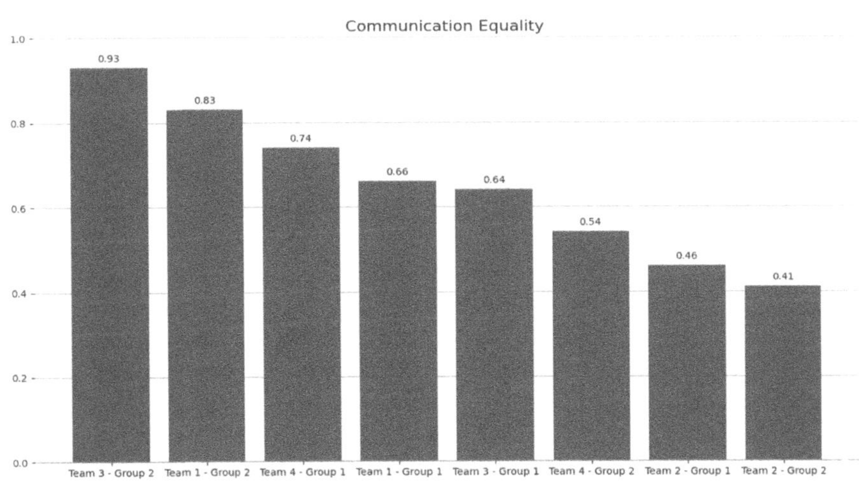

FIGURE 12.3 Communication equality comparison between two different groups of students.

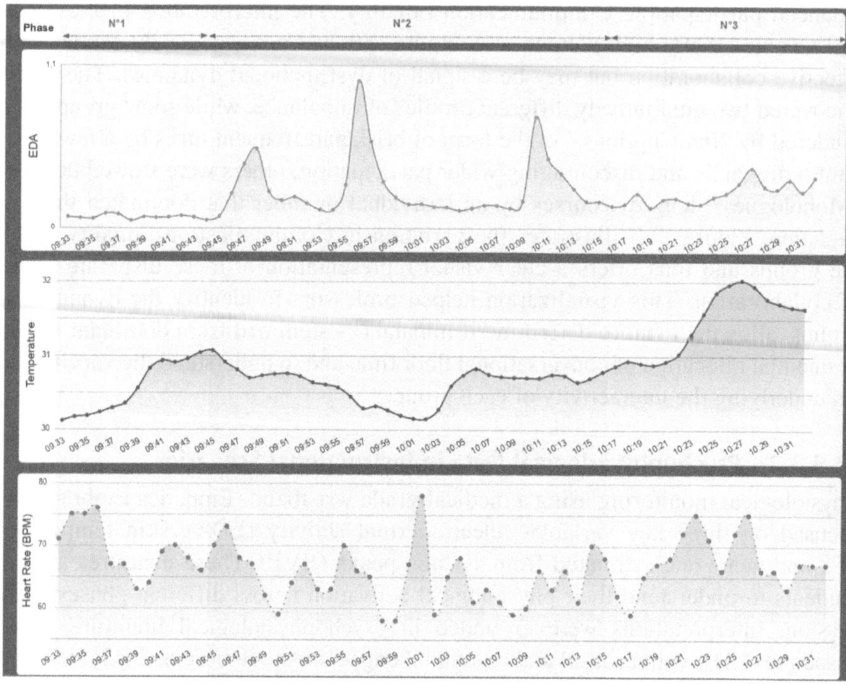

FIGURE 12.4 Temporal evolution of psychophysiological indicators (EDA, temperature, and heart rate) across three instructional phases. Example of a report provided to instructors.

classroom session. This visualization was particularly valuable for instructors, as it enabled them to identify calm states during the initial explanation, heightened arousal during performance, and sustained activation during feedback.

12.3.3.3 EEG-Based Cognitive–Emotional Indicators

In parallel, portable EEG headbands (Muse 2) were used to process alpha, beta, theta, and gamma brainwaves, generating relative measures of four indicators: alertness, concentration, fatigue, and stress. These metrics were interpreted using a machine learning–based model validated in prior academic studies (Pérez-Gómez et al., 2025; Torres-Rodríguez et al., 2025). Findings revealed consistently high levels of alertness (above 95%) and concentration (around 78%), minimal fatigue (0.6%), and elevated stress in approximately 75% of the records. This pattern indicates strong cognitive engagement and sustained energy, though accompanied by significant emotional load, particularly during evaluative stages. The distribution of cognitive–emotional indicators derived from EEG analysis was systematically reported to faculty as part of the feedback process. Figure 12.5 illustrates an example of these reports, showing the percentage of records classified as high versus medium/low across four indicators: alertness, concentration, fatigue, and stress. This visualization allowed instructors to quickly interpret student states during different phases of the session and to identify patterns of sustained activation or potential emotional overload.

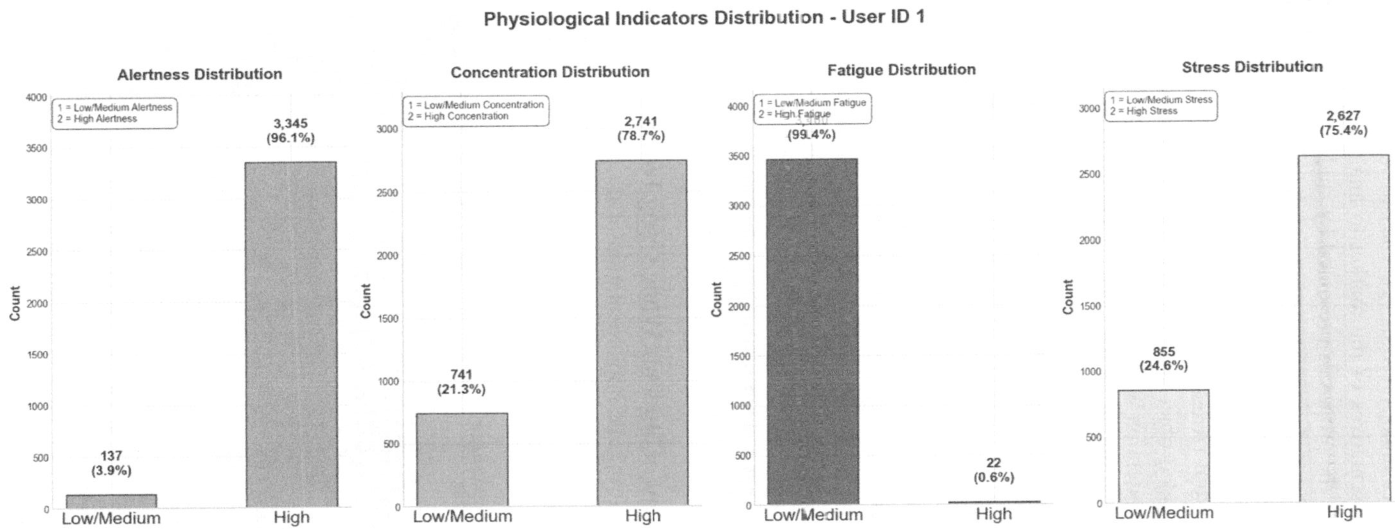

FIGURE 12.5 Distribution of physiological indicators (alertness, concentration, fatigue, and stress) obtained through EEG analysis. Example of a report delivered to instructors.

12.3.3.4 Eye-Tracking Indicators of Visual Attention

Mobile eye-tracking technology (Tobii Pro Glasses 3) was employed with participants acting as representatives of the market to analyze how external evaluators visually engaged with the proposals presented by students. This approach allowed the research team to determine which aspects of the presentations, such as textual components, product images, or the presenters themselves, attracted greater attention and for how long.

Metrics including AOI (Areas of Interest), fixation count, dwell time, and heat map distribution provided objective evidence of evaluators visual focus. In entrepreneurship sessions, attention was consistently concentrated on graphical elements that illustrated business models or prototypes, while textual descriptions received comparatively less visual engagement. Figure 12.6 presents an example of an AOI report generated during one of these sessions, showing the distribution of visual fixations across the main components of a student presentation. Such visualizations were shared with instructors and students to highlight which elements of their proposals effectively captured audience attention, offering valuable feedback to refine communication and persuasive strategies.

Together, these multimodal approaches demonstrate how integrating conversational and biometric analyses can enrich the teaching and learning process. By making visible aspects of collaboration, concentration, and emotional regulation that typically remain implicit, the IFE EC-LL projects positioned MMLA as a practical tool for guiding pedagogical decisions and fostering reflective, data-informed learning environments.

12.3.3.5 Engagement of Students While Using Technology

Student engagement during the implementation of six projects was measured using the UWES-S9 scale. The study comprised a sample of 70 participants. The analysis, carried out with OpenAI (2025), revealed that students did not show an increase in

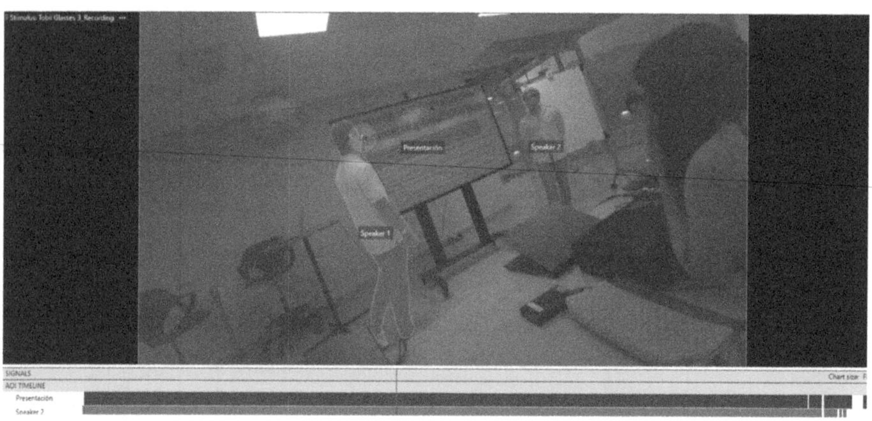

FIGURE 12.6 Example of an AOI report generated through eye-tracking with external evaluators during a student business proposal presentation.

their level of engagement after incorporating biometric technology into their courses, as illustrated in Figure 12.7.

12.3.3.6 Dimensions of Engagement of Students While Using Technology

When analyzing engagement by dimensions, it can be observed there is an increase in vigor and absorption. Vigor is characterized as having a great volunteer to dedicate to their studies regardless of their difficulties. Absorption refers to the total concentration and happiness they have during their classes. These can make them feel that time passes rapidly and when they have to leave their activities, they experience displeasure. This means that the students report being more persistent, really concentrated and with more happiness in their classes after using the different biometric technologies.

On the other hand, a slight decrease is observed in the dedication dimension Post-test application. This outcome may be partly explained by the fact that, although the novelty effect of incorporating biometric technologies can initially generate enthusiasm among students (81.7), over time some students might perceive a sense of being monitored, which could subtly influence their self-perception of dedication and/or commitment to the course content. It is therefore recommended, as noted by Creswell (2009), to triangulate these findings with qualitative techniques, deeper insights into student experiences, perceptions, and motivations regarding engagement with the course activities were obtained (Figure 12.8).

Also, it was of interest to examine the educational technology acceptance from students. A total of 70 students completed the questionnaire. Figure 12.9 illustrates that in a scale from 0 to 100 the dimension of engagement (86.5) while using technology and learning experience (85.9) were the ones with higher average. This means that students had a positive attitude towards educational technology, they felt happy using it in their classes and expected to use it in the future. Also, the use of technology helps them experience a better connection between theories and real-life experiences.

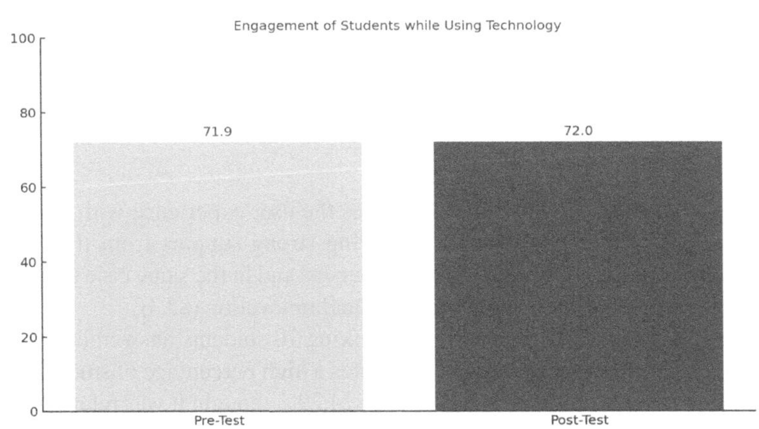

FIGURE 12.7 Engagement of students during the experience using biometric technology.

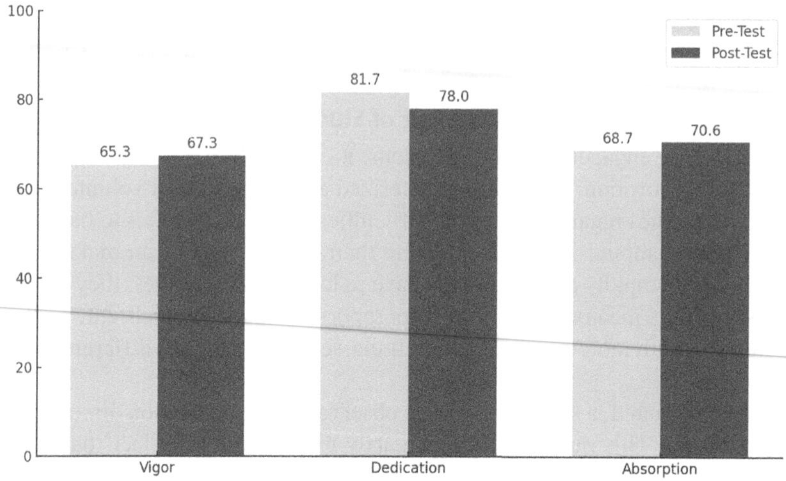

FIGURE 12.8 Dimension of engagement students during the experience using technology.

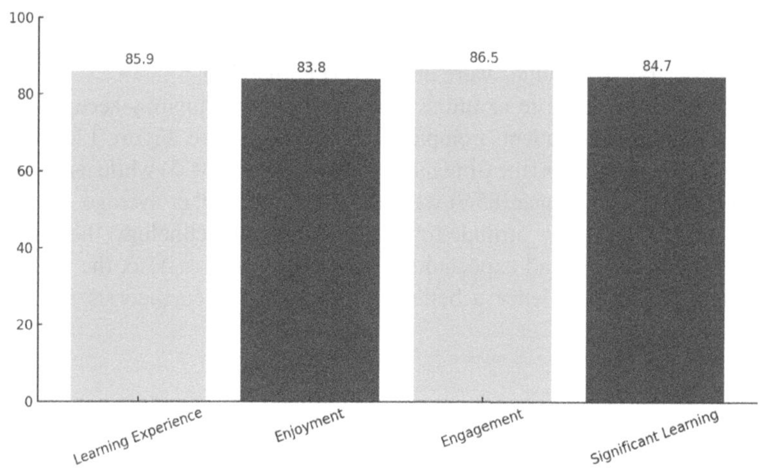

FIGURE 12.9 Educational technology acceptance.

On the other hand, Figure 12.10 illustrates the user experience with the technology, showing that students reported receiving strong support from their teachers (94.7) while using the technology on their courses, and in the same case they felt they really learned more while using the educational innovation (87.3).

Figure 12.11 represents the emotional ranking 70 students answered when asked how they felt using the technology. It illustrates a high percentage of students feeling happy with it in their courses (31.43%), also, 24.29% thought it was relevant using it. These results match with the ones found on Figure 12.6 where they had high levels of absorption.

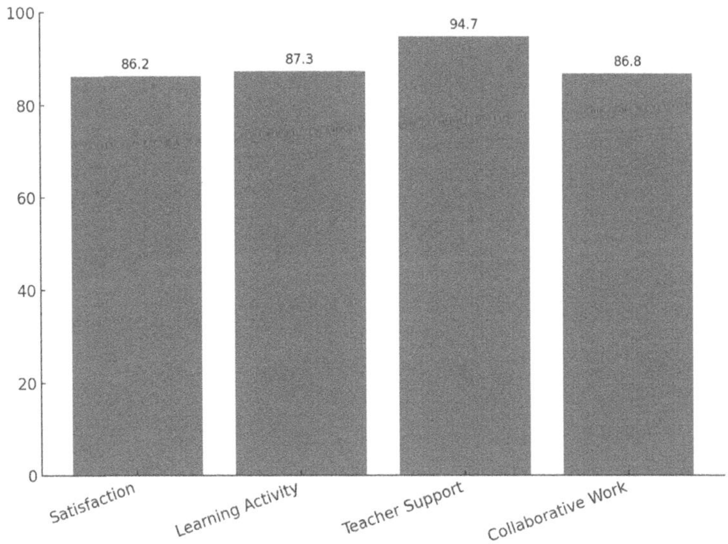

FIGURE 12.10 User experience.

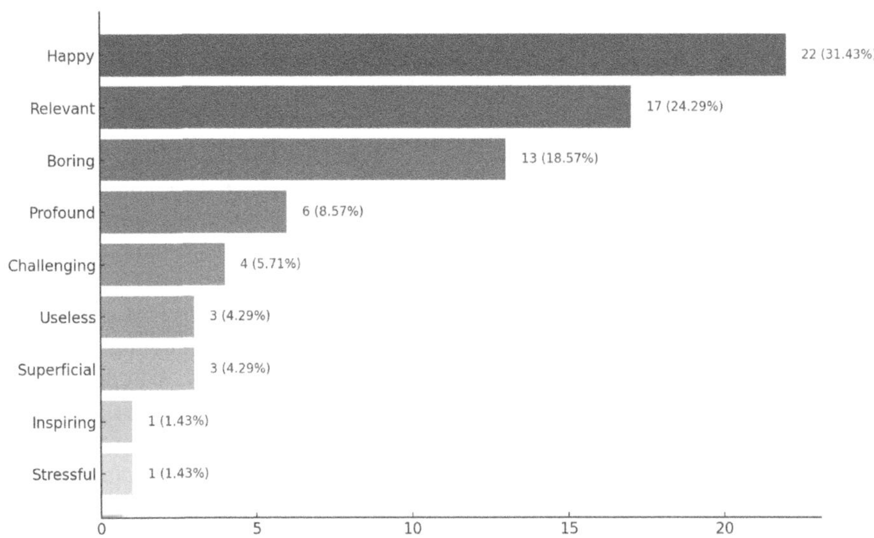

FIGURE 12.11 Emotional ranking felt during learning experience.

Finally, 95.7% of the students recommended having these kinds of experiences while learning new concepts in their classes and expressed appreciation for the support provided by teachers throughout the process. This highlights the importance of the human factor as a key facilitator when integrating new technologies into the learning environment (See Figure 12.12).

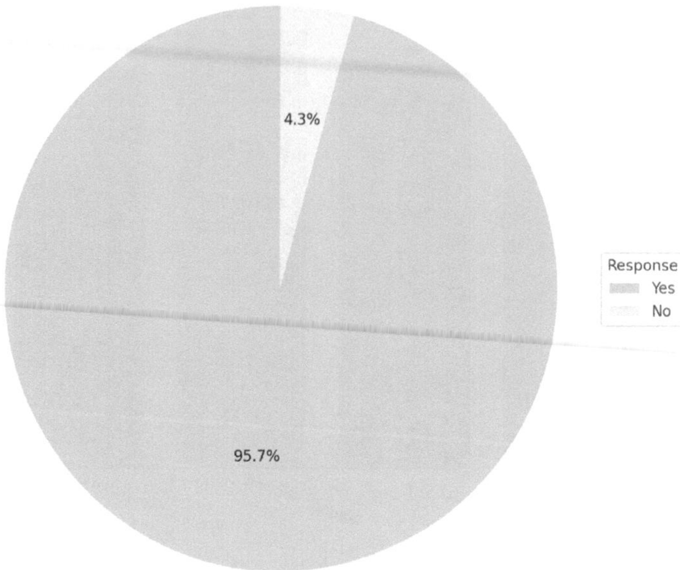

FIGURE 12.12 Students' recommendation.

12.3.4 Ethical Awareness and Student Experience

Despite the novelty of the technologies employed, student feedback was predominantly positive. Several projects, however, emphasized the importance of clearer communication regarding data privacy, signal interpretation, and the non-evaluative purpose of the recordings. These findings underline the central role of ethical safeguards in fostering student trust and ensuring responsible implementation of multimodal learning analytics.

All experimental sessions were conducted under the IFE Novus protocol, which established institutional guidelines for the ethical execution of educational research. Participants provided informed consent prior to their involvement, with procedures designed to guarantee voluntary participation and the right to withdraw at any stage. Although consent was collected through an informal yet documented mechanism, it followed established standards for transparency and clarity in research communication.

Data privacy was safeguarded through anonymization practices and secure storage of biometric and behavioral evidence. Faculty teams were instructed to avoid linking raw data directly to student identity and to restrict access exclusively to the research teams in charge of the projects. In addition, students were explicitly informed that the collected data would not be used for evaluative or grading purposes but solely for research and pedagogical reflection.

This ethical framework not only complied with institutional requirements but also contributed to positive student experiences by fostering an environment of openness and respect. As a result, students reported higher levels of confidence and willingness to engage with biometric technologies, recognizing the potential benefits of these tools when implemented under transparent and responsible conditions.

12.4 DISCUSSION

Multimodal learning analytics reveals that student engagement is not a static attribute but a dynamic process that fluctuates according to task complexity and the learning environment. This was observed across projects such as entrepreneurship and thermal systems, where EEG and physiological wristbands detected increases in attention and vigor during immersive or decision-based tasks (see Section 3.1). Schaufeli et al. (2002) conceptualize engagement as a persistent affective-cognitive state characterized by vigor, dedication, and absorption, a definition that aligns with the multimodal evidence gathered in this study. Consequently, engagement can be understood as a measurable, data-driven phenomenon that is both sensitive to contextual stimuli and central to designing effective pedagogical interventions.

Students' perceptions of their engagement throughout the course, both before and after implementation, reflect how the three dimensions of this process—vigor, dedication, and absorption—help to understand the way they experience educational intervention with biometric technology. Moreover, the findings regarding the increase in vigor and absorption levels after using the technology are consistent with the high level of acceptance of the employed technology. In this way, the perceived high level of teacher support and the perception of enhanced learning outcomes highlight the pedagogical significance of implementing biometric technology in higher education teaching.

Accordingly, the acceptance of biometric and immersive technologies emerges as a critical factor that shapes the success of experimental educational practices. Data from the Classroom of the Future project showed that students not only reported enjoyment and usefulness but also actively incorporated feedback from XR and wearable devices into their anticipatory scenario construction (see Table 12.1). According to Guerrero-Sosa et al. (2025), technological adoption in learning analytics depends on students' perceptions of ease of use and utility, which directly influence their intention to integrate these tools into their learning. This indicates that innovation in education requires not only robust methodologies but also attention to user-centered adoption processes, where acceptance functions as the bridge between technological novelty and pedagogical effectiveness.

MMLA advances the field of assessment by integrating physiological, behavioral, and interactional signals that provide a richer picture of learning beyond grades or surveys. In the negotiation and public speaking projects, indicators such as eye-tracking, stress levels, and voice patterns correlated with students' performance and confidence, offering insights that traditional self-reports alone could not capture (see Section 3.1). Blikstein and Worsley (2016) emphasize that multimodal data enable the measurement of complex learning tasks that are otherwise invisible to conventional evaluation systems. Therefore, multimodal evidence positions itself as a complementary tool to enhance the validity of educational assessments, allowing educators to address the multidimensional nature of learning.

The deployment of multimodal technologies demonstrates that ethical considerations are not peripheral but foundational to student participation and trust. This was particularly clear in projects where students initially expressed concern about privacy but later reported confidence once the IFE Novus protocol ensured informed consent, anonymization, and non-evaluative use of the data (see Section 3.3). Worsley et al. (2021) argue that commitments to transparency, consent, and participatory interpretation are essential for the sustainable growth of MMLA. Hence, ethical safeguards not only guarantee compliance but also operate as active pedagogical enablers, fostering openness and meaningful engagement with advanced technologies in learning contexts.

The IFE Experiential Classroom—Learning Lab model illustrates how institutional support and shared infrastructure can lower barriers for faculty to engage in multimodal experimentation. Evidence of this is reflected in the 29 structured data collection sessions involving more than 750 students, which would have been unfeasible without coordinated access to the IFE EC-LL facilities and methodological guidance (see Section 3.2). Bygstad et al. (2022) highlight that digital transformation in higher education requires not only new tools but also institutional ecosystems that sustain experimentation and scalability. This finding underscores that large-scale innovation in education depends on structured models that combine infrastructure, methodological alignment, and collaborative governance to produce sustainable impact.

12.5 CONCLUSION

The first Experiential Classroom Call at Tecnológico de Monterrey demonstrated the feasibility and potential of integrating multimodal learning analytics (MMLA) into real educational contexts. Six projects were successfully deployed during the first academic semester of 2025, engaging more than 750 students across undergraduate and postgraduate programs. These initiatives confirmed that multimodal experimentation can be embedded within authentic classroom dynamics while preserving methodological rigor and disciplinary relevance.

The results highlight three main contributions. First, MMLA enabled the identification of learning patterns that transcend traditional assessment methods, offering richer insights into engagement, cognitive load, and communicative performance. Second, the coordinated infrastructure of the IFE EC-LL proved capable of supporting large-scale multimodal data collection, positioning it as a scalable and reliable model for innovation in higher education. Third, the adoption of robust ethical protocols—anchored in informed consent, transparency, and anonymization—ensured that experimentation was conducted responsibly, fostering student trust and participation.

Beyond these contributions, the initiative also revealed challenges. Technical issues such as device calibration and signal synchronization required iterative adjustments, while the novelty of biometric tools demanded additional orientation for students and faculty. These lessons underscore that the success of multimodal deployments depends not only on technological availability but also on institutional support, clear communication, and adaptive pedagogical design.

In light of the non-significant results of the engagement variable, future phases of the study would benefit from incorporating qualitative methods, such as interviews and focus groups, to further contextualize the findings. Participants' voices could offer nuanced insights into their willingness to engage in learning activities, the effort and perseverance they dedicate to overcoming course challenges, and their commitment to the course content. Additionally, such perspectives may shed light on the degree of concentration and satisfaction they experience in relation to course activities.

Overall, this chapter illustrates how institutional calls that combine infrastructure, methodological guidance, and international evaluation can catalyze educational innovation. By aligning multimodal technologies with pedagogical goals and ethical standards, the IFE EC-LL has positioned itself as a model for evidence-informed transformation in higher education. The findings presented here provide actionable insights for academic communities seeking to advance the responsible, scalable, and pedagogically meaningful use of multimodal analytics.

REFERENCES

Assunção, H., Lin, S.-W., Sit, P.-S., Cheung, K.-C., Harju-Luukkainen, H., Smith, T., Maloa, B., Campos, J. Á. D. B., Ilic, I. S., Esposito, G., Francesca, F. M., & Marôco, J. (2020). University Student Engagement Inventory (USEI): Transcultural validity evidence across four continents. *Frontiers in Psychology, 10*, Article 2796. https://doi.org/10.3389/fpsyg.2019.02796

Blikstein, P., & Worsley, M. (2016). Multimodal learning analytics and education data mining: Using computational technologies to measure complex learning tasks. *Journal of Learning Analytics*, *3*(2), 220–238. https://doi.org/10.18608/jla.2016.32.11

Boucsein, W. (2012). *Electrodermal activity*. Springer Science & Business Media.

Bygstad, B., Øvrelid, E., Ludvigsen, S., & Dæhlen, M. (2022). From dual digitalization to digital learning space: Exploring the digital transformation of higher education. *Computers & Education*, *182*, C. https://doi.org/10.1016/j.compedu.2022.104463

Creswell, J. W. (2009). *Research design: Qualitative, quantitative, and mixed methods approaches* (3rd ed.). SAGE Publications.

Dollinger, M., Lodge, J. M., & Coates, H. (2019). Co-creation in learning analytics: Concepts, benefits, and challenges. *Journal of Learning Analytics*, *6*(3), 11–26. https://doi.org/10.18608/jla.2019.63.3

Eradze, M., Rodríguez-Triana, M. J., Milikic, N., Laanpere, M., & Tammets, K. (2020). Contextualising learning analytics with classroom observations: A case study. *Interaction Design and Architecture(s)*, *44*, 71–95. http://ixdea.org

Guerrero-Sosa, J. D. T., Romero, F. P., Menéndez-Domínguez, V. H., Serrano-Guerrero, J., Montoro-Montarroso, A., & Olivas, J. A. (2025). A comprehensive review of multimodal analysis in education. *Applied Sciences*, *15*(11), 5896. https://doi.org/10.3390/app15115896

Healey, J., & Picard, R. W. (2005). Detecting stress during real-world driving tasks using physiological sensors. *IEEE Transactions on Intelligent Transportation Systems*, *6*(2), 156–166. https://doi.org/10.1109/TITS.2005.848368

Kumari, R., Dwivedi, A., & Narsalay, R. (2020). Co-creation for social innovation in the ecosystem context: The role of higher educational institutions. *Sustainability*, *12*(1), 307. https://doi.org/10.3390/su12010307

Martinez-Maldonado, R., Echeverria, V., & Shum, S. B. (2023). Lessons learnt from a multimodal learning analytics deployment in-the-wild. *arXiv preprint*. https://arxiv.org/abs/2303.09099

Morán-Mirabal, L. F., Ruiz-Ramírez, J. A., González-Grez, A. A., Torres-Rodríguez, S. N., & Ceballos, H. G. (2025). Applying the living lab methodology for evidence-based educational technologies. In *2025 IEEE global engineering education conference (EDUCON)* (pp. 1–9). IEEE. https://doi.org/10.1109/EDUCON62633.2025.11016413

Ochoa, X., Lang, C., Siemens, G., Wise, A., Gasevic, D., & Merceron, A. (2022). Multimodal learning analytics: Rationale, process, examples, and direction. In *The handbook of learning analytics* (Vol. 2, pp. 54–65). Society for Learning Analytics Research (SoLAR).

OpenAI. (2025). *ChatGPT (Sept 2025 version)* [Large language model]. https://chat.openai.com/

Ouhaichi, K., Uskov, V., & Howlett, R. (2024). Exploring design considerations for multimodal learning analytics systems. *Frontiers in Education*, *9*, 1356537. https://doi.org/10.3389/feduc.2024.1356537

Pérez-Gómez, L. J., Morán-Mirabal, L. F., Ceballos, H. G., Torres-Rodríguez, S. N., & Ruiz-Ramírez, J. A. (2025). Assessing concentration levels in interactive digital tests through portable EEG technology. In *Proceedings of the 2025 World Engineering Education Forum – Global Engineering Deans Council (WEEF-GEDC)* (pp. 1–10). IEEE. https://doi.org/10.1109/WEEF-GEDC66748.2025.11256410

Ruiz-Ramírez, J. A., & Glasserman-Morales, L. D. (2021). Multimodal data value chain (M-DVC): A model to structure multimodal data for learning analytics. *Journal of Learning for Development*, *8*(3), 607–627. https://jl4d.org/index.php/ejl4d/article/view/525

Schaufeli, W. B., Bakker, A. B., & Salanova, M. (2006). The measurement of work engagement with a short questionnaire: A cross-national study. *Educational and Psychological Measurement*, *66*(4), 701–716. https://doi.org/10.1177/0013164405282471

Schaufeli, W. B., Salanova, M., González-Romá, V., & Bakker, A. B. (2002). The measurement of engagement and burnout: A two sample confirmatory factor analytic approach. *Journal of Happiness Studies*, *3*, 71–92. https://doi.org/10.1023/A:1015630930326

Torres-Rodríguez, S. N., Morán-Mirabal, L. F., & Ruiz-Ramírez, J. A. (2025). Multimodal data integration for assessing learner alertness. In *Proceedings of the 2025 World Engineering Education Forum – Global Engineering Deans Council (WEEF-GEDC)* (pp. 1–8). IEEE. https://doi.org/10.1109/WEEF-GEDC66748.2025.11256229

Worsley, M., Martinez-Maldonado, R., & D'Angelo, C. (2021). A new era in multimodal learning analytics: Twelve core commitments to ground and grow MMLA. *Journal of Learning Analytics*, *8*(3), 10–27. https://doi.org/10.18608/jla.2021.7361

Yurum, O. R. (2025). Technology-enhanced multimodal learning analytics in higher education: A systematic literature review. *IEEE Access*, *13*, 92057–92073. https://doi.org/10.1109/ACCESS.2025.3572467

Zhao, X., & Xu, R. (2024). Trends and challenges in mixed methods educational research: A comprehensive analysis of empirical studies. *International Journal of Asian Education*, *5*(4), 262–273. https://doi.org/10.46966/ijae.v5i4.450

13 Algorithmic Bias and Human Computer Interaction in Educational Platforms

A Qualitative Approach From Substantive Equity

Samuel Olmos-Peña,
Luisa Reyna Beatriz Ayón-Muñoz,
and Magally Martínez-Reyes

13.1 INTRODUCTION

The use of artificial intelligence (AI) techniques has proliferated across diverse fields such as medicine, finance, and education. In the educational domain, a specific subfield known as AIED, or artificial intelligence applied to education, has emerged, underscoring both its benefits and the challenges associated with its implementation. Among these challenges is the necessity of addressing ethical implications given the responsibility that comes with using models that directly affect end users, that is, students (Akgun & Greenhow, 2022; Dieterle, Dede, & Walker, 2022).

Within AI, machine learning is a set of techniques aimed at developing algorithms capable of making predictions or recommendations based on prior training. It is widely used to locate patterns within datasets through optimization processes and adjustments made autonomously. In this way, it allows for more accurate responses and contributes to automated decision-making in different areas, without relying on explicit programming (Beigang, 2022; Helm et al., 2020). In the field of education, they have been applied to complex problem-solving (Talavera & Luna, 2020), grade prediction, school dropout rates, exam evaluation, among others (Idowu, 2024).

However, a recurring problem in the adoption of these systems is the responsibility placed on their predictions, since errors in their results can have significant consequences for the people involved. A notable case outside the education sector was the COMPAS system, designed to predict criminal recidivism in the United States, whose results showed a systematic tendency to classify African Americans

DOI: 10.1201/9781003678250-13

as higher risk (Angwin et al., 2016). In the educational field, Baker and Hawn (2021), Yu et al. (2020), and Smith (2020) present different scenarios where students have been discriminated against based on characteristics related to their socioeconomic status and gender, illustrating how algorithmic biases not only affect technical accuracy but also the trust and access to opportunities of those who interact with such systems.

Research on algorithmic fairness has generated multiple formal metrics that allow for the quantification of bias and fairness in machine learning outcomes. However, these metrics are based on mathematical notions that, although necessary, do not comprehensively capture the user experience or consider the socio-technical context in which the systems operate. Several authors have pointed out the need to complement statistical approaches with qualitative instruments capable of assessing how different groups perceive and experience bias (Green, 2022).

In the absence of systematic and applicable qualitative instruments in the machine learning system design cycle, this chapter proposes an alternative evaluation framework. Since the user's perception of fairness is decisive in their perception of reliability (Szafran & Bach, 2024), it is imperative to involve them in the evaluation process. The objective of this study is to identify which sensitive variables can be used to determine the presence of bias in the results of educational models and how these variables can be operationalized in an assessable rubric. Therefore, this study aims to describe the bias perceived by different user profiles and broaden the definition of fairness beyond the strictly technical level.

The qualitative metric was constructed following the method of Nemoto and Beglar (2014), within the framework of substantive equity proposed by Fredman (2016). The proposal is composed of dimensions, indicators, and interpretive levels. Its preliminary validation was conducted through expert review and pilot testing, using hypothetical cases that simulated student profiles and their interaction with machine learning models. This process enabled the observation of the instrument's internal consistency and informed initial adjustments.

In an era where artificial intelligence is deeply integrated into school life, it is necessary to build systems that are not only intelligent but also fair, since, in the face of discriminatory results, what is at stake is not only the technical accuracy of the model but also the impartiality of the educational experience it offers. Quantitative metrics overlook how the model's decisions affect students' perceptions of fairness, motivation, and engagement with the platform, which are fundamental aspects from the perspective of human-computer interaction. This proposal contributes to a methodological alternative for bias assessment that takes user experience into account, complementing existing quantitative metrics. This chapter consists of a background section that contextualizes the relationship between artificial intelligence and human-computer interaction, machine learning, bias and algorithmic fairness, and substantive fairness. It then addresses the state of the art in bias assessment in machine learning and models applied to education, before going on to show the construction of the scale and pilot tests. Finally, it presents a discussion of the results, conclusions, and references used as a basis for developing the proposal.

13.2 BACKGROUND

13.2.1 Human-Computer Interaction and Artificial Intelligence

Human-computer interaction (HCI) is a field that involves principles from multiple disciplines such as cognitive psychology, ergonomics, graphic design, information technology, among others. Its objective is to optimize the end user's experience with a system or technology, ensuring efficiency, ease of use, and satisfaction (Geroimenko, 2025; Troussas, Krouska, & Sgouropoulou, 2025c).

Traditionally, HCI has been linked to the creative and intuitive design of interfaces. However, the incorporation of artificial intelligence into technological development has broadened the scope of the field, generating new challenges related to personalization, understanding, and management of models, as well as the need to ensure more complex interactions. In this sense, an intuitive interface is no longer sufficient to guarantee adequate interaction, as many systems require the implementation of additional tools and actions (Chang et al., 2023; Panda & Roy, 2024).

Based on this scenario, a proposal has emerged for human-centered artificial intelligence, which focuses on recognizing people's needs and capabilities, as well as ensuring fair treatment and ethical considerations. This is key to building user trust in systems of this type (Sahoo & Saurav, 2025). In this regard, Troussas, Krouska, & Sgouropoulou (2025a) propose a framework that combines principles of human-computer interaction and artificial intelligence to guide the design of educational platforms based on human-centered artificial intelligence. These principles include personalization, collaboration, adaptability, accessibility, and creativity. The authors emphasize that adaptability must guarantee criteria of equity and inclusion in order to avoid discriminatory practices and ensure that systems are accessible to all users.

Similarly, Sahoo and Saurav (2025) warn that if a system presents biases or discriminatory results, the consequences can directly affect the social and cultural sphere. Therefore, they highlight the importance of identifying and correcting such biases, involving the intervention of mitigation tools and people capable of detecting and correcting such problems. Finally, Paneru et al. (2024) and Wang (2024) highlight the importance of ensuring an adequate user experience in learning technologies. According to the authors, this condition encourages greater student participation, improves academic performance, and enhances the effectiveness of AI-mediated educational environments.

13.2.2 Machine Learning

Machine learning is a branch of artificial intelligence aimed at supporting automated decision-making. In the field of education, it has been used to develop adaptive systems capable of offering personalized learning paths, as well as to generate specific assessments and predictions (Troussas, Krouska, & Sgouropoulou, 2025b). Its main feature is the continuous improvement of models as they are fed with data that strengthens their training, without requiring linear programming that explicitly specifies each step in the decision-making process.

The machine learning life cycle consists of six stages (Suresh & Guttag, 2021; Spjuth, Frid, & Hellander, 2021): data collection, which will be used to train the algorithm; data preprocessing, to manage duplicate data, missing values, or noise in the data; algorithm selection and model training; evaluation of the predictions obtained, in order to validate the suitability of the model with respect to the training data; post-processing, where the responses obtained in the model are adapted to the requested context for user understanding; and model implementation, consisting of adding the necessary elements for easy user handling of the system. However, Fazelpour and Danks (2021) summarize it in three stages: preprocessing, in-processing, and post-processing. The latter is addressed in this chapter, as it is directly related to the handling of results and presentation to the end user (Pfeiffer et al., 2023).

13.2.3 Bias and Algorithmic Fairness

The concept of bias in artificial intelligence algorithms has been taken up by various authors who focus their research on the ethical use of this technology, with the aim of ensuring equity and inclusion. However, Kekez, Lauwaert and Ređep (2025) point out the lack of consensus regarding a precise and unified definition within the literature, as well as its link to the emergence of discriminatory results toward groups with shared characteristics. Given that different conceptualizations and types of bias can be found both in the phases of the machine learning life cycle and in the components of the system (e.g., training data, population sampling, results obtained, among others), it is essential to clarify the perspective from which the term will be used in this research.

This document adopts the approach used by O'Connor and Liu (2024), Uddin et al. (2024), and Fabris et al. (2022), which defines algorithmic bias as the occurrence of failures in systems that perpetuate discrimination based on sensitive or protected characteristics, such as gender (O'Connor & Liu, 2024; Uddin et al., 2024), socioeconomic status, age, sexual orientation, religion, and ethnicity, among others (Van Busum & Fang, 2024; Kekez, Lauwaert, & Ređep, 2025). These failures generate unfair results for individuals belonging to these groups (Simpson et al., 2025), raising growing concerns about ethics within artificial intelligence.

As already mentioned, algorithmic bias can manifest itself at different stages of the life cycle: in preprocessing, due to errors in data selection that reproduce disadvantages toward groups that have been historically discriminated against; during processing, through limitations in the algorithms used; and in post-processing, when there are flaws in the interpretation or implementation of the results (Mehrabi et al., 2021).

In the presence of bias, the concept of algorithmic fairness becomes relevant when understood as the absence of prejudice regarding the characteristics of individuals involved in decision-making and when seeking to avoid the propagation of existing biases or the generation of new ones (Mehrabi et al., 2021; Radanliev, 2025). This principle is part of the FATE framework (fairness, accountability, transparency, and ethics), an initiative promoted by Microsoft for the responsible development and deployment of artificial intelligence tools (Singhal, Tanveer, & Mago, 2023). According to the review by Behera et al. (2025), fairness is one of the most frequently addressed topics in the specialized literature.

In this context, various notions of fairness have been proposed from a quantitative perspective. These translate into metrics that use statistics and probability to measure the presence of fairness in the results of a machine learning model. Among the most widely used are metrics based on parity and the confusion matrix. The former focus on evaluating the rates of positive results among different groups. Notable examples include statistical parity, which considers a model to be equitable if all groups have the same probability of obtaining a positive result, and disparate impact, which evaluates the proportion of positive results among groups. Confusion matrix-based metrics, on the other hand, focus on the rates of true positives, true negatives, false positives, and false negatives. These include equal opportunity, equal probability, and conditional accuracy equality (Rzepka et al., 2022; Mehrabi et al., 2021).

However, the use of these metrics faces a limitation known as the impossibility theorem, which states that it is not possible to simultaneously satisfy more than one equity metric (Sahlgren, 2021; Caton & Haas, 2020; Pfeiffer et al., 2023; Erman, Furendal, & Möller, 2025). Consequently, a model may be considered fair under one definition of fairness but unfair under another. Furthermore, most of these metrics within models that allow for automated decision-making fall within the framework of so-called formal fairness (Green, 2022), understood as a vision of fairness in which all individuals are treated equally, assuming that they are in equal circumstances, have equal rights, and equal backgrounds (Grote, 2024). However, this approach has been criticized because, as Cohen and Tingruo (2025) point out, it is an abstract vision detached from reality, since not all of society shares the same conditions, which limits its effectiveness in truly guaranteeing fairness.

Given the previous scenario, various proposals have been made that seek to contribute a different vision of equity and model building, since, as this involves implementation within social environments, recommendations have been made regarding the consideration of the implementation context, the integration of a socio-technical perspective, and evaluation using methods applied to the social sciences according to the area where machine learning algorithms are applied (Hasan et al., 2022; Grote, 2024; Fazelpour & Danks, 2021; Green, 2022), express concern about expanding research in this area, highlighting that the development of qualitative metrics is a form of evaluation that has not yet been covered and developed for machine learning in the field of algorithmic bias.

13.2.4 Substantive Equity

This approach to equity suggests identifying social inequalities and hierarchies that have been marked throughout history based on certain categories or characteristics that individuals present. Once recognized, the aim is to remedy them or contribute to their eradication (Green, 2022; Fredman, 2016). Along the same lines, Grote (2024) describes it as "formal equity + x," where the variable "x" represents the identification of social relationships and hierarchies within a specific context.

It has been shown that there is a marked difference between evaluations using mathematical methods and the real impact of algorithms on everyday life. In this regard, Green (2022) argues for the need to shift to a substantive equity approach rather than a formal equity approach, adhering to the legal and philosophical theories of this approach. However, he warns that this type of equity should not be reduced to a mathematical model, as this would distort its definition.

According to Green (2022), promoting substantive equity in algorithms involves three steps: diagnosing inequalities, identifying possible reforms, and finally analyzing how algorithms can contribute to implementing those reforms. Complementarily, Fredman (2016) proposes a substantive equity framework consisting of four elements. First, repairing disadvantage, that is, identifying groups that have suffered systematic discrimination in order to grant them benefits that eliminate persistent barriers. Second, correcting stigma, stereotypes, and humiliation by recognizing prejudices and stereotypes based on attributes of individuals who make up the affected group. Third, incorporating a participatory dimension that promotes the social inclusion of historically marginalized groups. Finally, the fourth element is aimed at "accommodating difference" as a result of structural change by reducing discrimination in practice. For this chapter, we will focus on the first three dimensions of this framework, as the last one corresponds to a long-term assessment.

13.3 STATE OF ART

In the literature, the study of algorithmic bias in machine learning has been approached from different angles. A first approach has consisted of the theoretical description and classification of this phenomenon (Pagano et al., 2022; Mehrabi et al., 2021), as well as its link to sensitive variables such as gender, race, or socioeconomic status, which have been studied mainly in the field of education (Baker & Hawn, 2021; Yu, Lee & Kizilcec, 2021), encouraging further research on other documented variables. Simultaneously, technical mitigation strategies have been explored through specific tools and libraries (Deho et al., 2022). Another area of research focuses on reviewing the multiple definitions proposed around the concept of algorithmic bias (Panarese, Grasso, & Solinas, 2025), which consider it a phenomenon that is present in the social context and not only in the algorithm. However, the direct measurement of bias has not been fully addressed in the literature, which constitutes a significant gap.

On the other hand, the discussion on algorithmic fairness has evolved from conceptual and quantitative perspectives. Around 21 different notions of fairness have been identified, applicable to various models without establishing a defined context or field of study for their implementation (Ashokan & Haas, 2021). In the quantitative approach, metrics such as ABROCA, PreCOF, and other exploratory tools have been developed that combine accuracy calculations with notions of fairness linked to accuracy calculations. In the educational context, Idowu (2024) mentions ABROCA, group difference, and disparity metrics as the most widely used metrics, although the way to choose a metric in this field is to observe the one that has been most widely used by experts in the area.

Despite the large number of quantitative metrics, the applicability of a formal approach to equity has been observed and questioned due to the impossibility theorem, which has prompted the search for socio-technical approaches that allow bias to be addressed more comprehensively and promote equity and inclusion in artificial intelligence (Panarese, Grasso, & Solinas, 2025). Similarly, the use of approaches other than formal equity has been encouraged, with the emergence of substantive equity (Green, 2022) and procedural equity (Decker, Wegner, & Leicht Scholten, 2025).

In this regard, recent literature emphasizes the need to establish context-sensitive evaluations aimed at generating reliable systems for users (Hasan et al., 2022; Henry & Oliver, 2022, Sahlgren, 2021), joining efforts to explore how end users react or adapt to biases present in algorithms (Overbye-Thompson & Rice, 2025). In the educational field, this perspective is particularly relevant, as students are the direct recipients of the effects of a biased algorithm, and any discriminatory outcome has a significant impact on their academic future (Gaskins, 2022; Dieterle, Dede, & Walker, 2022).

Authors such as Hasan et al. (2022) propose involving the analysis of the interaction between end users and the responses obtained, with the aim of analyzing how fair the models involved are. Along the same lines, Szafran and Bach (2024) highlight that there are four dimensions of study in the literature regarding algorithmic fairness, emphasizing as one of them the impact of a low perception of fairness by end users, since it affects their trust in the system.

13.4 CONSTRUCTION OF THE PROPOSAL

In order to qualitatively operationalize algorithmic bias in the results of machine learning models, a Likert scale was chosen. This instrument is widely used in the social and educational sciences to assess unobservable constructs such as attitudes, opinions, or perceptions (Joshi et al., 2015; Jebb, Ng, & Tay, 2021), as well as in business settings to support decision-making processes and the selection of strategies aimed at improving performance. Its application is relevant for conducting an analysis of algorithmic equity in the educational field, as it allows data to be collected on participants' perceptions after their interaction with the system.

13.4.1 Method

The Likert scale was designed following the method proposed by Nemoto and Beglar (2014), which has been used in recent studies on people's perceptions of different issues (Ferrara et al., 2024; Machado et al., 2024; Mustafa, Malik, & Maqsoom, 2024). This method consists of five phases, which are described next:

1. Understanding the construct. This is where we understand what knowledge, skills, or other attributes should be evaluated, as well as the behaviors and tasks that manifest them in the field of study where we want to implement them (Messick, 1989; Gignac & Szodorai, 2024).
2. Developing of items. Based on the assumptions of the construct, clear and unambiguous items are developed, each focused on measuring a single idea. These can be organized into subscales or dimensions (Schrum et al., 2020; Willits, Theodori, & Luloff, 2016).

3. Determining the outcome space. Categories of between four and six options are defined, without including a neutral point, as this can be used as evasion or reflect ignorance of the construct being evaluated (Sturgis et al., 2014; Dykema et al., 2022).
4. Specifiying of the measurement model. This relates to how to interpret the responses obtained and achieve their operationalization. Nemoto and Beglar (2014) propose the Rasch model or the true score model of classical test theory (CTT) as alternatives. In this study, CTT was chosen, which assigns numerical values to the responses on the scale and allows a total score to be calculated by adding up the items, based on which interpretation intervals were established. This approach is widely used in education because of its simplicity (Polat, Turhan, & Toraman, 2022; Stemler & Naples, 2021).
5. Gathering feedback and plotting the questionnaire. This phase is linked to the feedback provided by people who are knowledgeable about the construct to ensure its validity. On the other hand, internal consistency for the present study was evaluated using Cronbach's alpha, a coefficient widely used in the validation of Likert scales (Mustafa, Malik, & Maqsoom, 2024; Souza & Reis, 2025).

13.4.1.1 Understanding the Construct

Based on the literature reviewed, we identified characteristics of students and the implementation context that have been reported in studies on algorithmic bias in education. We selected those that recurred in the research and were related to the promotion of equitable and inclusive education in accordance with criteria established by international organizations such as the ONU and UNESCO.

Likewise, contextual elements and their variations were included, understood as factors that condition the application of machine learning models. Sensitive variables or protected categories of students, linked to educational discrimination and bias in algorithms, have been studied by various authors (Rzepka et al., 2022; Kizilcec & Lee, 2021; Baker & Hawn, 2021; Smith, 2020; Akgun & Greenhow, 2022; Mayfield et al., 2019; Yu, Lee, & Kizilcec, 2021; Jeong et al., 2021; Sahlgren, 2021) and are summarized in the following list:

- Gender/Sex
- Sexual orientation
- Religion
- Political opinion
- Nationality
- Ethnic origin
- Race
- Language
- Disability
- Socioeconomic status
- Parental education level
- Migration background

Regarding variations in the implementation context, the following evaluation criteria were established (Hasan et al., 2022; Grote, 2024; Fazelpour & Danks, 2021; Sahlgren, 2021; Hernandez, 2023; Madaio et al., 2022, Henry & Oliver, 2022; Suresh & Guttag, 2021, Webb et al., 2020):

- Geographic context
- Temporal context
- Sociocultural context
- Original objective of the machine learning model evaluated

In addition, the substantive equity framework proposed by Fredman (2016), which comprises four dimensions, was adopted. For this proposal, three were considered: (1) redressing disadvantage; (2) countering prejudice, stigma, stereotyping, and humiliation associated with sensitive variables; and (3) the enhance voice and participation dimension, focused on inclusion. The fourth dimension, referring to the long-term impact of the model on society, was not incorporated as it exceeded the scope of this work.

Based on these elements, the following assumptions of bias were made:

- The results reflect a higher level of bias when there are indications of a lack of actions aimed at mitigating the disadvantages suffered by historically discriminated groups.
- The results reflect a higher level of bias when discrimination is identified toward one or more protected categories related to the labels used in the model or proxies.
- The results reflect a higher level of bias when excluding students with varied characteristics and belonging to the protected categories described previously.
- Bias tends to increase when a model is applied for purposes other than those for which it was originally designed.
- Bias tends to increase when a model is implemented in temporal, geographical, or sociocultural contexts other than those considered in its original design.

The constitution of the construct and these assumptions of bias allows the evaluation to be oriented both towards the results of the model and towards the perception of users in their interaction with the system. Depending on the purpose of the model, this perception can be evaluated in different roles of human-computer interaction: programmers during the training and validation phase; decision-makers in the education sector based on the results; and students when using adaptive models that consider their learning trajectories and styles. In this way, the aim is to determine whether users perceive fair, respectful, and stigma-free treatment; whether they understand the results obtained; and whether they consider that the model incorporates inclusion criteria, integrating a socio-technical perspective linked to substantive equity and the context of the implementation and deployment of the models.

13.4.1.2 Developing the Items

Based on the established assumptions, the following dimensions were defined in which the items were structured, as well as the indicators considered.

Dimension 1. Redressing disadvantage. Indicator. Results that do not benefit individuals belonging to different groups that have been historically discriminated against according to the sensitive variables identified.

Dimension 2. Correcting stigma, stereotypes, and humiliation. Indicator. Results that reflect unequal treatment based on the aforementioned characteristics of the student.

Dimension 3. Participatory dimension. Indicator. Results that do not benefit students from different groups belonging to the identified categories.

Dimension 4. Evaluation of the implementation context. Indicator. Results of the model implemented to solve a problem other than that for which it was designed; significant variations in the time period or temporal context with respect to when the model was trained and the training data was collected; considerable changes in the state, nation, or geographic context of implementation with respect to the originally planned location; relevant differences between the sociocultural environment in which the implementation was planned and the one in which it is ultimately applied.

Based on the indicators, 40 items were defined based on the relationship between the three dissensions of the equity framework proposed by Fredman (2016), the protected categories, and the context variations.

13.4.1.3 Determining the Outcome Space

In accordance with Nemoto and Beglar (2014), six descriptive anchors were determined to determine the level of disagreement or agreement with the statement, which are described in general terms in Table 13.1. For further analysis, they were assigned a score from 1 to 6, starting from the first level of disagreement (Alkharusi, 2022; Alhassan et al., 2022).

13.4.1.4 Specifying the Measurement Model

To interpret the results obtained when responding to the scale according to the model results, it is important to categorize variables in order to easily interpret the results based on cut-off points for the specific scale established from an identical distance between each category (Sayili et al., 2024). Using the equal intervals method, a class interval scale was developed by subtracting the minimum composite score from the maximum composite score; then calculating the width of the class intervals by dividing the previous result by the number of categories; and finally constructing the class intervals by adding the corresponding width (Alkharusi, 2022). This method allows for intuitive interpretation by the user, which facilitates its use by the different roles involved. As a result, and presentation to the user, the scores corresponding to each level of estimated bias are shown in Table 13.2 and 13.2a.

TABLE 13.1
Outcome Space

Level of Disagreement or Agreement	Assigned Score	Descriptor
Strongly disagree	1	No signs of bias are observed with respect to the variable evaluated.
Disagree	2	The model performs well, with minimal exceptions related to the variable evaluated.
Slightly disagree	3	The model performs acceptably, although with some exceptions that reflect possible biases in certain cases.
Slightly agree	4	The model presents several results with indications of bias with respect to the variable evaluated, although it incorporates partial attempts at fairness that fail to counteract these conflicts.
Agree	5	There is consistent evidence of unmitigated bias in the variable evaluated.
Strongly agree	6	There is clear and repeated evidence of unmitigated bias in the variable evaluated, with a significant impact on the results.

Source: Prepared by the authors

TABLE 13.2
Scores by Level of Bias

Level of Bias	Assigned Score	Descriptor
Very low	40–79	The perception of bias is minimal across the set of variables evaluated. In most cases, the model's decisions are perceived as fair. However, bias is present toward one or a few protected categories. An evaluation of this bias is recommended.
Low	80–119	A slight and localized bias is observed. The model shows certain disadvantages towards some of the protected categories. The differences must be considered to avoid affecting users
Medium	120–159	The bias is perceived as moderate. There are clear patterns of inequality in the model that affect several of the protected categories. Fairness is questionable, so a more in-depth evaluation of the model is required.
High	160–199	The perception of bias is considerable. The model's results affect a large proportion of user groups with sensitive attributes, impacting the educational experience. A review of the model is suggested.
Very High	200–240	The perceived bias is severe. The model reproduces or amplifies structural inequalities in most protected categories. The system is unreliable, so a review and redesign are suggested.

Source: Prepared by the authors

13.4.1.5 Gathering Feedback and Piloting the Questionnaire

Once the construction phase was complete, the questionnaire was reviewed by specialists in the field of human-computer interaction with expertise in ethical aspects related to the development of artificial intelligence systems. After incorporating the suggested adjustments, a pilot test was carried out to calculate Cronbach's alpha coefficient as a measure of internal consistency. Finally, the instrument was applied to open access models by establishing hypothetical cases (n = 10) and responding accordingly, in order to observe how the proposal worked.

Based on the observations received, adjustments were made to the wording of the items in order to make them more understandable to users without technical training. Likewise, the relevance of the protected categories was reviewed and validated, supported by the academic literature consulted. In the internal consistency analysis using Cronbach's alpha coefficient, the SPSS software reported the automatic elimination of items without variability, in accordance with the exploratory nature of the study. This occurs due to the small size of the selected sample. Nevertheless, the preliminary results are useful as an exploratory assessment and offer preliminary evidence of internal consistency in the remaining items, yielding a coefficient of 0.96. Their generalization requires further validation with a larger and more heterogeneous sample (Bujang et al., 2024).

Subsequently, and after making adjustments based on the feedback received, the questionnaire was adjusted, maintaining the organization in accordance with the dimensions evaluated. Figure 13.1 shows the dimension aimed at evaluating

A) The results obtained do not benefit individuals belonging to different groups that have been historically discriminated against based on their:						
Gender/Sex	Strongly Disagree	Disagree	Slightly Disagree	Slightly Agree	Agree	Strongly Agree
Sexual Orientation	Strongly Disagree	Disagree	Slightly Disagree	Slightly Agree	Agree	Strongly Agree
Religion	Strongly Disagree	Disagree	Slightly Disagree	Slightly Agree	Agree	Strongly Agree
Political Opinion	Strongly Disagree	Disagree	Slightly Disagree	Slightly Agree	Agree	Strongly Agree
Nationality	Strongly Disagree	Disagree	Slightly Disagree	Slightly Agree	Agree	Strongly Agree
Ethnic Origin	Strongly Disagree	Disagree	Slightly Disagree	Slightly Agree	Agree	Strongly Agree
Race	Strongly Disagree	Disagree	Slightly Disagree	Slightly Agree	Agree	Strongly Agree
Language	Strongly Disagree	Disagree	Slightly Disagree	Slightly Agree	Agree	Strongly Agree
Disability	Strongly Disagree	Disagree	Slightly Disagree	Slightly Agree	Agree	Strongly Agree
Socioeconomic Status	Strongly Disagree	Disagree	Slightly Disagree	Slightly Agree	Agree	Strongly Agree
Parental Education Level	Strongly Disagree	Disagree	Slightly Disagree	Slightly Agree	Agree	Strongly Agree
Migration Background	Strongly Disagree	Disagree	Slightly Disagree	Slightly Agree	Agree	Strongly Agree

FIGURE 13.1 Dimension: redressing disadvantage.

the redress of disadvantage, allowing respondents to analyze the trend of a model's results with respect to the established sensitive variables. Figure 13.2 illustrates the second dimension, which focuses on correcting stigma or discrimination toward a particular category.

Figure 13.3 shows the third dimension, which focuses on identifying whether there is a level of inclusion for students belonging to different groups. Finally, Figure 13.4 shows the fourth dimension, designed to evaluate the implementation context. In this way, the established indicators, the analyzed variables, and the previously designed results space are integrated.

To conduct the pilot test, open-access models hosted on GitHub (Prasad, 2021; Afzaal, 2021) were used, aimed at predicting mathematics grades in Portuguese secondary schools and final semester grades, respectively. These pre-trained models were evaluated using simulated cases designed to respond to the constructed questionnaire.

Figure 13.5 shows the relative distribution of failing cases associated with each sensitive category detected in the ten models evaluated. In Models 1 to 6, the highest proportion of bias signals is concentrated in socioeconomic status and parental literacy levels. However, the gender/sex category also shows a significant influence, given that most of these cases correspond to women. The high presence of socioeconomic status is explained by the fact that the models include proxies related to this variable, such as type of place of residence, school location, monthly salary, and

B) The results obtained reflect a negative bias towards one or more of the following characteristics of the student:						
Gender/Sex	Strongly Disagree	Disagree	Slightly Disagree	Slightly Agree	Agree	Strongly Agree
Sexual Orientation	Strongly Disagree	Disagree	Slightly Disagree	Slightly Agree	Agree	Strongly Agree
Religion	Strongly Disagree	Disagree	Slightly Disagree	Slightly Agree	Agree	Strongly Agree
Political Opinion	Strongly Disagree	Disagree	Slightly Disagree	Slightly Agree	Agree	Strongly Agree
Nationality	Strongly Disagree	Disagree	Slightly Disagree	Slightly Agree	Agree	Strongly Agree
Ethnic Origin	Strongly Disagree	Disagree	Slightly Disagree	Slightly Agree	Agree	Strongly Agree
Race	Strongly Disagree	Disagree	Slightly Disagree	Slightly Agree	Agree	Strongly Agree
Language	Strongly Disagree	Disagree	Slightly Disagree	Slightly Agree	Agree	Strongly Agree
Disability	Strongly Disagree	Disagree	Slightly Disagree	Slightly Agree	Agree	Strongly Agree
Socioeconomic Status	Strongly Disagree	Disagree	Slightly Disagree	Slightly Agree	Agree	Strongly Agree
Parental Education Level	Strongly Disagree	Disagree	Slightly Disagree	Slightly Agree	Agree	Strongly Agree
Migration Background	Strongly Disagree	Disagree	Slightly Disagree	Slightly Agree	Agree	Strongly Agree

FIGURE 13.2 Dimension: countering prejudice, stigma, stereotyping, and humiliation.

C) The results obtained do not benefit students from different groups belonging to the following categories:						
Gender/Sex	Strongly Disagree	Disagree	Slightly Disagree	Slightly Agree	Agree	Strongly Agree
Sexual Orientation	Strongly Disagree	Disagree	Slightly Disagree	Slightly Agree	Agree	Strongly Agree
Religion	Strongly Disagree	Disagree	Slightly Disagree	Slightly Agree	Agree	Strongly Agree
Political Opinion	Strongly Disagree	Disagree	Slightly Disagree	Slightly Agree	Agree	Strongly Agree
Nationality	Strongly Disagree	Disagree	Slightly Disagree	Slightly Agree	Agree	Strongly Agree
Ethnic Origin	Strongly Disagree	Disagree	Slightly Disagree	Slightly Agree	Agree	Strongly Agree
Race	Strongly Disagree	Disagree	Slightly Disagree	Slightly Agree	Agree	Strongly Agree
Language	Strongly Disagree	Disagree	Slightly Disagree	Slightly Agree	Agree	Strongly Agree
Disability	Strongly Disagree	Disagree	Slightly Disagree	Slightly Agree	Agree	Strongly Agree
Socioeconomic Status	Strongly Disagree	Disagree	Slightly Disagree	Slightly Agree	Agree	Strongly Agree
Parental Education Level	Strongly Disagree	Disagree	Slightly Disagree	Slightly Agree	Agree	Strongly Agree
Migration Background	Strongly Disagree	Disagree	Slightly Disagree	Slightly Agree	Agree	Strongly Agree

FIGURE 13.3 Participation dimension.

D) Regarding the context of implementation: The model's results are applied to solve a problem different from the one it was originally designed to address.						
	Strongly Disagree	Disagree	Slightly Disagree	Slightly Agree	Agree	Strongly Agree
The time period or historical context in which the model is implemented has different characteristics from the period when the training data were collected.						
	Strongly Disagree	Disagree	Slightly Disagree	Slightly Agree	Agree	Strongly Agree
The state, nation, or geographical context where the model is applied differs significantly from the context it was originally designed for.						
	Strongly Disagree	Disagree	Slightly Disagree	Slightly Agree	Agree	Strongly Agree
The sociocultural environment where the model is implemented differs substantially from the environment considered during its design.						
	Strongly Disagree	Disagree	Slightly Disagree	Slightly Agree	Agree	Strongly Agree

FIGURE 13.4 Evaluation of the implementation context.

parents' occupation. Models 7 to 10 also incorporate categories such as nationality, race, and migration background, derived from the hypothetical cases designed for this test. This complements the qualitative analysis by showing a comparison of the protected categories involved in the results, which reflect the presence of bias and allow the items formulated in the proposed metric to be answered.

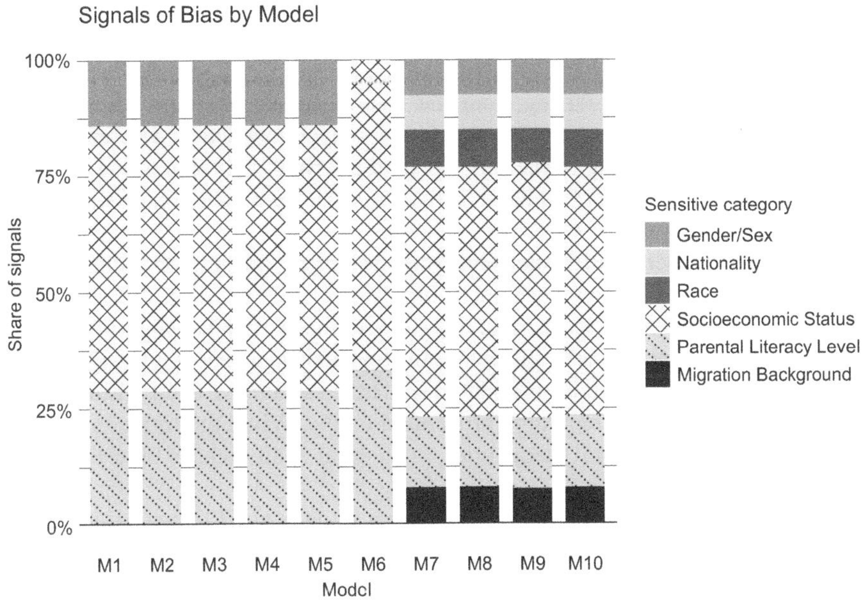

FIGURE 13.5 Distribution of sensitive variables in failed cases.

13.5 DISCUSSION

The results of the pilot test show that the proposed qualitative metric allows for the identification of perceived biases in educational models, particularly in specific sensitive variables that have been addressed in the literature on bias in machine learning applied to education (Baker & Hawn, 2021; Kizilcec & Lee, 2021; Rzepka et al., 2022: Smith, 2020). Based on this, it is possible to identify two important contributions: first, the user experience is integrated as a source of validation, contributing to the need to establish evaluations focused on humans and their interaction with the system (Rong et al., 2023); and secondly, the analysis of specific variables addressed within the educational area represents an advance in contextualization and sociotechnical approach that has been emphasized by various authors in the development of fair models (Panarese, Grasso, & Solinas, 2025; Fazelpour & Danks, 2021).

From the perspective of human-computer interaction, traditional user experience evaluation, focused on satisfaction, usability, and accessibility, is being expanded to incorporate equity as an important factor to consider. This aligns with the emergence of human-centered artificial intelligence (HCAI), which emphasizes the need to design systems that not only fulfill their technical objective but also meet ethical criteria of fairness and inclusion (Troussas, Krouska, & Sgouropoulou, 2025c).

The qualitative perspective does not seek to replace quantitative equity metrics, but rather to complement them. By focusing on outcomes rather than just input data, it allows biases to be identified even when they appear to be linked to proxies for sociodemographic variables (Giovanola & Tiribelli, 2022). Similarly, by adhering to the framework of substantive equity, which seeks to compensate for structural inequalities rather than starting from the idea of equal conditions in established cases (Green, 2022), we respond to the author's recommendation, who emphasizes the importance of seeking frameworks beyond a formal definition, since capturing the philosophical concept of equity in a mathematical formula is complex and leaves out various conditions.

In addition, placing all responsibility for assessing fairness on technical metrics means ignoring the human dimension of interaction (Szafran & Bach, 2024), which is a fundamental aspect in learning environments that use algorithms, since a fair algorithm contributes to student motivation and engagement (Onesi-Ozigagun et al., 2024). In this vein, it is pertinent to relate the substantive equity framework to Kizilcec (2016) findings regarding procedural equity. While the former focuses on compensating for structural inequalities, procedural equity relates to justice within the decision-making process.

From this perspective, and returning to what Rong et al. (2023) mentioned about the subjective dimension of equity, the proposed qualitative metric can act as an intermediate tool whose function is to identify perceived biases in the results and provide evidence on the need to add transparency and explainability mechanisms to the models, adapted to the educational and social context in which they are deployed. As a future proposal, systems could offer feedback according to the level of bias detected, avoiding excessive explanations that affect user confidence. Similarly, users themselves would have the possibility of reporting cases or requesting a review of the results based on perceived bias.

The limitations of the study include the fact that validation was restricted to a pilot test with a small number of cases. More extensive testing in real-world contexts is required, as well as the continuous adaptation of the variables analyzed as research in the area evolves. In conclusion, the preliminary results suggest that the proposed qualitative metric constitutes a significant contribution to the field of HCI and the development of artificial intelligence focused on educational contexts, by offering a way to detect biases that quantitative metrics alone fail to reveal.

13.6 CONCLUSIONS

This research showed that the proposed qualitative metric allows for the detection of perceived biases in educational contexts from a substantive equity perspective, thus complementing existing quantitative metrics and providing an assessment with a socio-technical perspective. This approach provides a new way of integrating user perception into the evaluation of algorithmic equity, highlighting first and foremost students as direct users, but also developers, who can use the metric to test their models, and decision-makers in the field of education, bringing the different actors closer to the evaluation process.

Given that validation was carried out through a pilot test, additional studies are required in specific contexts to further explore its implementation. This opens up avenues for future work, including the possible incorporation or exclusion of sensitive variables as academic research in the area progresses. If artificial intelligence in education can become a strategic ally in optimizing administrative processes and promoting user adaptation, the implementation of these systems is essential, as the perception of equity directly impacts the learning experience and trust in the platforms that comprise it.

REFERENCES

Afzaal, F. (2021). Student grade prediction project [Source code]. *GitHub*. https://github.com/fatimaAfzaal/Student_Grade_Prediction_Project/blob/main/Student_Grade_Prediction_Project.ipynb

Akgun, S., & Greenhow, C. (2022). Artificial intelligence in education addressing ethical challenges in K-12 settings. *AI and Ethics*, 2, 431–440. https://doi.org/10.1007/s43681021-00096-7

Alhassan, I., Asiamah, N., Opuni, F., & Alhassan, A. (2022). The likert scale: Exploring the unknowns and their potential to mislead the world. 9, 867–880. https://doi.org/10.47740/586.UDSIJD6

Alkharusi, H. (2022). A descriptive analysis and interpretation of data from Likert scales in educational and psychological research. *Indian Journal of Psychology and Education*, 12(2), 13–16.

Angwin, J., Larson, J., Mattu, S., & Kirchner, L. (2016). Machine Bias: There's software used across the country to predict future criminals. And it's biased against blacks. *ProPublica*. https://www.propublica.org/article/machine-bias-risk-assessments-in criminal-sentencing

Ashokan, A., & Haas, C. (2021). Fairness metrics and bias mitigation strategies for rating predictions. *Information Processing and Management*, 58(5), 102646–102663. https://doi.org/10.1016/j.ipm.2021.102646

Baker, R., & Hawn, A. (2021). Algorithmic bias in education. *International Journal of Artifcial Intelligence in Education*, 1–14. https://doi.org/10.1007/s40593-021-00285-9

Behera, A., Trivedi, P., Patra, S. K., & Makeni, C. (2025). Artificial intelligence and higher education: A systematic review. *American Journal of STEM Education*, 11, 27–52. https://doi.org/10.32674/0x43s107

Beigang, F. (2022). On the advantages of distinguishing between predictive and allocative fairness in algorithmic decision-making. *Minds and Machines*, 32(4), 655–682. https://doi.org/10.1007/s11023-022-09615-9

Bujang, M., Omar, E., Foo, D., & Hon, Y. (2024). Sample size determination for conducting a pilot study to assess reliability of a questionnaire. *Restorative Dentistry & Endodontics*, 49(1), Article e3. https://doi.org/10.5395/rde.2024.49.e3

Caton, S., & Haas, C. (2020). Fairness in machine learning: A survey. *arXiv*. https://arxiv.org/pdf/2010.04053.pdf

Chang, V., Eniola, R., Golightly, L., & Xu, Q. (2023). An exploration into human–computer interaction: Hand gesture recognition management in a challenging environment. *SN Computer Science*, 4, 441. https://doi.org/10.1007/s42979-023-01751-y

Cohen, J., & Tingruo, L. (2025). The reach of fairness. *ACM Journal of Responsible Computing*. https://doi.org/10.1145/3718989

Deho, O., Zhan, C., Li, J., Liu, J., Liu, L., & Duy Le, T. (2022). How do the existing fairness metrics and unfairness mitigation algorithms contribute to ethical learning analytics? *British Journal of Educational Technology*, 53(4), 822–843. https://doi.org/10.1111/bjet.13217

Decker, M., Wegner, L., & Leicht-Scholten, C. (2025). Procedural fairness in algorithmic decision-making: The role of public engagement. *Ethics and Information Technology*, 27(1). https://doi.org/10.1007/s10676-024-09811-4

Dieterle, E., Dede, C., & Walker, M. (2022). The cyclical ethical effects of using artificial intelligence in education. *AI & Society*. https://doi.org/10.1007/s00146-022-01497-w

Dykema, J., et al. (2022). Towards a reconsideration of the use of agree–disagree vs. alternative response formats in survey questions. *BMC Medical Research Methodology*. https://www.ncbi.nlm.nih.gov/pmc/articles/PMC8692311/

Erman, E., Furendal, M., & Möller, N. (2025). Algorithmic fairness and feasibility. *Philosophy & Technology*, 38(3). https://doi.org/10.1007/s13347-024-00835-8

Fabris, A., Messina, S., Silvello, G., & Susto, G. A. (2022). Algorithmic fairness datasets: The story so far. *Data Mining and Knowledge Discovery*, 36(6), 2074–2152. https://doi.org/10.1007/s10618-022-00854-z

Fazelpour, S., & Danks, D. (2021). Algorithmic bias: Senses, sources, solutions. *Philosophy Compass*, 16(8). https://doi.org/10.1111/phc3.12760

Ferrara, C., Sellitto, G., Ferrucci, F., Palomba, F., & De Lucia, A. (2024). Fairness-aware machine learning engineering: How far are we? *Empirical Software Engineering*, 29(9). https://doi.org/10.1007/s10664-023-10402-y

Fredman, S. (2016). Substantive equality revisited. *International Journal of Constitutional Law*, 14(3), 712–738. https://doi.org/10.1093/icon/mow043

Gaskins, N. (2022). Interrogating algorithmic bias: From speculative fiction to liberatory design. *TechTrends*, 67, 417–425. https://doi.org/10.1007/s11528-022-00783-0

Geroimenko, V. (2025). Key challenges in prompt engineering. In *The Essential Guide to Prompt Engineering: Key Principles, Techniques, Challenges, and Security Risks* (pp. 85–102). Springer Nature Switzerland. https://doi.org/10.1007/978-3-031-86206-9_4

Gignac, G., & Szodorai, E. (2024). Defining intelligence: Bridging the gap between human and artificial perspectives. *Intelligence*, 104, 101832.

Giovanola, B., & Tiribelli, S. (2022). Weapons of moral construction? On the value of fairness in algorithmic decision-making. *Ethics and Information Technology*, 24(1), 3.

Green, B. (2022). Escaping the impossibility of fairness: From formal to substantive algorithmic fairness. *Philosophy & Technology*, 35(90). https://doi.org/10.1007/s13347-022-00584-6

Grote, T. (2024). Fairness as adequacy: A sociotechnical view on model evaluation in machine learning. *AI and Ethics*, 4(2), 427–440. https://doi.org/10.1007/s43681 023-00280-x

Hasan, A., Brown, S., Davidovic, J., Lange, B., & Regan, M. (2022). Algorithmic bias and risk assessments: Lessons from practice. https://doi.org/10.1007/s44206-022-00017-z

Helm, J. M., Swiergosz, A. M., Haeberle, H. S., Karnuta, J. M., Schaffer, J. L., Krebs, V. E., Spitzer, A. I., & Ramkumar, P. N. (2020). Machine learning and artificial intelligence: Definitions, applications, and future directions. *Current Reviews in Musculoskeletal Medicine*, 13(1), 69–76. https://doi.org/10.1007/s12178-020-09600-8

Henry, J., & Oliver, M. (2022). Who will watch the watchmen? The ethic-political arrangements of algorithmic proctoring for academic integrity. *Postdigital Science and Education*, 4, 330–353. https://doi.org/10.1007/s42438-021-00273-1

Hernandez, C. (2023). (Some) algorithmic bias as institutional bias. *Ethics and Information Technology*, 25(24). https://doi.org/10.1007/s10676-023-09698-7

Jebb, A., Ng, V., & Tay, L. (2021). A review of key Likert scale development advances: 1995–2019. *Frontiers in Psychology*, 12, 637547. https://doi.org/10.3389/fpsyg.2021.637547

Idowu, J. (2024). Debiasing education algorithms. *International Journal of Artificial Intelligence in Education*, 34, 1510–1540. https://doi.org/10.1007/s40593-023-00389-4

Jeong, H., Wu, M., Dasgupta, N., Médard, M., & Calmon, F. (2021). Who gets the benefit of the doubt? Racial bias in machine learning algorithms applied to secondary school math education. In *35th Conference on Neural Information Processing Systems (NeurIPS 2021) Workshop on Math AI for Education (MATHAI4ED): Bridging the Gap Between Research and Smart Education*. https://fated2022.github.io/assets/pdf/FATED-2022_paper_Jeong_Racial_Bias_ML_Algs.pdf

Joshi, A., Kale, S., Chandel, S., & Pal, D. (2015). Likert scale: Explored and explained. *British Journal Applied Science*. https://doi.org/10.9734/BJAST/2015/14975

Kekez, I., Lauwaert, L., & Ređep, N. B. (2025). Is artificial intelligence (AI) research biased and conceptually vague? A systematic review of research on bias and discrimination in the context of using AI in human resource management. *Technology in Society*, 102818.

Kizilcec, R. (2016). How much information? Effects of transparency on trust in an algorithmic interface. In *Proceedings of the 2016 CHI Conference on Human Factors in Computing Systems* (pp. 2390–2395). https://doi.org/10.1145/2858036.2858402

Kizilcec, R., & Lee, H. (2021). Algorithmic fairness in education. In *The Ethics of Artificial Intelligence in Education* (pp. 174–202). Routledge.

Machado, E., Scavarda, L., Gusmão, R., & Silva, R. (2024). Industry 4.0 and sustainability integration in the supply chains of micro, small, and medium enterprises through people, process, and technology within the triple bottom line perspective. *Sustainability*, 16(3), 1141. https://doi.org/10.3390/su16031141

Madaio, M., Blodgett, S. L., Mayfield, E., & Dixon-Román, E. (2022). Beyond "fairness": Structural (in)justice lenses on ai for education. In *The Ethics of Artificial Intelligence in Education* (pp. 203–239). Routledge.

Mayfield, E., Madaio, M., Prabhumoye, S., Gerritsen, D., McLaughlin, B., Dixon-Román, E., & Black, A. W. (2019). Equity beyond bias in language technologies for education. In *Proceedings of the Fourteenth Workshop on Innovative Use of NLP for Building Educational Applications* (pp. 444–460). Association for Computational Linguistics.

Mehrabi, N., Morstatter, F., Saxena, N., Lerman, K., & Galstyan, A. (2021). A survey on bias and fairness in machine learning. *ACM Computing Surveys (CSUR)*, 54(6), 1–35. https://doi.org/10.48550/arXiv.1908.09635

Messick, S. (1989). Meaning and values in test validation: The science and ethics of assessment. *Educational Researcher*, 18(2), 5–11. https://doi.org/10.3102/0013189X018002005

Mustafa, M., Malik, M., & Maqsoom, A. (2024). Barriers to solar PV adoption in developing countries: Multiple regression and analytical hierarchy process approach. *Sustainability*, 16(3), 1032.

Nemoto, T., & Beglar, D. (2014). Likert-scale questionnaires. In N. Sonda & A. Krause (Eds.), *JALT2013 Conference Proceedings*. JALT.

O'Connor, S., & Liu, H. (2024). Gender bias perpetuation and mitigation in AI technologies: Challenges and opportunities. *AI & Society*, 39, 2045–2057. https://doi.org/10.1007/s00146-023-01675-4

Onesi-Ozigagun, O., Ololade, Y., Eyo-Udo, N., & Ogundipe, D. (2024). Revolutionizing education through AI: A comprehensive review of enhancing learning experiences. *International Journal of Applied Research in Social Sciences*, 6(4), 589–607.

Overbye-Thompson, H., & Rice, R. E. (2025). Understanding how users may work around algorithmic bias. *AI & Society*, 1–15. https://doi.org/10.1007/s00146-025-02498-1

Pagano, T., Loureiro, R., Lisboa, F., Ramos, G., Matos, R., Aragão de Sousa, G., Lisboa, L., Matos, M., Cruz, M., Lopez, E., Winkler, I., & Sperandio, E. (2022). Bias and unfairness in machine learning models: A systematic literature review. *arXiv preprint*. https://doi.org/10.48550/arXiv.2202.08176

Panarese, P., Grasso, M., & Solinas, C. (2025). Algorithmic bias, fairness, and inclusivity: A multilevel framework for justice-oriented AI. *AI & Society*. https://doi.org/10.1007/s00146-025-02451-2

Panda, S., & Roy, S. (2024). Reflections on emerging HCI–AI research. *AI & Society*, 39, 407–409. https://doi.org/10.1007/s00146-022-01409-y

Paneru, B., Paneru, B., Poudyal, R., & Shah, K. B. (2024). Exploring the nexus of user interface (UI) and user experience (UX) in the context of emerging trends and customer experience, human computer interaction, applications of artificial intelligence. *International Journal of Informatics, Information System and Computer Engineering (INJIISCOM)*, 5(1), 102–113.

Pfeiffer, J., Gutschow, J., Haas, C., Möslein, F., Maspfuhl, O., Borgers, F., & Alpsancar, S. (2023). Algorithmic fairness in AI: An interdisciplinary view. *Business & Information Systems Engineering*, 65(2), 209–222. https://doi.org/10.1007/s12599-023-00787-x

Polat, M., Turhan, N. S., & Toraman, Ç. (2022). Comparison of classical test theory vs. multi-facet Rasch theory in writing assessment. *Pegem Journal of Education and Instruction*, 12(2), 213–225.

Prasad, S. K. (2021). Predicting student performance using machine learning [Source code]. *GitHub*. https://github.com/skprasad117/Predicting-Student-Performance-Using-Machine-Learning

Radanliev, P. (2025). AI ethics: Integrating transparency, fairness, and privacy in AI development. *Applied Artificial Intelligence*, 39(1). https://doi.org/10.1080/08839514.2025.2463722

Rong, Y., Leemann, T., Nguyen, T., Fiedler, L., Qian, P., Unhelkar, V., Seidel, T., Kasneci, G., & Kasneci, E. (2023). Towards human-centered explainable AI: A survey of user studies for model explanations. *IEEE Transactions on Pattern Analysis and Machine Intelligence*, 46(4), 2104–2122.

Rzepka, N., Simbeck, K., Müller, H. G., & Pinkwart, N. (2022). Fairness of in-session dropout prediction. In *CSEDU* (Vol. 2, pp. 316–326). https://doi.org/10.5220/0010962100003182

Sahlgren, O. (2021). The politics and reciprocal (re)configuration of accountability and fairness in data-driven education. *Learning, Media and Technology*, 48(1), 95–108. https://doi.org/10.1080/17439884.2021.1986065

Sahoo, K., & Saurav, S. (2025). Designing AI systems with user empathy and inclusivity: Navigating bias and representation. In *Social, Ethical and Legal Aspects of Generative AI: Tools, Techniques and Systems* (pp. 1–11). Cham: Springer Nature Switzerland. https://doi.org/10.1007/978-3-031-87252-5_1

Sayili, U., Siddikoglu, E., Turgut, D., Arisli, H. E., Ceyhan, B., Gunver, M. G., Ozel Yildiz, S., Yurtseven, E., & Erginoz, E. (2024). Does categorizing scale scores with cutoff points affect hypothesis-testing results? *Discover Mental Health*, 4(1), 14. https://doi.org/10.1007/s44192-024-00067-4

Schrum, M., Johnson, M., Ghuy, M., & Gombolay, M. (2020). Four years in review: Statistical practices of Likert scales in human-robot interaction studies. In *Companion of the 2020 ACM/IEEE International Conference on Human-Robot Interaction* (pp. 43–52). https://doi.org/10.1145/3371382.338073

Simpson, S., Nukpezah, J., Brooks, K., & Pandya, R. (2025). Parity benchmark for measuring bias in LLMs. *AI and Ethics*, 5(3), 3087–3101. https://doi.org/10.1007/s43681-024-00613-4

Singhal, A., Tanveer, H., & Mago, V. (2023). Towards FATE in AI for social media and healthcare: A systematic review. https://doi.org/10.48550/arXiv.2306.05372a

Smith, H. (2020). Algorithmic bias: Should students pay the price? *AI & Society*, 35(4), 1077–1078. https://doi.org/10.1007/s00146-020-01054-3

Souza, R., & Reis, G. (2025). Avaliação Do Conhecimento Prévio Sobre A Física Quântica De Pessoas Em Meio Web: Uma Análise Utilizando Escala Likert E Alfa De Cronbach. *Ensino De Ciências E Tecnologia Em Revista—ENCITEC*, 15(1), 65–82. https://doi.org/10.31512/encitec.v15i1.1884

Spjuth, O., Frid, J., & Hellander, A. (2021). The machine learning life cycle and the cloud: Implications for drug discovery. *Expert Opinion on Drug Discovery*, 16(9), 1071–1079. https://doi.org/10.1080/17460441.2021.1932812

Stemler, S., & Naples, A. (2021). Rasch measurement v. item response theory: Knowing when to cross the line. *Practical Assessment, Research & Evaluation*, 26, 11.

Sturgis, P., Roberts, C., & Smith, P. (2014). Middle alternatives revisited: How the neither/nor response acts as a way of saying "I don't know"? *Sociological Methods & Research*, 43(1), 15–38.

Suresh, H., & Guttag, J. (2021). A framework for understanding sources of harm throughout the machine learning life cycle. In *Proceedings of the 1st ACM Conference on Equity and Access in Algorithms, Mechanisms, and Optimization* (pp. 1–9). https://doi.org/10.1145/3465416.3483305

Szafran, D., & Bach, R. L. (2024). "The human must remain the central focus": Subjective fairness perceptions in automated decision-making. *Minds and Machines*, 34(3), 24. https://doi.org/10.1007/s11023-024-09684-y

Talavera, A., & Luna, A. (2020). Machine learning: A contribution to operational research. *IEEE Revista Iberoamericana de Tecnologías del Aprendizaje*, 15(2), 70–75. https://doi.org/10.1109/RITA.2020.2987700

Troussas, C., Krouska, A., & Sgouropoulou, C. (2025a). A novel framework of human–computer interaction and human-centered artificial intelligence in learning technology. In *Human-Computer Interaction and Augmented Intelligence. Cognitive Systems Monographs* (Vol. 34). Springer. https://doi.org/10.1007/978-3-031-84453-9_9

Troussas, C., Krouska, A., & Sgouropoulou, C. (2025b). Case studies of interactive machine learning for adaptive learning technology systems. In *Human-Computer Interaction and Augmented Intelligence. Cognitive Systems Monographs* (Vol. 34). Springer. https://doi.org/10.1007/978-3-031-84453-9_8

Troussas, C., Krouska, A., & Sgouropoulou, C. (2025c). Human–computer interaction in education. In *Human-Computer Interaction and Augmented Intelligence* (Cognitive Systems Monographs, Vol. 34). Springer. https://doi.org/10.1007/978-3-031-84453-9_1

Uddin, S., Lu, H., Rahman, A., & Gao, J. (2024). A novel approach for assessing fairness in deployed machine learning algorithms. *Scientific Reports*, 14(1), 17753.

Van Busum, K., & Fang, S. (2024). Bias analysis of AI models for undergraduate student admissions. *Neural Computing and Applications*, 37(12), 7785–7795. https://doi.org/10.1007/s00521-024-10762-6

Wang, Y. (2024). Algorithmic decisions in education governance: Implications and challenges. *Discover Education*, 3(1), 229.

Webb, M., Fluck, A., Magenheim, J., Malyn-Smith, J., Waters, J., Deschênes, M., & Zagami, J. (2020). Machine learning for human learners: Opportunities, issues, tensions and threats. *Educational Technology Research and Development*, 69, 2109–2130. https://doi.org/10.1007/s11423-020-09858-2

Willits, F., Theodori, G., & Luloff, A. (2016). Another look at Likert scales. *Journal of Rural Social Sciences*, 31(3), 6.

Yu, R., Lee, H., & Kizilcec, R. (2021). Should college dropout prediction models include protected attributes? In *Proceedings of the Eighth ACM Conference on Learning@ Scale* (pp. 91–100). https://doi.org/10.1145/3430895.3460139

Yu, R., Li, Q., Fischer, C., Doroudi, S., & Xu, D. (2020). Towards accurate and fair prediction of college success: Evaluating different sources of student data. *Proceedings of the 13th International Conference on Educational Data Mining* (pp. 292–301). https://eric.ed.gov/?id=ed608066

14 Digital Microcredentials in Latin America and the Caribbean

Ecosystem Maturity, Regulatory Frameworks, Blockchain Infrastructure, and Credential Analytics for Regional Governance

*Frank E. Melendez-Anzures,
Claudia Camacho-Zuñiga, Genaro Zavala,
Carlos Alario-Hoyos, Oscar Jerez-Yañez,
Miguel A. Morales-Chan, and
Carlos Delgado-Kloos*

14.1 INTRODUCTION

14.1.1 Contextualizing the Global Rise of Microcredentials

Over the past decade, digital microcredentials have consolidated as a strategic instrument to address the growing demand for lifelong learning and to introduce greater flexibility in competency accreditation processes across higher education and continuing professional development. They are defined as short-term certifications focused on specific learning outcomes, enabling the recognition of concrete skills in a modular, portable, and verifiable manner (OECD, 2021; UNESCO IESALC, 2025).

Their rapid expansion is driven by two converging dynamics. On one hand, there is a pressing need to make visible the learning acquired in non-formal and informal contexts, which have traditionally been excluded from formal accreditation systems (CEDEFOP, 2022). On the other hand, the structural transformation of the digital economy demands the continuous updating of both technical and transversal skills (OECD, 2023a).

DOI: 10.1201/9781003678250-14

Multilateral organizations such as the OECD, UNESCO, and the European Commission regard microcredentials as a key instrument to bridge the gap between educational provision and the evolving requirements of the labor market, while fostering flexible and personalized learning pathways (Bideau & Kearns, 2022; OECD, 2021, 2023a; UNESCO IESALC, 2025). In Europe, the adoption of the European Approach to Microcredentials—aligned with the European Credit Transfer and Accumulation System (ECTS)—has facilitated their integration into national qualifications frameworks and quality assurance systems, establishing normative benchmarks that are increasingly being considered as transferable models by other regions (CEDEFOP, 2022; OECD, 2023a).

At the international level, countries such as Australia and New Zealand have implemented specific national frameworks for microcredentials, embedding them within their formal qualifications systems (OECD, 2023b). In the United States, adoption has been primarily led by universities and technology companies, which have developed alternative credentials with a strong emphasis on employability (Athey & Palikot, 2024). These developments have been further supported by the adoption of open technical standards such as Open Badges 3.0 and Verifiable Credentials, promoted by 1EdTech, which enable interoperability and global portability of credentials (1EdTech, 2024).

Recent studies have highlighted the potential of microcredentials to strengthen employability, enhance academic mobility, and foster adaptive learning trajectories aligned with contemporary demands (Gamage & Dehideniya, 2025). At the same time, international debate has emphasized that their effective implementation depends on critical structural conditions, including coherent regulatory frameworks, robust quality assurance mechanisms, and clear schemes for cross-border recognition (Ahsan et al., 2023; Zdunek et al., 2024).

Overall, microcredentials represent an emerging global instrument with transformative potential. Nevertheless, their consolidation as legitimate certification mechanisms will depend on convergence toward common standards, trusted digital infrastructures, and public policies that ensure their systemic integration within contemporary educational ecosystems. While some countries and regions are advancing toward integrated frameworks, others, such as Latin America and the Caribbean (LAC), face specific challenges that demand adaptive approaches and context-sensitive governance strategies.

14.1.2 Opportunities and Challenges for Latin America and the Caribbean

In LAC, interest in microcredentials has expanded significantly in recent years. Institutional diagnostics reveal an emerging ecosystem characterized by pioneering experiences and pilot projects, yet marked by substantial heterogeneity in regulatory, technical, and conceptual dimensions (MOCHILA Project, 2025a, 2025b; UNESCO IESALC, 2025).

Three major opportunities stand out. First, student enthusiasm: multiple surveys indicate that students perceive microcredentials as valuable tools to enhance employability and complement formal education (MOCHILA Project, 2025a). Second, their inclusive potential: as short, flexible, and accessible programs, they expand opportunities for historically excluded groups in higher education, including women, low-income youth, and rural populations (Tinsley et al., 2022; UNESCO IESALC, 2025). Third, technological innovation: the adoption of technologies such as blockchain reinforces the authenticity, traceability, and portability of credentials, thereby fostering greater trust among employers and learners (Mohammad & Vargas, 2022; OECD, 2023a).

Nonetheless, the challenges are equally significant. Most countries in the region lack specific regulatory frameworks for microcredentials, generating institutional ambiguity and limiting their official recognition in both academic and labor markets (MOCHILA Project, 2025b; Semigina & Rashkevych, 2023). Many higher education institutions also face technical and pedagogical constraints in designing, issuing, and integrating them coherently into curricula (MOCHILA Project, 2025a). Added to this is the limited interoperability among digital platforms, which fragments the ecosystem and hinders cross-border recognition of credentials (MOCHILA Project, 2025d; Varadarajan et al., 2023).

The territorial distribution of initiatives is also uneven. While countries such as Mexico, Colombia, Chile, and Ecuador lead with robust institutional experiences, other subregions, particularly Central America and the Caribbean, display more incipient progress (MOCHILA Project, 2025c). Notable cases include Tecnologico de Monterrey (Mexico), a pioneer in leveraging blockchain for credential issuance; Universidad Galileo (Guatemala), which has implemented digital badges for continuing education; and UTPL (Ecuador), which has integrated microcredentials into its curricular model (MOCHILA Project, 2025c).

Compared to Europe, where microcredentials are already integrated into qualification frameworks, quality assurance systems, and international portability mechanisms, LAC still faces considerable regulatory and institutional fragmentation. Although blockchain offers advantages for verification and portability, it also poses complex challenges related to data governance, digital privacy, and specialized technical training, particularly in contexts where data protection policies remain nascent. Notably, governance frameworks for credentialing institutions remain underdeveloped (de Alwis et al., 2025), while broader challenges such as interoperability, regulation, high implementation costs, and privacy concerns persist (El Koshiry et al., 2023; Mohammad & Vargas, 2022).

In summary, LAC stands at a dual crossroads: on the one hand, a fertile ground for educational innovation grounded in employability, inclusion, and digital trust; on the other, a set of regulatory, institutional, and technological gaps that must be addressed through strategic vision and regional cooperation to ensure the legitimacy and scalability of microcredentials.

14.1.3 Purpose and Contribution of the Chapter to Existing Knowledge

This chapter aims to critically analyze the gaps and opportunities facing LAC in consolidating an ecosystem of blockchain-based digital microcredentials, proposing a regional governance model to foster their effective adoption. Based on a comprehensive literature review of technical reports, academic literature, and institutional cases, the chapter makes three main contributions:

1. A comprehensive vision of the regional ecosystem: The chapter identifies and categorizes the regulatory, technological, and institutional heterogeneity across LAC, highlighting the main gaps that hinder interoperability and mutual recognition.
2. A proposal for credential analytics: The concept of credential analytics is introduced as a strategic tool to monitor, evaluate, and optimize the use of microcredentials, addressing their potential to guide public policy and improve employability and academic mobility.
3. An interoperable governance model: The chapter proposes a regional governance framework based on open standards and blockchain, integrating regulatory, technological, and quality assurance recommendations to strengthen the trust and traceability of credentials.

By offering a critical synthesis of current progress and challenges, this work contributes to academic discussion and provides guidance to policymakers, universities, and productive sectors on how to scale microcredentials in the region in a sustainable and equitable manner.

14.2 METHODOLOGICAL APPROACH

14.2.1 Type of Review and Thematic Scope

This study is based on a structured narrative review with a scoping review orientation, designed to map the development of digital microcredentials in Latin America and the Caribbean (LAC). It integrated three types of sources: (1) peer-reviewed academic publications, (2) policy reports and technical documents from international and regional organizations, and (3) institutional case studies. The analysis addressed microcredentials, digital credentials, blockchain-based verification systems, and credential analytics, with an emphasis on both implementation barriers and opportunities. To broaden the perspective, references were included to consolidated frameworks and regulatory experiences in Europe and North America.

14.2.2 Search Strategy, Sources, and Inclusion/Exclusion Criteria

The bibliographic search was conducted between March and August 2025, covering publications from 2010 to 2025. The international databases Scopus and Web of Science were consulted, complemented by targeted searches in Google Scholar and institutional repositories. Combinations of keywords in English and Spanish were used (e.g., microcredentials, microcredenciales, digital badges, credential analytics, blockchain infrastructure, Latin America and the Caribbean).

Selected documents had to meet three criteria: (1) thematic relevance, meaning they contributed to the debate on the design, issuance, governance, or adoption of microcredentials or blockchain-based digital credentials; (2) geographic relevance, with a focus on LAC or lessons that could be extrapolated from other regions; and (3) academic or institutional quality, prioritizing peer-reviewed articles and reports with explicit methodologies. Press releases and other materials without substantive analysis were excluded, as were technical studies of blockchain not linked to higher education.

In total, 22 indexed academic publications, 11 international reports, 4 institutional case studies, and 4 recent comparative regional reports were reviewed. Additionally, 12 complementary sources, including technical specifications, book chapters, and conference proceedings, were integrated, providing institutional diagnostics, regulatory analyses, and empirical evidence across 17 LAC countries.

14.2.3 Thematic Categorization and Documentary Analysis Process

The corpus was organized into four analytical categories, consistent with the theoretical framework:

1. Emerging microcredential ecosystem: levels of institutional adoption and educational purposes.
2. Regulatory framework in Latin America and the Caribbean: existence and alignment of national or sectoral policies with qualification frameworks and quality assurance mechanisms.
3. Digital governance and blockchain: platforms, interoperability, and the use of blockchain in digital credentials.
4. Credential analytics: potential for using data for institutional management, employability, and public policy design.

A qualitative content analysis was applied to identify trends, convergences, and divergences, triangulating the findings from academic literature with regional reports and case studies.

14.3 RESULTS OF THE REVIEW

14.3.1 Emerging Microcredential Ecosystem

The microcredential ecosystem in Latin America and the Caribbean (LAC) is in an early stage, characterized by rapid expansion and growing institutional interest. An analysis of regional trends reveals that one in three students has already earned at least one microcredential, motivated primarily by employability. This is coupled with increasing demand from the productive sector: more than 50% of companies report difficulties in finding workers with the required skills, positioning these credentials as a strategic instrument to bridge skills gaps. Furthermore, it is estimated that 65% of institutions that have not yet implemented microcredentials plan to adopt them within the next five years, signaling sustained growth of the model (UNESCO IESALC, 2025).

Based on documentary analysis and institutional diagnostics, four levels of maturity in microcredential management can be identified, classified according to the degree of formalization, curricular integration, and validation mechanisms. At the exploratory level, informal or extracurricular initiatives prevail, without curricular integration or institutional recognition. The initial level is characterized by the use of commercial platforms such as Credly, Badgr, or Acreditta, without the allocation of academic credits or alignment with regulatory frameworks. At the advanced level, microcredentials are integrated into formal study programs, with defined instructional design and, in some cases, the use of technologies such as blockchain to ensure traceability. Finally, the ecosystemic level involves articulation with national qualifications frameworks and quality assurance agencies, enabling formal recognition both within and beyond the institution (MOCHILA Project, 2025a, 2025c).

This classification is summarized in Table 14.1, which presents the four levels of institutional maturity according to their characteristics, degree of formalization, and representative examples in the region.

The formative purpose of microcredentials in LAC is oriented toward three central objectives: employability, inclusion, and flexible learning pathways.

1. Employability stands out as the predominant motivation, with credentials focused on highly demanded technical and digital skills such as programming, cybersecurity, and data analytics. Recent data indicate that more than 80% of students consider microcredentials to strengthen their employment opportunities (MOCHILA Project, 2025a).
2. Inclusion initiatives target marginalized populations or those with limited access to formal education, such as adult learners, students from rural areas, or individuals without prior university experience. In this regard, microcredentials provide shorter, more accessible, and adaptable formats that respond to diverse needs (Tinsley et al., 2022; UNESCO IESALC, 2025).

TABLE 14.1
Institutional Maturity Levels of Microcredentials in Latin America and the Caribbean (LAC)

Maturity Level	Main Characteristics	Examples in LAC
Exploratory	Pilot or isolated initiatives. Informal issuance of badges in extracurricular courses. No curricular integration or institutional recognition.	Public universities in Central America offering badges for extension workshops.
Initial	Microcredentials issued through commercial platforms (Credly, Badgr, Acreditta). Limited recognition. No academic credit assigned.	INTEC (Dominican Republic) in continuing education programs; Universidad Autónoma de Chile.
Advanced	Credentials linked to the formal curriculum. Use of blockchain for verification. Defined instructional design aligned with qualification frameworks.	Tecnológico de Monterrey (Mexico) with blockchain diplomas; Universidad Técnica Particular de Loja (Ecuador).
Ecosystemic	Integration with national qualifications frameworks and quality assurance agencies. Institutional and external (employer) recognition.	Emerging pilots in Panama, Colombia, and Puerto Rico where credentials are officially recognized.

3. Finally, experiences oriented towards flexible learning pathways are beginning to consolidate. These enable the accumulation and articulation of modular credentials toward higher-level certifications. Although still at an early stage, promising models can be found in institutions such as Tecnologico de Monterrey and UTPL, which have incorporated stackable microcredentials into formal academic programs (MOCHILA Project, 2025c; Peters et al., 2025).

In terms of regional distribution, initiatives display an uneven pattern. Mexico, Colombia, Chile, and Ecuador concentrate the majority of developments, while in Central America and the Caribbean, fragmented efforts prevail. This asymmetry reveals institutional and regulatory gaps that may hinder the scalability of the model. In response, a regional consultation process has been launched to develop a common framework for microcredentials, aimed at strengthening interoperability, quality, and regional recognition of these credentials (UNESCO IESALC, 2025).

14.3.2 Regulatory Framework in Latin America and the Caribbean

The regulatory landscape of microcredentials in LAC is marked by significant heterogeneity, with uneven progress in their institutionalization, legal recognition, and integration into national qualifications frameworks. While some countries have developed explicit regulations that formalize their existence, in most cases, regulatory development remains incipient, partial, or entirely absent (MOCHILA Project, 2025b; UNESCO IESALC, 2025).

Recent comparative analyses suggest that countries in the region can be grouped into five regulatory categories, each reflecting distinct levels of institutional consolidation (MOCHILA Project, 2025b). This diversity is summarized in Table 14.2, which classifies the region's regulatory frameworks into five comparative categories.

1. Explicit regulation and interoperable platforms: Panama, Colombia, Ecuador, and Puerto Rico have enacted regulations that legally recognize microcredentials and integrate digital verification mechanisms. The Dominican Republic, still in transition, is developing guidelines through its Ministry of Higher Education, Science, and Technology (MESCyT), as reported in the MOCHILA Project (2025b).
2. Regulatory transition: Mexico, Chile, and Uruguay are in phases of discussion or pilot testing, without yet consolidating specific legislation. In these contexts, microcredentials generally function as institutional projects without official validity (Arroyave Villa, 2023; MOCHILA Project, 2025b).
3. Initiatives without legal backing: Argentina, Brazil, Bolivia, and Paraguay show a proliferation of microcredentials issued by universities or private platforms but without state recognition, limiting their portability and legitimacy (Ling & Ling, 2023; MOCHILA Project, 2025b).
4. Qualifications frameworks without explicit mention: Costa Rica and Guatemala operate active national qualifications frameworks, but these do not formally incorporate microcredentials as a differentiated category (Carțiș et al., 2023; MOCHILA Project, 2025b).

5. Absence of regulation: Honduras, El Salvador, and, until recently, the Dominican Republic lack legal references or educational policies that recognize these credentials, making their use for academic or labor purposes difficult (Iniesto et al., 2022; MOCHILA Project, 2025b).

The absence of coherent regulatory frameworks generates three major structural risks. First, the fragmentation of quality criteria across institutions prevents the accumulation, transfer, or mutual recognition of microcredentials (Iniesto et al., 2022). Second, the lack of quality assurance mechanisms undermines confidence in their academic or labor market value (Ling & Ling, 2023). Finally, in deregulated contexts, a market of low-value credentials may emerge, amplifying educational inequality and creating confusion among employers and students (Carţiş et al., 2023; Kušić et al., 2022).

National examples illustrate these dynamics and the coexistence of regulatory gaps with pioneering initiatives. In Chile, microcredentials remain internal projects without curricular integration or official recognition, which limits their systemic impact. In Mexico, the Ministry of Public Education has not issued specific guidelines, forcing innovative institutions such as Tecnologico de Monterrey to operate in a legal vacuum, relying solely on their institutional prestige to support their digital credentials (Arroyave Villa, 2023). Despite these challenges, some countries are moving toward greater formalization. In the Dominican Republic, the Ministry of Higher Education, Science, and Technology (MESCyT) is developing guidelines to incorporate microcredentials into the National Qualifications Framework. In

TABLE 14.2
Comparative Classification of Regulatory Frameworks in LAC Countries

Regulatory Category	Description	Main Countries
Explicit regulation and interoperable platforms	Countries with laws or decrees that formally recognize microcredentials and provide digital verification mechanisms.	Panama, Colombia, Ecuador, Puerto Rico
Regulatory transition	Countries with partial guidelines or pilot projects under discussion for the incorporation of microcredentials.	Mexico, Chile, Uruguay
Initiatives without legal backing	Microcredentials issued by institutions or private platforms without official recognition.	Argentina, Brazil, Bolivia, Paraguay
Operational qualifications framework without mention of microcredentials	Countries with active national qualifications systems that do not yet include microcredentials as a category.	Costa Rica, Guatemala
No specific regulation	Countries with no legal or administrative reference to microcredentials.	Honduras, El Salvador, Dominican Republic (in transition)

Guatemala, the Technical Commission for Quality Assurance has proposed specific guidelines for their evaluation. Meanwhile, Panama has proposed integrating them into its official electronic certification platform (MOCHILA Project, 2025b; UNESCO IESALC, 2025).

At the international level, frameworks such as that of the European Union, linking microcredentials to the European Qualifications Framework and the ECTS system, as well as national policies in Australia and New Zealand, demonstrate how formal integration fosters the scalability and legitimacy of these credentials (OECD, 2023a, 2023b).

Without common regulatory frameworks, the LAC region faces the risk of deep institutional fragmentation in the development of microcredentials. There is an urgent need to move toward national standards articulated with regional mechanisms of interoperability. Organizations such as UNESCO and the OECD have stressed that supranational coordination is essential to ensure the trust, scalability, and social impact of microcredentials in the region.

14.3.3 Digital Governance and Blockchain

Digital governance has become a central component in the transformation of educational systems, particularly with regard to the management and verification of credentials. In this context, emerging technologies offer solutions to overcome long-standing challenges of trust, fragmentation, and interoperability. Among the most prominent is blockchain, recognized as an infrastructure capable of ensuring reliable and verifiable records. Blockchain is a distributed ledger technology that organizes information into cryptographically linked blocks, ensuring transparency, traceability, and immutability without the need for a central authority (Gräther et al., 2018). These features have made blockchain a strategic tool in domains where trust and verification are essential, such as digital credentials in higher education.

In LAC, the adoption of blockchain as an infrastructure for digital credentials remains incipient, yet it is increasingly recognized as a key enabler of trust and interoperability within accreditation systems. In a regional context characterized by fragmented regulatory frameworks, uneven institutional development, and limited confidence in traditional verification mechanisms, blockchain offers added value as a trust infrastructure. Its advantages go beyond the immutability of records: by anchoring credentials on a blockchain, traceability and decentralized verification are guaranteed, reducing fraud and facilitating cross-border portability. In addition, credential holders can manage their records through digital wallets, reinforcing data sovereignty and enabling selective disclosure of information, without depending exclusively on institutional or governmental repositories (McGreal, 2023; Samala et al., 2024).

Pioneering experiences in the region already illustrate this potential. Tecnologico de Monterrey (Mexico) has issued more than 4,000 diplomas anchored on blockchain, granting graduates direct control over verifiable credentials. Similarly, the National University of Colombia, Universidad Tecnica Particular de Loja (Ecuador), and Universidad Galileo (Guatemala) have developed pilots based on Blockcerts or LACChain, exploring decentralized verification mechanisms (Jaramillo & Piedra,

2020; MOCHILA Project, 2025c; Vargas & Piedra, 2023). Recent studies in Ecuador highlight the positive reception of these initiatives among students, while also pointing to challenges related to data protection and institutional readiness (Barreto Pin et al., 2024).

Nevertheless, implementation poses substantial governance challenges. The immutability of records complicates the correction of errors, making hybrid models (on-chain and off-chain) necessary to comply with data protection regulations (Gräther et al., 2018). Moreover, most institutions lack the capacity to manage decentralized digital identities (DIDs) or adopt verifiable credential (VC) protocols. At the national level, few strategies clearly define who administers educational blockchain nodes, how open standards will be adopted, and how cross-border interoperability and user privacy will be ensured (Subramanian et al., 2024; Turkanović et al., 2018). This regulatory ambiguity generates operational uncertainty and limits the scalability of projects.

In terms of platforms, four solutions concentrate the active projects in LAC: Credly, based on Open Badges with optional blockchain integration; Acreditta, developed in Colombia with regional support and LinkedIn integration; Badgr/Canvas Badges, widely adopted by universities but lacking native blockchain functionality; and Blockcerts, which relies on public blockchains (Bitcoin, Ethereum) for verifiable credentials managed through digital wallets. Their characteristics are summarized in Table 14.3, which highlights the technological and functional diversity of these initiatives.

There is an emerging consensus on the need to align regional projects with international standards such as Open Badges 3.0 (IMS Global) and Verifiable Credentials

TABLE 14.3
Technical Comparison of Blockchain-Enabled Platforms Active in LAC

Platform	Underlying technology	Key features	Countries/institutions using it
Credly	Based on Open Badges; optionally integrable with blockchain	Customizable badge design, open APIs, large-scale issuance, badge analytics	Universities in Mexico, Colombia, Chile; companies such as IBM
Acreditta	Blockchain (Hyperledger) and Open Badges	Verifiable credentials, LinkedIn integration, Spanish-language support, regional focus	Institutions in Colombia, Ecuador, Peru, Dominican Republic
Badgr/ Canvas Badges	Based on Open Badges; no native blockchain	LMS integration, badge pathway tracking, student portfolios	Universities in Brazil and Argentina; MOOC platforms
Blockcerts	Public blockchain (Bitcoin, Ethereum)	Credentials with cryptographic signatures and blockchain hashes; user-controlled digital wallets	Tecnologico de Monterrey (Mexico), UNAL (Colombia), projects in Brazil

(W3C) to ensure interoperability. In Europe, the European Blockchain Services Infrastructure (EBSI) already enables the cross-border verification of university diplomas, while in LAC isolated pilots still predominate, without integration into national strategies or regional frameworks (OECD, 2023a, 2023b). A promising alternative is the use of federated networks such as LACChain, promoted by the Inter-American Development Bank, which can reduce costs, enhance transparency, and strengthen the scalability of the regional ecosystem (Pardo et al., 2023; Porto & Presant, 2023).

From a governance perspective, the opportunities and challenges identified can be synthesized into a reference architecture for blockchain-enabled credentials, which illustrates the full credential life cycle:

1. The issuing institution creates and digitally signs the credential.
2. A hash is generated and stored on the blockchain (e.g., LACChain, EBSI, or another network).
3. The credential is delivered to the holder through a digital wallet.
4. Verifiers, such as employers or other universities, consult the blockchain to confirm authenticity.
5. Verification records feed into credential analytics systems, generating insights on usage, mobility, and impact.

This model emphasizes that blockchain governance in education is not merely a technical challenge but requires institutional coordination, clear regulatory frameworks, and the adoption of open standards that ensure trust, scalability, and meaningful use of credential data.

In brief, blockchain has the potential to become the trust infrastructure for microcredentials in LAC, provided that current institutional fragmentation is overcome. Without clear governance frameworks, shared standards, and supranational coordination, these initiatives risk remaining limited to experimental pilots. Moving toward a federated model of digital governance is key to ensuring trust, interoperability, and the social impact of digital credentials in the region.

14.3.4 Credential Analytics

Credential analytics refers to the systematic use of data generated by digital credentials (such as microcredentials, digital badges, or blockchain-based diplomas) to inform academic, institutional, and policy decision-making. These data include credential metadata (certified competencies, issuing institution, workload), usage patterns (frequency and type of verification), and their integration into broader educational and career trajectories. Conceptually, credential analytics extends the field of learning analytics by shifting the unit of analysis from course-level performance to the recognition, validation, and impact of certified skills across multiple contexts (Brown et al., 2021; Varadarajan et al., 2023).

In higher education, credential analytics enables institutions to monitor program effectiveness, identify skill gaps, and realign curricula with labor market demands. For employers, aggregated data on verified microcredentials provide evidence-based insights into candidate competencies, allowing more accurate recruitment processes and better alignment between academic preparation and workforce needs (Ahsan et al., 2023; Lang & Sharp, 2023). At the policy level, credential analytics has the potential to generate intelligence for workforce development, informing strategies aimed at closing regional skill gaps, fostering mobility, and promoting inclusive growth (OECD, 2023a; UNESCO IESALC, 2025).

From the perspective of learners, credential analytics can enhance transparency in how microcredentials are recognized, supporting cross-border validation, portability, and accumulation of learning outcomes. This can improve motivation and engagement, as learners gain visibility into how specific credentials contribute to employability and lifelong learning pathways (Bideau & Kearns, 2022; Oliver, 2022).

The key dimensions of credential analytics are summarized in Table 14.4. Relevant variables include the following:

1. Issuance data (date, duration, institution), which allows the monitoring of program growth and temporal trends.
2. Learner profile (including gender, age, place of residence, and prior education), useful for inclusion and equity studies.
3. Usage and validation data (number of verifications, type of verifier, time between issuance and validation), which provide insights into labor market acceptance.
4. Accumulation pathways (sequences of microcredentials and stackable credentials) demonstrate how learners construct flexible learning trajectories.
5. Labor market outcomes (employment after credentialing, sector of hiring, initial salary), which measure the impact of microcredentials on employability.

TABLE 14.4
Educational and Labor Data Categories for Credential Analytics

Dimension	Variables/Indicators	Possible analyses
Issuance data	Date of issuance, issuing institution, duration (hours), thematic area	Identify peaks in training supply; analyze distribution of thematic areas over time
Learner profile	Gender, age, place of residence, prior education level	Assess women's participation in STEM microcredentials; detect regional disparities
Usage and validation data	Number of verifications, time to first validation, type of verifier (employer, HEI)	Determine which credentials have highest labor demand; measure speed of uptake
Accumulation pathways	Sequence of microcredentials obtained, stackable pathways toward diplomas	Analyze learning patterns (competency combinations); design recommended pathways
Labor market outcomes	Time to employment after credentialing, sector of hiring, initial salary	Evaluate employability effectiveness; correlate credentials with emerging sectors

In practice, these dimensions can be modeled and visualized through interactive dashboards that display demographic distributions, the most frequent accumulation pathways, and the economic sectors most engaged in credential validation. Such visualization tools transform data into actionable intelligence for universities, employers, policymakers, and learners alike (Lumina Foundation, 2025).

Nevertheless, the implementation of credential analytics raises significant governance and ethical challenges. A central issue concerns data ownership: it remains unclear whether data should belong to learners, issuing institutions, or credentialing platforms. Ensuring privacy and consent requires robust anonymization protocols, secure storage, and compliance with data protection regulations. Risks of algorithmic bias are also considerable, as predictive models trained on incomplete or skewed datasets may reproduce existing inequalities in access to education and employment. Moreover, the growing commercialization of educational data by private platforms risks transforming learning trajectories into commodities (Kayyali, 2025; Narong, 2025).

From a technological standpoint, international standards such as Open Badges 3.0 (IMS Global) and W3C Verifiable Credentials provide the necessary infrastructure for interoperability, transparency, and cross-border recognition of digital credentials. Embedding these standards into credential analytics frameworks ensures that data can be exchanged securely and meaningfully across institutions, employers, and countries (IMS Global, 2021; W3C, 2019).

At the international level, initiatives such as Europass and the European Blockchain Services Infrastructure (EBSI) illustrate how credential analytics can be embedded into national qualification frameworks, linking educational records with employment services to enhance labor mobility (CEDEFOP, 2022; OECD, 2023a). In LAC, organizations such as UNESCO IESALC and the Inter-American Development Bank have highlighted the potential of credential analytics to strengthen employability strategies, although regional practices remain fragmented and hindered by the lack of common metadata standards (Mateo-Berganza Díaz et al., 2019; Porto & Presant, 2023; UNESCO IESALC, 2025).

In conclusion, credential analytics represents a strategic tool for building evidence-based higher education and labor market policies. Its contribution extends beyond improving the quality and relevance of educational provision: it generates institutional and regional intelligence to guide strategies for inclusion, employability, and sustainable development. However, its transformative potential will only materialize if robust ethical and governance frameworks, interoperable infrastructures, and shared standards are established, ensuring that credential data serve the public good rather than corporate interests.

14.4 PROPOSED MODEL FOR REGIONAL GOVERNANCE

The preceding analysis suggests that Latin America and the Caribbean (LAC) require an integrated governance model to enable blockchain-based microcredentials to achieve legitimacy, interoperability, and scalability. Such a model must combine regulatory articulation, technical standards, quality assurance practices, and monitoring mechanisms. The following lines of action are proposed.

14.4.1 Normative Articulation: Structural Recommendations for LAC

The first component involves building a regional regulatory framework that provides shared guidelines without imposing uniformity. Current ambiguity in defining what constitutes a microcredential undermines recognition in both academic and labor markets (Brown et al., 2021; OECD, 2023a). Without a common baseline, institutions risk generating fragmented initiatives that remain disconnected from national and regional qualifications frameworks. Three actions are recommended:

1. Define and categorize microcredentials by establishing official definitions that differentiate between badges, nanocourses, and digital diplomas, specifying minimum requirements such as duration, learning outcomes, and assessment criteria. Experiences in Europe show that a lack of clarity weakens recognition, whereas consensual definitions facilitate integration into qualifications frameworks (Council of the European Union, 2022; European Commission, 2021; OECD, 2023a).
2. Incorporate microcredentials into higher education legislation and quality assurance regulations. This would enable mechanisms for validation and accumulation within formal programs, overcoming the current fragmentation. Linking microcredentials with national qualifications frameworks (NQFs) and academic credit systems has proven effective in international contexts (Council of the European Union, 2022; Oliver, 2019). In LAC, such integration would also allow recognition in public-sector recruitment and professional licensing.
3. Establish mutual recognition agreements across countries. Inspired by the Buenos Aires Convention for university degrees, such agreements would ensure that a microcredential issued in one country carries equivalent value in another. Multilateral organizations, including UNESCO IESALC, have encouraged progress toward a regional framework with minimum standards, which represents a key opportunity for articulation (UNESCO IESALC, 2025).

14.4.2 Interoperability and Decentralized Governance Through Blockchain

The second component is to guarantee technical interoperability and distributed governance. Evidence suggests that without open standards, microcredentials risk fragmentation into isolated platforms, thereby reducing their value for both learners and employers (Brown et al., 2021; Oliver, 2019). Key recommendations are as follows:

1. Adopt open standards such as Open Badges 3.0 and W3C Verifiable Credentials, which ensure that credentials are readable across platforms while preserving data sovereignty (IMS Global, 2021; W3C, 2019). Shared

standards prevent duplication and promote learner mobility (OECD, 2023a).
2. Deploy a regional blockchain infrastructure, modeled on initiatives such as LACChain by the Inter-American Development Bank, where credentials are anchored in a shared ledger. This reduces costs, improves verification, and distributes governance among participating institutions (Allende López & Colina Unda, 2018; Pardo et al., 2023). Each university could serve as an issuing node, while a regional consortium would define governance and security protocols. Compliance with data protection laws would require complementary off-chain mechanisms (Turkanović et al., 2018).
3. Create self-sovereign digital identities (DIDs) for learners and graduates, enabling them to manage their own credentials in personal wallets and share them with third parties without the need for intermediaries. This strengthens portability and trust across borders (Gräther et al., 2018; Grech et al., 2021).

In this governance model, governments, higher education institutions, the productive sector, and technology platforms interact through a regional framework coordinated by a quality assurance agency that supervises standards, interoperability, and formative impact.

14.4.3 Common Indicators and Standards for Monitoring

The third component is the establishment of indicators and monitoring tools, fundamental to evaluating the relevance, quality, and impact of microcredentials in LAC. The credibility of microcredentials depends on transparent monitoring systems that allow stakeholders to measure effectiveness (Brown et al., 2021; Oliver, 2019; Tamoliune et al., 2023). Suggested dimensions include:

1. Issuance and usage indicators: number of credentials issued by type, percentage validated by employers, and average time between issuance and first validation. These indicators measure market acceptance (Brown et al., 2021; OECD, 2023a).
2. Quality indicators: student and employer satisfaction, course completion rates, and alignment between learning outcomes and national qualifications frameworks (OECD, 2023a).
3. Inclusion indicators: distribution of credentials by gender, region, and socioeconomic group; percentage of participants from vulnerable populations. Alignment with the SDGs, particularly inclusive and equitable education, would provide social legitimacy (OECD, 2023a).
4. Metadata standards: each credential should include mandatory fields (issuing institution, date, duration, assessment criteria, validity period), in line with the Inter-American Development Bank's Digital Credential Framework, which establishes a "Critical Information Summary" (Porto & Presant, 2023).

14.4.4 Role of the Regional Observatory on Microcredentials

The fourth component is the creation of a Regional Observatory on Microcredentials, coordinated by multilateral organizations and leading universities. This observatory would serve as a hub for coordination, monitoring, and knowledge transfer, contributing to the consolidation of a transparent and sustainable regional ecosystem. Its main responsibilities would include:

1. Data collection and transparency: systematically publishing information on microcredential initiatives across LAC, including programs, disciplines, platforms used, and the number of credentials issued.
2. Analytical reports: producing periodic diagnoses to identify trends, best practices, and gaps.
3. Capacity-building: providing technical assistance and training to governments and institutions in the design, issuance, and assurance of microcredentials.
4. Facilitation of recognition agreements: mediating between stakeholders to ensure the adoption and implementation of regional standards.

Comparable models in other regions demonstrate the feasibility of such initiatives. For instance, the European MOOC Consortium developed the Common Microcredential Framework (CMF) to harmonize standards across MOOC platforms, while the MicroHE project piloted recognition and portability mechanisms for microcredentials within European higher education (Varadarajan et al., 2023). These experiences, together with proposals for maturity models to assess institutional capacity (Iatrellis et al., 2024), provide relevant benchmarks for LAC, where a Regional Observatory could accelerate institutional adoption and ensure policy alignment.

In summary, the proposed governance model integrates normative articulation, interoperable infrastructure, indicator-based evaluation, and a regional coordinating body. Its gradual and collaborative implementation would allow the consolidation of a trustworthy, transparent, and inclusive microcredential ecosystem in LAC. Table 14.5 synthesizes these strategic recommendations by stakeholder—governments, higher education institutions, the productive sector, and technology platforms—organized across short, medium, and long-term horizons.

14.5 CONCLUSIONS

This chapter provides a comprehensive and critical perspective on blockchain-based microcredentials in Latin America and the Caribbean (LAC). By analyzing academic literature, reports from international organizations, and selected institutional case studies, it identifies regulatory, technical, and institutional gaps that explain the still-limited diffusion of credentials in the region. It also systematizes the main purposes of microcredentials (employability, inclusion, and flexible pathways) and proposes a typology of institutional maturity. The introduction of credential analytics as

TABLE 14.5
Strategic Recommendations by Stakeholder for a Regional Ecosystem

Stakeholder	Short term	Medium term	Long term
Governments	Revise higher education laws to recognize microcredentials; join regional framework initiatives.	Integrate microcredentials into qualifications frameworks and employment programs; finance blockchain pilots.	Promote regional mutual recognition agreements; update regulations based on Observatory findings.
Higher Education Institutions (HEIs)	Establish innovation units for credentialing; train faculty in microcredential design.	Align microcredentials with formal programs and qualifications frameworks; adopt open standards (Open Badges, VCs).	Consolidate internal credential ecosystems; join regional consortia for issuance and verification.
Productive sector	Co-design microcredentials with HEIs; recognize them in recruitment processes.	Build sectoral consortia with HEIs to certify skills; offer internships linked to microcredentials.	Develop corporate credentialing systems interoperable with regional frameworks; fund content updates.
Technology platforms	Ensure compliance with metadata standards; provide training and support in Spanish.	Integrate self-sovereign identities and regional blockchain; reduce costs for low-resource HEIs.	Develop credential analytics tools aligned with data protection regulations; feed insights into the Observatory.

a strategic tool to measure impact and inform policies represents a novel contribution. Finally, the chapter presents a regional governance model that integrates normative recommendations, decentralized infrastructure, monitoring standards, and the role of a regional observatory.

To move toward a sustainable and trustworthy ecosystem, several recommendations emerge:

1. Develop and adopt a regional framework with the participation of governments, quality assurance agencies, universities, and employers. This framework should serve as an umbrella for national regulations, enabling harmonization and mutual recognition.
2. Promote articulated pilot projects that integrate microcredentials into formal programs and use blockchain for verifiable issuance. Evaluating these pilots with clear indicators will provide evidence of return and guide improvements.
3. Foster inter-institutional collaboration and the creation of blockchain consortia nodes. Interoperability cannot be achieved in isolation; cooperation is required to share infrastructures, expertise, and costs.

4. Prioritize capacity building for faculty, technical staff, and managers in microcredential design, open standards, and data protection practices. Regional training programs could accelerate this process.
5. Ensure inclusivity and equity by offering microcredentials not only in high-demand labor areas but also in socially relevant fields such as basic education, health, and soft skills. Targeted funding and support policies should ensure access for vulnerable populations.

Given that the field of microcredentials in LAC remains emergent, further research is needed to inform decision-making. Priority lines include the following:

1. Longitudinal studies to evaluate the long-term impact of microcredentials on employability and academic mobility.
2. Comparative studies across countries and regions (e.g., LAC versus the European Union) to identify transferable best practices and analyze the influence of different normative and cultural contexts.
3. Cost and sustainability analyses of blockchain platforms and business models for microcredentials, to determine their economic viability in both public and private institutions.
4. Ethics and data protection research, exploring decentralized identities (DIDs), privacy safeguards, and risks of surveillance in blockchain-based credentialing.
5. Credential analytics and artificial intelligence applications to support the design of personalized learning pathways and identify regional skills gaps.

While this review provides an integral overview, certain limitations must be acknowledged. First, the scope of the literature search was restricted to a defined time window and to sources available in major academic databases and institutional repositories, which may have excluded relevant work published in other languages or less visible outlets. Second, academic research on microcredentials in LAC remains limited; much of the available evidence comes from institutional reports or pilot projects, which do not always meet the methodological rigor of peer-reviewed studies. Third, given the rapid evolution of technologies such as blockchain and the fluid nature of regulatory frameworks, some findings may become outdated in a relatively short period. Despite these constraints, triangulation across multiple types of sources helped strengthen the robustness of the analysis. These limitations also underscore the need for ongoing, systematic, and comparative research in the field.

The success of a blockchain-based microcredential ecosystem in LAC will depend on the ability of stakeholders to articulate regulatory frameworks, build interoperable infrastructures, generate trust through quality and transparency, and leverage credential data to improve both education and employment. The agenda outlined in this chapter calls for concerted action and continuous research to transform the potential of microcredentials into an effective mechanism for inclusion and sustainable development.

DECLARATION OF INTEREST STATEMENT

The authors declare no conflict of interest.

ACKNOWLEDGMENTS

This research was developed within the framework of the MOCHILA project—Microcredentials in Higher Education for Latin America and the Caribbean (Project No. 101179172), co-funded by the European Union under the Erasmus+ Capacity Building in Higher Education Programme (ERASMUS-EDU-2024-CBHE).

REFERENCES

1EdTech. (2024). Open badges 3.0 specification. *1EdTech Consortium*. https://www.imsglobal.org/spec/ob/v3p0

Ahsan, K., Akbar, S., Kam, B., & Abdulrahman, M. D.-A. (2023). Implementation of micro-credentials in higher education: A systematic literature review. *Education and Information Technologies*, 28(10), 13505–13540. https://doi.org/10.1007/s10639-023-11739-z

Allende López, M., & Colina Unda, V. (2018). Blockchain: How to develop trust in complex surroundings to generate social impact value. https://doi.org/10.18235/0001139

Arroyave Villa, N. A. (2023). El enfoque de las microcredenciales en la Educación Superior. *Rastros Rostros*, 26(1). https://doi.org/10.16925/2382-4921.2024.01.09

Athey, S., & Palikot, J. (2024). The value of non-traditional credentials in the labor market. *arXiv*. https://arxiv.org/abs/2405.00247

Barreto Pin, J. X., Reina Paredes, J. D., Barreto Pin, L. Y., & Rodríguez Rodríguez, A. (2024). Tecnología Blockchain y la gestión de registros educativos en la Educación Superior. UNESUM—Ciencias. *Revista Científica Multidisciplinaria*, 8(3), 169–187. https://doi.org/10.47230/unesum-ciencias.v8.n3.2024.169-187

Bideau, Y. M., & Kearns, T. (2022). A European approach to micro-credentials for lifelong learning and employability. *Journal of European CME*, 11(1). https://doi.org/10.1080/21614083.2022.2147288

Brown, M., Mhichil, M. N. G., Beirne, E., & Mac Lochlainn, C. (2021). The global micro-credential landscape: Charting a new credential ecology for lifelong learning. *Journal of Learning for Development*, 8(2), 228–254. https://doi.org/10.56059/jl4d.v8i2.525

Carțiș, A., Leoste, J., Iucu, R., Kikkas, K., Tammemäe, K., & Männik, K. (2023). Conceptualising micro-credentials in the higher education research landscape: A literature review. In M. Dascalu, P. Marti, & F. Pozzi (Eds.), *Polyphonic Construction of Smart Learning Ecosystems* (pp. 191–203). Springer Nature Singapore. https://doi.org/10.1007/978-981-19-5240-1_13

CEDEFOP. (2022). *Microcredentials for Labour Market Education and Training: First Look at Mapping Microcredentials in European Labour-Market-Related Education, Training and Learning: Take-up, Characteristics and Functions (Cedefop Research Paper No. 87)*. Publications Office of the European Union. https://doi.org/10.2801/351271

Council of the European Union. (2022). Council Recommendation of 16 June 2022 on a European approach to micro-credentials for lifelong learning and employability. *Official Journal of the European Union*, C 243, 10–18. https://eur-lex.europa.eu/legal-content/EN/TXT/?uri=uriserv:OJ.C_.2022.243.01.0010.01.ENG de Alwis, A., Shrestha, A., & Sarker, T. (2025). Exploring governance for accreditation in the education sector using blockchain technology: A systematic literature review. *Discover Education*, 4(1), 57. https://doi.org/10.1007/s44217-025-00449-y

El Koshiry, A., Eliwa, E., Abd El-Hafeez, T., & Shams, M. Y. (2023). Unlocking the power of blockchain in education: An overview of innovations and outcomes. *Blockchain: Research and Applications*, 4(4), 100165. https://doi.org/10.1016/j.bcra.2023.100165

European Commission. (2021). *Proposal for a Council Recommendation on a European Approach to Micro-Credentials for Lifelong Learning and Employability*. COM(2021) 770 final. European Commission. https://eur-lex.europa.eu/legal-content/EN/TXT/?uri=celex:52021DC0770

Gamage, K. A. A., & Dehideniya, S. C. P. (2025). Unlocking career potential: How micro-credentials are revolutionising higher education and lifelong learning. *Education Sciences*, 15(5), 525. https://doi.org/10.3390/educsci15050525

Gräther, W., Kolvenbach, S., Ruland, R., Schütte, J., Torres, C., & Wendland, F. (2018). Blockchain for education: Lifelong learning passport. In W. Prinz & P. Hoschka (Eds.), *Proceedings of the 1st ERCIM Blockchain Workshop 2018* (Reports of the European Society for Socially Embedded Technologies, ISSN 2510–2591). https://doi.org/10.18420/blockchain2018_07

Grech, A., Sood, I., & Ariño, L. (2021). Blockchain, self-sovereign identity and digital credentials: Promise versus praxis in education. *Frontiers in Blockchain*, 4, 616779. https://doi.org/10.3389/fbloc.2021.616779

Iatrellis, O., Samaras, N., & Kokkinos, K. (2024). Towards a capability maturity model for micro-credential providers in european higher education. *Trends in Higher Education*, 3(3), 504–527. https://doi.org/10.3390/higheredu3030030

IMS Global. (2021). *Open Badges 3.0. IMS Global Learning Consortium*. https://www.imsglobal.org/spec/ob/v3p0/

Iniesto, F., Ferguson, R., Weller, M., Farrow, R., & Pitt, R. (2022). Introducing a reflective framework for the assessment and recognition of microcredentials. *The Open/Technology in Education, Society, and Scholarship Association Journal*, 2(2), 1–24. https://doi.org/10.18357/otessaj.2022.2.2.37

Jaramillo, M. P., & Piedra, N. (2020). A blockchain model proposal for the decentralized management of academic credentials in Ecuadorian universities. In *2020 9th International Conference on Software Process Improvement (CIMPS)* (pp. 94–102). IEEE. https://doi.org/10.1109/CIMPS52057.2020.9390104

Kayyali, M. (2025). Defining micro-credentials: Concepts, theories, and pedagogies. In M. Kayyali (Ed.), *Navigating Quality Assurance and Accreditation in Global Higher Education* (pp. 219–246). IGI Global Scientific Publishing. https://doi.org/10.4018/979-8-3693-6915-9.ch009

Kušić, S., Vrcelj, S., & Zovko, A. (2022). Micro-credentials—Improvement or fragmentation in higher education? In *Education and New Developments 2022* (Vol. 2, pp. 152–156). https://doi.org/10.36315/2022v2end033

Lang, G., & Sharp, J. H. (2023). Micro-credentials in us higher education: An empirical analysis. *Information Systems Education Journal*, 21(1), 2–10. https://files.eric.ed.gov/fulltext/EJ1385272.pdf

Ling, P., & Ling, L. (2023). Micro-credentials and higher education: The bottom line. In C. Subasinghe & B. Giridharan (Eds.), *Introducing Multidisciplinary Micro-Credentialing: Rethinking Learning and Development for Higher Education and Industry*. Emerald Publishing Limited. https://doi.org/10.1108/978-1-80382-459-820231009

Lumina Foundation. (2025). *Micro-Credentials Impact Report 2025: Insights from Students and Employers*. Lumina Foundation. https://www.luminafoundation.org/wp-content/uploads/2025/05/Micro-Credentials-Impact-Report-25.pdf

Mateo-Berganza Díaz, M. M., Rucci, G., Amaral, N., Arias Ortiz, E., Becerra, L., Bustelo, M., Cabrol, M., Castro, J., Caycedo, J., Duryea, S., Groot, B., Heredero, E., Hincapie, D., Magendzo, A., Navarro, J. C., Novella, R., Rieble-Aubourg, S., Rubio-Codina, M., Scartascini, C., & Vezza, E. (2019). The future is now: Transversal skills in Latin America and the Caribbean in the 21st century. https://doi.org/10.18235/0001950

McGreal, R. (2023). Blockchain and micro-credentials in education. *International Journal of E-Learning & Distance Education*, 38(1), Article n1. https://doi.org/10.55667/10.55667/ijede.2023.v38.i1.1250

MOCHILA Project. (2025a). Informe WP2.1—Diagnósticos en instituciones de educación superior de LAC en relación con la adopción de microcredenciales. *Erasmus+ Capacity Building Project*. http://www.proyectomochila.org/wp-content/files/Informe_WP_2.1._v8.pdf

MOCHILA Project. (2025b). Informe WP2.2—Análisis de la normativa actualizada en relación con la emisión de microcredenciales en LAC. *Erasmus+ Capacity Building Project*. http://www.proyectomochila.org/wp-content/files/Informe_WP_2.2.pdf

MOCHILA Project. (2025c). Informe WP2.3—Estado del arte de las iniciativas existentes en relación con la utilización de microcredenciales en LAC. *Erasmus+ Capacity Building Project*. http://www.proyectomochila.org/wp-content/files/WP2.3_Estado_del_arte_de_las_iniciativas_existentes_en_relacion_con_la_utilizacion_de_microcredenciales_en_LAC.pdf

MOCHILA Project. (2025d). Informe WP2.4—Marco referencial para el diseño y emisión de microcredenciales en las IES en América Latina y el Caribe. *Erasmus+ Capacity Building Project*. http://www.proyectomochila.org/wp-content/files/D2.4_MarcoMOCHILA.pdf

Mohammad, A., & Vargas, S. (2022). Challenges of using blockchain in the education sector: A literature review. *Applied Sciences*, 12(13), 6380. https://doi.org/10.3390/app12136380

Narong, D. K. (2025). Research trends on micro-credentials: A keyword co-occurrence analysis and science mapping. *Journal of Further and Higher Education*, 49(7), 919–937. https://doi.org/10.1080/0309877X.2025.2509578

OECD. (2021). Micro-credential innovations in higher education: Who, what and why? *Education Policy Perspectives, No. 39*. OECD Publishing. https://doi.org/10.1787/f14ef041-en

OECD. (2023a). Micro-credentials for lifelong learning and employability: Uses and possibilities. *Education Policy Perspectives, No. 66*. OECD Publishing. https://doi.org/10.1787/9c4b7b68-en

OECD. (2023b). Public policies for effective micro-credential learning. *Education Policy Perspectives, No. 85*. OECD Publishing. https://doi.org/10.1787/a41f148b-en

Oliver, B. (2019). *Making Micro-Credentials Work for Learners, Employers and Providers*. Deakin University. https://dteach.deakin.edu.au/wp-content/uploads/sites/103/2019/08/Making-micro-credentials-work-Oliver-Deakin-2019-full-report.pdf

Oliver, B. (2022). *Towards a Common Definition of Micro-Credentials*. UNESCO. https://unesdoc.unesco.org/ark:/48223/pf0000381668

Pardo, A., Latorre, L., Allende, M., Leal Batista, A., Gutierrez, M., & Puerto, F. (2023). *Tech Report: Blockchain*. https://doi.org/10.18235/0005109

Peters, M., Beirne, E., & Brown, M. (2025). Micro-credentials and their implications for lifelong learning–global insights and critical perspectives. *Distance Education*, 46(1), 1–7. https://doi.org/10.1080/01587919.2025.2463137

Porto, S. C., & Presant, D. (2023). The IDB digital credential framework: Principles and guidelines for creating and issuing credentials. https://doi.org/10.18235/0004903

Samala, A. D., Mhlanga, D., Bojic, L., Howard, N.-J., & Coelho, D. P. (2024). Blockchain technology in education: Opportunities, challenges, and beyond. *International Journal of Interactive Mobile Technologies (iJIM)*, 18(1), 20–42. https://doi.org/10.3991/ijim.v18i01.46307

Semigina, T., & Rashkevych, Y. (2023). Microcredentials as an educational trend and a challenge for higher education. *International Scientific Journal of Universities and Leadership*, 16, 77–89. https://doi.org/10.31874/2520-6702-2023-16-77-89

Subramanian, S. S., Krishnan, A. S., & Seetharaman, A. (2024). Blockchain revolution in education. In Y. Ramakrishna & P. Keer (Eds.), *Frameworks for Blockchain Standards, Tools, Testbeds, and Platforms* (pp. 96–130). IGI Global Scientific Publishing. https://doi.org/10.4018/979-8-3693-0405-1.ch005

Tamoliune, G., Greenspon, R., Tereseviciene, M., Volungeviciene, A., Trepule, E., & Dauksiene, E. (2023). Exploring the potential of micro-credentials: A systematic literature review. *Frontiers in Education*, 7, 1006811. https://doi.org/10.3389/feduc.2022.1006811

Tinsley, B., Cacicio, S., Shah, Z., Parker, D., Younge, O., & Luke Luna, C. (2022, March). Micro-credentials for social mobility in rural postsecondary communities: A landscape report. *Digital Promise*. https://doi.org/10.51388/20.500.12265/151

Turkanović, M., Hölbl, M., Košič, K., Heričko, M., & Kamišalić, A. (2018). EduCTX: A blockchain-based higher education credit platform. *IEEE Access*, 6, 5112–5127. https://doi.org/10.1109/ACCESS.2018.2789929

UNESCO IESALC. (2025). Mapping micro-credentials in Latin America and the Caribbean: Towards a common framework. *UNESCO International Institute for Higher Education in Latin America and the Caribbean*. https://unesdoc.unesco.org/ark:/48223/pf0000393794

Varadarajan, S., Koh, J. H. L., & Daniel, B. K. (2023). A systematic review of the opportunities and challenges of micro-credentials for multiple stakeholders: Learners, employers, higher education institutions and government. *International Journal of Educational Technology in Higher Education*, 20, Article 13. https://doi.org/10.1186/s41239-023-00381-x

Vargas, F., & Piedra, N. (2023). Decentralized issuance and verification of university micro-credentials. In *2023 12th International Conference on Software Process Improvement (CIMPS)* (pp. 90–99). IEEE. https://doi.org/10.1109/CIMPS61323.2023.10528844

W3C. (2019). *Verifiable Credentials Data Model 1.0*. World Wide Web Consortium. https://www.w3.org/TR/vc-data-model/

Zdunek, K., Dobrowolska, B., Dziurka, M., Galazzi, A., Chiappinotto, S., Palese, A., & Wells, J. (2024). Challenges and opportunities of micro-credentials as a new form of certification in health science education—a discussion paper. *BMC Medical Education*, 24(1), Article 1169. https://doi.org/10.1186/s12909-024-06174-8

Index

Note: Page numbers in *italic* indicate a figure and page numbers in **bold** indicate a table on the corresponding page.

B

C

F

G

H

I

L

M

Q

R

S

T

U

V